INTIMATE PERSONAL VIOLENCE IN CANADA

Anastasia Bake

St. Clair College

PEARSON

Toronto

Vice-President, Editorial Director: Gary Bennett
Editor-in-Chief: Michelle Sartor
Acquisitions Editor: Carolin Sweig
Signing Representative: Kerry Hollingsworth
Marketing Manager: Lisa Gillis
Supervising Developmental Editor: Madhu Ranadive
Developmental Editor: Toni Chahley
Project Manager: Ashley Patterson
Production Editor: Mohinder Singh, Aptara®, Inc.
Copy Editor: Kelli Howey
Proofreader: Judy Sturrup
Compositor: Aptara®, Inc.
Permissions and Photo Researcher: Christina Beamish
Art Director: Julia Hall
Cover Designer: Miguel Acevedo
Cover Image: Getty Images / Stone / Andy Ryan

Credits and acknowledgments of material borrowed from other sources and reproduced, with permission, in this textbook appear on the appropriate page within the text and on page 351.

If you purchased this book outside the United States or Canada, you should be aware that it has been imported without the approval of the publisher or the author.

Library and Archives Canada Cataloguing in Publication

Bake, Anastasia
        Intimate personal violence in Canada / Anastasia Bake.
Includes index.
ISBN 978-0-13-257201-9
        1. Family violence—Canada. 2. Intimate partner violence—
Canada. I. Title.
HV6626.23.C3B35 2013   362.82'920971   C2012-903504-1

ISBN 978-0-13-257201-9

I would like to dedicate this book to my Moonbeams,
my daughters Hannah and Roberta.

Brief Contents

Contents

Chapter 8   **Services to
Victims** 278

Foreword

I am pleased to write a foreword for *Intimate Personal Violence in Canada*. This is a well-written teaching text that lays IPV groundwork for undergraduate or graduate students in social work and/or law, as well as their cognate disciplines. It is a comprehensive overview of IPV that is topical, timely, and presented in one source. There is a sense of completeness about the overall handling of this topic to achieve this goal.

Often, students must seek, probe, and investigate a variety of disparate search engines for this content. When they do, it is presented in a range of different forms that include legal documents, social policies, various media forums, case materials, best or promising practices, anecdotal materials, theoretical studies, and empirical and multi-disciplinary reports written in their respective language "speak." Teachers and students alike now can have the full gamut of IPV information in one complete text, with each chapter clearly written and consistently formatted. Ms. Bake should be applauded for the scholarly sifting and sorting out of this mass of materials and for presenting it creatively in this text.

Each chapter nicely cascades core issues from one to the next. The eight chapters in these knowledge waterfalls include the history of violence, theoretical explanations of violence and violence against children, violence against women, family violence, violence in same-sex relationships, laws, services to women, and services for victims. In each chapter, the author first sets the stage with historical context (with the exception of Chapter 2, where this is not needed). Then she effectively braids laws, social policies, and their noteworthy gaps with real case material to actually see how clients "fall through the cracks" in institutions of care where, for them, systemic oppression is the norm, not the exception. Instructors will find it easy to add their own case materials to supplement the ones presented herein. They will also find it very convenient to have both well-crafted multiple choice and discussion questions at the end of each chapter, as well as a glossary of key terms.

Stylistically, her written cadence is clear and uncluttered. She presents critical insights and a freshness of thought throughout the text. Her tone is candid, factual, appropriately rhetorical, and written directly to post-modern students in the ways that they converse, for example through TV shows and musical references, and in the ways that they understand knowledge, for example condensed into "take-away points," using 5¢ rather than 10¢ words, websites, and pictures, and presenting paradoxical contradictory facts and opinions to trigger debate and discussion. It is often difficult for academics to actually reach out to their audience's ears and cerebrums (the thinking part of our brains). This seems to be easy for Ms. Bake, as she does it so naturally and effectively.

In sum, this is a first-rate teaching text written from the perspective of Canadian clients and helping professionals in a "bottom-up" approach. Ms. Bake has done an admirable job of throwing a net over this much-needed Canadian content *ad mari usque ad mare—*

from sea to shining sea. I highly recommend this text to students and practitioners interested not only in having fingertip information about this important topic, but also in having "hands-on" data that can inform and direct their practice with the numerous marginalized and vulnerable victims of IPV in Canada.

Michael J. Holosko, Ph.D.
Pauline M. Berger Professor of Family and Child Welfare,
University of Georgia, Athens, GA

About the Author

Anastasia Bake, known as Stasi by most, is a registered, licensed M.S.W. social worker. She has worked extensively with children and families for nearly 30 years in a variety of capacities. Stasi's passion to advocate for the rights and protections of others was ignited through her work and lengthy experience in the field of child welfare. Beyond child welfare, Stasi worked for eight years as a school board social worker and nearly 15 years as an educator and professor in both social work and liberal arts.

Throughout Stasi's varied career, she has provided crisis intervention, clinical counselling services, and group treatment to child, adolescent, and adult victims of interpersonal violence. She has comprehensive experience in the family court and criminal justice systems on behalf of victims. Always an innovator, Stasi developed and implemented treatment and prevention programs for adolescents around date rape, sexual harassment, and bullying. She has been interviewed on local TV, CBC radio, and in the *Windsor Star* regarding her uniquely designed and executed programs. Stasi has participated in numerous board and community committee working groups to improve services for clients.

Stasi's work has been recognized by her peers and her home community. In 2001, she was the recipient of the Ontario Association of Social Workers (South Western Branch) Distinguished Service Award, honouring that year's theme of Social Advocacy. In 2004, she was the recipient of the New Beginnings Community Excellence Award, Social Worker of the Year.

Currently, Stasi is a sessional instructor for the School of Social Work at the University of Windsor and a full-time professor at St. Clair College of Applied Arts and Sciences, where she has developed and offered many new courses for the Department of Community Studies including, Drugs and Addictions, Human Sexuality, and Intimate Personal Violence. Professor Bake's integrity, energy, knowledge, and interest in her students make her a popular professor. She is a committed academic and lifelong learner.

Preface

Why do we need a Canadian introductory textbook on intimate personal violence? That is a tough question. Most people do not want to think about violence or its consequences; yet, it is an unavoidable fact that interpersonal violence is embedded in our culture. Over the past 40 years, many encouraging advancements in laws, policy, treatments, and public awareness have been achieved. Despite these positive and progressive gains, violence within intimate relationships persists.

In 1983, while completing my undergraduate degree, I found myself working part-time for the emergency on-call service of my city's Children's Aid Society. My shift was 5 p.m. to 9 a.m., Monday through Friday plus weekends. Back then, there were no cell phones or other convenient electronic devices. Instead, I would be awakened at night by the shrill blare of an old-fashioned pager. Many of these pager calls would ultimately send me on my way to investigate the circumstances of a child potentially in need of protection. There were few positive stories, but there were moments of great satisfaction knowing that the work I was doing stopped, or better yet prevented, a child from being abused or mal-treated. From here on, interpersonal violence remained part of my everyday awareness.

During that same period, important legislative enactments occurred: the *Charter of Rights and Freedoms* in 1982, and in 1983 Bill C-12 ushered new sexual assault laws and language. Sweeping revisions were also being made to child protection legislation in the province of Ontario. Momentum was mounting to recognize victims' rights and needs. Over the years, the fight for protective legal measures would ensue, but so too would the equally important resolve to discover the best ways of providing assistance to victims to ensure that they healed and became survivors.

My early days in child protection fueled my passion for this topic. For the next 20 years, I provided direct services to victims of all ages, genders and sexual orientations. I learned a great deal. Sometimes observing "other professionals" at work also taught me how not to be! For the past 8 years, I have been teaching students about the history, con-text, dynamics and experiences of interpersonal violence. It is my hope to draw on my background of clinical knowledge, practice wisdom, and teaching experience to produce a textbook that provides a meaningful overview of IPV for students. My foremost goal is to bring to light and honour the authentic human element of intimate personal violence.

HOW THE BOOK IS ORGANIZED

This textbook is organized into eight chapters. The first two chapters set the stage with an overview of the history of violence in Canada and theoretical explanations of interpersonal violence. The next four chapters address specific forms of violence. The book concludes with an overview of laws and services for victims.

Each of the four chapters addressing specific forms of violence is structured in a modular format:

- Module 1—Defines the particular form of violence

- Module 2—Explores the impact of each of the identified forms of violence

- Module 3—Outlines the prevalence and relevant statistics pertaining to each form of violence

These modules provide teaching flexibility. Different aspects of each form of violence can be covered within the class lecture, while others can be assigned as individual or group projects.

PEDAGOGICAL FEATURES

The pedagogical features of this text are informed by a desire to structure the book to include the ingredients of a good class lesson. Over the years, I've found that a near perfect lesson combines a clear description of the theory, a great narrative that speaks to the facts (everyone loves a good story), and, if and when possible, an expert perspective on a particular theme or issue. It is a great gift to share and acknowledge the stories and deeds of outstanding Canadians. It was with these ideas in mind that I organized the text.

Pedagogical features found in this textbook include the following:

- **"From the Pen of . . ." Boxes:** These boxes provide a forum for experts and leaders in the field to speak directly to the student. These outstanding individuals all provide a vital and informative perspective on the topic of intimate violence. The vastness of their experiences is impressive, and so is the contribution each has made to Canadian society.

- **Canadian Headline News Boxes:** These authentic stories highlight significant cases in intimate personal violence and provide invaluable insight into the topic at hand. These publicly recorded victimizations not only address the content being analyzed, they also illustrate Canada's response to victims and their needs, and the resulting call for legislative changes, the enactment of new laws, essential services, and the realization that Canadians can become advocates! While many of the cases discussed expose some dark moments in Canada's history, they also illuminate the strength of our society.

- **Key Terms:** Key terms are bolded within the text, and defined in a glossary at the end of each chapter.

- **Multiple Choice Questions:** At the end of each chapter, students will find 10 multiple choice questions to help recap the chapter contents. Answers to these questions are found in an appendix at the end of the book.

- **Discussion Questions:** Also found at the end of each chapter are three to five discussion questions. These questions could be assigned individually or used to spark in-class discussion and debate.

INSTRUCTOR'S SUPPLEMENTS

Instructor's Manual (ISBN 978-0-13-307399-7)

The Instructor's Manual includes teaching tips and discussion and project ideas in a chapter-by-chapter format. The Manual provides instructors a base from which to generate classroom discussion as well as encourage students to further apply the concepts and ideas presented in the text.

PowerPoint Presentations (ISBN 978-0-13-307400-0)

The PowerPoint Presentations provide a comprehensive selection of slides highlighting key concepts featured in the text and is a useful supplement to your classroom lectures.

Test Item File (ISBN 978-0-13-307397-3)

The Test Item File contains approximately 400 multiple-choice and true-and-false questions. Each question is classified by level of difficulty (easy, moderate, challenging) and is correlated to chapter topics.

CourseSmart for Instructors (ISBN 978-0-13-261171-8)

CourseSmart goes beyond traditional expectations, providing instant, online access to the textbooks and course materials you need at a lower cost for students. And even as students save money, you can save time and hassle with a digital eTextbook that allows you to search for the most relevant content at the very moment you need it. Whether it's evaluating textbooks or creating lecture notes to help students with difficult concepts, CourseSmart can make life a little easier. See how when you visit www.coursesmart.com/instructors.

Technology Specialists

Pearson's technology specialists work with faculty and campus course designers to ensure that Pearson technology products, assessment tools, and online course materials are tailored to meet your specific needs. This highly qualified team is dedicated to helping schools take full advantage of a wide range of educational resources by assisting in the integration of a variety of instructional materials and media formats. Your local Pearson Canada sales representative can provide you with more details on this service program.

Pearson Custom Library

For enrolments of at least 25 students, you can create your own textbook by choosing the chapters that best suit your own course needs. To begin building your custom text, visit www.pearsoncustomlibrary.com. You may also work with a dedicated Pearson Custom Library editor to create your ideal text—publishing your own original content or mixing and matching Pearson content. Contact your local Pearson representative to get started.

peerScholar

Firmly grounded in published research, peerScholar is a powerful online pedagogical tool that helps develop students' critical and creative thinking skills through creation, evaluation, and reflection. Working in stages, students begin by submitting written assignments; peerScholar then circulates their work for others to review, a process that can be anonymous or not, depending on instructors' preferences. Students immediately receive peer feedback and evaluations, reinforcing their learning and driving development of higher-order thinking skills. Students can then re-submit revised work, again depending on instructors' preferences. Contact your Pearson representative to learn more about peerScholar and the research behind it.

STUDENT SUPPLEMENTS

CourseSmart for Students (ISBN 978-0-13-261171-8)

CourseSmart goes beyond traditional expectations, providing instant, online access to the textbooks and course materials you need, at an average saving of 60 percent. With instant access from any computer and the ability to search your text, you'll find the content you need quickly, no matter where you are. And with online tools like highlighting and note-taking, you can save time and study efficiently. See all the benefits at www.coursesmart.com/students.

PERSONAL THOUGHTS

I would like to include a few thoughts that I regularly share with my students. None of us who work with victims, teach this theory, or study this topic live in a vacuum. We are all part of families and communities. The type of material presented in this text can bring about and perhaps unearth personal issues. It is difficult to study this topic or work with victims without being emotionally challenged on some level. Some personal introspection and reflection might be necessary, and beneficial.

Acknowledgments

When I began to consider whom I wanted to acknowledge, I knew I had many people to thank; for this, I am truly grateful.

To begin, I wish to acknowledge the countless people, many of them our youngest Canadian citizens, who trusted me to share their most painful personal experiences. I learned a great deal from my clients, and they touched my soul in countless ways during the 20 years I worked as a child protection worker, and later as a school social worker. Their courage inspired me to honour their dignity by attempting to be both a better person and an informed, skilled clinician. They were in my thoughts as I planned and wrote this book.

On a very different note, I would like to acknowledge and thank an incredible professional team at Pearson Canada. First, my deepest gratitude is extended to Joel Gladstone, my acquisitions editor. I am honoured to have been given this opportunity. Joel's ongoing support and guidance were invaluable. Of course, there is also my developmental editor Toni Chahley. I think it is fair to say that Toni did a lot of the heavy lifting. Her encouragement, critical guidance, and unwavering patience to educate me about her world, book writing, were never-ending; thank you Toni! Later when production began, continuous support and direction were generously provided by Supervising Developmental Editor: Madhu Ranadive, Project Manager: Ashley Patterson, Production Editor: Mohinder Singh, Copy Editor: Kelli Howey, Proofreader: Judy Sturrup, and Photo Researcher: Christina Beamish.

Last to acknowledge is Kerry Hollingsworth. Kerry's support was omnipresent as we began and ended this extremely rewarding professional journey!

Next to thank is Dr. Michael Holosko, who wrote the foreword to this book. I am proud to say he was one of my favourite, yet most demanding professors. Dr. Holosko nurtured my academic pursuits while in graduate school, and as my career unfolded, whenever needed, he provided genuinely valued advice and support.

The others to whom I am extremely grateful are the "From the Pen of . . ." authors. Their contribution to the text has provided all of us with a very authentic and rich learning experience. On a much grander level, they teach all of us how to be in the world. Their advocacy and efforts changed Canadian society. I would specifically like to thank

Sandy Clark
Marion Crawford
Michael Harris
Lynn Kainz
Greg Monforton
Colette Mandin
Jane M. Oxenbury
Corinne Robertshaw
Wendy van Tongeren Harvey

Many of these individuals also generously supported my research process. I would especially like to thank Sandy Clark, Marion Crawford, Colette Mandin, Corinne Robertshaw, and Wendy van Tongeren Harvey. My research was also enhanced by Deputy Chief Constable Doug LePard of the Vancouver Police Department, who authored the "Missing Women—Investigation Review." Also assisting me in the research of this text was a former student Tammy St. Louis.

A special thank-you is also extended to the instructors who provided feedback on this manuscript at various stages of development:

Liora Barak, Fanshawe College
Lori Stinson O'Gorman, University of Ottawa
Lisa Barnoff, Ryerson University
Jan Blaxall, Fanshawe College
Susanne Otenheimer, Memorial University
Donna Mansfield, Sault College of Applied Arts and Technology
Bruce Hardy, Douglas College

Next on my list are my students, past and present. It has been almost 15 years since I first became a sessional instructor in the School of Social Work at the University of Windsor. Later, in 2004, I was given a great gift: the opportunity to become fully immersed in the profession of teaching when I was hired as a full-time faculty member at St. Clair College. These two schools of learning have provided me an opportunity to meet countless students from all ages and backgrounds. The classroom is a joyful place for me, and teaching has enriched my life.

I would also like to thank Dr. G. Brent Angell; Director of the School of Social Work at the University of Windsor. As a sessional instructor in the school of social work, Dr. Angell has, and continues to support me professionally, as well as encouraging my learning and teaching.

The most important individuals to highlight are a special group of colleagues who throughout the years have become lifelong friends. All of them in their own right have provided unwavering social justice advocacy; Joan Reid, Alice Barron, Lynn Kainz, Dr. Andrea Dinardo, and Tina DiSimmone.

Anastasia Bake

Chapter 1
History of Intimate Personal Violence in Canada

All things are subject to interpretation. Whichever interpretation prevails at a given time is a function of power and not truth.

Friedrich Nietzsche, philosopher (1844–1900)

Chapter Objectives

1   Describe the historical victimization of children, and when and how legal protection from harm evolved.

2   Describe the historical victimization of women, and when and how legal protection from harm evolved.

3   Describe the historical victimization of homosexuals, and when and how legal protection from harm evolved.

4   Describe the history of the development of the *Diagnostic and Statistical Manual of Mental Disorders* (DSM), and its role in labelling and victimizing citizens.

INTRODUCTION

Intimate personal violence creates victims. Today, when we think about crime or a victim, we could reflect upon a person's pain or perhaps upon the criminal justice system. Thinking of the justice system may even prompt us to recall a recent news story or a television crime show. Many of us might think of *Law & Order*; you may even be hearing the tune from the show's theme in your head. And as much as that iconic theme song became imprinted in our psyches, so too did the lines that open each show. The narration alerted us, the listener, to the importance of the criminal justice system and the two existing and important groups that work within it; the police and the prosecution.

Two equally important groups emphasized were the police, and the district attorneys (the Crown, in Canada)—but where are the victims? The fact is, unless you have worked in the criminal justice system, needed the system, or more importantly, been a victim, you may not have asked this question. But trust that many have, and many will continue to do so. The manner in which our laws and the Canadian criminal justice system have historically defined and treated "victims" must therefore be examined. To examine the history of violence, we will explore two important areas:

1. The various forms of violence
2. How laws and rights were eventually acquired to provide protection from harm

The term "rights" can be explained as legal, social, or ethical principles of freedom or entitlement. Better stated, rights are rules that define what people are permitted to do, and what is owed to them. Historically in Canada, opinions about what constitute rights were determined by a dominant group. Different people were granted different rights: some had more, while others had none. As such, many groups of people were oppressed, harmed, and violently treated. Before we look at Canada's history, we present some key definitions. It is important to be mindful of these 21st-century descriptions as we take a step back in history.

Today, the Department of Justice Canada refers to the term *child abuse* as "the violence, mistreatment, or neglect that a child or adolescent may experience while in the care of someone they either trust or depend on, such as a parent, sibling, other relative, caregiver or guardian. Abuse may take place anywhere and may occur, for example, within the child's home or that of someone known to the child" (Department of Justice Canada, 2012).

Further, the **United Nations (UN)** defined violence against women in its 1993 *Declaration on the Elimination of Violence against Women* as "any act of gender-based violence that results in, or is likely to result in, physical, sexual or psychological harm or suffering to women, including threats of such acts, coercion or arbitrary deprivation of liberty, whether occurring in public or in private life."

Other definitions of violence have also been articulated. They vary depending on the objectives of a particular research study, policy, or law. But what is a definition? According to a number of sources, a definition is a statement of what a thing is, a statement of the meaning of a word or phrase, or a statement conveying fundamental character. Why do you need to know this? Concepts tell us how "things" are defined. Words paint a picture of the meaning of the time, and they are based on the writer's understanding of the world. Historically in Canada, beginning around the 19th century, the notions of rights were determined by a dominant group: white men of British or French heritage. They dictated the social norms and rules of Canadian society. In fact, it was these men who would draft the *British North America Act* of 1867, in which the female voice was effectively silenced.

The meaning of words, therefore, is relative. How people have described or not described rights can help us understand how acts of violence against children, women, and homosexuals were permissible and legal at that time. Let us begin our examination of the history of intimate personal violence with the history of violence against children.

1.1 CHILD VIOLENCE AND MALTREATMENT IN EARLY CANADA

Any time we examine the treatment of people in a historical perspective, we learn about their history. In this chapter, we will examine specific populations of children.

Aboriginal Residential Schools

Long before Europeans settled in Canada, the Aboriginal people nurtured and protected their children. The abusive treatment of Aboriginal children—or, better stated, the trajectory of the historical abuse—began in the 1600s with the story of the Récollets. Although they are not routinely discussed in Canada, their history is noteworthy because they played an important part in the inception of what would eventually become the residential school movement. Knowledge of the consequences of this movement would expose the racist views of the Canadian government, as well as the brutality directed toward a very vulnerable population of Canadian children.

The Récollets were a French branch of the Roman Catholic Church that was sent to the French colonies to fulfill their missionary role: the implementation of a "civilization" policy. This policy specifically stated that "By royal edict at the beginning of the seventeenth century, the French were, 'to seek to lead the natives . . . to the profession of the Christian faith, to civilization of manners, an ordered life' and of course to a 'submission to the authority and dominations of the crown of France' . . . Aboriginal children would be made French in heart and mind" (Milloy, 1999, pp. 13–14).

Assimilation was at the heart of the "civilization policy." **Assimilation** required all groups to be brought together, *after* the dominant group had determined the rules, customs, and attitudes of the prevailing culture. With **colonization** as the goal, and propelled bythe "civilization edict," the Récollets would establish the first boarding schools for Aboriginal youth, thus creating the foundation for the residential schools. The Récollets ran these schools until 1680, when they were displaced by the Jesuits and the Ursulines, a Roman Catholic female order. The goal remained: the conversion of the Huron people to Christianity.

By the late 1700s and early 1800s, many historical events took place in Canada that affected Aboriginal people. Specifically, after the Seven Years' War ended in 1763, King George III of England signed a Royal Proclamation intended to protect Aboriginal groups from being exploited by the European settlers and colonial officials in Canada. The proclamation recognized Aboriginals as autonomous and self-governing within the colonial system. Despite this, Aboriginals and their cultures were viewed by the Canadian settlers as uncivilized, inferior, and incompetent. In 1842, the Bagot Commission produced one of the earliest official manuscripts that recommended education as a means of ridding the Canadian society of Indians (Leslie, 1982).

These beliefs justified the creation of the first of many policies used to control and assimilate Aboriginal persons: the *Gradual Civilization Act,* 1857; the *British North America Act,* 1867; and the *Indian Act,* 1867.

At the time of Confederation (1867), the policy changed from fostering native autonomy through industry to assimilating them through education and forcing them to fit into mainstream "colonial" Canada. In 1879, a more aggressive assimilation approach was conceived. Prime Minister Sir John A. Macdonald introduced houses of industry, the system that would eventually become residential schools for Aboriginal children. Residential schools were now federally run under the Department of Indian Affairs. Later that year, the Davin Report called for church-run, off-reserve, aggressive "civilization" schools. Attendance was now mandatory, and agents employed by the government ensured that all native children attended.

During the 1870s the government began to partner with various Christian churches, establishing and operating the boarding and residential schools for First Nations, Inuit, and Métis children. In addition to the Catholics, the Protestant, Anglican, and Methodist religions became active in the education of native children. The Canadian government believed Aboriginal people could be successful, productive members of Canadian society if they learned English and adopted Christian and Canadian customs. Through education they would learn new lifestyles, pass them on to their children, and in a few generations native language, culture, and traditions would be abolished.

This ethos would continue to be reinforced during the period of 1913 to 1932 by Dr. Duncan Campbell Scott, the head of the Department of Indian Affairs. He is quoted as saying, "I want to get rid of the Indian problem . . . .. Our objective is to continue until there is not a single Indian in Canada that has not been absorbed into the body politic and there is no Indian question, and no Indian Department, that is the whole object of this Bill" (National Archives of Canada, Record Group 10).

This state-funded system was carried out with tremendous zeal for over a century. The belief that Aboriginal assimilation would build a prosperous nation gained further momentum in 1920, when the *Indian Act* was amended. Now all Aboriginal parents were legally required to send all their children to Indian residential schools.

Soon, 130 Indian residential schools dotted the nation, with a common goal: to make Aboriginal children productive members of "white" society. In 1861, the first Indian residential school was established at Mission, British Columbia, and was operated by the Roman Catholic Church. The last federally run residential school, the Gordon Residential School in Saskatchewan, was closed in 1996. More than 70 percent were run by the Roman Catholic Church (see Figure 1.1).

Childhood stories have slowly emerged in recent decades. These narratives describe extra-ordinarily harsh and violent existences for many Aboriginal children. Neglect, physical, and emotional abuses were constant occurrences. Overcrowding, poor sanitation, and a lack of medical care led to high rates of tuberculosis, with death rates that reached 69 percent (Milloy, 1999). Violent acts were numerous, and harmful deeds were

Figure 1.1 Map of Residential Schools in Canada

Map of Canada with dots indicating residential school locations.

Source: The Aboriginal Healing Foundation's "Directory of Residential Schools In Canada,"
www.afn.ca/residentialschools/history.html#

broad in scope. Presents and letters from family were withheld, and brothers and sisters were separated. When children were caught speaking their native language, needles were inserted into their tongues. If they disobeyed, they were locked in closets and cages. Children were also frequently stripped naked, and menstruating girls were often publicly shamed and beaten.

Children, in their own way, tried to cope or end their suffering, and running away was common. Christine Haines explained to the Williams Lake residential school inquest why she ran away on two separate occasions:

> The Sisters didn't treat me good—they gave me rotten meat to eat and punished me for not eating it . . .. I have been sick from eating it . . . I use to hide the meat in my pocket and throw it away . . . (Milloy, 1999, p. 143)

For her disobedience, Christine claimed that she had been locked in a "cold and dark" room, fed bread and water and beaten with a strap, sometimes on the face.

> And sometimes they took my clothes off and beat me—this is why I ran away . . ..
> (Milloy, 1999, p. 143)

Milloy (1999) reports a historical account of the consequences of one child's decision to run from the abusive conditions of his residential school in Alberta. After being caught, he was

> . . . shackled to a bed, had his hands tied, was stripped and was "most brutally and unmercifully beaten with a horse quirt until his back was bleeding." The accused, P.H. Gentleman, in the course of his explanation, admitted using a whip and shackles and that the boy might have been marked. (p. 146)

Other forms of violence have also been recorded. Children were burned, scalded, and beaten until unconscious. Sexual assaults also took place, and so did forced abortions of staff-impregnated girls. The guardians of the residential schools sapped the Aboriginal children's souls, bodies, and beings.

Today, it is clear that the actions of the governments and bureaucratic machines that supported and perpetuated the residential schools represent a shameful and atrocious piece of Canadian history. But assimilation practices did not end with the residential school system; new strategies were used, and they too were supported through legislation.

The Sixties Scoop

In 1951, the *Indian Act* was again amended. At this point the Aboriginal assimilation strategy was modified. Instead of placing Aboriginal children in residential institutions, the child welfare system removed them from their family homes and placed them in non-Aboriginal foster homes. The practice of using legal apprehensions to remove children has been referred to as the "Sixties Scoop"; it began in the early 1960s and lasted until the early 1980s (Johnston, 1983). Between 1959 and 1970, the percentage of Aboriginal children who were apprehended from their homes and made legal wards of the state jumped from one percent to approximately 30 to 40 percent (Fournier & Crey, 1997).

According to the Canadian Council on Social Development, in 1955 there were 3433 children in the care of British Columbia's child welfare branch. Of that number, it was estimated that 29 children, or less than one percent of the total, were of Indian ancestry. By 1964, however, 1446 children in care in B.C. were of Indian extraction. That number represented 34.2 percent of all children in care (Johnston, 1983).

The devastation of these 20 years would eventually become public. Aboriginal people had, however, immediately condemned the practice. During the Aboriginal Justice Inquiry of Manitoba in 1999, Anthony Wood of God's River told the inquiry:

> There was no publicity for years and years about the brutalization of our families and children by the larger Canadian society. Kidnapping was called placement in foster homes. Exporting Aboriginal children to the U.S. was called preparing Indian children for the future. Parents who were heartbroken by the destruction of their families were written off as incompetent people. (Aboriginal Justice Implementation Commission, 1999)

The historical policies that mandated the enforced separation of Aboriginal children from their parents and communities during their critical developmental years is considered one of the most egregious issues in child welfare. The accepted position, confirmed and underscored by researchers today, is that the forced removal of children from their families was devastating for Aboriginal individuals, families, communities, and cultures.

Pre-Industrial Child Welfare: Pre-1890

At the same time in Canada—separate from the treatment of Aboriginal children—was a specific ethos of the day regarding the expectation of other Canadian children. Canadian culture of the time was influenced by the belief system set out in English **common law**. The English courts utilized the concept of *parens patriae*, which referred to the right of the King to act in the best interests of the child. There is little evidence, however, to suggest that the courts used this power to protect children from abuse and neglect. In England as early as 1535, laws allowed children who were identified as neglected or delinquent to be put to work or placed in **poor-houses** (Radbill, 1987; Sanders, 1945). These provisions were not an attempt to protect but to maintain control over children who were resistant to parental punishment.

By the 1700s and early 1800s, English common law and culture were exported to and implemented in Canada, and children were treated harshly. Early legislation in Canada, such as the *Orphans Act* in 1799 and the *Apprentices and Minors Act* of 1874, upheld the harsh British tradition. Specifically, Canada's *Orphans Act* gave town wardens the power to bind a child under age 14 as an apprentice or labourer. Moreover, able-bodied Canadian men who needed and wished to obtain government support were obligated, along with their wives and children, to move into workhouses. Children were separated from their fathers; families were broken up. All family members living in these workhouses were required to work in return for their bed and board, including children over the age of 7 (Turner & Turner, 2010).

Canada's "British Home Children"

Starting in the early 1600s, Britain was overpopulated and poverty and disease were overwhelming. The abundance of homeless and poverty-stricken children was not helped either by the Industrial Revolution or the Great Famine that swept across Europe. Hundreds of thousands of people flocked to England's industrial centres, which were ill-prepared to accommodate them. Slums and their problems grew. Children were turning to crime, and Britain's established reformatories and industrial schools were bursting (though a child's crime often involved stealing food, often taking just enough to eat). These pressing problems required swift and meaningful intervention by government.

Government action was essential; something—anything—had to be done. Consequently, child **migration** became viewed as the cheapest way of saving children while lessening a costly social, economic, political, and moral problem. The government would rescue children from their families, the streets, and workhouses, and distribute them to developing British colonies. Whilst Britain's problem occurred, Canada had its own unique challenges. England realized that Canada required an increase in its English population to counterbalance the larger French factor in Lower Canada (known today as Quebec). In addition, Canada's farming needs and open spaces created an easy outlet for the development of child migration.

The prevailing thought of the day was that "it would offer the poor waifs and strays a better fait than keeping them in squalor and consigning them to crime, degradation and an early death at home" (Kohli, 2003, p. xii). In 1854, a committee in Canada formed and began to receive children from England's institutions (Kohli, 2003). Consequently, two years after Confederation, in 1869, the Home Children movement started. Children from the industrial and reformatory schools were sent to the colonies, including Canada. Under the law, between 1869 and the Great Depression, well-intentioned philanthropists sent as many as 100 000 Home Children to Canada to serve as cheap labour. Boys came as farm labourers, and girls were mothers' helpers. Most were between the ages of 7 and 14; many were younger, some older.

While most of the children were called orphans, two-thirds of them had parents who were too poor to provide for them. In time, as many as 50 agencies exported children to Canada without the knowledge or permission of their parents, a move made legal by the British Parliament. Even more children were sent through philanthropic organizations (Kohli, 2003).

While it is true that many were treated well, Home Children were generally denied affection because they were merely "hired hands." In addition to the personal losses, trauma, and abuses experienced, many of these children also faced societal discrimination. As Kohli (2003) noted, although the government of Canada placed great importance on the immigration of these children, the rest of Canadian society did not. The **stigma** attached to these children was considerable and, through no error of their own, they were scattered across Canada.

Migration slowed during the Great Depression. Agencies in the U.K. continued to send children over age 14 until 1939, when the last distribution home closed in Toronto. Farmers could no longer afford the pittance required to pay the children. The agencies closed and took the children's personal records back to England. Home Children were left with no one to defend them, protect them, or follow up on their well-being. They were separated from country, culture and family. They simply fell through the cracks.

In 2010, England's Prime Minister Gordon Brown issued an apology and recognized the actions of its past. Only a small number of those children, then in their 80s and 90s, were alive to hear the British government's apology. The Australian Prime Minister had apologized earlier, in November 2009. Canada has never apologized! But that did not stop other Canadians from stepping forward. Thanks to the work of a group of special Canadians, the story of the British Home Children would be told. In "From the Pen of . . ." (Box 1.1), Marion Crawford has generously contributed an overview of the level of commitment and collaboration devoted to ensure that these child victims were acknowledged and remembered. This group would succeed: the Canadian government designated 2010 the Year of the British Home Child. Canada Post also issued a commemorative stamp that year. These two events recognized the experiences of the more than 100 000 Home Children who were sent to Canada between 1869 and the end of the Second World War.

1.1 From the Pen of Marion Crawford: Recognition for the British Home Children

Work on obtaining recognition for the more than 100 000 children sent to Canada began in earnest in 2008 by the Middlemore Atlantic Society (MAS) and our sister organization, the Nova Scotia Home Children and Descendants Association (NSHCDA). With the help of group members, president of MAS Marion Crawford and chairs of the NSHCDA Cecil and Marilyn Verge began letter writing campaigns to provincial and federal Members of Parliament. We also sent requests for a commemorative coin and stamp to honour the British Home Children.

Letters were sent from MAS alone to more than 100 Premiers, Lieutenants Governor, the Prime Minister, the Governor General of Canada, leaders of the federal parties, and many current Members of Parliament. Our response rate in 2008 was a mere 10 percent. This was a very sad showing of support and acknowledgment from the government. Yet within New Brunswick and Nova Scotia there was support on the provincial level. With the help of Hon. T. J. Burke (New Brunswick, Minister of Consumer & Corporate Affairs) and his office, the Middlemore Atlantic Society was able to achieve provincial recognition with the unanimous

passing of Motion #24 on December 16, 2008. The NSHCDA were able to attain October 2009 as the Month of the British Home Children. A request was forwarded from the Nova Scotia Premier's office on behalf of all three parties, asking the federal government to support this effort.

In the spring of 2009, the Canadian Stamp Advisory Board stated that it would produce a commemorative stamp to be issued in October 2010. Canada Post agreed to allow the image of the stamp to be presented on one of the two British Home Children memory quilts that have travelled within Canada on display. The block was made by Marion Crawford and was released for the quilt to its creator, Hazel Perrier of Alberta. Because Canada Post was making its formal release of the stamp in June 2010, for any displays of the quilt prior to that date it was expected that the stamp quilt block would be covered.

Catherine West was elected as new chair with the NSHCDA and, together with Marion Crawford, branched out in quest of assistance. Notices were placed on the Britishhomechildren. org mailing list, and very soon descendants from

(continued)

across Canada and even the United States were writing letters to Members of Parliament calling for the need to support the Year of the British Home Children effort. One particular volunteer in Alberta wrote an email to each and every federal MP—more than 300—to help bring awareness and ask for support. Helen Atkinson was very instrumental in this campaign and she is not even a descendant of British Home Children.

Even with all our efforts to get recognition, we still had no member willing to bring it forward for us. Alexa McDonough, NDP from Nova Scotia, had begun work for us on a Private Member's Bill; however, she retired from her position when the election came up in 2009.

With no one person to advance our cause, I contacted my local MP, the Honourable Greg Thompson. I had not previously heard back on my original request for support, but after explaining our situation to his secretary in Apohaqui, New Brunswick, I had an immediate reply. My email was forwarded to Mr. Thompson's Ottawa office and I received a phone call that same day.

Mr. Thompson provided strong support and asked his party members if one could bring a motion for the Year of the British Home Children. Mr. Phil McColeman took up the offer and further communications began with him and his parliamentary secretary, Barbara Mottram. Behind-the-scenes work was very active for his office to secure support from all parties, including the Honourable Jason Kenney and the Honourable Gilles Duceppe (who is a fellow descendant and made a point of being present for the motion and speaking in support of the motion).

The federal government of Canada declared 2010 the year of the British Home Children.

Review Question

This story enriches our understanding of how and by what means our country was formed. How does this knowledge resonate with you today?

Source: Provided to Anastasia Bake by Marion Crawford.

Studies showed that, apart from being exploited, more than two-thirds (over 66 000) of the British Home Children were abused by their patrons in Canada. It is a wonder that so many survived. Yet survive they did, and many are still with us today. Most continue to live the quiet lives of unsung heroes. They triumphed over adversity, raised loving families, and contributed to the stability of their communities. Thousands served in the two World Wars for their adopted country and hundreds—perhaps thousands—gave their lives for it. It has been estimated that Home Children and their descendants make up 11.5 percent of Canada's population.

Legal Rights of Children Begin to Emerge

The first legal challenge to the absolute rights of parents over their children occurred south of the Canadian border, in New York City in 1874. While visiting an older woman in a tenement house, a church worker learned there was a child being abused by her adoptive parents. The child was also seriously malnourished and neglected. After appeals to protective agencies including the police and the district attorney's office proved ineffective, the woman appealed to Henry Bergh, who was a member of the American Society for the Prevention of Cruelty to Animals.

She pointed out to Bergh that the child was being treated like an animal and was certainly a member of the animal kingdom. Based on this argument, the Society for the Prevention of Cruelty to Animals brought about an action that resulted in the child's removal from her parents (Fontana, 1964). One year later, in 1875, the New York Society for the Prevention of Cruelty to Children was established. At that moment, organized child protection was born; it was the first child protection agency in the world.

That it took the persistence of a church worker to convince an organization devoted to the prevention of cruelty to animals to take a position to protect children is a profound statement about the values of the time. Canada, unfortunately, shares the same priority legacy. Animal protection legislation existed in Canada before legalized child protection. Eventually, legislation was enacted in Toronto, and the Canadian child welfare movement began.

Canada's Child Welfare

One of the most influential figures in the development of the Canadian child welfare system and the protection of children was an Irish immigrant and newspaper reporter named John Joseph Kelso. In his capacity as a police reporter, he noticed a large number of young children being left unattended on city streets, and that many were living in deplorable conditions. The response of the courts and jails to which many of these youth were sent was also inadequate. Kelso wrote passionately about these children, and as a result of his narratives Canada's child welfare movement gained momentum.

Kelso's newspaper articles spurred a public outcry that led to the passage of the *1888 Act for the Protection and Reformation of Neglected Children in Ontario.* Later, in 1893,

Children taken in by J.J. Kelso.

Ontario passed *The Act for the Prevention of Cruelty and Better Protection of Children.* This act was considered to be the first comprehensive piece of legislation in North America to protect children. The act granted provision for municipal governments to voluntarily organize and financially support Children's Aid Societies as a means of providing local services to abused and neglected children. Further, the state could decide whether or not parents were capable, and it now had authority to remove children from their homes and put them in care. Elsewhere in Canada, other jurisdictions followed Ontario's lead, and they too would introduce child welfare legislation. Ontario's legislation placed Canada at the forefront of child protection and welfare.

Despite these laws, few considered the treatment of children to be a matter of public concern. This changed in 1962, when C. Henry Kempe, Brandt F. Steele, and colleagues delivered their first presentation about the "battered child syndrome" at the 30th annual meeting of the American Academy of Pediatrics in Chicago.

Public awareness of child maltreatment soon grew with the coining of the term. **Battered child syndrome** referred to the repeated mistreatment or beating of a child that resulted in physical and psychological injuries. In Canada and in the world, knowledge of the battered child led to new laws that included mandatory reporting. In the 1980s, the American Medical Association cited the identification of battered child syndrome as one of the 60 most important contributions of American medicine in the 20th century.

In that same time period, the ***Badgley Report*** was released in 1984. This report disclosed the high rate of child sexual abuse cases in Canada. These findings led to drastic policy and legislative changes, which included the addition of 16 new assault charges being added to the sexual assault provisions of the ***Criminal Code of Canada*** (Bill C-15). These *Criminal Code* offences did not remove the legal authority of child welfare agencies to investigate child sexual abuse cases. What these legal provisions did do was to ensure that the police would be involved in investigations and that charges for *Criminal Code* offences could be laid.

The 1980s ushered in new legislative changes in child welfare. An attempt was made not only to address the abuse and neglect of children but also to determine the meaning of the best interest of a child. In 2009, the United Nations' *Convention on the Rights of the Child* marked its 20th anniversary by declaring "Children Are Persons Too!" Twenty years earlier, in 1989, the original Convention was passed. Article 3.1 of the Convention states:

> In all actions concerning children, whether undertaken by public or private social welfare institutions, courts of law, administrative authorities or legislative bodies, the best interests of the child shall be a primary consideration. (*Convention on the Rights of the Child,* 1989)

The strength of the convention's conviction placed a child's needs front and centre, providing a vital guiding light for all those who intervened in the lives of children.

Conclusion

At the end of the 1980s, much had changed in Canada regarding the beliefs and views regarding children, and more importantly their rights and entitlements. But this was only the beginning. As a society moves forward, it must also take responsibility for its past actions in order to improve its future. We now look at the history of violence against women and the rights and the laws that were needed to ensure protection from oppression, harm, and violence.

1.2 THE HISTORY OF VIOLENCE AGAINST WOMEN AND THE "FIGHT FOR RIGHTS"

Historically, laws and rights established for most men were not extended to women. An overview of women's rights in Canada illustrates a struggle of courage and perseverance. Women fought hard for all of the following:

- the right to vote (suffrage)
- the right to be educated
- political and social equality
- the right to hold public office
- bodily integrity and autonomy; the right to choose
- legal protection from violence

Canada's history of gender inequality and lack of rights for women had a dreadful impact on women's lives. Today's view of victimization is quite different from those that have slowly rolled out since the 1970s. The nation's emotional and legal reaction to violent crime has changed dramatically. In the last four decades the victims' movement in Canada has emerged as a powerful source of social, political, and legal change. Yet, the momentum—and, perhaps, the "right"—to demand equality and protection grew from the early work and solid foundation laid by the pioneers of the "first" women's movement. Through their persistence and courage they sounded the alarm and set the stage for what was possible when women rallied with a unified voice to demand redress and worked together to transform the status quo.

Who were these women, and what did they do? Canada's first women's movement had the enormous task of confronting the dominant thought of the day (that is, the male view), which was that women were essentially irrational by nature, weak-minded, and frail—unlike men, who were steadfast in opinion and inherently rational beings (Calixte, Johnson, & Motapanyane, 2010). At the same time, a similar perception of women was being challenged in England. The idea that the concept of equality for women was attainable was encouraging to white European and Canadian women.

Although white women became hopeful, the **patriarchal** and racist ideals regarding Aboriginal persons existed in Canada. Thus, the Aboriginal woman's plight was different. Canada's Aboriginal people suffered a diminished political and social status under the enactment of Canada's Indian policies. These acts of forced control and assimilation had tremendous impact on Aboriginal children and women. In the *Indian Act* of 1867, women became subject to their husbands and fathers, just as European women had been. This mindset forced European values upon the Aboriginal people, destroying the strong nurturing family structures and parenting practices that existed long before the Europeans arrived (Stevenson, 1999). Prior to this, Aboriginal women enjoyed meaningful political participation and high status in their societies.

The *Indian Act* also determined who was and who was not an Indian. If a woman was born a registered Indian but married a non-status Indian, the law stated she was no longer an Indian: she would be removed from the register and denied the rights and protections set out by the Act. An Indian man, however, could marry whomever he wanted, and that individual would gain Indian status through marriage even if she was not of Aboriginal parentage (Stevenson, 1999).

The First Women's Movement Begins

In Canada, challenges and change began with what has been called the first women's movement. The momentum started in the 19th century with the temperance movement; their goal was to control alcohol consumption. Concerns regarding alcohol consumption came about in the early 19th century, when social aid was negligible and the majority of Canadians were self-employed as farmers, fishermen, or small businessmen. Also, given the social **mores** of the time, it was more common for men to abuse alcohol. Women were resultantly affected by the economic fallout and subjected to the violence associated with alcoholism.

To organize, they formed the Woman's Christian Temperance Union (WCTU). The temperance battle brought white women together. With every victory their momentum increased. Eventually, women set their sights on the federal vote. Canadian women began to lobby. To challenge the accepted male perspective regarding women's intellect, women signed petitions, held demonstrations, and staged mock parliamentary debates to ridicule the men who upheld women's political and legal inequalities. Nellie McClung is quoted as stating:

> Our worthy opponents will emphasize the fact that women are the weaker vessel. Well I should think that a woman who cooks for men, washes and bakes and scrubs and sews for her family could stand the extra strain of marking a ballot every four years. (CBC, 2001)

It was through this common ground and their ability to organize that women began to feel and experience political power. Eventually, on May 24, 1918, their activism paid off, and the *Act to Confer the Electoral Franchise upon Women* was enacted. This legislation gave (white) women the right to vote in federal elections. Many provincial governments followed. Native women covered by the *Indian Act* continued to be prohibited by federal legislation from voting for band councils until 1951.

By the 1920s, women's groups were making headway in a number of social causes. In the early 1900s, particularly in the 1920s, the **Famous Five** emerged. These five Alberta women—Nellie McClung, Emily Murphy, Louise McKinney, Irene Parlby, and Henrietta Edwards—were persistent critics of male society's refusal to grant women political and social equality. With the help of then-Prime Minister William Lyon Mackenzie King, a legal and political battle was waged to have women recognized as persons under the *British North America (BNA) Act,* referred to as the Persons Case.

The Persons Case was brought to the British Privy Council, the highest level for legal appeals in Canada at the time. Success followed: with a landmark decision on October 18, 1929, Lord Sankey, Lord Chancellor of the Privy Council, announced that yes, women are persons. The Famous Five succeeded in having women defined as "persons" in section 24 of the *BNA Act,* which had originally used the word "persons" to refer to more than one person and "he" to refer to one person. Women were now eligible for appointment to the Senate. This milestone victory symbolized the right of women to participate in all facets of life, and is considered one of Canada's most important historical achievements.

The women's movement continued to change with the times. Other events taking place outside of Canada would also breathe life into the movement. By the late 1940s two world wars had ended, the First World War (1914–1919), and the Second World War (1939–1945). The grievous and sadistic acts perpetrated against targeted groups during the Second World War exposed the world to the unthinkable, the unimaginable. Prisoners (some of them Canadian) and victims across Europe had been abandoned. Concern for victims and the rights of all human beings were now on the world agenda.

In response, following the end of the Second World War, the General Assembly of the United Nations adopted and proclaimed the *Universal Declaration of Human Rights* on December 10, 1948. Following this historic act the Assembly called upon all member countries to publicize the text of the Declaration and "to cause it to be disseminated, displayed, read and expounded principally in schools and other educational institutions, without distinction based on the political status of countries or territories." Canada signed on in 1949. This Declaration provided a global human rights reference point and vital common ground.

The next wave of feminist activism took place in the 1960s and 1970s in Canada and in the United States. Building on earlier successes and attempting to right some wrongs, the forcefulness of the women's movement intensified. Human rights, civil rights, gay rights, and women's rights were put on the agenda. With a growing percentage of women in the workforce, going to university, and attending law school, feminist critics of the law soon emerged.

The Fight for the Right of Bodily Integrity and Autonomy

Women activists soon turned their attention to the existing gender discrimination and inequality that had persisted throughout the decades. Cognizant of the *Universal Declaration of Human Rights,* feminist groups focused. One area quickly addressed was the law specific to reproductive choice and freedom. The **World Health Organization (WHO)** defines reproductive rights as follows:

> Reproductive rights rest on the recognition of the basic right of all couples and individuals to decide freely and responsibly the number, spacing and timing of their children and to have the information and means to do so, and the right to attain the highest standard of sexual and reproductive health. They also include the right of all to make decisions concerning reproduction free of discrimination, coercion and violence. (WHO, 2010)

Reproductive freedom: to be or not to be pregnant? Plus, the reassurance of knowing that if one chooses pregnancy, one will be fully aware, informed, and in control of the child's birth and destiny. Today, this right is taken for granted. The moment a child is born, infant and mother are united. Today, women are not exposed to the fear, exploitation and heinous acts of violence that historically were inflicted upon countless women. Today, therefore, the discrimination, coercion, violence, and the confusion and shame of a pregnancy resulting even from rape and incest are acts of violence that must be highlighted.

In "Canadian Headline News" Box 1.2 and "Canadian Headline News" Box 1.3, you will read about two dark moments in Canadian history. In both cases, not having the legal right to control reproductive destinies created grave outcomes—pun intended—for women and their children.

The story described in Box 1.2 takes place in Nova Scotia, where women were stigmatized and exploited and their children sold and murdered.

1.2 Canadian Headline News: The Butterbox Babies of the 1920s, '30s and '40s

Located in East Chester, Nova Scotia, the Ideal Maternity Home was operated by William and Lila Young from the 1920s to the 1940s. William was a chiropractor and Lila was a midwife (despite advertising herself as an obstetrician). They offered maternity care for local married couples and discreet birthing and placement for children of unwed mothers.

Initially, in 1928, the Youngs worked out of their four-bedroom home. When they began their business they had barely enough money to buy cots for their patients to sleep on. By 1943, after several renovations, their cottage became a vast structure with 14 bathrooms and 54 rooms. Their home became fashionable and their property expansive. But what activities transpired within these expanding walls? Opportunity and death—but how?

The city of Halifax was a major Canadian naval port during the years of the First and Second World Wars, when numerous ships crossed the North Atlantic to England. Yet many of these ships never completed the journey. Some sailors died, some never returned. Women were left pregnant and unmarried, or became widowed expectant mothers. The Ideal Maternity Home offered more or less the only place for these women and their children. The Youngs met a demand for women because birth control and abortion were illegal in Canada.

When the women first arrived, they envisioned a safe place to give birth. Instead the women faced inconceivable abuses. Mothers were charged $500 for the home's services. At a time when the average wage in the area was $8 a week, few women could afford this fee and were forced to work at the home for up to 18 months to pay their bills. Plus, elaborate contracts were signed by the women, giving Mr. Young the power of attorney and legal authority over their babies and their adoptions.

Sparse, if any, community sympathy existed for the women who decided to have their babies (Cahill, 1992). Families would disown their pregnant daughters. The shame and stigma experienced would silence these women when they witnessed infant neglect and the unhealthy conditions of the delivery rooms. Yet it did not stop there.

In some cases, married couples went to the home exclusively for birthing services but were told their baby died shortly after birth. In actual fact, their babies were stolen and sold on the black market to couples from New York and New Jersey. Desperate for a child, these couples would arrive and purchase a baby for approximately $10 000. To meet the needs of their prospective customers, twins were separated or randomly "matched," depending on what the customers wanted.

The black market babies were, however, the fortunate ones. Hundreds of other babies were left to die because of the home's inadequate medical facilities. Sick, deformed, disabled infants, or infants of mixed race, were considered unmarketable. They would be fed molasses and water until they starved to death. Babies who died were buried in small wooden grocery boxes typically used for dairy products, hence the term Butterbox Babies. The bodies were buried either on the property bordering a nearby cemetery or at sea; sometimes they were burned in the home's furnace. A caretaker would later admit to Canadian journalist Bette Cahill that he was paid to bury the babies in open graves (Cahill, 1992).

One could say the Youngs benefited from being at the right place at the right time. With a wealthy adoption market in the United States, Youngs' greed caused them to craft a piece of history in which women and their babies were exploited, violated, and in some cases killed.

The Youngs were unconstrained by laws governing adoptions—at that time, there weren't any. In 1940 the *Maternity Boarding House Act* was amended, and the Youngs applied for a licence but were turned down. On November 17, 1945, based on findings from inspections, the Ideal Maternity Home was ordered closed. While they were eventually tried for various crimes involving the home, including manslaughter, the entire truth of the horrors perpetrated there was not widely known until much later. It is estimated that between 400 and 600 babies died at the home, while at least another thousand survived and were adopted. Most women who gave up their babies did so with the hope that their children would be part of a loving family and have a bright future, and many were.

Reflection Questions

1. How were the lives of these women and children violated?

2. How secretive do you think this maternity home had to be—or was the stigma so great that no one really cared?

Sources: Cahill, 1992; Hartlen, 2001.

Box 1.3 describes the exploitation of Quebec women in the 1940s, and the grievous results that occurred when rights and laws were nonexistent or ignored. This story illustrates the outcome of being stigmatized; of having no power or, worse yet, protection in society. It also punctuates the acts of oppression, prejudices and influence of the Catholic Church and the medical profession. The fact that many of these girls became pregnant due to rape would indeed re-victimize them and their children. Interestingly, the fallout continues today.

1.3 Canadian Headline News: The Duplessis Orphans—Quebec's "Children of Sin"

Coerced by those in power and forced to surrender their children, these unwed mothers gave away their children, unaware of their fate. The Duplessis Orphans were named after Quebec Premier Maurice Duplessis; he and his government were responsible for the orphans and their ultimate fate.

Most of the orphans' mothers were teenage girls at a time when unwed parenthood carried deep social stigma. Others were children of rape or incest. Others were from families too poor to provide for another child. Most of these children were cut off from society, cut off from their mothers.

What happened? During the 1940s and 1950s the Roman Catholic Church in Quebec operated nearly all of the province's charitable institutions, as well as the public schools and hospitals. Orphanages and schools were the financial responsibility of the provincial government. Funding for mental institutions (the mentally ill) was a federal responsibility. Federal subsidies paid more to hospitals than to orphanages. When this fact was realized, Maurice Duplessis, in cooperation with the Roman Catholic Church, which ran the orphanages, began to conceptualize a shrewd and cunning fiscal plan in order to receive more money per child. They did this with no regard, respect, or compassion for hundreds of human lives.

Suddenly, an alarming number of healthy children were fraudulently and hastily diagnosed as mentally incompetent psychotics and were shipped to Quebec asylums. Children went to bed as orphans and woke up psychiatric patients. Also, since nuns operated the orphanages, many of these establishments were suddenly relabelled as asylums and these children were now labelled mentally deficient. Larger subsidies (for the mentally ill) rolled in.

Although this was a horrific act of human injustice, the worst was yet to come. Children were physically and sexually abused, many were restrained in straitjackets, and some endured experiments with new anti-psychotic and medical procedures: electroshock and lobotomies. Proof of lobotomies existed. Paul St. Aubin, for instance, received electroshock therapy, and has scars from the lobotomies he endured during his 18 years at Cite de St. Jean de Dieu.

Sylvio Vincent, who lived at the same hospital as Paul St. Aubin, had the job of washing the bodies of those who died in the operating ward. He said many of the bodies he saw had holes in their heads. Additionally, in Quebec, in 1942, a law was passed that allowed the nuns to sell the orphans' unclaimed bodies to medical schools for $10. The selling of orphans' bodies continued into the 1960s.

Once these patients were released from the hospitals, these treatments left many orphans unprepared to cope in the outside world. Years later, long after these institutions were closed, the children who survived began to speak about the harsh treatment they endured at the hands of the psychiatrists and the priests, nuns, and church administrators. For the rest of their lives they would struggle to bring attention to their story and demand compensation. Collectively, the Duplessis Orphans began to speak their truth. As their voices grew, and the legitimacy of their lives became undeniable, the government had to reply.

Adding a voice to this movement in 1991, Alice Quinton and author Pauline Gill published *Les Enfants de Duplessis*. The memoir chronicled Quinton's experiences growing up in Hôpital Saint-Julien. In her account, Quinton recalled receiving electroshock therapy and doses of the tranquilizer Largactil and the painkiller Demerol. Fifty years after her first assessment, Alice Quinton underwent a second psychiatric evaluation at the Louis-H Lafontaine Hospital in Montreal. Dr. Claude Choquette stated, "She is of completely sound mind, and very intelligent. She is completely normal. What happened to her was unbelievable" (*Gazette,* April 7, 1991).

Daniel Simard, a social worker in 1951, recalled the Quebec orphanages as uncaring. "It was as though they were making the children expiate the sin of being born illegitimate" (*Gazette,* Nov. 22, 1992). Further, Dr. Denis Lazure, a psychiatrist and the Health and Social Services Minister, stated that social dictums were extremely rigid in the 1940s and 1950s. "The taboo of the illegitimate child was extremely strong—we can't imagine how strong," he told the *Vancouver Province.* "So we shut them away. Everyone closed their eyes—doctors, judges, lawyers, teachers, journalists, everyone."

Government Reaction to the Duplessis Orphans

- In 1997, Quebec's ombudsman recommended the orphans be paid $1000 for each year they spent inside the institution and an additional sum (between $10 000 and $20 000) to those who endured physical and sexual abuse. These recommendations were not accepted during the premiership of Lucien Bouchard.
- On March 4, 1999, Premier Lucien Bouchard offered the first public apology to the Duplessis Orphans. However, he did not blame or hold anyone legally responsible, and defended the benevolence of the church.
- The financial battle would wage on until the Duplessis Orphans unanimously accepted an offer, but with a clear message that the offer was insufficient, and they accepted it because they were reaching the ends of their lives (Bruno Roy in the *Toronto Star,* July 1, 2001).

Many of the Duplessis Orphans were excluded from the settlement. Only those who had been improperly diagnosed as mentally deficient were included in the offer; the average Canadian criminal court award for sexual abuse was $250 000.

A New Chapter Unfolds in 2004

The story did not end there. A group of orphans were fighting to have the bodies of children exhumed to prove that children within those orphanages were also experimented upon and buried in unmarked graves at Cite de St. Jean de Dieu insane asylum, and then buried in a cemetery in east-end Montreal. They believed that the cemetery may be the final resting site of orphans who were used in medical experiments. They wanted the bodies exhumed so autopsies could be done.

Again, in the end, a searing injustice seems to have been the collusion of doctors, church officials, and government leaders who falsely diagnosed the most defenceless wards of the province to boost the flow of funding to needy institutions.

Update: *Justice at Last?* On November 29, 2010, US attorney Jonathan Levy of Washington

(continued)

D. C. filed a complaint at the United Nations Human Rights Council against Canada for egregious human rights abuses. The act was the culmination of 18 years of political agitation by hundreds of victims of what has come to be known as the Duplessis orphans scandal. *This story is not done . . . to be continued.*

Reflection Questions

Canada signed the Universal Declaration of Human Rights in 1949. Article 3 states:

Everyone has the right to life, liberty and security of person.

1. What thoughts come to mind now that you have just read the fate of the Duplessis Orphans?

2. Do you think the Canadian public should also demand further investigation into the alleged unmarked graves?

Sources: CBC, 1992, 1993, 2004.

Birth Control and Abortion Rights

Today, women have the "legal right" to control their fertility. Birth control is available and there is a product to suit most needs. We take our many options for granted. However, birth control, like most rights, did not come easily, and has a long and controversial history.

Preventing conception was illegal in Canada from the time the first *Criminal Code of Canada* was enacted in 1892 until 1969 when contraception became legal. There were varying degrees of tolerance toward people who provided support to women and couples who wanted to control their fertility, but essentially this was an illegal act. Contraception was also opposed by religious and political interest groups. Their attacks on the "birth controllers" were frequent and often defamatory.

Eventually, women earned the right to have legal control over their own reproductive lives. In 1969, Parliament passed Bill C-150, which amended section 251 of the *Criminal Code,* decriminalizing contraception. Decriminalizing contraception gave *all* Canadians the legal right to prevent pregnancy and protect themselves against sexually transmitted infections.

Further, with the introduction of Bill C-150 abortions became legal under certain conditions. A woman was permitted an abortion if a committee of three doctors felt the pregnancy endangered the mental, emotional, or physical well-being of the mother. The committee, called a Therapeutic Abortion Committee (TAC), would decide whether an abortion fit an exemption to the *Criminal Code of Canada*. But this was not enough!

Bill C-150 did not provide all the reproductive rights women demanded. Women wanted abortion legalized. Challenges and protests persisted. Women began to do what they had historically done: they rallied. But it was a rally fit for the 1970s; it was a raucous and rolling rally on wheels called the Abortion Caravan. For the full story, see "Canadian Headline News" Box 1.4.

1.4 Canadian Headline News: The Abortion Caravan

The Abortion Caravan began in Vancouver, on April 27, 1970, and travelled 4500 kilometres to eventually end in Ottawa. It was one of many victories that created the strength and momentum necessary to successfully repeal the abortion law of 1969.

On April 27, 1970, the Abortion Caravan set out from Vancouver with several vehicles and about 19 women. On its way to Ottawa, the group stopped at many towns and cities, gathering up hundreds of supporters. As they travelled they would publicize their cause by hosting demonstrations and providing public meetings. They financed their mission through the generosity of supporters across Canada. Canadians voluntarily fed and sheltered these women.

The Abortion Caravan's journey to Ottawa provided valuable publicity. They had planned for and executed two days of demonstrations. On May 9, a scheduled meeting in Ottawa with the Minister of Justice ended in disappointment after the Minister refused to attend. In response, hundreds of women decided to crash Prime Minister Trudeau's residence at 24 Sussex Drive.

When they arrived, they placed a coffin on Prime Minister Trudeau's front lawn to represent the deaths of thousands of Canadian women who died from illegal and unsafe abortions. The coffin was ceremoniously covered with objects women used for abortions, such as knitting needles, a Lysol container, and a vacuum cleaner hose.

However, they had more extensive plans; the big event was scheduled for the next day. Caravan members selected about 30 women to attend Parliament as visitors. With their visitors' tickets in hand, and bicycle chains and a photocopied speech hidden in their purses, they selected seats apart from each other in the Visitors' Gallery. Then they discreetly chained themselves to their chairs.

In the middle of question period in the House of Commons, one woman stood up and began loudly reciting the speech demanding repeal of the abortion law. When security guards approached her, another woman sitting elsewhere in the Gallery would stand up and continue the same speech, one after another. Security guards darted around to silence the women, and after quite some time were able to cut the chains off all the women (Thomson, 2008).

This day was historic on many accounts, including that, for the first time in its history, on that day Parliament was closed. The next day, nearly every newspaper in the country carried the story of the Abortion Caravan. Awareness was achieved.

Reflection Question

What risks (if any) do you think these women (and men) faced as a result of their association with or participation in the Abortion Caravan in 1970?

Source: Thomson, 2008.

Following the Caravan, Dr. Henry Morgentaler continued to challenge the legal system and the existing abortion laws. He would emerge as one of Canada's most controversial advocates when he broke the law and opened the country's first abortion clinic. Over the next two decades, the Montreal doctor would be heralded a hero by some—and called a murderer by others—as he fought for women's right to have a legal abortion.

Abortion was eventually decriminalized on January 28, 1988. This ruling has left Canada without a law regulating abortion. Twenty years later, in 2008, in recognition of Dr. Morgentaler's contribution to Canadian society, amidst anger and abhorrence *and* adulation and applause, Dr. Morgentaler was made a member of the Order of Canada.

The Aboriginal Woman's Oppression, and Physical and Sexual Victimization

Elsewhere in Canada, concerns were being raised regarding the historical treatment and discriminatory actions and language of the *Indian Act*. Although this movement was taking place in the 1980s, the violence and **oppression** experienced by Aboriginal women dated back long before the enactment of the *Indian Act* of 1897. In fact, beginning in the 1600s, colonization, racism, violence, and patriarchal values were forced upon Aboriginal women. This colonialist belief system led to the immediate subjugation of Aboriginal women; sexual oppression and degradation occurred.

"Mrs. Faries' working class of Indian women—a branch of the W.A. at York Factory."
[ca. 1910].

Aboriginal women, however, were useful. Europeans came to Canada with the hope of prosperity and good fortune. Those coming to Canada, most of them men, understood the wealth of the fur trade, and would use Aboriginal women to help guide them into unexplored territories. When the British and French used the influence of Aboriginal women to secure new markets they became an integral part of trade. Some native women married fur traders and thus provided an important link between the two cultures. The fur trader secured the trade of his wife's band or tribe, and he learned from her survival skills, native customs, and languages. However, for most Aboriginal women, their position in the new society was that of slave.

The Aboriginal women who were part of the fur trade economy were usually confined to York Factory (Absolon, Herbert, & MacDonald, 1996). York Factory was the Hudson's Bay Company's most valuable post, because it was perfectly situated geographically for exporting and importing goods. According to Kathleen Barry (1984), it was a form of hostage-taking, where Aboriginal women were forced to accept the Western values of capital and private property. As First Nations society became altered through this new policy of capitalism, First Nations women also became sexual commodities (Absolon et al., 1996). Women were purchased through a system of exchange. For example, women were sold for alcohol and other European goods. In Barry's book *Female Sexual Slavery,* she wrote, "the traffic in women, like the traffic in drugs or black market babies, depends upon a market . . . the demand for sexual service is most significant where men congregate in large groups separated from home and family" (1984, p. 70).

Some European men took First Nations women as their "country wives," lived with them, and had children (Bourgeault, 1989). While, on the surface, this might appear to be highly regarded behaviour, all too often these women and their children were deserted by the white men at a later date. According to Barry (1984), the phenomenon of the "country wife" was a more clever form of sexual exploitation that was used by the officer class. In these relationships, First Nations women were concubines—secondary wives without legal sanctions. These relationships, particularly when First Nations women became reliant on white men, created serious conflict between the women and their culture. "Country wives" and their children were not considered legitimate property of men by English common law. These families were therefore forsaken (Barry, 1984).

The Aboriginal women's fate would soon be sealed with the passage of the 1876 *Indian Act.* Native women who married non-native men immediately lost their status and relinquished the right to live on reserves. All these forces systematically created women's subservience to men. This history coupled with the devastating results of the residential school system caused irreversible damage to First Nations culture and women in particular. See "Canadian Headline News" Box 3.7 in Chapter 3 to read the eventual apology of the Canadian government.

In 1985, with the enactment of Bill C-31 a huge victory for Aboriginal women was achieved. Specifically addressed were the historical sexually discriminatory rules that had stripped Indian women of their rights. These changes also brought the Act into line with the provisions of the *Canadian Charter of Rights and Freedoms* in 1982. The changes were intended to:

- treat men and women equally
- treat children equally whether they are born in or out of wedlock and whether they are natural or adopted
- prevent anyone from gaining or losing status through marriage
- restore Indian status for those who lost it through discrimination or disenfranchisement
- allow first-time registration of children (and in some cases descendants of subsequent generations) of those whose status is restored
- allow for the registration of children born out of wedlock if either parent was a registered Indian, regardless of their date of birth

While changes were being made to address the discriminatory laws regarding Aboriginal women, and the fight for reproductive rights was being waged, a new victim-oriented perspective on justice was also gaining international recognition. Two important positions were taken within five years of each other by the United Nations. The first was the *Convention on the Elimination of All Forms of Discrimination against Women,* which Canada signed on July 17, 1980.

The second event took place in 1985, with the United Nations *Declaration of Basic Principles of Justice for Victims of Crime and Abuse of Power.* This document encouraged countries already addressing victim rights, and it spurred others to start or expand victim rights and services. The Declaration, with an emphasis on rights and protection, boded well with the changing mood of the Canadian citizenry.

Women's rights advocates also saw sexual assault and domestic violence and the poor response of the criminal justice system as potent illustrations of a woman's lack of protection, respect, power, and influence. Many deficiencies and abuses were exposed, and the methods and means to effect change were identified. As with the temperance movement in the 1800s, women combined their intellect, wisdom, compassion, and social justice advocacy to fight for a better and safer world.

History of Domestic Violence

The historical record of marriage and violence has been written about for centuries, as illustrated in 1602 by English writer William Shakespeare. The following is a quote by Shakespeare's character Othello, who is speaking to his wife, Desdemona:

> *By heaven, I saw my handkerchief in's hand.*
> *O perjured woman! Thou dost stone my heart,*
> *And makest me call what I intend to do*
> *A murder, which I thought a sacrifice; I saw the handkerchief.*

In *Othello,* Shakespeare presents one of his grimmest tragedies. Iago is a bitter and perhaps jealous soldier bent on destroying his commander, Othello. In carrying out his plan, Iago convinces Othello of Desdemona's infidelity, of which she is not guilty.

Othello's anger and jealousy gradually fester until he lashes out at Desdemona. He begins with veiled insults, then moves to berating her about his lost handkerchief and striking her, and finally directly calls her "that cunning whore of Venice that married with Othello." Othello ultimately accuses Desdemona of adultery and then kills her by smothering her in bed.

Accusations, degradation, fear, pain, and even death; violence against women is not confined in time and space. It is as common now as it was as described by Shakespeare in 17th-century England. In fact, physical dominance of wives by husbands has been a topic dating from the first marriage law instituted by Romulus in 750 BC. The concern, however, at the time was not in *preventing* domestic violence; to the contrary, the concern was in support of "wife beating"—legally and culturally (Danis, 2003; Lemon, 1996). The intent of the law was to protect the husband from potential legal harm, because during this time period a husband was held liable for the crimes committed by his wife (Lemon, 1996).

This belief system, the culturally sanctioned authority men had over women, would continue to prevail from the Middle Ages (900–1300) until the 19th century (Martin, 1976). In England by the late 1500s, an entrenched culture was solidified, the "Golden Age of the Rod," also known as the "rule of thumb" (Martin, 1976; Walker, 1979). Perhaps you have heard the expression but never gave it much thought. It was a reference to the common-law principle that permitted men in England to beat their wives as long as they didn't use a rod thicker than the circumference of their thumb (Lemon, 1996; Walker, 1979).

Despite the emergence of some differing views, the "golden age" mindset would continue to dominate and define English common law. Wife beating remained acceptable. As such, until relatively recently women were unable to divorce their husbands or obtain legal protection from assault. These beliefs and this legal **precedent** would therefore lay the foundation of the legal and cultural mores of a developing Canadian society.

By the early 20th century women were gaining an increase in political power in Canada. New rights were gained. However, legislation to protect them from the brutality they experienced in their homes was not forthcoming. This was in spite of the fact that legislation had been enacted to protect children from harm. Instead, when it came to wife assault, "marital privacy" became the standard; essentially, abuse was considered a family problem (Turekheimer, 2004). Inequalities still needed to be addressed, and domestic violence, much like sexual assault, would be a problem that would take many decades to confront and change.

Battered Women and the Women's Shelter Movement

Not until the second-wave women's movement of the late 1960s and 1970s was public interest in domestic violence piqued (Danis, 2003; Schechter, 1982). Interestingly, in 1980 Richard Gelles (1980) conducted a review of the family violence literature. He noted that while academic interest in the issue of child abuse became ignited by the publication of Henry Kempe's "The Battered Child Syndrome" in 1962 (Kempe et al., 1962), there was no specific seminal scholarly research or publication on women abuse.

The late 1960s in Canada, similar to Europe and the United States, saw a new women's movement emerge and take hold. Feminists rejected all limits to the equality of women's rights. Women were greatly influenced by books and articles written by feminists such as Betty Friedan (*The Feminine Mystique,* published in 1963), Kate Millett (*Sexual Politics,* published in 1970), Germaine Greer (*The Female Eunuch,* published in 1970), and Gloria Steinem, who in 1970 cofounded *Ms. Magazine.*

These authors wrote about gender power imbalance and described the domination and oppression of women by men. In the area of violence toward women, in 1974 a groundbreaking book entitled *Scream Quietly or the Neighbours Will Hear* was authored by British writer Erin Pizzey. It was the first published book on the subject of battered wives. Predating the release of this book, however, was the opening of England's first shelter for battered women.

The shelter existed initially as a community agency called the Chiswick Women's Aid, which opened in London, England, in 1971. It was located in a derelict old building, at the time awaiting demolition, and quickly became a meeting place for women. One day an abused woman showed up and was taken in; others followed (Dobash & Dobash, 1992). As is often the case in major social movements and societal wake-up calls, this shelter's origin was unplanned. The ethos of the policy set out at Chiswick Women's Aid was "no one should ever be turned away" (Dobash & Dobash, 1992; Okun, 1986).

Chiswick House catapulted violence against wives into the public spotlight. But on a more intimate level, it connected an abused woman with other women who could relate to her fear and pain. Through this growing support system women became empowered to take action and hold government and its laws accountable to this form of violence. Soon the private pain of many became a public matter. Relationships with the media were forged, which helped transform violence against women into a social problem (Dobash & Dobash, 1992; Mahony, 1994). Erin Pizzey is credited with setting up the world's first refuge for battered women in 1971, and she went on to establish an international movement for victims of domestic violence.

During the same time period two other important pieces of literature were published. In 1979, American Lenore Walker wrote *The Battered Woman.* Walker would later, in 1984, write *The Battered Woman Syndrome.* In Chapter 2, the "learned helplessness" theory of battered women and the "cycle of violence" explain why battered women are often caught up in a cycle of violence over which they have no control.

The second book that seared the issue of wife assault into the North American psyche was *The Burning Bed,* written by Faith McNulty in 1980. The book was based on the real-life story of Francine Hughes, who had endured 13 years of domestic violence at the hands of her husband, James Berlin ("Mickey") Hughes. In 1977, Francine set fire to her husband's bed while he slept, and he was killed and the house destroyed in the resulting blaze. She then drove her children and herself to the police station and confessed. Francine Hughes was later tried in the state of Michigan and found not guilty by a jury of her peers, by reason of temporary insanity. McNulty's book did a skillful job demonstrating what intense and prolonged trauma can do to a human. It also illustrated Lenore Walker's explanation of learned helplessness and the resultant battered woman syndrome (see Chapter 2). In 1984, the book became a television movie starring Farrah Fawcett. Thanks to television, mainstream Canada and the United States were introduced to the problem of domestic violence; it could no longer be denied.

Canada's Domestic Violence Movement

Coast to coast in Canada, organizations were being formed. Some initially focused on self-help or consciousness-raising, while others promoted social change. Initially the movement consisted of smaller radical groups, but the movement's base gradually expanded to incorporate women from all parts of Canada, including those with diverse viewpoints.

A unique challenge did emerge early in Canada: the struggle to include distinct voices. Domestic violence and how it was defined and understood was not the same among various groups of women. Canada's Aboriginal women, their views, and the subsequent services they wanted were quite different from the white feminist voice that had dominated the political arena; they did not share the same opinions.

Feminists believed violence against women was a direct result of the unequal power that existed between men and women; an expression of the patriarchal society. Aboriginal women understood their experience differently, which resulted from Canada's historical treatment of Aboriginal persons. As Janovicck wrote, "racism, unfair child welfare practices, and discrimination against women in the *Indian Act* made it even more difficult for Aboriginal women to leave violent families" (2007, p. 1). Even if Aboriginal women needed and desired help, the distrust created by the residential school system and the "Sixties Scoop" caused women to fear that support they deserved would not be given and, worse yet, that their children would be taken from them by child protection workers.

What's more, under the *Indian Act* women who chose to leave their communities would be involuntarily removed from the Indian registry when they left or married outside of it. Aboriginal women were placed between a rock and a hard place: they could choose to leave an abusive home, or to lose their own as well as their children's entitlement to treaty rights.

Early in the Aboriginal women's movement, activists realized that many battered women had also been sexually assaulted. This, coupled with the legacy of the devaluation of indigenous culture, would consequently direct their efforts toward developing specialized counselling that focused on nurturing pride in their Aboriginal culture (Janovicek, 2007). Simply stated, the white feminist and Aboriginal women's histories, their realities, and their fears were profoundly different and undisputable. Although mainstream white feminist perspective was vital in challenging and changing the dominant culture, the reality of the Aboriginal women's experience was real. They therefore took a different approach, and developed theories of violence against women that reflected their cultural values and personal and political histories.

In time, the women's movement grew in Canada and various methods were used to shine the light on serious gender inequalities. Government and political parties were lobbied to educate and raise concerns regarding the inequalities. In response, the Canadian government stepped up in 1967 and commissioned the **Royal Commission on the Status of Women (RCSW)**.

Published in 1970, the 488-page RCSW report contained 167 recommendations. It became known as the Bird Commission, named after Chairperson Florence Bird (see Photo 1.3). The report bolstered the efforts of the women's movement. Urgent women's needs were addressed, including abortion services and daycare options. However, looking back, it was clear that not all critical women's issues were addressed, or even revealed.

The Bird Commission did not mention the problem of violence against women. In 2001, during an interview 30 years after the RCSW was published, former executive

Florence Bird, commissioner for the Council on the Status of Women.

secretary of the Commission, Monique Bégin, stated that the common belief of the time was that violence was not talked about: "Violence toward women—we had never talked about that—because at the time, that was still viewed as something personal, not collective, it was not public, it was private, so today violence is a major problem for society" (CBC, 2001, n.p.).

Fortunately, women in the grassroots organizations did respond to the "private" violence being experienced by women. Feminists were becoming aware that numerous women needed support and assistance; public awareness was also growing. Canadians embraced the chant "We will not be beaten," and it became the mantra of women across the country in their organization to eradicate domestic violence. Grassroots efforts transformed the public consciousness. The common belief was twofold: that women face brutality from their husbands, and that the indifference from social institutions had to change (DeKeseredy & MacLeod, 1997; Dobash & Dobash, 1979).

Also discovered was the fact that when women left abusive relationships they frequently lacked basic necessities, including housing and financial resources. Services to address these needs were initially unavailable. Therefore, women's drop-in centres allowed women to stay overnight, while other women volunteered their homes as a place of refuge.

In Canada, the first shelter opened in 1973: Vancouver's Transition House. By 1975, 18 shelters had been opened in Canada and another 57 were opened between 1975 and 1979 (Rodgers & MacDonald, 1994, cited in Tutty, 2006). Beendigen, a shelter for Aboriginal women and children, opened in Thunder Bay in 1978 (Janovicek, 2007).

The Shelters

In early shelters, staffs were comprised of volunteers or former residents. If shelter workers were paid it was usually minimum wage or from a short-term federal grant (MacLeod, 1989). The first shelters used a holistic and empowering approach in which women supported women to move on in their lives. By the end of the 1980s the number of Canadian shelters had increased to 400, and the problem of abused women became accepted as a legitimate social issue (Denham & Gillespie, 1998). It was also at this point when the federal, provincial, and territorial governments began to provide funding to shelters. Eight years after the first transition home opened in Vancouver, Linda MacLeod, in 1980, made the first attempt to suggest the incidence of wife assault, and suggested that 1 in 10 Canadian women were victims of intimate violence.

The conflicting views that existed between groups of women caused unease. The early shelter groups were anchored in a feminist ideology and saw wife abuse as resulting from the differences in power between men and women. This position did not support, or respect, the Aboriginal women's reality. Aboriginal women wanted to develop theories that strengthen the family, which included involving the abuser. Feminists and the Aboriginal women had different goals, but both agreed that domestic violence was a serious problem.

As time passed it became clear that other voices were not represented in the feminist model; the awareness of lesbian partner abuse had emerged. In accepting the fact that violence exists in these intimate relationships, feminists were forced to acknowledge that women can be and also are abusive.

History of Rape Laws

Rape is distinct from and dissimilar to any other crime; perpetrators are overwhelmingly male (97 percent), and 85 percent of victims are female (Brennan & Taylor-Butts, 2008). Added to rape's uniqueness is the alarming fact that most incidents of rape go unreported, despite evidence describing the devastating impact of this crime, which has long been a part of Canada's history. An accurate appreciation of its history requires an understanding of the laws and how they evolved. It also requires an understanding of time and place, which includes the existing social, cultural, and political forces and how they in turn shaped public opinion and legislation.

Today when we think of rape or sexual assault laws, we might immediately think of the *Criminal Code of Canada*. But the *Criminal Code* did not exist until 1892. Up until that point in Canada, rape was a common-law offence and the laws of England were applied. Although it is not the intent of this chapter to discuss and trace the complete legal historical record of rape, there are important points in history to mention. Society's views shaped the meaning of rape, the legal or the judiciary's position of this crime, and the rights and worth of women.

Ancient Rape Laws During ancient times the concept of **false allegations** and its consequences was introduced to the social consciousness. The legendary story of Potiphar's wife (MacFarlane, 1992) was a significant morality example in Hebrew, Christian, and Muslim folklore. It describes what can happen to an honourable man if a vengeful woman deliberately and falsely claims to have been raped. It was during this period when certain myths and **stereotypes** began to develop, and they would continue to plague the Anglo-Saxon system of criminal justice until the second millennium. A summary of the story is as follows (MacFarlane, 1992).

Joseph the Israelite was a highly regarded slave in the Egyptian household of Potiphar. Potiphar's wife was attracted to Joseph. She would regularly cast a lecherous eye on Joseph, and relentlessly invited Joseph to lie with her. The moral Joseph always reminded her of the important role of their master: her husband. One day, Joseph and Potiphar's wife were alone in the house. Taking advantage of this opportunity, Potiphar's wife grabbed Joseph by his clothes and demanded he lie with her. Joseph was able to flee; however, he left behind a torn item of clothing.

When Potiphar returned home his wife showed him Joseph's torn piece of clothing and claimed that she had been raped by him. Potiphar's rage was instant, and he placed Joseph in prison. Joseph, however, was a good man, and his devoted service to the

Pharaoh ultimately led to his release from jail and later appointment as ruler of Egypt (MacFarlane, 1992).

The story of false accusation from a spurned and vengeful lover contributed greatly to a common-law belief that viewed alleged victims of sexual assault with doubt and distrust. The resultant effect was to shift the focus from an inquiry into the conduct of the accused to that of the moral merit or character of the complainant: the victim (MacFarlane, 1992). And, as you will soon read, the issue of a false accusation or the concept of consent did and would influence the unfolding development of the crime of rape, and the eventual sexual assault legislation.

Canada's Rape Laws Now we will move to Canada. Canadian law derives from English common law and quickly took hold in early Canadian society. After Confederation, Canada's *Criminal Code* became the project of Sir John Sparrow David Thompson, then minister of justice. Previously, English precedent (a determined standard) became a convenient if not compulsory starting point for early Canadian courts (MacFarlane, 1992).

The original meaning of the word rape was "to steal." A historical examination of the descriptions of sexual assault crimes paints a picture of the belief that rape was an offshoot of abduction. Specifically, carrying a woman off was of greater offence to her husband or father than to the woman herself (Tang, 1998). From a historical perspective, rape laws were produced to ensure the protection of a woman as property of either the father or the husband. This discriminatory view of women as property consequently formed the basis of early Canadian rape legislation.

In 1892, rape became codified in the *Criminal Code of Canada* (*An Act to Amend the Criminal Code, 1892*, S.C. 1893, c. 32). Before you read the definition of Canada's first rape law it should be mentioned that the term "carnal knowledge" is an archaic or legal euphemism for sexual intercourse. In 1892, sec. 266 defined rape as:

> [T]he act of a man having carnal knowledge of a woman who is not his wife without her consent, or with consent which has been extorted by threats or fear of bodily harm, or obtained by personating the woman's husband, or by false and fraudulent representations as to the nature and quality of the act.

So here began the writing of Canadian rape laws. As the saying goes, time stands still for no one, but this was not so in the case of Canada's rape laws. Many many decades later, change would be demanded. Societal pressure mounted. Transformation in how Canadian law defined rape and how the victim was treated began to unfold, and this reform did not occur in isolation. Legislative response occurred due to a growing citizenry of critics and, most importantly, women's groups. Collectively, they recognized the deficiencies and adverse consequences of the rape laws; changes had to be made.

Significant legal reform also began to transpire during the passing of the *Canadian Charter of Rights and Freedoms* in 1982. The *Charter* ensured the legal guarantee that gender equality would be protected by law. The *Charter* also allowed women the right to have greater input in the drafting of gender-related legislation. The lobbying efforts of organizations such as the National Action Committee on the Status of Women (NAC) were successfully improving the lives of women in other areas of Canadian society.

Rape laws were now on the national agenda. The laws received ruthless criticism— and why not! First, rape laws did not protect women. Second, the laws were biased and based on belittling or disparaging assumptions against and toward women. A woman's sexual history and her credibility were callously viewed. Equally significant was the fact that rape laws did not apply to men.

Most pressing was the undeniable fact that rape was a crime primarily inflicted upon women by men. A long time had passed since the initial writing of the Canadian *Criminal Code*. Those writings were based on the social perception of white men. Sexual assault, like any other crime, is "socially constructed," and this construct needed changing. Sexual assault crimes for the most part were processed in the criminal justice system, in what had been chiefly a white male domain. Put simply, current cases in our courts are based on precedent (the outcomes of previously determined cases). Most had been shaped by the ideological cultural perceptions that were created and shared by men. Consequently, the rape laws that had benefited white men were reinforced, over and over and over.

Added to the legislative failure was the treatment of the sexual victims in Canada. How victims were treated in the criminal justice system discouraged them from reporting. The rules of evidence that applied in sexual assault cases strongly supported the accused, which permitted many rapists to avoid conviction. But the combined voices of many distinct groups of women ultimately influenced and created sexual assault legislative change.

Canada's Rape Laws Begin to Change: Bill C-127

In August 1982, Canada's then-Justice Minister Jean Chrétien introduced Bill C-127. The goal was to transform the existing historical rape laws. Prior to the 1982 amendments, the legal construction of rape placed considerable importance on a woman's sexual history and her credibility as a victim. The amendments made to the *Criminal Code* specifically abolished some rules that perpetuated biases against women. The bill also changed the description and definition of rape to make it easier for women to report and easier for the Crown to prosecute these crimes. These legal changes were enacted in 1983, are viewed as an important victory. A number of key concerns that had been exposed were changed. Table 1.1 highlights the key issues.

Table 1.1 Rape Law Limitations Prior to the Enactment of Bill C-127 and the Subsequent Changes

	Original Rape Law Concerns	Bill C-127 Changes
1	Women's sexuality was defined by men's sexuality. Vaginal penetration by a penis was the only standard with which a woman's body could be sexually violated in rape. Without penile penetration, a forced sexual act was not rape. If an object other than a penis was used it was not considered rape.	The definition of sexual assault was broadened. A three-tiered structure of sexual assault offences was introduced, including a full range of sexual activities.
2	Language: the specific description of rape was gender-biased. Rape was defined only as penetration of a vagina by a penis, which meant a man of any age could not be raped.	The offence was redefined in gender-neutral terms. A man could now, in the eyes of the law, be sexually assaulted. This degendering was upheld by the *Charter of Rights and Freedoms*, which guaranteed gender equality.
3	Patriarchal basis of marriage gave a husband legal unlimited sexual access to his wife. Marital rape was not recognized; wives could not charge their husbands with rape.	Spousal immunity in sexual assault cases was eliminated
4		Consent obtained by fear of force would not be considered consent. New legislative requirement obligated judges to instruct juries to consider the reason-ableness of any grounds for belief by the accused that the complainant consented to the assault.
5	Women were considered morally under-developed, therefore a woman's testimony under oath could not be trusted and could not convict the defendant. Corroboration (substantiated; support) was needed. The rape complaint had to be recent in order for it to be considered in court. Rape complaints that were not made immediately after the attack were invalidated.	Corroboration was not required for a conviction. The doctrine of recent complaint no longer applied.
6	The way rape was legally defined placed importance on the victim's sexual history and credibility *rather than* on the perpetrator's guilt. A woman's credibility depended on her sexual reputation. Her previous sexual conduct could be freely questioned. The complainant's sexual conduct with men other than the accused was considered important in establishing her consent, as were the stereotypes associated with women at the time (many still exist, including the notion that women who led a man on or dressed provocatively deserved what they got).	The complainant's sexual history with the accused could not be used, except in limited mitigating circumstances. Under the new law, with the enactment of the rape-shield provision, victims no longer had to defend their reputations in court.

Sources: Criminal Code of Canada; Tang, 1998; Roberts & Grossman, 1994.

Bill C-127 was also designed to change public opinion. Those goals were:

- to encourage a more positive attitude toward reporting crimes to the police
- to change public notions of what constitutes a crime of sexual aggression (e.g., by informing people about legal changes such as the removal of spousal immunity)
- to stress the aggressive (as opposed to the sexual) nature of these crimes (Roberts & Grossman, 1994).

The 1982 sexual assault law reform eliminated some discriminatory rules against rape victims. Plus, the rape-shield law limited a defendant's ability to cross-examine rape complainants about their past sexual behaviour. Yet, like all laws in Canada, they must also be guided by the *Charter of Rights and Freedoms*. What ultimately unfolded thereafter in courtrooms across Canada were legal challenges to confront and clarify: 1) access to complainants' (victims') records, and 2) the meaning of consent or mistaken belief in consent. These important issues will be discussed in Chapter 7.

Conclusion

Thanks to achievements of the women's movements, monumental changes were made to legally protect women from many forms of oppression and sexual violence. Yet, as you will read, legal and cultural challenges continue and an ongoing commitment to these rights is vital.

1.3 THE HISTORICAL VICTIMIZATIONS OF GAY, LESBIAN, BISEXUAL, AND TRANSGENDER CITIZENS

For gay and lesbian citizens, historically, their right to choose whom to love, sexually desire, or live with was once considered a sin, psychiatric disorder and a criminal offence. Gay and lesbian Canadians were not allowed these human entitlements. As such, when homosexuals chose to be intimate they would experience community disapprobation and criminal penalties. Take this concern one step further and imagine the reality for a GLBT individual who was a victim of intimate personal violence. Who would—or could—they turn to for help, protection, and justice? The answer, of course, is regrettably, no one. In order to study violence in same-sex relationships, the historical values, policies, and laws that perpetrated violence against gay and lesbian citizens will be addressed.

At this point, our discussion will take a brief walk back in time to examine society's understanding of homosexuality. As in the case of other populations of people and how they are described, homosexuality bore a considerable social stigma. The word *homo-sexuality* historically has been associated with concepts of sin, criminality and pathology.

Homosexuality: Historical and Religious Perspectives

Today's views on laws have come from ancient Greek, Roman, and British cultures. Within these societies, homosexuality was viewed differently throughout history. Although there have been periods when homosexuality was accepted, there also were times when it was scorned, or worse, methodically and violently targeted. Literature and art, however, has revealed that in some ancient societies, especially Greek society, male-male sexual behaviour was not only present but openly accepted. There is a wealth of material from ancient Greece pertinent to issues of sexuality, ranging from dialogues of Plato, such as the *Symposium,* to plays by Aristophanes and expansive collections of Greek artwork and vases (Carroll, 2010).

As for lesbianism, the word lesbian itself comes from the island of Lesbos, in Greece, where the poet Sappho lived about 600 BC. Unlike male homosexuality, less information is available regarding lesbians (Carroll, 2010). In fact, there is no direct testimony by a female of how women in ancient times experienced love between women, or of how they viewed its role in their lives (Bullough, 1979). As such, this has perhaps erroneously encouraged a hypothesis that there was a greater acceptance of lesbianism than the evidence actually shows. This also cast another historical world view of women through the male lens.

Compared to today's Christian beliefs, up until the late sixth century the Roman Empire had few restrictions about sexuality, including homosexuality (Boswell, 1980). Consequently, Romans had very permissive attitudes toward homosexuality and bisexual behaviours. Further, in the entire Bible, same-sex sexual behaviour is explicitly mentioned only in the prohibition in Leviticus, and it refers only to men (Carroll, 2010).

By the ninth century, almost every part of Europe had some sort of local law code based on Church teachings. Although these codes included some sanctions for sexual transgressions, including rape and incest, homosexual relations were not forbidden in any of them, and the church's indifference to homosexuality lasted well through the 13th century (Boswell, 1980; Kuefler, 2006; Siker, 1994).

It was in the latter part of the 12th through to the 14th century that witnessed a sharp rise in hostility toward homosexuality. A new intolerance grew, and homosexuality became punishable by death (Boswell, 1980; Kuefler, 2006). This intolerance developed in part from the pressing social problems of the day. Plagues had scourged Europe throughout the 13th century, forcing the Catholic Church to advocate for the repopulation of Europe. The Catholic Church also had another pressure. Papal (i.e., having to do with the Pope) power regarding the right to divorce was challenged, which led to the birth of the Protestant faith in the 16th century. The church responded by changing the Catholic doctrine with respect to sexuality.

From that moment the Church focused to increase its populace. Suddenly, all sexual practices were considered "unnatural" if they did not lead to procreation, and they were considered mortal sins. The Church started to appeal to a conception of "nature" as the standard of morality, and crafted it in such a way so as to forbid homosexual sex. From that point on, religious teachings were incorporated into legal sanctions (Boswell, 1980; Hunt, 1999; Kuefler, 2006; Siker, 1994). Reference to natural law still plays an important role in contemporary debates about homosexuality in religion, politics, and even court-rooms. You can read a story that exemplifies this point in Chapter 6, "Canadian Headline News" Box 6.2, about a 2002 Supreme Court case that demonstrates how the natural-law legal strategy has been used in the second millennium.

Homosexuality in the 18th and 19th Centuries

By the 18th and 19th centuries, secular (worldly) views and interpretations were increas-ing. Probably the most important discussions regarding homosexuality were in medicine and psychiatry. The prestige of medicine was also taking hold, and medicine and psychia-try were effectively competing with religion and the law for jurisdiction over sexuality. As a consequence, discussions about homosexuality expanded from the realms of sin and crime to include pathology (Greenberg, 1988). The application of the medical viewpoint now allowed sexuality to be conceptualized as innate or biologically driven. This shift was considered progressive because a sick person was less blameful than a sinner or a criminal (D'Emilio & Freedman, 1988; Duberman, Vicinus, & Chauncey, 1989). This meant homosexuality was not chosen, nor were its acts; therefore, it made less sense to criminalize it.

Soon, doctors were called in by the courts to examine sex-crime defendants (Foucault, 1980; Greenberg, 1988). Now doctors, especially psychiatrists, campaigned for the **repeal** or reduction of criminal penalties for consensual homosexual sodomy, but they would continue to "rehabilitate." Physicians and scientists also believed homosexu-ality was not a sin but an illness that, if left untreated, would spread like a contagious disease. The dangers of this extremely perilous perspective were realized in Nazi Germany, when homosexuals were imprisoned and murdered along with Jews and others as part of the program to purify the Aryan race (Adam, 1987; Hunt, 1999).

The Third Reich and Homosexuality

The Nazi Party, ruled by the dictatorship of Adolf Hitler, gradually took over many civic organizations, local governments, and courts (Giles, 2002). The Nazis dictated the mood of the country and controlled and sanctioned all public opinion by destroying and ridding the country of divergent points of view, whether they existed in academia, literature, or art. While homophobia was widespread but not universal in Germany, it was the attitude of a handful of leaders who eventually shaped the campaign against homosexuals (Giles, 2002). Soon Hitler identified homosexuals, particularly gay men, among the groups that the Nazis targeted. Thus, gay organizations were banned and academic books regarding homosexuality and even sexuality were destroyed (Hunt, 1999; Steakley, 1974).

In September 1935, the campaign against homosexuals was escalated by the introduction of the *Law for the Protection of German Blood and German Honour,* (*paragraph 175a*). This law brought about sweeping extensions of the legal criteria for "lewd and unnatural behaviour" (Steakley, 1974). It now included a variety of new illegal behaviours, such as kissing, embracing, and even having homosexual fantasies (Steakley, 1974). Once enacted, ordering the police "pink lists" became a priority. Noteworthy was the fact that in the early 1900s the German police had begun compiling lists of suspected homosexual men.

Since homosexuals were a targeted group, they too were arrested and sent to concentration camps. Upon arrival, prisoners had to wear downward-pointing triangles on their jackets. The colour of the triangle denoted the category to which the individual belonged. The **pink triangle** was used to identify male prisoners who were sent to camps because of their homosexuality status (Giles, 2002; Hunt, 1999; Steakley, 1974). Prejudice was also vividly present inside the concentration camps. Giles pointed out that,

> . . . some 2,100 castrations had been carried out by the middle of 1941 . . . .. From the actions of Ernst Kaltenbrunner, and of various doctors working with the police and SS, it begins to look as though castration was not simply used as a preventive measure, but as a rather satisfying punishment. (2002, pp. 16–17)

Following the Second World War, the world would realize the scope of the murderous actions of Hitler and the Nazi Party. The Third Reich demonstrated how easy it was for a government to scapegoat and brutally target groups of people; brand their sexuality as a sex crime, and soon other citizens could be at ease to "look the other way" while the Nazis went about their torture, beatings, castration, and out-and-out killing of homosexuals (Giles, 2002; Steakley, 1974). And as devastating as these facts might be, the treatment of gay people was still injurious in post-war North America and continued into the 1970s and beyond (Giles, 2002).

Pathologizing, criminalizing, and stigmatizing, one might say, also signify the three sides of the triangle that hampered efforts to commemorate over 100 000 homosexual victims of the Third Reich. Today, the downward pink badge is turned upward and worn as a sign of courage and pride. It is fitting that these victims of violence are memorialized.

Homosexuality in 20th-Century North America

Much like laws, the definitions and descriptions of mental disorders and their subsequently permitted actions had significant impact on the treatment, rights, and protections of children, women, and homosexuals. Previously in this chapter, references have been made to homosexuality being viewed as a mental illness. But where does this label or thought begin? In Canada and in the world up until the 1970s physicians and psychiatrists viewed homosexuality as a mental disorder. The psychiatric position is an imperative topic, because it wielded great influence. Psychiatrists were "definers" of individual worth; the profession garnered immense power and prestige.

For this reason, we now explore the development of the *Diagnostic and Statistical Manual of Mental Disorders (DSM)*. The *DSM* provides a common language regarding mental disorders; therefore, its inception and how it has evolved are important. As you will read in future chapters, the *DSM* is quoted often to describe psychological impact and diagnoses resulting from various forms of violence. Even more specific to this chapter is the discussion regarding homosexuality as a mental disorder.

The History of the *Diagnostic and Statistical Manual of Mental Disorders (DSM)*

Currently, the ***DSM-IV-TR*** is the most up-to-date manual being used. The manual provides a classification of mental disorders. Its purpose is threefold:

- to provide a helpful guide to clinical practice
- to facilitate research and improve communication among clinicians and researchers
- to serve as an educational tool for teaching psychopathology

The *DSM* is a vital reference taught to students and consulted by psychiatrists, physicians, social workers, psychologists, health care workers, and those employed in social service fields. Our understanding begins by examining why and by whom the *DSM* was first developed, and what, how, and why specific notable changes occurred in subsequent editions.

The roots of the *DSM* go back to the 1840s. Before the first edition was conceived or published, a classification system was developed by a group of superintendents from American insane asylums and hospitals (AMSAII) who in 1921 would become the American Psychiatric Association (APA) (Adam, 1987). Their original goal was to count the numbers of patients confined in mental hospitals and create a uniform system of naming, classifying, and recording the cases of mental illness. This group, together with the National Commission on Mental Hygiene, developed a guide for mental hospitals called the *Statistical Manual for the Use of Institutions for the Insane,* and over the years it would be revised several times by the APA.

Similar to other significant moments of change described in this chapter, world events and their consequences set in motion the need to transform thinking and action. Key to furthering the development and understanding of mental illness were the two world wars. During the First World War and the Second World War, military psychiatrists who treated soldiers suffering from mental disorders believed their conditions resulted from their traumatic war experiences: **shell shock**. "It consists of a lingering anxiety, a tendency toward nightmares, 'flashback memories' of battle, and the avoidance of activities that might provoke a sensation of danger" (McHugh, 1999, p. 4).

These war years witnessed the large-scale involvement of U.S. psychiatrists. This consequently redirected the psychiatric focus away from mental institutions, "the asylums," and the traditional clinical perspective. The conception of the *DSM,* one could say, came about due to these changes. In 1943 a committee developed a new classification scheme called *Medical 203.* It was used to help psychiatrists treat soldiers whose mental health was harmed as a result of their war experiences (Regehr & Glancy, 2010). Soon confusion existed because of the numerous classification systems being used. In 1950 the APA decided to examine the various manuals. The ultimate goal was to create one system that could be used for diagnostic and statistical purposes, plus a glossary of definitions for the different illnesses. A decision was made to call the new document the *Diagnostic and Statistical Manual of Mental Disorders (DSM).* In 1952, *DSM-I* was published.

The medical profession carried immense authority, and its diagnoses controlled the lives of many citizens. Many Canadian headline news stories have pointed to this fact, for example the "erroneous" psychiatric labelling of the Duplessis Orphans by psychiatrists, and the right of "medical doctors" to determine which women were entitled to a therapeutic abortion. The time when a person lived and the descriptions found or not found in the *DSM* had great impact on a life. This statement is no more true than when we examine the historical treatment of homosexual citizens and the impact the gay rights movement had, which categorically (pun intended) forced change.

The Gay Rights Movement and Challenges to the *DSM*

Much like the women's movement, the gay rights movement began to demand changes— but why? In the *DSM-I* and the *DSM-II,* homosexuality was considered to be a mental illness. For decades homosexuals were pathologized by the medical profession, and as such, social and legal constraints were severe. Hence, the designation of homosexuality as a mental illness needed to be eliminated. In the early 1970s activists began to campaign against the *DSM* classification of homosexuality as a mental disorder.

From 1970 to 1973 angry but determined protesters began to disrupt the APA offices and annual meetings. In the early 1970s members of the American Gay Liberation Front (GLF) and the Gay Activists Alliance (GAA) demanded the right to take a seat at the table and participate in the conversation regarding the damage that psychiatric "therapies" were doing to the lives of gays and lesbians (Hunt, 1999; Marcus, 1992).

Eventually, the weight of empirical data coupled with the changing mood and power of the U.S. gay community forced the Board of Trustees to remove homosexuality as a disorder category from the *DSM* in 1974. By 1986, the diagnosis was removed entirely from the *DSM.* The only remnant in the revised *DSM-III* occurred under "Sexual Disorders Not Otherwise Specified," which included persistent and marked distress about one's sexual orientation (American Psychiatric Association, 1987). Since this time the

APA has worked intensively to eradicate the stigma historically associated with a homosexual orientation (APA, 1987).

Gay Rights in Canada and Protection from Violence

The post-war period sentiments regarding homosexuality that existed in Europe and the United States also were present in Canada. The sodomy laws that remained in Europe were equally true for Canada; overt legal oppression of gays and lesbians continued.

Modelled on British law, the Canadian government had criminalized sexual relations between people of the same sex, even if it was consensual and occurred in the privacy of a home. Buggery remained punishable by death from 1841 to 1869.

In 1892, a broader law targeting all homosexual male sexual activity was enacted called "gross indecency." Criminal penalties pertaining to sexual behaviour between males went beyond anal intercourse and included all sexual relations between males. When the *Criminal Code* was revised in 1953–1954, this law was extended to gay women. Additionally, in 1948 and 1961 new *Criminal Code* changes were used to brand gay men as "criminal sexual psychopaths" and "dangerous sexual offenders." These criminal convictions led to an indeterminate prison sentence. Now gays and lesbians suspected of consensual homosexual relations were liable to prosecution (Hunt, 1999).

While all these *Criminal Code* changes were unfolding, inspired by the gay rights activism taking place in the United States, in 1964 the Association for Social Knowledge (ASK) was founded in Vancouver. ASK maintained a community centre and published a newsletter. ASK relied upon experts in the field of psychology and medicine to help educate its membership on the nature of homosexuality and to argue that existing criminal penalties punishing homosexual behaviour were irrational. ASK also organized Canadian gays and lesbians to oppose Canadian laws that criminalized sodomy and gross indecency (Hunt, 1999).

In time, however, homosexuality would become a fundamental Canadian issue. Unlike the **Stonewall Riots** in New York that ignited gay communities in the United States, one might say that Canada's gay rights movement began not with rioting chants and broken windows, but in the quiet discriminatory arrest of a man named Everett George Klippert in August, 1965. Accordingly, his voice, this voice, would eventually become louder and louder and the fight for gay rights would begin.

The Everett George Klippert Story On the morning of August 16, 1965, in Pine Point, Northwest Territories, the RCMP detained mechanic Everett George Klippert. They questioned him about an arson case they were investigating in the community. Mr. Klippert was known to police as a homosexual. Although he was found to have no connection with the fire, the intense and protracted questioning did bring out details of his sexual activities which included times and places. Mr. Klippert admitted to having had consensual homosexual sex with four separate adult men. He was arrested and charged with four counts of "gross indecency" under section 149 of the *Criminal Code.*

Later, Mr. Justice Sissons found Klippert guilty and declared him a dangerous sexual offender and sentenced him to "preventive detention"; he was sentenced indefinitely. The "preventive detention" determination was the result of a court-ordered psychiatric assessment that determined him to be an "incurable homosexual."

Mr. Klippert appealed this decision to the Northwest Territories Court of Appeal, but his appeal was dismissed. He then appealed to the Supreme Court of Canada. The Court, however, dismissed the appeal in a controversial 3–2 decision. There was also a growing consensus that Klippert should not face such a penalty for a victimless "crime."

Canadians responded by sending hundreds of letters; some were supportive, but many were abusive. Moreover, the day after Klippert's conviction was upheld by the Supreme Court, New Democratic Party leader Tommy Douglas invoked Klippert's name in the Canadian House of Commons, stating that homosexuality should not be considered a criminal issue. On December 21, 1967, Prime Minister Pierre Elliott Trudeau uttered his famous and often cited quote in a media scrum outside the House of Commons:

> Take this thing on homosexuality, I think the view we take here is that there's no place for the state in the bedrooms of the nation, and I think what's done in private between adults doesn't concern the *Criminal Code.* When it becomes public this is a different matter . . .

Those remarkable or haunting words, famously made by Pierre Trudeau caused a swell of controversy that surged across Canada. The Omnibus Bill brought the issue of homosexuality to the forefront for the first time, changing the political and social landscape in Canada forever. Trudeau however, was motivated by this glaring example of how the government regulated and punished sexuality. Within six weeks, Trudeau presented the *Criminal Law Amendment Act, 1968–69* (Bill C-150), an omnibus bill that, among other things, decriminalized homosexual acts between consenting adults. The presentation of this *Act* generated considerable debate. Divergent views were plentiful, and many statements were fuelled by anger and perhaps fear.

Furthermore, Trudeau also acknowledged that the Bill contained some of the most extensive revision of the *Criminal Code* since the 1950s, (contraception was decriminalized) which helped bring the laws of the land up to contemporary Canadian society. The presentation of this *Act* generated considerable debate. Divergent views were plentiful, and many statements were fuelled by anger and perhaps fear.

Then the third and final reading took place on April 16, 1969. After what would be considered an impassioned debate, in 1969 the House passed Bill C-150 by a 149–55 vote, decriminalizing homosexuality. Bill C-150 went on to pass in the Senate and received Royal Assent on Aug 26, 1969

The specific amendments to the *Criminal Code* made certain sex acts committed in private between any two consenting persons 21 or older no longer illegal. Despite these changes, Klippert wasn't released from the maximum security penitentiary until mid-1971. He died in 1996 at the age of 70. Following the enactment of Bill C-150, ASK would disappear (Hunt, 1999).

On August 28, 1971, a protest on Parliament Hill was held to mark the anniversary. Charlie Hill, representing Toronto Gay Alliance, spoke at the event. It was the second anniversary of Bill C-150. Soon after, the first issue of *The Body Politic* was published and sold.

The Body Politic Energized and motivated by the success of the march on Parliament Hill, members of Toronto's gay and lesbian community formed a united newspaper called *The Body Politic* (Bébout, 1995). *The Body Politic* published 135 issues over its 15-year existence from 1971 to 1987. Based in Toronto, it was the leading journal of gay liberation in Canada, and became an internationally respected voice of radical gay thought. Despite the publication and the growing strength of the collective gay voice, police in various cities across the country would steadily increase their harassment. One targeted area was gay bathhouses; this is where the story of Operation Soap begins (Bébout, 1995).

Operation Soap What would continue to unfold despite the enactment of Bill C-150 was a societal belief system regarding homosexuality and, for some Canadian police forces, the right to continue to administer the law in the manner they saw fit. Bill C-150 had only decriminalized certain limited homosexual actions (Bébout, 1995; Hunt, 1999). The bill amended the buggery and gross indecency sections to ensure that sex between two consenting adult gay men was no longer a crime, but only providing it took place in private and between participants aged 21 years or older.

The bill forced legal gay sexuality into constricted private spaces (Bébout, 1995). Therefore, in 1969, armed with the bill's broad definition of "public," police promptly stepped up their patrols. Generated by the police and the government, this legal window of "opportunity" led to the conception and implementation of Operation Soap. Operation Soap marked a major turning point. The bathhouse raids and their aftermath are widely considered to be the Canadian equivalent of the 1969 Stonewall riots in New York City. What happened?

Operation Soap was part of a deliberate campaign by government and police to push gay baths and bars out of business, to silence the gay press, and to remove the gay voices from public discourse. On February 5, 1981, at least 150 Toronto police simultaneously raided four of Toronto's most popular gay bathhouses; over 300 innocent men were arrested. It was the largest mass arrest in Canadian history, comparable only to the October Crisis of 1970 when the *War Measures Act* was proclaimed and all civil rights were thus curtailed. To draw a comparison, during the October Crisis between 450 and 500 people were arrested without warrants.

But Operation Soap and those actions did not end. Whatever the catalyst for the unprecedented response, and despite all the years of harassment, this event inspired a spontaneous wave of fury. Mass protests and rallies grew denouncing Operation Soap. By midnight on February 6, 1981, 3000 people had gathered in Toronto. They blew whistles, waved homemade signs, and chanted "No more raids!" and "Stop the cops!" The protestors blocked traffic at several major intersections. The police were undermanned and unprepared, and could do little except reroute traffic.

This 1981 event is now considered one of the crucial turning points in Canadian GLBT history. The gay community continued to fight for rights that had always been entitled to heterosexuals: the right to legally marry and to embrace a life free from harassment.

CHAPTER CONCLUSION

We are the sum total of our history. Our attitudes and beliefs reflect all our historical influences. The great difficulty that challenges today's society and each of us individually is in recognizing that our own collection of beliefs, feelings, and moral thought regarding children, women, and sexuality are a product of our particular time and place and, hopefully, are in a constant state of evaluation and evolution.

Multiple Choice Questions

1. The history of child maltreatment in Canada begins with which of the following groups?

    a. Ursulines   **b.** Jesuits
    c. Récollets   **d.** Christian Brothers

2. One of the most influential figures in the development of the Canadian child welfare system and the protection of children was John Joseph Kelso. What was his profession?

    a. justice of the peace
    b. lawyer in the criminal court system
    c. newspaper reporter
    d. medical doctor

3. Who said, "I want to get rid of the Indian problem"?

    a. Prime Minister Sir John A. Macdonald
    b. Dr. Duncan Campbell Scott
    c. King George III
    d. Dr. C. Henry Kempe

4. The Butterbox Babies of the 1920s, 30s and 40s were in what province?

    a. Nova Scotia   **b.** Ontario
    c. Newfoundland   **d.** Prince Edward Island

5. After years of oppression, Aboriginal women achieved a significant victory in 1985, when a particular bill was enacted that specifically addressed the historical sexually discriminatory rules that stripped Aboriginal women of their rights. What was the name of the bill?

    a. Bill C-150
    b. Bill C-86
    c. Bill C-31
    d. the Gradual Civilization Bill

6. The battered woman theory was conceptualized to explain why battered women remain in abusive relationships. Who conceptualized this theory?

   a. Betty Friedan   **b.** Lenore Walker
   c. Germaine Greer   **d.** Erin Pizzey

7. Who is credited with starting the world's first shelter for battered women?

   a. Florence Bird   **b.** Lenore Walker
   c. Germaine Greer   **d.** Erin Pizzey

8. The Royal Commission on the Status of Women (RCSW) was published in what year?

   a. 1950   **b.** 1960
   c. 1970   **d.** 1980

9. From the time the *Criminal Code of Canada* was written, it took how many years for the laws governing rape (sexual assault) to be amended?

   a. 30   **b.** 50
   c. 70   **d.** 90

10. Which of the following did Bill C-150 provide?

    a. the legal right to use contraception
    b. the legalization of homosexual sex between consenting adults in a private place who were over the age of 21
    c. the right to a legal abortion under certain conditions
    d. all of the above
    e. none of the above

Discussion Questions

1. Describe what "Sixties Scoop" refers to.
2. According to Canadian history, the expression "bodily integrity and autonomy" related to what injustices and acts of violence? As a consequence, what rights and protections were won by the feminists?
3. What is the *DSM,* and how is it significant to the history of homosexuality?

Key Terms

assimilation: the process by which minority groups gradually adopt the cultural patterns of the dominant majority group.

Badgley Report: Canadian report published in 1984 that outlined the extent of child sexual abuse in Canada. It painted an alarming picture of the scope and history of this problem.

battered child syndrome: the repeated mistreatment or beating of a child resulting in physical and psychological injuries.

Canadian Charter of Rights and Freedoms: the constitutional document that sets out the rights and freedoms affecting people of Canada; the people entitled to the specific rights and freedoms vary by the particular right or freedom.

colonization: when radical or ethnic groups from one society take over and dominate the racial or ethnic groups of another society.

common law: a legal rule or a body of legal principles, established through judicial decision, that deals with particular legal issues or subject areas.

Criminal Code of Canada: first enacted in 1892; the most important source of criminal law in Canada. It is divided into 28 parts and contains the full listing and explanation of criminal offences and procedures in Canada.

DSM-IV-TR: the *Diagnostic and Statistical Manual of Mental Disorders.* Published by the American Psychiatric Association, the *DSM* is used by clinicians and psychiatrists to diagnose psychiatric illnesses and covers all categories of mental health disorders for both adults and children. The manual is non-theoretical and focused mostly on describing symptoms as well as statistics concerning which gender is most affected by the illness, the typical age of onset, the effects of treatment, and common treatment approaches.

false allegation: when a person makes up something about someone that is not true.

Famous Five: five Alberta women, Nellie McClung, Emily Murphy, Louise McKinney, Irene Parlby, and Henrietta Edwards, who were persistent critics of male society's refusal to grant women political and social equality.

migration: the movement of persons from one country or locality to another.

mores: norms that have a moral base.

oppression: the exercise of authority or power in a cruel or unjust manner.

paragraph 175a: a provision in the German Criminal Code that made homosexual acts between males a crime.

parens patriae: a doctrine that holds that the state has a responsibility to look after the well-being of children and to assume the role of parent, if necessary.

pathologizing: interpreting the victim's reaction to his or her victimization as an "illness," sickness, or pathology.

patriarchal: part of a tradition in which families are male-dominated.

pink triangle: a symbol used to identify male prisoners who were sent to camps because of their homosexual status.

poor-houses: also referred to as workhouses; places where those unable to support themselves were offered accommodation and employment.

precedent: a court decision that influences or binds future decisions on the same issue or similar facts.

repeal: to terminate the application of a statute.

shell shock: a term commonly used after the First World War to refer to what is now known as post-traumatic stress disorder.

stereotypes: prejudicial attitudes toward racial and ethnic groups based on false or inadequate group images.

stigma: social disapproval of actions or beliefs that are against cultural norms.

Stonewall Riots: a series of spontaneous, violent demonstrations against the police in New York City that occurred in 1969; considered the first instance when the homosexual community in the United States fought back against a government-sponsored system that persecuted homosexual persons.

Royal Commission on the Status of Women (RCSW): published in 1970; a 488-page report that contained 167 recommendations. Known as the Bird Commission, after Florence Bird, its chairperson.

United Nations (UN): an international organization of independent states, with headquarters in New York City, formed in 1945 to promote peace and international cooperation and security.

Universal Declaration of Human Rights: the 1948 Declaration adopted by the United Nations that arose directly from the experience of the Second World War. It represents the first global expression of rights to which all human beings are inherently entitled, and it consists 30 articles that have been elaborated in subsequent international treaties, regional human rights instruments, and national constitutions and laws.

World Health Organization (WHO): an agency of the United Nations that monitors outbreaks of infectious disease and sponsors efforts to prevent and treat diseases.

Chapter 2
Theoretical Explanations of Violence

The only person you are destined to become is the person you decide to be.

Ralph Waldo Emerson, poet (1803–1882)

Chapter Objectives

1   Present the ecological framework as an organizational model to guide our understanding of the various perspectives used to explain intimate personal violence.

2   Present, define, and explain how the micro, mezzo, and macro levels of society contribute to our understanding of intimate personal violence.

3   Present, define, and explain the major theoretical explanations under the micro, mezzo, and macro levels of organization.

2.1 INTRODUCTION TO THEORETICAL EXPLANATIONS OF VIOLENCE

Within the past 40 years, many measures have unfolded to provide protection to Canadians. Yet, even despite these changes, the question remains: How is it possible, after four decades of progressive collective work, that the choice to be violent survives over knowledge and laws? In this chapter, we provide an overview of some of the major theoretical explanations of interpersonal violence in an attempt to answer this question. Today, most professionals who work in the field of interpersonal violence, regardless of their area of specialization, consider theories that propose only a single cause for something as complicated as interpersonal violence to be inadequate. Therefore, within this chapter a number of theories will be presented.

While the topic of intimate violence can be challenging to study, for those who work within the field understanding the theoretical explanations can be multifaceted yet necessary. Since 1962, when intimate violence was first academically unearthed by C. Henry Kempe's *The Battered Child Syndrome,* and 1974, when Erin Pizzey authored *Scream Quietly or the Neighbours Will Hear,* numerous explanations, insights, and perspectives have been articulated. To help organize the various theories or "ideas" available, we will use the **ecological model**. This framework involves understanding the individual, the family, the daily systems they live and work within, and the larger society's laws and values, as well as how these parts are connected.

The Ecological Model

People at any given time are influenced by others and their surroundings. Bronfenbrenner (1979) was one of the first academics to realize it was not just our human relationships that affected us, but also our environment and the culture in which we live. As such, Bronfenbrenner's research began with the primary purpose of understanding human development and behaviour within this context and its many layers.

The ecological approach accentuates the complex interrelationships among all systems, the individuals, family, communities, and the larger society. Thus, a unified perspective that stresses the interrelationships that exist among people and other influences in their lives is necessary. Plus, systems are goal directed (Bronfenbrenner, 1979; Heise, 1998). Humans and their social systems do their utmost to accomplish their goals. Needs must be addressed and met, and the family is the one system (we hope) that can provide the essential human needs of food, shelter, love, belonging, and encouragement. Our communities, cities, and country serve similar roles to ensure needs are met, and if we are lucky they help foster human potential.

Building on Bronfenbrenner (1979), we will use a three-level approach to human systems. This three-level ecological framework tends to focus more on a person's dignity and human rights than on individual physical impairment or limitations; *there has been enough victim blaming in our society*. As such, this perspective places a greater emphasis upon, and underscores the connections among problems, and the limits in a person's specific environment such as home, school, and society. These levels are *micro, mezzo,* and *macro,* and they are defined below and in Figure 2.1.

Micro Level At the **micro** level the major emphasis is on the individual, and this system encapsulates the smallest social interactions within primary relationships. They are *usually* based on enduring, intimate (close) relationships. This level's main characteristic focuses on personal development. As such, in this level all theories that include explanations about individual behaviour, personality, and individual motivation as well as psychopathology are important.

What is noteworthy is that the individual, even within his or her own intimate microsystem, is also shaped by other encounters. Common sense tells us that it would be unreasonable to believe that a child is solely a product of the family environment. There are multiple, simultaneous influences that nurture and create a child's development and learning. The process of human growth and learning can carry on throughout adolescence and even during adulthood. We have to believe this, or how else do we challenge and change the status quo? So, what are the other places or sources that provide further opportunity to look beyond our own homes, that will enable an individual to become who they choose to be and, for some, to create a different *type* of home? At this point we will describe the next level—the mezzo system.

Mezzo Level The **mezzo** level incorporates family, neighbourhoods, communities, and schools (teachers and peers). These include the shared cultural values and beliefs

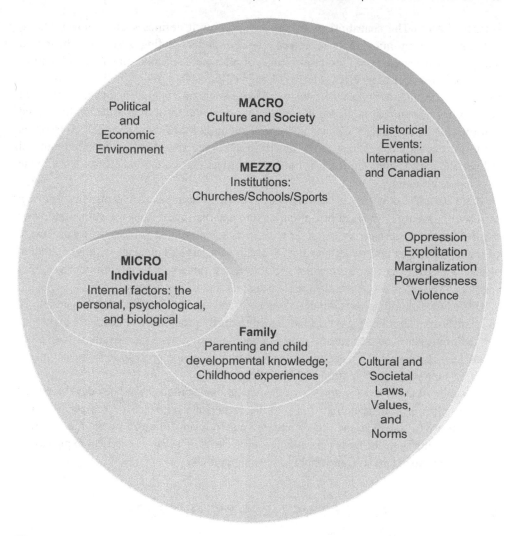

Figure 2.1 The Micro, Mezzo, and Macro Levels

about what is appropriate or inappropriate at any given time. Woven throughout all these systems are the rules—written, spoken, or simply "understood." Examples include:

- the types of parenting methods or discipline methods that are used and endorsed
- the types of spousal relationships that are celebrated, and the expressions of human sexuality that are allowed or prohibited

And, similar to the interrelationship that exists between the micro and the mezzo levels, the overarching macro level also influences.

Macro Level The contributions of culture and how it defines societal **norms**, laws, policies, and economics are at the **macro** level. An understanding of society's historical and present-day treatment, and prohibitions of all aspects of governmental and institutional policies and their effects on the larger culture takes place at the macro level. Significant moments in Canada's history forced societal change, for instance, the two world wars. Partnering in global world and international initiatives such as the United Nations has also shaped Canada's social structure. Moreover, national civil rights activities have forced change at the macro level. Some specifically addressed cultural values and norms that diminished human dignities; consequently, efforts were made to promote equality.

Yet various social forces and changes are not always based on episodic historical events or influences. They are part of our culture and our times. They are values and ideas that influence us; perhaps we can refer to them as social trends. Sometimes we are aware of these influences and sometimes not. Sometimes a large percentage of the population agrees with them and sometimes not. And there are times when only a minority group requires a specific change, despite the fierce opposition of the majority.

The last example to consider describes how Canada, in recent decades, has attempted to identify special interest groups (also called minority groups) by deliberately highlighting their uniqueness—their needs—and responding accordingly. One example took place when legislative changes were made to the criminal justice process to help victimized children cope while participating in the justice system.

Within all these levels a number of theoretical explanations have been developed that help expand our understanding of how intimate personal violence occurs and is maintained. We will start with the big picture, the macro level, followed by the mezzo level, and concluding with the most personal, the micro level. The key theoretical explanations identified at the macro level are oppression and patriarchy.

2.2 THE MACRO LEVEL AND VIOLENCE: THE BIG PICTURE

Today, despite all the challenges and changes made to address violence in our society, we continue to live in a very violent world. Tragic and heartbreaking stories tend to stir people. Once aroused, a common reaction is to want to understand why violence happens, why it is allowed, and how to stop it. At the macro level there are cultural and societal factors that contribute to an environment that can either foster or directly cause, and also condemn or punish, acts of violence. Culture includes a society's historical record, and its current beliefs, values, and rules. Consider Canada's history; acts of violence not only were allowed, but legally sanctioned. Thus, understanding the forms of violence and *when* they occurred is critical.

To begin, we will examine the meaning of oppression and the role it has in explaining intimate personal violence.

Oppression

To begin this chapter, the examination of "oppression" is obligatory. Many historical acts of oppression and violence were supported and enforced by legislation, governmental policies, and medical assessments. As such, incredible hardship and acts of cruelty have been perpetrated against many citizens.

What is vital to our understanding of oppression is the power and authority some groups have over others. This gives them the capacity to define and enforce their beliefs, and to deny other groups specific entitlements, protections, and services. An academic who has extensively studied the issue of oppression and its role in creating social problems is Bob Mullaly (2007, 2010). Mullaly puts forward the point that before an understanding of oppression can be made, it is first important to know what oppression is *not* (Mullaly, 2007).

We all live in a society where our choices are restricted. We are told we can't text or talk while driving, and some professors do not allow texting or talking on cell phones in class. These examples restrict our freedom, take away our right to choose, and for some may cause frustration. But these are not forms of oppression. Not everything that restricts our freedom is oppressive (Mullaly, 2007). To understand oppression, one has to look at the social context of a particular restriction and if and how it impacts our choice or opportunity. **Oppression** exists when restrictions of choice are due to a person's status or membership in a group, not because of individual worth or failure. Furthermore, as Fry (2001) writes, "The experience of oppressed people is that the living of one's life is confined and shaped by forces and barriers which are not accidental or occasional and hence avoidable" (p. 141).

Another feature of oppression is that it is not accidental. To have oppression in society the two-sided coin is needed: the privileged and the oppressed. The oppressor occupies a position of power, influence, and very often prestige. Oppression is perpetrated systematically by the dominant majority, as observed in Canada's early Indian policies, and the treatment of the British Home Children discussed in Chapter 1. Oppression existed to ensure that a certain "type" of citizenship was protected, and that its level of importance, its superiority, was elevated. These legal sanctions protect and ensure the oppressor's access to better quality and more of whatever is most valued and prized at any given time and place.

Oppressors also view the oppressed as a group that must be controlled for the good of society (Mullaly, 2007). This was clearly articulated during colonization with the government of Canada's determined effort to rid society of the "Indian problem." Historically, myths have been perpetrated and perpetuated to support oppression. One example in particular that Canadian culture appears to have not evaded is **victim blaming**. This type of false accusation has existed for centuries and continues today. The sentiment is echoed in statements such as, "if she wanted to leave she could," or "she did something to bring on the assault." A judicial decision as recently as 2011 implied that if women dress a certain way then they are asking to be raped; see "Canadian Headline News" Box 8.1.

Moreover, many myths relate to the notion of normal or abnormal. For centuries the medical and legal communities defined the normal perspective regarding sexuality, which was dominated by the white, male, heterosexual Christian perceptive. Bishop (2002) further suggested that historically every oppressed group has been assigned at least one negative sexual myth. These stereotypes are socially constructed, and justify or even legitimate one group's opinion or importance at the expense of another's group's human dignity and integrity. We also see the issue of sexuality highlighted in existing cultural views within Canada; one example is discussed later in this chapter in "Canadian Headline News" Box 2.2.

Forms of Oppression Chapter 1 identified numerous groups that have suffered different forms of oppression at various times, and within Chapters 3 to 6 we will continue to discuss present-day expressions of oppression and violence. Iris Young (1990) developed a set of five categories or types of oppression. What is noteworthy is that every oppressed group might not experience the same type or similar level of severity. Table 2.1 presents examples of oppression.

So how do we overcome oppression? One would think, based on the positive historical gains made, that one vehicle to eliminate oppression would be through the acquisition of rights and legal sanctions (that is, laws). As Chapter 1 demonstrated, historically some

Table 2.1 Types of Oppression

	Type	Definition
1	Cultural Imperialism	Arises when the dominant group universalizes its experiences and culture to establish the norm; also referred to as ethnocentrism. All others are measures by the standards of the dominant group; they are the "ideal." Stereotypes are born from these perspectives. As such only the dominant group's story or culture was celebrated. All others were undervalued, or even branded as, sinful, deviant and inferior.
2	Exploitation	Refers to those social processes whereby the dominant group is able to accumulate and maintain status, power, and assets from the subordinate groups.
3	Marginalization	Excludes entire groups of people from meaningful participation in society.
4	Powerlessness	The overarching impact denies the opportunity to develop one's capacities and to not have the right or power to make decisions regarding one's life.
5	Violence	Includes physical attacks, and harassment, ridicule, or intimidations that stigmatize. Group members not only experience direct acts of violence, but constantly fear victimization.

Sources: Young, 1990; Mullaly, 2010, 2007.

groups of people have had certain rights and entitlements while others have not. Nevertheless, even when legal rights are granted we cannot assume that they are always available. One significant point to note is that many Canadians do not know exactly what rights and forms of protection are available to them. They might not be in a position (due to location, age, finances) to access those rights. As such, we can reflect upon the quote that opens this chapter. Simply because people are afforded rights, entitlements, and protection does not ensure they will have the same options. Equal access does not always occur. At this point, we will move to the second theoretical explanation under the macro level, which involves the reality of privilege, power, and control—patriarchy.

Patriarchy: Privilege, Power, and Control— A Feminist Theory

For centuries we have witnessed the fact that children and women, as well as gay and lesbian citizens were not protected and valued, but harmed. This hierarchical, white heterosexual male-dominated and entitled "family system" was exported to Canada by the Europeans and ultimately supported a cultural tradition in which women and children were victimized in their homes.

With the advent of the second-wave women's movement in the late 1960s and 70s, combined with the naming or exposing of child abuse, domestic violence, and rape, came investigative questions regarding the "who, why, where, when, and how much" of male-perpetrated violence began. The most salient clarification resulting from the analysis was the fact that violence was the result of male power and the privileged position men held over women. Rosenberg and Duffy (2010) wrote that men's "historical property right over women and children, along with their contemporary position in the social order—as heads of household, as fathers, as husbands, as brothers, as employers, as professors, and so forth provided them with the power to oppress and victimize women. In this sense violence is a reflection of male power and privilege in society" (p. 175).

In an effort to address this problem, over the last 40 years measures aimed at breaking the silence over patriarchal violence and oppression have been introduced in Canada and in the world. Patriarchy and its centuries-old value base structure is what many theorists (particularly feminist theorists) believe to be one of the main theoretical explanations of violence.

Patriarchy is the term used to describe a society characterized by historical and current unequal power relations between women and men whereby women were systematically disadvantaged and oppressed. Much of patriarchy has its roots in Christianity. The Christian Bible states boldly that women should be submissive to men. Patriarchal cultures traditionally upheld the privileges of men based on gender, social structures, religious practices, and legal codes. With those instilled societal beliefs, women have to struggle to gain strength, rights, and opportunities for their gender.

Today, patriarchy can differ in expression but remains rooted in the perceptions of male superiority and female subordination. This sense of superiority is often a last resort in the male effort to maintain existing power structures when women and girl children question and challenge the status quo. Generally the status quo deprived females of specific rights and entitlements that were enjoyed by men and boys *simply* because they were born male.

This dominance takes place across almost every level of life but is particularly noticeable in women's underrepresentation at the macro level in key government institutions, in decision-making positions, and in employment and industry. For instance, although Canadian women earned the right to vote in 1918, and became "persons" in 1929, they did not begin to have access to most political offices until well into the late 1970s. And even today, women are found in political office at a rate far lower than one would expect from a group that represents one-half of Canada's population.

Reports supporting patriarchal violence often point to the power structure under which women and men are assigned different roles. These roles go far beyond the obvious biological ones. For instance, in the case of religion, standards such as "culture," "tradition," and "attitudes" are often interpreted by men and tend to be "man-made" constructs of **gender stereotypes**, which provide the rules of how people are to behave, relate to one another, and dress.

The issue of "dress" is an element that often is part of patriarchal oppression. The fact that how a woman dresses is still noteworthy in the 21st century is serious. A case discussed within this textbook exemplifies this point. In 2011, a Toronto police officer, addressing a class of university students, suggested women should stop dressing like "sluts" if they didn't want to be raped (see the description of the slut walk in Chapter 8). A statement of this "spirit" at this particular level of power and privilege demonstrates a special characteristic of violence, in that it is openly encouraged and endorsed. These assertions—sanctions—force women to confirm their sexual identities, and thus their rights on a day-to-day basis, by choosing assertiveness or obedience, the clothing they wear, whether to be bold or passive, and so forth. Plus, these assertions are aggressive and blaming. In Finney Hayward's book *Breaking the Earthen Jar,* she quotes a woman NGO leader as saying, "Before, I defined violence as blows, rape or sexual abuse. Now I see it as everything that violates my right to be treated as a human being" (2000, p. 207).

This is only one example in a discussion of existing present-day forms of patriarchal violence. A distressing story occurred in June 2011, when Canadians and the world once again would be awakened to a vicious act of violence directed at a woman. "Canadian Headline News" Box 2.1 tells the story of a husband who, accusing his wife of infidelity, gouged her eyes and almost bit off her nose. The fact that the husband's belief (whether erroneous or not) would allow him to think he could commit such an act of brutality toward another human being is unacceptable. As this case illustrates, a system of beliefs can severely curtail individual freedom (of choice) in fundamental areas of life and security.

2.1 Canadian Headline News: Husband Accuses Wife of Infidelity, Gouges Her Eyes and Bites Her Nose

After studying for nine months at the University of British Columbia in the political science master's program, Ms. Rumana Monzur returned home to Bangladesh to see her family, which included her daughter. But, in her words, that opportunity did not last long. Angered by a set of beliefs he had, her husband, Hasan Syeed, blinded her and partially bit off her nose.

This vicious act of violence was so severe that her father took her to India for additional treatment. Soon after the attack, an ophthalmologist confirmed that her left eye was blinded permanently while the retina of the other one was not responding to her brain.

Responding to this event, on June 15, 2011, UBC president Stephen Toope wrote a statement acknowledging the community's sadness at the incident. "This tragic occasion is a poignant marker of the need to work to protect the fundamental human right of all women to pursue education," he said.

A week later, on June 21, 2011, Dr. Toope would write that "Doctors atSankara Nethralaya in Chennai and at the Aravind Eye Hospital in Pondicherry have regretfully agreed that no further treatment is possible for Ms. Monzur. I understand that Ms. Monzur is now recovering with the care and support of her family in Dhaka." The president would further state that the university was "working to prepare options for Ms. Monzur to complete her Masters degree

in Political Science. While this cannot, of course, be Rumana's immediate priority, we want her to know that everyone at UBC is thinking of her and of her future."

Ms. Monzur was an assistant professor in the International Relations Department at Dhaka University. She was in Canada pursuing her master's degree in political science at UBC while her family remained in Dhaka. Reports suggest her husband accused her of cheating before the attack. Many have since condemned his comments. Her husband was arrested 10 days after the attack. Following his arrest he confessed to torturing Rumana.

Later, in December 2011, Hasan Syeed was found dead on a blanket in the bathroom of the Bangabandhu Sheikh Mujib Medical University. The news report said he had been transferred from the Dhaka Central Jail in November.

Reflection Question

Rumana Monzur's highly publicized case of brutal domestic violence is cited in the excerpt as a violation of her fundamental human rights as a woman to "access education." If you were asked to be the spokesperson for Canada's position on the human rights violation(s) inherent in the story of Rumana Monzur, what message would you want to emphasize to the world?

Sources: Toope, 2011a and 2011b; The Daily Star, 2011; Mahoney & Nolen, 2011; Ryan, 2011.

Yet the most extreme example of culturally motivated violence occurs in the form or action of an honour killing. Although this occurs more frequently in other parts of the world, various cultural beliefs do exist in Canadian society, which led to tragic murders of females. To read these stories, see "Canadian Headline News" Box 2.2.

There is no conceivable excuse or justification for the killing of one's daughter or wife because her behaviour is *believed* to have brought shame to the family. And defining the word "shame" or "shameful behaviour" again forces us to ask: who is the definer of appropriate behaviour? Cultural definitions are generally defined by the dominant group—those who hold the power and who have right to impose their will upon others.

Nothing short of condemning honour killing is acceptable. There is no allowed cultural respect or sensitivity to the different values of other ethnicity in Canadian society that could ever ask any Canadian, any human being, to "understand" or justify how a father or brother could kill a daughter, sister, or mother in the name of honour—whatever that honour represents. Nor is it comprehensible that a mother could be a sympathetic witness to such a savage act of violence.

2.2 Canadian Headline News: Death in the Name of Honour

In June 2010, the father and brother of 16-year-old girl, Aqsa Parvez, pleaded guilty to second-degree murder in the matter of her death and were sentenced to life in prison. Ms. Parvez lived in Mississauga, Ontario, was of Pakistani descent, and wanted to wear Western clothes, get a part-time job like her Canadian friends, and stop wearing the hijab.

During the sentencing hearing, an agreed statement of facts released in court revealed that when Ms. Parvez entered her teen years, she began rebelling against her father's rules, especially his requirement that she wear traditional Muslim clothing. She and her family experienced tremendous conflict because of the divergent values that existed between Pakistani and Canadian culture. She had previously told her father she did not wish to wear the hijab, wanting instead to dress in Western clothes with the same freedoms as the other girls in her high school.

Prior to her murder in September 2007, Ms. Parvez told a counsellor at Applewood Heights Secondary School in Mississauga that she was "afraid her father wanted to kill her." The school made arrangements for Ms. Parvez to stay at a shelter, but she stayed only three days. Soon after, she was permitted to wear non-traditional clothes to school but the conflicts within the family did not subside. Ms. Parvez occasionally spent time living with friends, but each time her father or another family member would ask her to return home.

On December 10, 2007, Ms. Parvez was picked up at the school bus stop by her brother at approximately 7:20 a.m. Just 36 minutes later, her father called 911 and told police he had "killed his daughter." Peel Regional Police later took Muhammad Parvez into custody and charged him with murder. But, according to the statement of facts, it was Waqsa Parvez, her brother, who killed Ms. Parvez. His DNA was found beneath his sister's fingernails.

As this case demonstrates, although honour killings have often been linked to sexual issues such as adultery and premarital sex, other perceived "offences" have also prompted such killings, and one significant example stems from a woman's desire and push for independence.

Regardless of the violent action or perceived reason, honour killings reflect an extreme example of a male sense of honour. These acts of violence are executed by men who feel they haven't received their owed respect—men who consider "their" women, whether daughter or partner, to be their chattel, to do with as they choose.

A 2008 report co-written by Dr. Amin Muhammad, a psychiatrist at Memorial University in St. John's, Newfoundland, suggests honour killings date back to ancient societies. According to the report, Incan law allowed husbands to starve their wives as punishment for adultery, while the Aztecs permitted stoning or strangulation as punishment for such crimes. In Pakistan, this is referred to as *karo-kari*, and it was only recently outlawed—though, the report said, "perpetrators are rarely brought to justice."

Reflection Question

How should our courts respond to these types of crimes? Do you think these victimizations should be treated any differently than other acts of violence?

Sources: City News, 2007, 2010; Cohen, 2010; Gill, 2006.

The last point to make involves another flagrant manifestation of gender inequality, yet one that is perhaps not so clearly labelled as such, and it relates to a lack of bodily integrity. Remember, gaining this right required persistent perseverance! And although it is a legal right for all Canadians to have knowledge of and access to birth control and an abortion if they choose, some women, based on their cultural and religious beliefs, are forbidden this right—this choice. In fact, in the "publicly funded" Catholic school systems in Ontario, birth control and abortion are not included in the educational instruction. This deprivation of liberty defines another form of patriarchal violence. But unlike open violence, which is easier to detect as a result of the injuries it causes, deprivation can be more subtle. It is important to remember that the boundary between violence and oppression tends to be indistinct.

Macro Conclusion

The root causes of all patriarchal violence must be addressed by challenging perceptions of male superiority and female subordination as well as interpretations of masculinity that reinforce patriarchal structures and male violence. Oppression and violence limits individual freedoms and the range of personal choice and well-being. It makes it more difficult for people to obtain the education and profession they would like to choose, and despite all earnest intentions, it can affect the person you are destined to become—*the person you decide to be.*

As an examination of the macro level illuminates, the culture of a society encompasses its attitude, values, and beliefs. A culture's ethos therefore serves as a blueprint for human behaviour. As such we can think of the family as the primary institution through which children and adults learn the influence of the macro level. We will now discuss the theories that focus on the mezzo level of the ecological system.

2.3 THE MEZZO LEVEL

Intergenerational Violence: The Cycle of Violence Hypothesis

An old adage states:

The apple doesn't fall far from the tree.

But through my years of clinical work with children and families, I have learned that:

There have been many tremendously blustery days.

Introducing individuals as wives, husbands, partners, mothers, fathers, sons, daughters, or "steps" positions them in a special set of relationship roles, expectations, and responsibilities. The attributes assigned to these roles have a significant impact on how an individual perceives themselves and others. What's more, regardless of our current or past family living arrangements or our family's societal description (two-parent family, blended, divorced), most of us will consider family central to our self-identification. There are, however, no simple or straightforward explanations regarding the activities people undertake in supporting or working within and maintaining their families.

A family's life is a busy place full of activity, communication, change, success, tragedy, reminiscence, regret, anticipation, and hope. What happens in families also involves silence—and not just in the sense of quietness, but in the sense of what is unspoken; this includes secrets!

Couples are also an important subsystem at the mezzo level. They impact the lives of their children whether they are married, divorced, cohabiting, same-sex, or in a nurturing and loving or a conflicted and violent relationship. During the developing years children are exposed to the relationship patterns of their family, and the most critical teachers are their parents.

Learning involves discovering how parents interact with the outside world, with their children, with each other. It also involves understanding how to express warmth and gratitude (if they do) and how to respond to conflict. All this information, this teaching, will ultimately affect the values, knowledge, and skills a child learns. The reality is that many children experience abuse and witness violence within their homes. We therefore question whether they will learn to be violent.

What grows and takes flight when a child's life begins in an abusive and hostile home? Many have studied this very question. Studies have provided important information. The short answer is that there has been a mixture of results. This is not surprising since interpersonal violence is a very complex problem. Several variables intervene in the lives of people. Some abused children do grow to repeat the life they had, some abuse their children and/or their spouses, and some are victimized again in their adult intimate relationships. But this is not always the case. The following is an overview of research that addresses the positive and negative correlations of intergenerational violence.

Positive Correlations: Violence Begets Violence The intergenerational theory suggests that a childhood history of abuse predisposes the survivor to violence in later years. Various types of violence, whether physical, emotional, or sexual, and even witnessing violence may influence the child to believe that violence is normal (Elliott & Mihalic, 1997; Fagan 2005). If the child views the violence as normal, if this is what he or she is learning, then why think otherwise? Remember, children do not have many learning sources to draw upon in early life.

Numerous studies have found evidence to support a direct link between violence and future offending. This suggests that violent and abusive adults learned this behaviour as a result of being the victims of, or witnesses to, aggressive and abusive behaviour as children (Babcock, Miller, & Siard, 2003; Chapple, 2003; Dutton, 1998; Elliott & Mihalic, 1997; Fagan 2005). Siegel (1992) specifically noted that "the boy who witnesses his father repeatedly strike his mother will more than likely become an abusive parent and husband" (p. 170).

Some studies have noted not only that those who experience childhood victimizations will become victimizers later in life, but that some children may also have anger and aggression problems or even become criminal offenders during childhood and adolescence. For some, the impact of intergenerational violence occurs sooner rather than later (Choice et al., 2006; Elliott & Mihalic; 1997; Fagan 2005; Nicholas & Rasmussen, 2006).

Researchers are not sure of the exact mechanism by which this happens, but they do have several theories. The first theory is at the heart of the intergenerational theoretical explanation: learning. In general, learning theories assert that development results from an accumulation of experiences. Learning theories are aligned with the early philosophy of John Locke, who said that children are born with neither good nor bad tendencies, but their behaviour is shaped, for better or worse, by their environments. "Empiricism is the view that humans possess no innate tendencies, that all differences among humans are attributed to experience. As such, the blank slate view suggests that adults can mould children into whatever they want them to be" (Boyd, Johnson, & Bee, 2009, p. 3). Further, a learning perspective maintains that a long-lasting change in behaviour is based on experiences, or adaption to the environment (Boyd et al., 2009). As such, by examining environmental influences, behaviour can be explained or understood.

We will now briefly examine key theories on learning and how they are related to the transmission of violence: behavioural learning theory, social learning theory, and cognitive learning theories.

Learning Theory: Behaviourism

Behaviourism is a mechanistic theory, which describes observed behaviour as a predictable response to experience (Boyd et al., 2009). Although our biology sets restrictions on what we can do (we can't all play hockey like Jason Spezza), behaviourists view the environment as a much more influential force. They support the belief that human beings at all ages are continually able to learn about their world the same way other organisms do; by reacting to conditions or aspects of their environment. This includes determining what they find enjoyable, painful, or frightening. Behaviourists also look for events that determine whether or not a particular behaviour will be repeated. They focus on associative learning, in which a mental link or a connection is formed between two events. Two types of associative learning to be discussed are classical conditioning and operant conditioning (Boyd et al., 2009).

Classical Conditioning Classical conditioning was first discovered by Nobel Prize winner Ivan Pavlov (1849–1936). Pavlov can be credited with providing the first theory on learning when he executed his experiments in which dogs learned to salivate at the sound of a bell. This salivation, this *response,* would not naturally take place unless there had been some form of manipulation, some "learning"—and this was Pavlov's goal. What Pavlov demonstrated was that each incident of learning begins with a biologically programmed stimulus–response connection, or a reflex (Ciccarelli, Harrigan, & Fritzley, 2009). When a biological response exists naturally and it is associated with (linked to) another event that is not biologically programmed (called a neutral stimulus), a new response will be learned and a new behaviour will be born. As such, a bell sound, a conditioned stimulus, had caused dogs to salivate—now a conditioned response.

Pavlov's original work and theory would not stop there. In 1920, American child behaviourist John Watson would apply Pavlov's classical conditioning theory to humans by using an 8-month-old child named Little Albert. Watson's experiment began by implementing Pavlov's key concepts of classical conditioning. The following provides an overview of his study (Ciccarelli et al., 2009).

Watson and Little Albert Albert was situated in the middle of a room. A white laboratory rat was deliberately placed near him. At this point he showed no fear of the rat. As the rat moved around, Albert began to reach out to him; this was the first step. The white rat was the *neutral stimulus* (NS). Albert had never before seen a white rat, therefore he had *no* initial reaction.

In further trials, Watson made a loud and surprising sound behind Albert's back by striking a suspended steel bar with a hammer when the baby touched the rat. Not surprisingly, because Albert was startled and frightened, Albert did what most babies do—he cried and showed fear when he heard the loud unexpected noise.

> The frightening noise was the unconditioned stimulus (UCS).
> The response—Albert's fear, crying—was the unconditioned response (UCR).

After several such pairings of the two stimuli (white rat, *NS,* and noise, *UCS*), Albert was presented with only the rat. Despite the absence of the noise, he became very distressed as the rat appeared in the room. He cried, turned, and tried to move away from the rat.

Albert had associated the white rat (original *neutral stimulus,* now the *conditioned stimulus*) with the loud noise (*unconditioned stimulus*) and an emotional response; crying was produced. Albert was now afraid of white rats.

Albert would also generalize his fear: when presented with other furry objects he would become upset. **Stimulus generalization** occurs when a conditioned response follows a stimulus that is similar to the original conditioned stimulus; the more similar the two stimuli are, the more likely generalization is to occur. As such, he showed similar fear when Watson appeared in front of him wearing a Santa Claus mask, made with white cotton balls to represent his beard. (Conditioning a child to fear Santa—or to fear anything, for that matter, would never pass an ethics committee today!)

Although these two experiments took place decades ago, this type of learning does continue to happen, and it does not have to take place in a precisely designed and executed laboratory setting. Classical conditioning learning takes place without our knowledge and without deliberate intervention. Children learn to react (so do adults) to certain stimuli in their environment, and sometimes the reaction is not "normal" or "expected." When this occurs it should be a signal that somewhere a specific connection has been made.

An example to illustrate this point took place one summer many years ago, when I worked as a child protection worker. I was working with a very young child who had been sexually abused; this fact was documented through her bodily injuries, yet many questions were still unanswered. One day, when she was at the agency for her weekly therapy session, I offered her a freezie from the agency freezer. Her physical reaction was one of repulsion. Her entire demeanour changed; her reaction to the offered treat was startling. In time, it was discovered that part of the abuse ritual had involved providing her with freezies or ice cream. Most children enjoy freezies, but for this child they triggered the traumatic and painful memories of her sexual victimization. Here, learning was demonstrated.

An essential point to remember is that when you spend time with a child you become aware of how they act and react when they feel happy, safe, nervous, and afraid. Children, especially young children, have minimal self-awareness and are not generally conscious of their behavioural cues, so they don't hide them. It is therefore up to the adults who nurture, love, and protect them to notice any significant "unnatural" changes in a child's behaviour.

Operant Conditioning Psychologist B. F. Skinner (1953) was following the work of Pavlov and Watson when he developed his operant conditioning theory (sometimes also referred to as Skinnerian conditioning). Through operant conditioning, an association is made between behaviour and a consequence for that behaviour: rewards and punishments. To understand operant conditioning we need to first understand the basics of operant conditioning.

Operant conditioning is the learning in which a voluntary response is strengthened or weakened, depending on its favourable or unfavourable consequence (Skinner, 1953). Thus, when we say a response has been weakened or strengthened we mean that it has been made more or less likely to occur regularly. *Reinforcement* is the central concept in operant conditioning. Similar to Pavlov's theory, operant conditioning has key terms that will help us analyze behaviour and understand how learning unfolds. The key concepts in operant conditioning are positive reinforcers and negative reinforcers, and positive punishment and negative punishment.

Positive Reinforcers A positive reinforcer is a stimulus added to the environment that brings about an increase in a preceding response. An example, which involves intergenerational violence, takes place when a child grows up observing one parent being violent, physically intimidating, verbally abusive, or controlling. If a child observes that these actions do, in fact, yield a specific desired outcome, they will learn that violence is an effective means of getting what one wants from a partner. This learning also influences adults. For instance, when a sexual abuse victim hears how a defence lawyer speaks to a sexual assault victim during a court trial, or how a judge describes a victim negatively, they may question the value of reporting their victimization. As such, the victim's public experience in the criminal justice system affects the number of victims willing to go forward and report their victimization.

Negative Reinforcers A negative reinforcer occurs when a particular behaviour strengthens or increases in the hope that a negative consequence can be avoided. In these situations, a response is strengthened by the removal of something considered unpleasant.

Punishment is the presentation of an adverse event or outcome that causes a decrease in the behaviour it follows. There are two kinds of punishment: positive punishment and negative punishment.

Positive Punishment Positive punishment involves the presentation of an unfavourable event or outcome in order to weaken the response it follows. An example would result when a neighbour sees or hears a parent abuse their child, prompting them to call their local child protection agency. Following an investigation, when it is determined that a child has been abused, the child is removed from the parent's home. This demonstrates to the parent that there are consequences when they abuse their child. It also teaches society that their calls of concern are heard.

Negative Punishment Negative punishment (also known as punishment by removal) occurs when a favourable event or outcome is removed following a behaviour. An example would be a spouse who stops verbally abusing his partner after she leaves the home and/or seeks counselling.

In order to stop violence within families, individual members must realize that violence is wrong and not tolerated. To achieve this, the protective systems—police, child protection workers, and the courts—must act judiciously. Moreover, abusive individuals must have access to experiences (counselling) that help and support new ways of coping and living; new behaviours can be learned.

Negative Correlation: "The Violence Stops with Me" The discussion so far could easily lead to the conclusion that growing up in an abusive home will automatically cause a child to be abusive toward their children and partner as an adult. There is no doubt that violence impacts victims and the witnesses. The child and adult reflect the world in which they were raised. Living in an abusive home, or perhaps even a violent community or culture where violence was condoned, does not ensure every child will automatically become abusive. Studies inform us that a negative correlation also exists; in fact, "research shows that the relationship between the early experience and later perpetration of violence is far more complex than one might assume" (Choice et al., 2006, p. 327).

Even though the probability of being violent toward one's spouse is higher for a previously abused person, not everyone follows this pattern (Dutton, 1998). One study estimated that 40 percent of child abuse victims grew up to become abusive themselves; thus, 60 percent of abused children do not become abusive adults. Similar research conducted by Kaufman and Zigler suggests that intergenerational transmission appeared to occur in 30 percent of their sample, and another study found that approximately one-third of those who had suffered physical or sexual abuse or neglect as a child would subject their own children to some form of abuse (Elliott & Mihalic, 1997). The important number to emphasize here is that 70 percent would not.

So what takes place in the lives of these children that creates a different outcome—the choice to not be violent? Elliott and Mihalic (1997) noted that the cycle is less likely to be repeated if a child had the love and support of one parent, loving supportive relationships as adults, and fewer stressful events in their life. This finding was also supported in Dutton's (1998) study which found that having at least one supportive or loving parent or other adult in the life of a child may also help overcome the effects of living in a hostile home with an abusive parent. This is where the larger mezzo system can play an important role. Supportive and positive role models can exist in other significant relationships, such as coaches, teachers, and even neighbours.

Most interesting was the finding of *choice*. Research found that a critical variable in halting or ending intergenerational abuse takes place when people make the choice to acknowledge their childhood abuse and specifically make a determined decision not to repeat it (Elliott & Mihalic, 1997). The issue of choice requires thought—cognition—and this is the gift that makes us human.

With this in mind, we will now explore additional theories that help expand how we understand learning. Those who grew up exposed to violence, whether in a home, institution, or community (places that they did not choose), can and do make the choice not to repeat the cycle of violence.

Social Learning Theories and Cognition

In the early days of behaviourism, the original focus of Pavlov, Watson, and Skinner was on observable behaviour. Anything that might be occurring inside a person's mind was once considered to be of no interest to the behaviourists because it could not be seen or directly measured. But in the 1950s, and more intensely in the 1960s, many psychologists became aware that cognition, the mental events that take place inside a person's mind while behaving, could no longer be ignored (Ciccarelli et al., 2009). Albert Bandura's social learning theory has become perhaps the most influential theory of learning and development.

Social cognitive approaches to learning emphasize the influence of cognition—thoughts, feelings, expectations, and values, as well as the observation of other's behaviour—on personality. This supports the intergenerational "cycle of violence" hypothesis, which suggests that violent and abusive adults learn these behaviours as a result of being the victims of, or witnesses to, aggressive and abusive behaviour as children. But exposure to violence does not ensure learning (Bandura, 1969).

An equally important theoretical process put forward by Bandura emphasized the idea that people also have the ability to become self-regulated learners. Self-regulation occurs when individuals have their own thoughts about what is appropriate or inappropriate behaviour and choose their actions accordingly (Bandura, 1997).

Unlearning What Was Learned It is important to encourage and nurture self-regulation in those who did not have the benefit of a non-violent childhood or life. As mentioned earlier, Bandura was interested in child development and understanding violence in aggression. As a result, he also thought that if aggression was diagnosed early in a child's life, the child could learn to refrain from being aggressive when a different way of acting (intervention) was taught (Bandura, 1975; 1997). Counselling is one option, but so, too, is society (macro level), when schools, social service agencies, or legal authorities recognize and identify that what has happened is violence. Without this, acts of violence can remain framed as acceptable, or simply "misunderstandings."

The next theory that helps to explain why the cycle of violence can potentially be stopped is called cognitive theory.

Cognitive Theory

An essential aspect of cognitive theory is the emphasis placed on the ability of a person to perceive, interpret, and process the events in any given situation (Todd & Bohart, 1994). When someone behaves violently or aggressively, their behaviours are being influenced by thought patterns. This involves what they perceived and interpreted prior to the behaviour. Changing these thought patterns, then, will theoretically contribute to a change in behaviour.

Cognitive theory, therefore, emphasizes the point that violence and aggression are choices, which involve individual internal processes. Contrary to claims that they were "forced" to act and behave abusively, a cognitive theory approach encourages the individual to acknowledge that they chose to behave aggressively and violently. Conversely, their free will also allows them to choose whether they will be violent or non-violent.

The last point to make is that many people, after having been a victim of violence—whether inflicted by a parent, sibling, or spouse, or in a school, sport, or religious institution—in time will be able to cognitively reframe the experience by stating, "I have been given many examples of how NOT to be in this world."

Conclusion

The application of an intergenerational understanding of violence requires sensitivity. People are more complex than a simple action–reaction. We must be cautious and aware of becoming untrusting and suspicious of another person simply because he or she was abused as a child. In doing so, we would in fact be re-victimizing the person by our unfair and prejudicial attitudes. Remember that most abused children do not grow up to abuse their children or spouses. At this point we begin to examine the individual factors: the micro level.

2.4 MICRO-LEVEL THEORIES THAT EMPHASIZE THE INDIVIDUAL

The following theories are those that zero in on "internal" factors: the personal, psychological, and biological. At this level, violence is viewed as resulting from personal and parenting inadequacies, inadequate self-control issues, or various psychological and biological abnormalities.

Personal Attributes and Characteristics

This textbook provides examples of various forms of interpersonal violent acts which encompass a range of perpetrators, or "abusers." As such, categorically explaining how each of these individuals looks or behaves is difficult to do. Although there is no "one size fits all," some significant theoretical explanations have been put forward. We begin by addressing some known personal characteristics that relate to those who abuse their children and/or spouses.

Perpetrators: Those Who Abuse Their Children and Spouses In addition to the increased risk of violence associated with a history of being abused or witnessing violence, a number of other risk factors (explanations) have been noted. With respect to a person who abuses his or her children and/or spouse, the following perpetrator characteristics have been noted:

1. *Family relationship factors: Perceptions about their child and their role as a parent.* A noted risk factor relates specifically to a person's lack of parenting knowledge and knowledge regarding child development, and it becomes even more elevated when the parent's expectations about child's behaviour are not developmentally appropriate. Additionally, when a child in the family is fussy or has other problems there is increased risk of child abuse (Emery & Laumann-Billings, 1998; Milner & Chilamkurti, 1991; Wekerle & Wolfe, 2003). Children with physical or mental disabilities or who have difficult temperaments are more likely to be abused than others.

   A further noted risk factor is social isolation. Abusive families tend to:

   - withdraw from social involvement, be more isolated

   - lack good support networks

   - avoid involvement with outside recreational or extracurricular activities in their schools or communities.

   And, as stated earlier, additional experiences and other relationships are of utmost importance for a child, and for any family member who is living within an abusive home.

2. *Alcohol and drug use/abuse.* Although a popular theme in explaining intimate personal violence, the relationship between alcohol and battering is not clear. Batterers are not all alcoholic, and they can usually control their anger (Kindschi & Gosselin, 2010; Walker, 1984). Obviously, more violence occurs when people drink alcohol than when they do not, but a causal link between alcohol and violence has not been established. Although individuals often are drinking when they engage in abuse, this behaviour does not in and of itself explain where these violent tendencies originate, or why alcohol and drugs do not have similar results for everyone who uses alcohol. The primary suggestion is that alcohol and drugs act as **disinhibitors**, thereby releasing violent tendencies within an individual.

3. *"Locus of control."* **Locus of control** is a concept from social psychology that refers to the degree to which people feel able to control their circumstances and outcomes

in their own lives. One's locus can be either *internal,* meaning the person believes that they control their life, or *external,* meaning they believe that their environment or others (people and systems) control their life (Rotter, 1990). Parents who are seen as being at risk of becoming abusive seem to have a high external locus of control, or a feeling that their lives are controlled by things external to themselves.

4. *Self-esteem and ego strength.* In studies of battering research it was discovered that men who batter may react with more anger and hostility to conflict situations as compared to other men. A batterer may have a "machismo" attitude that may allow him to feel he can dominate his partner. This controlling behaviour actually makes a batterer appear helpless and dependent (Hofeller, 1982). Because of this, Tolman and Bennett (1990) noted that these men may view themselves as low in masculinity and use violence to strengthen their masculine image. This directly impacts the feeling of self-worth. Milner and Chilamkurti (1991) confirmed that a relationship between self-esteem and abuse exists; problems can arise when these men are faced with stress and conflict over issues pertaining to children, money, sex, or alcohol.

5. *Anger and aggression theories.* There is a great deal of evidence that suggests those individuals who are consistently more aggressive in a variety of situations are influenced to be this way, at least in part, by their biology. However, anger and aggression theories are complex. Men who batter their spouses or abuse their children usually do not have generalized anger or aggression problems. They do not beat up strangers, colleagues, or neighbours (Kindschi Gosselin, 2010; Walker, 1984). This suggests that men who batter possess at least average anger control skills. The problem, therefore, is not a deficit in anger control skills; it is more an issue of choosing not to use the skills they possess with their intimate partners.

    Further, interpreting the genetic basis of aggressiveness is complicated by the fact there is also a related personality characteristic that has a genetic component. Empirical studies have found that those who are more empathetic are less aggressive. When one is empathetic, one is more sensitive to how others feel (Broidy et al., 2003; Miller & Eisenberg, 1988). If aggressive behaviour hurts someone physically or emotionally, the empathetic individual can feel that person's pain. Such feelings would tend to keep one from inflicting pain on others even if the aggression one feels is high.

    Empathy is an important characteristic to possess; however, it too is a tricky quality to categorize. Although it is believed to have a genetic basis, its development is also related to child rearing, or, more specifically, "mothering" (Hoffman, 1981; Ruston et al., 1986). Children with mothers who were more involved in their care and who inhibited their aggression were more likely to grow up to be concerned about other people (Koestner, Franz, & Weinberger, 1990).

The Duluth Model: Spousal Violence Theory The need to understand why the batterer batters began in the 1980s. One of the leaders in addressing this question grew from a program that originated in Duluth, Minnesota. The Domestic Abuse Intervention Program (DAIP) was initiated in 1980 to help reform the criminal justice system.

Through this work, hundreds of battered and sexually abused women were interviewed to better understand how the men in their lives controlled them. As such, they developed the **power and control wheel** (see Figure 2.2), which depicts behaviours batterers possess that they use to dominate their intimate partners and/or children. Batterers have the need to control and dominate. Violent acts are not driven from a place of aggression, but rather the central issues are control and domination, and they are commonly perpetrated by the stronger against the weaker.

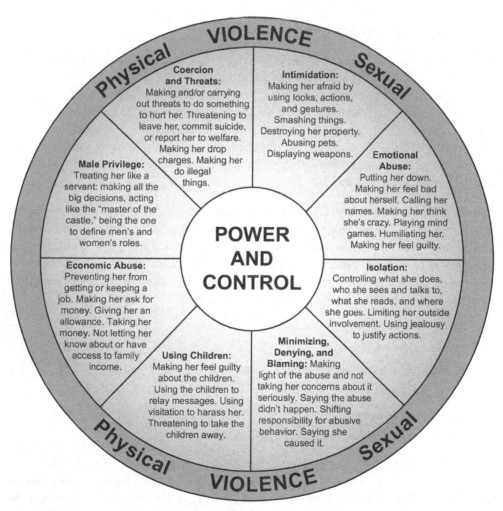

Figure 2.2 The Power and Control Wheel

Source: Domestic Abuse Intervention Program, Duluth, Minnesota

Over the past 30 years, the Duluth model has evolved and changed. It continues to work toward ending violence against women through its programs in Duluth and in partnership with domestic violence practitioners around the world.

Typology research also seeks to understand why people are violent (Holtzworth-Munroe & Stuart, 1994). This is particularly true when the issue of mental health is raised, sometimes referred to as pathology. This leads to the next category or explanation of abusive and violent behaviour. It includes the degree to which an individual has a psychological or "mental health" problem. The following classifications provide examples of people who commit acts of intimate violence: borderline and antisocial personality disorders; pedophilia and sexual offending; and Munchausen syndrome by proxy.

Psychological Explanations

According to the *Diagnostic and Statistical Manual of Mental Disorders* (*DSM-IV-TR*; see Chapter 1), personality disorders are "enduring patterns of perceiving, relating to, and thinking about the environment and oneself that are exhibited in a wide range of social and personal contexts," and "are inflexible and maladaptive, and cause significant functional impairment or subjective distress" (American Psychiatric Association, 2000, p. 686). The *DSM-IV-TR* lists 10 types of personality disorders. Personality disorders that are associated with violence and abusive behaviour are borderline personality disorder and antisocial personality disorder.

Borderline Personality Disorder Borderline personality disorder causes intense mood swings, impulsive behaviours, and severe problems with relationships and self-worth; they lead tumultuous lives (Butcher et al., 2009). Everyone has problems with emotions or behaviours sometimes, but a borderline personality disorder causes the problems to be serious, repeated, and life-disrupting. The most common symptoms (Barlow, Durand, & Stewart, 2009; Butcher et al., 2009) include:

- relationship problems
- intense emotions and mood swings
- problems with anger and aggression, such as violent temper tantrums
- low self-worth
- impulsive behaviours
- a frantic fear of being left alone (abandoned)

One research study conducted by psychologist Don Dutton and his colleagues at the University of British Columbia indicates a line between borderline personality disorder and spousal abuse (Barlow et al., 2009). Several studies completed by the team indicate that men who abuse their spouses are high in borderline characteristics. Further, their extreme affective instability combined with their high levels of impulsivity often lead to erratic self-destructive behaviour (Dutton, 1995, 1998, 2007; Dutton & Starzomski, 1993).

Generally, signs of the disorder first appear in childhood. But problems often don't start until early adulthood. Treatment can be difficult, and positive change can take years. Borderline personality disorder is possibly the most difficult mental disorder to treat; this is because problems with emotions and behaviours are hard to improve.

Antisocial Personality Disorder Antisocial personality disorder (APDS) is a mental illness that involves a pervasive pattern of disregard for or abuse of the rights of others. People with antisocial personality disorder are among the most dramatic of individuals, and have a history of failing to comply with social norms. They behave in ways most of us would find deplorable, such as stealing from friends and family. They also tend to be irresponsible, impulsive, and deceitful (Widiger & Corbitt, 1995). Barlow and colleagues (2009) quote Robert Hare's description of the antisocial personality disorder as

> . . . social predators who charm, manipulate, and ruthlessly plow their way through life, leaving a broad trail of broken hearts, shattered expectations, and empty wallets. Completely lacking in conscience and empathy, they selfishly take what they want and do as they please, violating social norms and expectations without the slightest sense of guilt or regret. (Hare, 1993, p. xi)

Deception, exploitation, and manipulation are behaviours utilized to gain personal profit or pleasure by people with antisocial personality disorder. It is the mental disorder most highly correlated with crime. In a scientific study, Porter and his colleagues (2000) conducted research to study whether psychopathy would contribute to the understanding of sexual violence. More than 300 Canadian federal sex offenders and non–sex offenders participated in the study. Their sample concluded that all the sex offenders scored higher in the callous personality aspect of psychopathology relative to the non-sex offenders (Barlow et al., 2009). The *DSM-IV-TR* defines seven clinical features; two key examples include a reckless disregard for the safety of self and others, and a lack of remorse after having hurt, mistreated, or stolen from another person.

Antisocial personality disorder usually develops during childhood or early adolescence and continues into adulthood.

Pedophilia and Sexual Offending People who sexually abuse children are a diverse group. Virtually all research overwhelmingly identifies offenders to be male. What are the varieties of sexual offenders? One way to explain the unthinkable act of the sexual violence that is perpetrated against children involves the clinical descriptions in the *DSM-IV-TR*. The sexual violence discussed in this textbook is classified as sexual offences. It is important to note that sex offending is a legal definition; a sex offender is someone who has been sanctioned by the law that is outlined in the *Criminal Code*. Although "sexual offence" is a more widely used term for those who engage in sexual behaviours that are illegal, the term **pedophile**, which often is used interchangeably with sex offender, child molester, etc., is a "clinical diagnosis." This term describes a specific group of people who engage in adult–child sexual behaviours.

The *DSM-IV-TR* classifies pedophilia within a broader category of paraphilias (sexual disorders in which there are strong, recurring sexually stimulating urges, fantasies, or behaviours).

An explanation or an understanding of the "characteristics" of those who sexually abuse children is far too complex in scope for this textbook. Yet, it is important to include a brief description of what is known regarding "child molesters," or those clinically known as "pedophiles," and pedophilia. Nicholas Groth first published his book, *Men Who Rape: The Psychology of the Offender,* in 1979. Groth and the equally respected Suzanne Sgroi (*Handbook of Clinical Intervention in Child Sexual Abuse,* 1985) have been considered by many to be the original theorists to blaze a path in our understanding of child sexual abuse.

Groth's Typology of Pedophilia

What might be a disturbing fact for the reader is that "most persons who commit incest cannot be distinguished from those who do not, at least in regard to any major demographic characteristics. Such offenders do not differ significantly from the rest of the population in regard to level of education, occupation, race, religion, intelligence, mental status, or the like essentially defined sexually offenders as belonging to one of two types" (Groth, 1985, p. 215).

Yet, if you reflect upon known sexual abuse cases, this fact has been demonstrated over and over again. Most parents would not willingly hand their children over to a sexual offender; therefore, if a molester's characteristics actually mirrored the meaning of the monstrous acts they commit, most of us would run the other way. This, of course, is not the case. Children and adults have for centuries been betrayed and tricked by sexual predators. Groth divided those who sexually abuse children into two basic types with regard to their primary sexual orientation and their level of sociosexual development; he called these types fixated and regressed offenders (Groth, 1985; 1990).

Fixated Offenders Fixated offenders are males who at the onset of their sexual maturation develop a major or exclusive attraction to children. Children are their preferred sexual interest. These men can also be married and engaged in sexual relations with people their own age. But psychologically their sexual preference remains predominantly fixed on children.

Regressed Offenders Regressed offenders do not exhibit an early sexual predisposition toward children, but show a more conventional peer-oriented sociosexual development. Their sexual interest and activities focus primarily on their own age. As they enter adulthood, their adult relationships become conflicted due to the increased responsibilities (job, bills, etc.) causing a sharp increase in their stress level. Thus if an unanticipated hardship occurs; they find it difficult to manage.

The outcome for men of this "type" is that they will find themselves becoming sexually attracted to children. Groth specifically states that "In general, fixated child molesters are drawn to children sexually in that they identify with the child and appear in some ways to want to remain children themselves. They tend to adapt their behavior and interest to the level of the child in an effort to have the child accept them as an equal" (1985, p. 216). Figure 2.3 provides an overview of specific characteristics used to differentiate between the fixated and regressed offender.

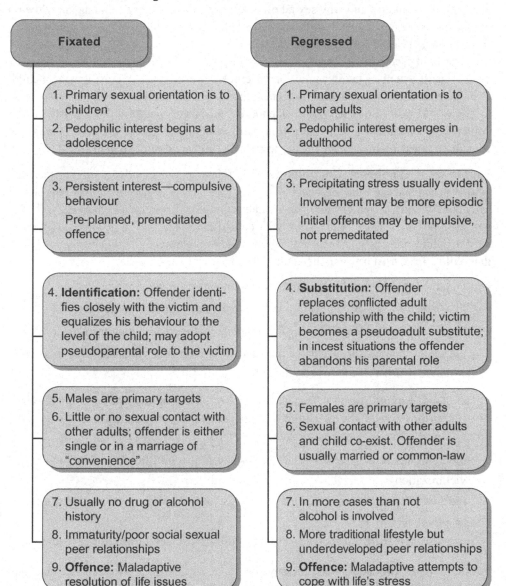

Figure 2.3 Groth's Typology of Pedophilia

Sources: Groth, 1979; Sgroi, 1985

Finkelhor's Multifactor Model: Incest Theory In addition to Sgroi (1985) and Groth (1979), David Finkelhor (1984; 1986) is respected and well known for his work involving children and the sexual or incest offender. An important point to stress from Finkelhor's research is that only 30 to 60 percent of identified offenders had themselves been sexually victimized. Therefore, like other forms of violence, more than one factor is needed to explain how and why sexual offenders develop as they do. And again, while no consensus exists to completely explain the complex problem of incest, Finkelhor's multi-factor model (1984) theory will be discussed.

The multifactor model theory does not diagnose a psychiatric disorder or describe symptoms. It examines the dynamics or the process involved in sexually abusing a child. Finkelhor proposed a four-factor theoretical model for understanding what causes people to commit violent sexual acts against children. His theory emphasized the *preexisting conditions* that enabled a perpetrator to actually commit the abuse. The four factors that contribute to a perpetrator's propensity to abuse a child are described below.

Factor One: Emotional Congruence This refers to the emotional fit between the adult's needs and the child's characteristics of accessibility. For some reason, the sexual offender feels more comfortable with children. Emotional congruence must exist for the abuser to build a trusting relationship with the child. If necessary, a pedophile will work hard to achieve this by coaxing or luring the child into pleasurable or game-like activities that build a false trust between the adult and child. Key points are that:

- they relate to children because they are emotionally immature
- they have low self-esteem and it can be overcome by dominating children
- they deal with their experiences of childhood trauma by becoming the abuser
- the child(ren) they are sexually attracted to are versions of themselves as a child whom they are trying to love and care for

Factor Two: Sexual Arousal This is defined as a physiological arousal in the presence of children or photographs of children. Simply stated, offenders must become sexually aroused by children. Key points are that:

- their childhood sexual experiences are re-played in adult life (early childhood sexual victimization)
- the normal parental or affectionate feelings toward children are misinterpreted as sexual
- many have learned to become aroused by children through exposure to pornography

Factor Three: Blockage Fixation develops at a particular developmental stage that leaves the individual incapable of progressing to a mutually satisfying adult relationship. A key point to consider from a developmental perspective is that:

- their emotional and sexual needs cannot be met in an adult heterosexual relationship

Key points to consider from a situational perspective are that:

- the first adult sexual experience they had with an adult woman was so traumatic they turned instead to children

- their relationship with their spouse has broken down but they do not seek sexual satisfaction outside of the family so they turn to incest with their children

Factor Four: Disinhibition Disinhibitors do not cause sexual violence. This refers to the pedophile's ability to be free of inhibition motivators, causing him to be incapable of inhibitory behaviour; therefore, he becomes aroused and subsequently abuses a child. Also connected to this factor is the acknowledgement that these individuals often have numerous personality factors that facilitate their ability to abuse. Many were noted earlier. Key points to consider are:

- they don't have inhibitions against sex with children

- their judgment is impaired through alcohol/drugs or brain injury

- great personal stress lowers their inhibitions and leads them to seek sex with children

- they lack proper control of their impulses

- society rarely prosecutes sexual offences against children so they interpret this as permission to offend

There is probably no one theory or explanation that can account for sexually abusing children. The four-factor model is one way to explain the complex dynamics that take place. It can be used as a checklist to gather information.

All these theories provide useful frameworks in our understanding of a very complex and serious form of violence. And even though personality, social, and situational variables have been teased out in various research studies as possible explanations of violent behaviour, the literature on these characteristics is still inconsistent.

Stopping Sex Offenders in Their Tracks

Underscoring the importance of understanding how pedophiles or sexual offenders choose and groom their victims grew into a preventative strategy by Carla van Dam. In her book *The Socially Skilled Child Molester: Differentiating the Guilty from the Falsely Accused* (2006), van Dam provides some key points to "stop sex offenders in their tracks." These strategies complement Canada's child abuse reporting laws by reinforcing the significance of educating the public, and the public's role in ending child sexual abuse. Her five key points do not relate to treatment, but they are prevention strategies for adult members of the public to use. They include the following:

1. A willingness to consider the possibility that known and trusted adults sexually molest children.

2. Ability to identify the behaviour patterns used by socially skilled sex molesters.

3. Increasing competence at recognizing potentially abusive behaviour.

4. Inoculation of society through communication, awareness, and action.

5. Ability to stand firm; setting boundaries and rules that are respectful and nurturing of child development and needs, then choosing to *never* negotiate.

Munchausen Syndrome by Proxy Munchausen syndrome occurs because of psychological problems in the adult (the parent), and is generally an attention-seeking behaviour. **Munchausen syndrome by proxy (MSbP)**, also called factitious disorder by proxy, is a form of child abuse in which a parent induces real or apparent symptoms of a disease in a child. Although some experts believe MSbP to be a mental illness, it is not officially recognized in the *DSM-IV-TR.*

This syndrome generally involves a mother abusing her child by seeking needless medical attention for the child (Parnell & Day, 1997). For instance, by adding blood to a child's urine or stool, withholding food, falsifying fevers, or secretly giving the child drugs to make the child throw up or have diarrhea, the mother *knowingly* creates false symptoms. Based on the confused group of symptoms created (they don't quite fit any known disease), children are often hospitalized and are made to suffer through unnecessary tests and uncomfortable medical procedures—even surgeries. Further, the frequent medical and hospital visits keep the child close at hand so the mother can continue to create symptoms. Changes in the child's condition are almost never witnessed by hospital staff and almost always occur only in the mother's presence (Tammy et al., 2007; Venneman et al., 2005). Additional tragedy results from the parent's deception if the child does require essential medical care. Some children may die from infections or other injuries inflicted by parents with Munchausen syndrome by proxy (Tammy et al., 2007; Venneman et al., 2005).

Biological Theories

Not all behaviour is psychologically driven, some is biologically or "chemically" based. These theories concentrate on the physical substrate of our nature and behaviour (Eller, 2005). This includes our body, our chemicals, and our genes.

History of Biological Theories Trying to understand, explain, and perhaps predict violence or a "violent type" biologically has long been a part of human civilization. For instance, according to Greek and Roman myth, evilness was thought to reside in persons with red hair. Plus, "being ugly was an indictment of a bad person, one predisposed to commit crime" (Kindschi Gosselin, 2010, p. 71), and so were even "more fanciful things like our facial features or the shape and texture of our skull" (Eller, 2005, pp. 35–36). One of the earliest criminal anthropologists to provide this type of theory was Franz Joseph Gall (1758–1828). Gall's theory of phrenology (also called craniology) hypothesized that the shape of the human skull was indicative of personality, and could be used to predict criminality. Johann Gaspar Spurzheim (1776–1853) would bring Gall's theory to North America, and even Sherlock Homes (author Conan Doyle's fictional character) would described principles of phrenology when solving a number of crimes (Schmalleger & Volk, 2008).

Other biological approaches to violence and crime continued to be developed into the mid-20th century. Sheldon proposed a new theory that combined personality types, which included a rather detailed biopsychological constitutional typology (Schmalleger & Volk, 2008). Humans were divided into three categories: endomorph (heavy and round), ectomorph (light and slender), and mesomorph (intermediate and muscular). The belief was that certain body shapes were more inclined toward deviance than others.

Needless to say, today these early theories have limited application in our understanding of intimate violence. Yet, these early explanations underscore the fact that for centuries most societies have asked the question of who commits crime. In time, similar to all fields and professions, theoretical advances occurred.

Biological Theories Today In a more scientific vein, recent biological work has focused on the brain both in terms of its physiology and its chemistry. Research in the area of nutrition has produced some limited evidence that the old maxim "you are what you eat" may contain more than a morsel of truth. Biocriminology has made some strides in linking violence or disruptive behaviour to eating habits (Schmalleger & Volk, 2008).

Biochemical theories include a number of factors that contribute to violence, the first being low sugar levels or hypoglycemia (Burke, 2005). It has become an accepted scientific hypotheses that hypoglycemia can produce too much insulin, which reduces the mind's capacity to reason or to judge the long-term consequences of behaviours.

For instance, in June 2011, *National Post* reporter Jane Switzer authored a story that described a Toronto police officer who was given a conditional discharge after he threatened to Taser two handcuffed burglary suspects in the genitals. The Ontario Provincial Court Justice who heard the case believed his actions could be attributed to hypoglycemia. The defence lawyer argued during the trial that his client, Const. Hominuk, was a type 1 diabetic, and on that day his sugar levels were aggravated by lack of sleep and skipping a meal prior to his shift. In Canada, hypoglycemia (low blood sugar) is considered to be a "non-mental disorder automatism" under section 16 of the *Criminal Code.* This consideration, this defence, can be determined by a trial judge alone and it could potentially result in a complete acquittal (Department of Justice, November 2002).

Hormones Biochemical theories have also suggested hormonal imbalances and adrenalin sensitivities as possible cause of criminal behaviour (Burke, 2005). Kindschi Gosselin (2010) writes that "the raging hormones of women and the excess of testosterone in men have alternatively been accepted and rejected as a cause of criminal behaviour during this century" (p. 73). The most pervasive theory is a perceived link between testosterone and male aggressions (Burke, 2005; Kindschi Gosselin, 2010; Schmalleger & Volk, 2008). Specifically, "more focused studies have unveiled a direct relationship between the amount of the chemical present and the degree of violence used by sex offenders, while other researchers have linked steroid abuse among bodybuilders to destructive urges and psychosis" (Schmalleger & Volk, 2008, p. 178).

The next section provides information regarding victims and their behaviours. Key theories have developed to help us understand more about victims of spousal violence.

2.5 VICTIM THEORIES

The Battered Woman Syndrome

The concept of **battered woman syndrome (BWS)** has evolved from its inception in 1979 in the book entitled *The Battered Woman.* This theory does not explain why violence occurs; rather, it explains what happens in abusive relationships. The term was coined by author, psychologist, and feminist academic Lenore Walker to refer to specific psychological and behavioural symptoms that are caused by protracted exposure to intimate partner violence. Walker also suggested that the violence moves through a predictable sequence of stages or phases, a model known as the cycle of violence.

From 1978 to 1981, Dr. Walker interviewed 435 women in the Rocky Mountain region of Colorado who had been, or were at the time, victims of domestic violence. The interviews were conducted to identify and examine key psychological and sociological variables that made up the proposed battered woman syndrome. She was interested in testing two specific theories about battered women: the *cycle theory of battering,* and an adaptation of Martin Seligman's *learned helplessness theory* (Walker 1984). (We will examine learned helplessness theory next.) What set Walker's study apart from others in her field, and which would later allow her theory to achieve legal and social-psychological status, was that it combined the results of an extensive clinical study with those two theoretical models to produce a clear description of the patterns of violence in intimate relationships and their psychological and behavioural sequelae for female victims.

Although BWS is not specifically listed in the *DSM-IV-TR,* it is generally recognized as a psychological condition association with **post-traumatic stress disorder (PTSD)** that results from exposure to severe trauma, which includes being battered or fearing battering. Because of this trauma certain behaviours existed, including flashbacks and other intrusive experiences when a woman perceives a situation to be dangerous (even when it is not). The victim's exhibited symptoms are comparable to those exhibited by persons who have undergone other traumatic life experiences, such as prisoners of war, or even our soldiers who today are returning from war emotionally harmed and wounded.

BWS is included in the World Health Organization's *International Classification of Diseases.* On the basis of these classifications, researchers have attempted to define BWS, in diagnostic terms, as the development of physical, psychological, and social abnormalities and symptoms, such as depression, low self-esteem, and isolation, which follow the direct personal experience of a series of violent acts by an intimate partner

(Walker, 1995). As mentioned earlier, at the heart of the BWS theory is Seligman's theory of learned helplessness.

The Theory of Learned Helplessness

Learned helplessness is a condition (not a disorder; you will not find it in the *DSM-IV-TR*) that is used to explain a victim's inability to protect herself against the batterer's violence following repeated, but failed, efforts to do so (Walker, 1977/78).

Walker's study did *not* assume a relationship between mental illness and subsequent susceptibility to intimate violence. Rather, it attempted to show how the symptoms commonly connected with specific forms of mental illness, such as depression, low self-esteem, and helplessness, appeared in women who had suffered long-term domestic abuse (Walker 1984; 1995).

In the process of developing her theory, she used social learning theories to explore ways in which environmental factors (mezzo) could interact with individual personality traits (micro) to create particular behavioural, cognitive, and emotional responses. Specifically, she used and modified Seligman's theory of learned helplessness to explain why so many battered women are unable to leave their abusers (Walker 1984).

Seligman's theory sought to explain certain forms of psychological paralysis by utilizing social learning and cognitive/motivational theoretical principles. It is based on a study conducted with laboratory animals whereby the animal was repeatedly and non-contingently shocked until it became unable to escape the painful situation. The theory suggested that once this took place, this animal would not attempt to escape, even when escape was both possible and obvious to other animals that had not undergone the previous shock treatment. These distorted perceptions, according to Seligman, resulted from an inability to predict the effectiveness of one's actions.

Drawing from Seligman's work, Walker hypothesized that continual exposure to battering, like electric shocks, would, over time, diminish a woman's motivation to react. In other words, a woman who stayed in a violent relationship was more likely to exhibit signs of learned helplessness than one who had never been in or had escaped a violent relationship (Walker, 1984).

Violence Overtime: Walker's Cycle of Violence

Onset, type, and frequency of abuse can vary across relationships. Even violent physical aggression is often preceded by nonviolent verbal abuse and can be accompanied by attentive and loving behaviour. Violent relationships do not involve continuous abuse; episodes are uneven. While no two abused women share the identical experience, experts have documented that abuse usually follows a cycle made up of three phases. The first to write about the cyclical or phase component of abusive relationships was Lenore Walker in 1979 when she proposed a cycle theory of violence. The **cycle of violence** includes the tension-building phase, the acute battering phase, and the tranquil or loving phase. They are summarized as follows:

- *Tension-building.* The victim senses there will soon be an explosive violent incident. Tension rises and the victim's fear escalates; belittling and threatening leads to a slap. To calm her partner she becomes happy—agreeable. She has one goal: to prevent an escalation in violence. Some women find this episode so foreboding and unbearable that many simply antagonize the batterer to just get it over with.

- *Acute battering incident: Out of control, destructive, brutal, and even savage.* The violence escalates from tension building to violence severe enough to lead to death. The victim has no control over when it will stop. She does not try to leave because she would be at greater risk of harm.

- *Respite phase:* Called the "honeymoon" or "flower" phase, because the abuser apologizes profusely. He may cry and plead for forgiveness, all the while promising to never hurt her again.

Early in abusive relationships women possess hope. Hope that the incident is isolated, and hope that it will never take place again and things will improve, because of the abusive partner's sincere expression of remorse and the kindness that often follows an abusive episode. As time passes, the number of violent episodes increases and the cycle is repeated. Eventually, the loving contrition component disappears.

Generally, without intervention (legal intervention) or treatment the cycle continues—and escalates. When chronic violence is present, aggression often becomes more frequent or severe (Pence & Paymar, 1993; Straus, 1993; Walker, 1984).

CHAPTER CONCLUSION

Theories can help explain why intimate personal violence occurs. They include the most intimate human explanations, extending to the larger world we live in, plus all the "in-between" influences. Needless to say, this explains why interventions are required at all levels. Professionals who provide indirect or direct services for victims must work together. The collective voices and collaboration of legal and policy experts must complement the knowledge and wisdom from those who provide clinical work, and even more specifically those who have experienced violence. Most important, it is the responsibility of people to become less tolerant of intimate personal violence and speak up when it occurs.

Multiple Choice Questions

1. Social processes whereby the dominant group is able to accumulate and maintain status, power, and assets from the energy and labour expended by subordinate groups describes which of the following forms of oppression?

   a. marginalization   **b.** powerlessness
   c. exploitation   **d.** cultural Imperialism

2. Which theorist is most associated with the ecological model?

    a. Bronfenbrenner   **b.** Pavlov
    c. Watson   **d.** Belsky

3. A three-level approach to human systems is utilized in an ecological model. Which level encapsulates the smallest social interactions within primary relationships?

    a. micro   **b.** milo
    c. mezzo   **d.** macro

4. The contribution of culture and how it defines societal norms, laws, politics, and economics occurs at which level of the ecological model?

    a. micro   **b.** milo
    c. mezzo   **d.** macro

5. Personal attributes and characteristics plus mental health difficulties and disorders are best described at which level of the ecological model?

    a. micro   **b.** milo
    c. mezzo   **d.** macro

6. John Watson's research demonstrates how a child could learn to fear a specific object. This type of learning can take place in or outside of a scientific experiment. What type of learning did his study support?

    a. classical conditioning   **b.** operant conditioning
    c. social learning   **d.** cognitive learning

7. With respect to a person who abuses their children and/or spouse, which of the following was NOT identified as a possible perpetrator characteristic?

    a. perception about their child; child development knowledge
    b. perception about their role as a parent
    c. locus of control
    d. gender stereotyping rigidity

8. Abusive families present all of the following risk factors EXCEPT which one?

    a. social isolations
    b. don't have good support networks
    c. overinvolvement with religious institutions
    d. minimal outside recreational or extracurricular activities

9. Specific psychological or "mental health" problems have been used to classify those who commit intimate violent acts. Which of the following was NOT identified?

    a. bipolar disorder   **b.** antisocial personality disorder
    c. pedophilia   **d.** Munchausen syndrome by proxy

10. "Predators who charm, manipulate, and ruthlessly plow their way through life," are best described by which of the following disorders?

    a. bipolar disorder
    b. antisocial personality disorder
    c. pedophilia
    d. Munchausen syndrome by proxy

Discussion Questions

1. Describe and explain Lenore Walker's cycle of violence theory.

2. What are the cultural and social influences that are believed to contribute to the impact of violence and maltreatment?

3. What are the "individual-level" influences that are believed to contribute to the impact of violence and maltreatment?

Key Terms

battered woman syndrome (BWS): a set of specific psychological and behavioural symptoms that are caused by protracted exposure to situations of intimate partner violence.

cycle of violence: a theory developed by Dr. Lenore Walker to explain how violence in an intimate relationship is not even but waxes and wanes. Three stages were identified: tension-building phase; explosion or acute phase; and the calm loving respite phase.

disinhibitor: something that causes a loss or reduction of an inhibition.

ecological model: tries to understand phenomena within the context of interacting social environments.

gender stereotypes: the application of the belief or attitude that certain characteristics are specific to one's gender that indirectly affect one's abilities; such attitudes are based on the beliefs of traditional stereotypes.

stimulus generalization: occurs when a conditioned response follows a stimulus that is similar to the original conditioned stimulus; the more similar the two stimuli are, the more likely generalization is to occur.

learned helplessness: a condition used to explain a victim's inability to protect herself against the batterer's violence that develops following repeated, but failed, efforts to do so.

locus of control: can be either internal or external.

macro: literally means "large"; in a system-organizational sense, used to refer to large units, especially at the cultural and societal level.

mezzo: literally means "middle"; in a system-organizational sense, used to refer to medium-sized units, especially at the level of families or small groups.

micro: literally means "small"; in a system-organizational sense, used to refer to small units, especially at the level of single individuals.

Munchausen syndrome by proxy: a pattern in which a parent inflicts harm on a child in order to get attention from others, including doctors and nurses.

norms: socially defined rules of behaviour including folkways, mores, and laws.

operant conditioning: learning in which a voluntary response is strengthened or weakened, depending on its favourable or unfavourable consequence.

oppression: the exercise of authority or power in a cruel or unjust manner.

pedophile: a clinical diagnosis that describes a specific group of people who engage in adult-child sexual behaviours.

patriarchy: the tradition of male dominance.

post-traumatic stress disorder (PTSD): a disorder recognized in the *DSM-IV-TR* that is characterized by the presence of a trauma-inducing experience, intrusive symptoms, avoidance of situation that triggers intrusive symptoms, and hyperarousal.

power and control wheel: a diagram used in the Duluth program that depicts the coercive strategies used by batterers against their intimate partners.

victim blaming: attributing responsibility to victims for the bad things that happen to them.

Chapter 3
Violence Against Children

Someday, maybe, there will exist a well-informed, well considered and yet fervent public conviction that the most deadly of all possible sins is the mutilation of a child's spirit.

Erik H. Erikson, psychoanalyst (1902–1994)

Chapter Objectives

1   Identify the different categories of child abuse and neglect and explain their significance.
2   Describe the physical and psychological consequences of child abuse and neglect.
3   Interpret the statistics regarding the prevalence of child abuse and neglect.

3.1 DEFINING CHILD ABUSE AND NEGLECT

As recently as 1961, few considered the treatment of children to be a matter of public concern. But Henry Kempe and his colleagues challenged this belief when in 1962 they published "The Battered Child Syndrome" in the *Journal of the American Medical Association*. At the time, the **battered child syndrome** was based on a narrow definition of abuse—emphasizing a history of characteristic physical injuries, generally perpetrated upon young children by their principal caregivers. Today, definitions are much broader than Kempe's. Over the years, the range and complexities of child maltreatment have been recognized and expanded.

While no universally agreed-upon definition of abuse exists, the overarching descriptions contain similar themes. Descriptions of abuse and neglect have been provided by many theorists, government agencies, and laws. The phrase *child abuse and neglect* generally refers to abuse perpetrated by parents and other caregivers. According to the Canadian Children's Rights Council, child maltreatment refers to the harm, or risk of harm, that a child or youth may experience while in the care of a person they trust or depend on. This may include a parent, sibling, other relative, teacher, caregiver, or guardian.

Harm may occur through someone's direct actions, which is referred to as an *act of commission,* or through a person's neglecting to protect or provide an element of care necessary for healthy child growth and development, which is called *omission*. One form of neglect that will be referred to in this and other chapters relates to the institutions or "systems" that are legally responsible for providing care and services to children. Many cases involving the omission to protect would become known years later when adults reported their childhood victimizations. Many of these cases revealed the fact that systems did not take the steps to protect children when incidences of alleged victimizations were disclosed.

Various forms of child abuse and neglect have been cited in the literature. Table 3.1 identifies the five overarching forms identified.

Table 3.1 Types of Child Abuse and Maltreatment

Type of Maltreatment	Definition	Example
Physical Abuse	The application of unreasonable physical force by a parent, caregiver, or youth to any part of a child's body	Harsh physical discipline, grabbing, shaking, pushing, throwing, kicking, biting, hitting with a hand, hitting with an object, punching, choking, strangling, stabbing, burning, and the excessive use of restraints
Neglect	Failure by a parent or caregiver to provide to a child the physical or psychological necessities of life	Failure to supervise: leads to physical or sexual harm; physical, medical, and educational neglect; failure to provide psychological treatment; abandonment
Emotional Abuse	Behaviour by a parent or caregiver that harms a child psychologically, emotionally, or spiritually	Unreasonable, hostile, and abusive treatment; frequent or extreme verbal abuse; frightening and humiliating behaviours; emotional neglect, causing *non-organic failure to thrive* (a diagnostic term applied in cases of children less than age 3 who have suffered a slowing or cessation of growth for which no physical or physiological causes can be identified)
Exposure to Violence	Circumstances that permit a child to be aware of violence occurring between a caregiver and his/her partner or between other family members	Permitting a child to see or overhear violent episodes, or be exposed to signs of the violence; permitting a child to see physical injuries on their parent or caregiver
Sexual Abuse	A parent or caregiver involving a child or youth in an act of sexual gratification, or exposing a child to sexual activity, behaviour, or contact	Voyeurism, sex talk, sexual exploitation, fondling, oral sex, attempted penetration, penetration

Sources: Finkelhor, 2008; Kolko et al., 1992; Monteleone & Brodeur, 1994; Trocmé et al., 2005.

Despite variations in definitions, when a child protection investigation is being conducted the important definition is the one confirmed in child protection legislation. Each province and territory in Canada has unique legislation defining and describing abuse, and although they are not uniform, they are similar. One critical difference is the legal age of a child; this varies across Canada. For instance, in Ontario a child is someone up to age 16, but in British Columbia a person is considered a child up to age 19 (for a complete listing, see Table 7.1 in Chapter 7).

We will now present descriptions and examples of the five forms of maltreatment: physical abuse, neglect, emotional abuse, exposure to violence, and sexual abuse.

Physical Abuse

Physical abuse includes any non-accidental action that causes or could cause physical harm to a child, such as hitting or shaking, or the unreasonable use of force to restrain a child which results or may result in a non-accidental injury. Specifically, physical abuse may include shaking, choking, biting, kicking, burning, poisoning, drugging, holding a child under water, or any other harmful or dangerous use of force or restraint.

Whether due to a personal experience or from hearing a story of abuse reported through the media, most people are emotionally affected by these cases involving our youngest and most vulnerable citizens. It is easy to be outraged by this victimization, because often the injuries are visible and difficult to ignore.

But what really constitutes physical abuse, and how do the authorities determine whether abuse is present? The simple fact is that evidence of physical abuse of children is not always so apparent. However, the law in each province and territory defines child abuse and describes how to respond. Many factors must be considered. The presence or absence of physical evidence is not the only factor considered by child protection workers (those who are legally mandated to enforce child protection legislation). Parental behaviour or attitudes regarding the child, coupled with the presence of suspicious physical injuries, may indicate the presence of physical abuse. Figure 3.1 provides examples of signs and symptoms of physical abuse that have been cited.

Although the language or the words chosen to describe child physical abuse may be clear, there are a number of variables that can make the determination of abuse difficult. Research and practice have demonstrated that many parents and guardians who physically abuse their children never leave observable marks. Even when a mark is present, the question remains: Is the mark itself enough to prove or warrant a child abuse finding?

Moreover, investigators focus not only on the visible or medically known injury, but also on the frequency. Frequency is important. Imagine a parent who one day leaves a very clear hand mark on a child's arm as the result of an unyielding attempt to prevent the child from running into traffic. Is there a mark? Yes, but is this abuse? Now consider the parent who never leaves a mark but who, as a matter of parenting "style," slaps the

---

SIGNS AND SYMPTOMS OF PHYSICAL ABUSE IN CHILDREN

1   Arrives at school too early or does not want to leave school; possible fear of going home

2   Shies away from touch

3   Flinches at sudden movements, or seems afraid to go home

4   Is always watchful and "on alert," as if waiting for something bad to happen

5   Cheats, steals, or lies, which may be related to high expectations at home and fear of failure

6   Shows fearlessness or extreme risk taking

7   Wears inappropriate clothing to cover up injuries, such as long-sleeved shirts on hot days

8   Has frequent injuries or unexplained bruises, welts, or cuts

9   Has injuries that appear to have a pattern, such as marks from a hand or belt

10   Acts out; displays aggressive or disruptive behaviour

THE FOLLOWING ARE SPECIFIC TO THE ADULT OR OTHER CAREGIVER WHICH MAY LEAD ONE TO CONSIDER THE POSSIBILITY OF PHYSICAL ABUSE

11   Refers to the child as a "liar" or describes a child using derogatory language

12   Describes child as "clumsy," "accident prone"

13   Offers conflicting, unconvincing, or no explanation for the child's injury

14   Uses harsh physical discipline with the child, which often relates to a lack of understanding regarding realistic developmental abilities

---

Figure 3.1 Signs and Symptoms of Child Physical Abuse

Sources: Finkelhor, 2008; Flaherty et al., 2006; Monteleone & Brodeur, 1994; Trocmé et al., 2005.

child each and every time the parent feels frustration. An important question to explore would be whether slapping is the only method of discipline known to the parent. This raises the issue of discipline, and this is a significant variable to consider.

Reasonable Discipline Recently, Canada's Supreme Court was asked to determine whether any form of violence toward a child was acceptable—but, more importantly, whether physical discipline violated a child's rights under the *Charter of Rights and Freedoms* or children's constitutional rights (for details, see "From the Pen of Corinne Robertshaw; Founder/Coordinator, Repeal 43 Committee" Box 7.2 in Chapter 7). Simply stated, is there an acceptable level of force, and if so, what is acceptable when disciplining a child? Is a slap on the hand okay for some children and not okay for others? Is it ever okay to use an object when disciplining a teenager?

In 2004, the Supreme Court determined a child's constitutional rights were not violated (the legality of this issue will be discussed in Chapter 7), but the Court did provide legal standards of physical force as noted in the list below. Under Canadian law, physical punishment of children is deemed reasonable if:

1.   It is administered by a parent (teachers are NOT permitted to use corporal punishment).

2.   The child is between the ages of 2 and 12, inclusive.

3.   The child is capable of learning from correction.

4. It constitutes "minor corrective force of a transitory and trifling nature."

5. It does not involve the use of objects or blows or slaps to the head.

6. It is used for "educative or corrective purposes" and does not stem from a caregiver's "frustration, loss of temper, or abusive personality" (2004 SCC 4, [2004] 1 S.C.R. 76).

A significant fact that must be considered involves age. Age does matter! An example to demonstrate this point involves shaking a child; age would drastically alter the outcome. Shaking an adolescent, for instance, might be considered acceptable by some. But imagine the potential for injury when a parent's level of frustration is so great, and their ability to cope so diminished, that in an effort to silence the crying demands of their young child they would resort to severely shaking the child. This type of act is perilous enough to cause significant injury or even death. See Box 3.1 for a description of shaken baby syndrome.

The last point to consider is child development. This question does not relate just to the age of a child, but also to their cognitive and emotional developmental stage. What is the child's ability and or inability to learn, understand, find protection, and seek help? These questions must also be addressed and answered by child protection workers and our courts.

3.1 Shaken Baby Syndrome

Shaken baby syndrome (SBS) is also called abusive head trauma/inflicted traumatic brain injury, or AHT. Abusive head trauma occurs because someone has vigorously shaken the child. Victims are mostly infants younger than one year old. This type of trauma is occasionally seen in children up to 4 years old; however, the average age of victims is between 3 and 8 months.

The perpetrators are usually parents or caregivers. A common explanation or trigger is frustration or stress when the child is crying. Unfortunately, the shaking may have the desired effect: although at first the baby cries more, he or she may stop crying as the brain is damaged. Damage can be even greater if there is impact during a shaking episode (hitting a wall or a crib mattress, for example). Following the shaking the brain swells, which can cause enormous pressure within the skull, compressing blood vessels and increasing overall injury to its delicate structure.

What Are the Effects of SBS?

SBS often causes irreversible damage. The majority of infants who survive severe shaking will have some form of neurological or mental disability, such as cerebral palsy or mental retardation. Some injuries may not be fully apparent before 6 years of age, or until the child begins school and they exhibit behavioural problems or learning difficulties

Damage can include partial or total blindness, hearing loss, seizures, impaired intellect, speech and learning difficulties, and problems with memory and attention. But by that time, it is more difficult to link these problems to a shaking incident from several years before. In the very worst cases, children die due to their injuries.

Source: Canadian Medical Association Journal, 2003.

Neglect

Neglect, or failure to provide, is a form of child abuse that occurs when a child's parents or caregivers do not provide the mandatory thought, care, and response to a child's emotional, psychological, or physical development. Further, true neglect is chronic, involving repeated incidents. A child missing one lunch at school does not indicate neglect. Many missed lunches should cause concern.

As a student reading what is perhaps your first textbook on violence, you may wonder how the issue of neglect fits under the title of this text. Dubowitz (1994) pointed out in his review of the literature that the results of neglect can be as bad as or worse than those associated with other forms of child maltreatment. In Canada, a case that made the news involved a 35-day-old infant who died of starvation while in the care of his mother and several government organizations. See "Canadian Headline News" Box 3.2 for a full account of this heartbreaking story of the perilous result of neglect.

3.2 Canadian Headline News: Jordan Heikamp's Starvation Death a Homicide

Homicide was the coroner's jury verdict in the death of baby Jordan Heikamp, who starved to death in a Toronto shelter in 1997, just 35 days after his birth. Pictures presented at the inquest showed a baby so thin he was nothing more than skin and bones. Jordan weighed four pounds and two ounces when he died—four ounces less than when he was born.

Renee Heikamp, Jordan's 19-year-old mother, was homeless at the time she gave birth to him in hospital. Medical staff identified Jordan and his mother as high risk, and turned them over to the Catholic Children's Aid Society. Renee and Jordan were placed in the Anduhyaun Shelter for Women in Toronto, where they spent the next 27 days. Jordan was rushed to hospital but died on arrival, the victim of "chronic starvation." Criminal charges were laid. Renee Heikamp and Toronto Catholic Children's Aid Society worker Angie Martin were charged with criminal negligence causing death.

The pre-trial judge said that everyone involved with the case—from doctors and nurses to the women's shelter—seemed confused as to who was taking what role in caring for the baby. The judge suggested Ms. Heikamp was a troubled woman inexperienced in raising a baby: "How should Ms. Heikamp have known anything was wrong with Jordan when no one else did?"

Social workers and hospital staff denied they were to blame, and testified that Renee repeatedly rebuffed their efforts to help. They said she showed little interest in parenting information and lied about Jordan's condition. They also blamed provincial cutbacks to social service agencies for creating an excessive workload. Renee blamed the death of her son on the lack of assistance from social workers, who she said should have shouldered more responsibility. She also blamed her own lack of education, stating she didn't realize how sick Jordan was. It became clear that the professionals also did not know exactly how sick Jordan had become.

In 1998, after a 13-month preliminary hearing into the death, Madam Justice Mary Hogan of the Ontario Court of Justice ruled that the case would not proceed to trial because of a

(continued)

lack of evidence of "wanton and reckless disregard" for the life or safety of another person, the requisite element for criminal negligence causing death on the part of either Ms. Heikamp or Ms. Martin *(R. v. Heikamp and Martin, 1999, at 2)*.

Later, following the conclusion of the pretrial, in April 2001, after a four-month investigation, a coroner's inquest ruled that the death was a homicide, and made recommendations for changes to the child protection system to prevent a similar death in the future. It was accompanied by 44 recommendations directed at all the parties involved in the inquest, including the Catholic Children's Aid Society, young

mothers, the hospital where Jordan was born, and shelter workers, hospitals, public health departments, and the Ministry of Community and Social Services (Ontario).

For more information on a description of pre-trial hearings and coroner's inquests, see Chapter 8.

Reflection Question

This case raises many questions. At first it is easy to blame Ms. Heikamp, a 19-year-old woman; however, what other issues do you think must be examined?

Sources: Blanchard, 1999; CBC News, 2001a, 2001b, 2001c; *R. v. Heikamp*, 1999.

Neglect also extends beyond food and water; it consists of failing to provide a child with clothing, shelter, cleanliness, education, medical care, and protection from harm. Understanding basic human needs is fundamental to recognize the signs of child neglect. Figure 3.2 provides a list of potential signs of physical neglect.

Assessing neglect requires a consideration of child developmental needs, poverty, and other family and community factors. With poverty, food is one of the first basic needs that is neglected. Does this mean there is neglect if suitable nourishment is not provided when a family is stricken with poverty? If neglect by definition is a choice, then the answer to this question must be a resounding no. Families—parents—

SIGNS AND SYMPTOMS OF CHILD NEGLECT

1 Child is frequently late or missing from school

2 Child is frequently sleepy and always tired

3 Child is frequently unsupervised

4 Child is left in a car unattended

5 Child is left alone or allowed to play in unsafe situations and environments. This includes ensuring children are not left unattended around hot stoves, ovens, furnaces, hot water, etc.

6 Child's clothes are ill-fitting, or inappropriate for the weather

7 Child has body odour, and clothes are filthy

8 Child is looking through the garbage for food; is stealing food and/or lunch money from others

9 Child has untreated illnesses; not getting a child to the doctor in a timely manner when the child is not well, is in pain, has a fever, and/or is vomiting

10 Child has rotting teeth and chronic bad breath

11 Child has untreated physical injuries

12 Infants: Failure to thrive

Figure 3.2 Signs and Symptoms of Child Neglect: Physical Needs

Sources: Finkelhor, 2008; Monteleone & Brodeur, 1994; Trocmé et al., 2005.

also need support and assistance. Knowledgeable child protection workers and judges must weigh a great number of variables when addressing, and assessing, the problem of neglect.

Emotional Neglect In addition to unmet physical needs, the emotional needs of a child can also be neglected. Emotional neglect includes failing to provide a child with love, safety, and a sense of worth. Neglect also occurs when an adult fails to attend to a child's emotional needs in a sensitive and responsive manner. Being detached and uninvolved and interacting only when necessary is a form of neglect.

Emotional Abuse

Emotional child abuse (maltreatment) involves specific acts or omissions by parents or caregivers that cause or could cause serious behavioural, cognitive, emotional, or mental disorders. Emotional maltreatment can include the following: verbal threats, socially isolating a child, intimidation, exploitation, terrorizing, or routinely making unreasonable demands on a child. So how would these behaviours appear in daily life? Let's examine a few examples of emotional maltreatment.

Rejecting a child is considered to be emotionally harmful and serious. This could be demonstrated when a parent or guardian refuses to acknowledge a child's presence, value, or worth. Communicating to a child that she or he is useless or inferior and devaluing her/his thoughts and feelings are other examples. A further example involves repeatedly treating one child differently from their siblings in a way that suggests dislike, resentment, or rejection of the child. The ultimate rejection would be to tell a child their birth was a mistake and they have never been wanted.

Isolation includes physical confinement such as locking a child in a closet or room. It can also involve restricting normal contact with others, such as withholding contact with a favourite family member or not allowing a child to attend an age-appropriate event such as a classmate's birthday party. As I write this, I am reminded of a client I once worked with who refused to allow her young child to go "trick-or-treating" on Halloween night even though the child's siblings were allowed to go out. Underscoring the cruelty of the mother's methodical plan to emotionally hurt her child is the fact that she had built up the child's anticipation by making her Halloween costume.

Coercing by intimidation is a more severe type of emotional abuse. Placing or threatening to place a child in an unfit or dangerous environment is an example of intimidation. A common and harmful example of intimidation that stands out from previous child protection days was when a parent, as a discipline strategy, would threaten their child by telling them they would call the child protection agency and have them taken away if they did not behave. They would also describe child protection workers as uncaring and dangerous. This would exacerbate a child's fear if/when child protective services was asked to intervene. Figure 3.3 highlights some signs of emotional abuse.

SIGNS AND SYMPTOMS OF EMOTIONAL ABUSE
1   Child is anxious about doing something wrong
2   Child is excessively fearful
3   Child shows extremes in behaviour: extremely compliant or extremely demanding; extremely passive or extremely aggressive
4   Child acts inappropriately; either adult-like, taking care of other children, or inappropriately infantile; rocking, thumb-sucking
5   Doesn't seem to be attached to the parent or caregiver

Figure 3.3 Signs and Symptoms of Emotional Abuse

Sources: Fortin & Chamberland, 1995; Kaplan et al., 1999; Kolko et al., 1992; Kurtz et al., 1993; Trocmé et al., 2005.

Exposure to Violence

Children who witness or who are exposed to violence are also affected by the emotional, physical, and sometimes sexual assaults on their mothers. This form of violence therefore represents another category of child abuse.

In relation to other forms of violence, it is a relatively newly identified category of concern. When the battered woman became a focus more than 40 years ago, very few researchers considered the impact on the children who witnessed the violence. The specific focus at the time was on raising awareness of the existence and scope of wife battering and the inadequate response from society. Only when children were physically abused along with their mothers did the child factor into the battered woman equation. Yet, as child abuse issues began to intersect with those of wife battering, a growing concern and understanding emerged.

Children today are no longer considered unaffected bystanders in violent homes (Jaffe, Wolfe, & Crooks, 2003; Kelly, 1996; Kolko, Blakely, & Engleman, 1992; Krane & Davies, 2007). Witnessing violence can significantly affect a child's social development and mental health. And, although some children might be harmed in the crossfire of violence and violent acts (e.g., a mother, while holding her child, is assaulted by her partner), the majority of children are hurt through indirect violence—because they are close by, or because they personally witness the violence directed at their mothers or siblings.

Some acts of violence children witness are unimaginable. For instance, in Toronto in 2000 a man poured a litre of sulphuric acid over his partner, who was in the process of breaking up their long-term relationship. The woman was left in critical condition with caustic burns to 80 percent of her body. Her six-year-old son witnessed the grisly attack (*Toronto Star,* 2000).

Although "witnessing violence" is a frequently used expression, the term "exposure to violence" is also helpful because it encompasses the range of situations to which a child might be subjected. Exposure to intimate partner violence was researched in the

Canadian Incidence Study of Reported Child Abuse and Neglect (CIS, 2008). This study identified four separate forms of exposure to intimate violence:

1. *Direct witness to physical violence:* The child is physically present and witnesses the violence between intimate partners.

2. *Indirect exposure to physical violence:* Includes situations where the child overhears but does not see the violence between intimate partners; or sees some of the immediate consequences of the assault (e.g., injuries to the mother); or overhears or is told about conversations about the assault. This also involves the times when a child hears the abuser's threats to injure or kill himself, the children, and/or their mother.

3. *Exposure to emotional violence:* Includes situations in which the child is exposed directly or indirectly to emotional violence between intimate partners, for instance forcing a child to listen to the degradation of his or her mother, or hearing the abuser's threats to injure or kill himself, the children, and/or their mother.

4. *Exposure to non-partner physical violence:* A child has been exposed to violence occurring between a caregiver and another person who is not the spouse/partner of the caregiver (e.g., between a caregiver and neighbour, grandparent, aunt, or uncle).

Additional examples of exposure to intimate violence have been noted in the literature (Fantuzzo & Lindquist, 1989; Jaffe, Wolfe, & Wilson, 1990; Kaufman, Kantor, & Little, 2003; Kolko et al., 1992; Kolko, Blakely, & Engleman, 1996; Krane & Davies, 2000):

- a child fears for his/her own and his/her mother's life
- a child watches the aftermath of abuse, such as a parent or parents arrested and removed by police
- a child witnesses the mother's suicide attempt; the child might need to call for help
- a child is used as a pawn or weapon against their mother
- a child is interrogated or involved in spying on their mother

Moreover, children may see or hear their fathers hitting their mothers or siblings, and may feel helpless in their ability to answer their cries for help. Some children observe sexual assaults or even murder (Eth & Pynoos, 1994; Jaffe et al., 1990). The fact that these forms of violence are taking place in a child's core relationships is serious. As one would therefore imagine, exposure to indirect violence has harmful effects on children (Fantuzzo & Lindquist, 1989; Jaffe et al., 1990; Kolko et al., 1996). This issue is discussed later in this chapter.

Sexual Abuse

It is not uncommon to see stories about sexual assault, child sexual abuse, or incest in the media. It seems next to impossible to turn on a computer or television or to pick up a newspaper or magazine without encountering a news story or disclosure of a child sexual abuse case. This public awareness of sexual abuse became widespread only in the late 1980s; despite the long documented history of child sexual abuse in Canada, this form of violence began to receive academic and public attention only during the mid 1980s.

Today, however, when many child abuse cases, particularly sexual abuse, become public, it is because of their involvement in the criminal justice system. It is important to remember that a great number of child sexual abuse cases (all child abuse cases, for that matter) that take place in the "here and now" are not known to the general public. The identities of child victims involved with the child welfare system are confidential; these cases are not reported in the daily news unless *Criminal Code* charges are laid. Even when this occurs, victims are not named. Nor are the victims who choose not to pursue criminal charges.

More often, the cases of sexual abuse that become known to the public are historical cases—these include situations when the abused child, who is now a teenager or an adult, chooses to come forward and report her or his childhood victimization. When this occurs the victim's anonymity is still protected; however, the alleged perpetrator can be identified.

So what do we know about the existence of child sexual abuse? According to Benjamin Schlesinger's 1980s review of the literature, from the period of 1937 to 1974 there were only 32 published articles relating to child sexual abuse. By contrast, he pointed out that during the period of 1975 to 1980, 85 articles were published (Schlesinger, 1980). From that point on, many theorists began to research and study the prevalence of sexual abuse, and clinicians began to study the impact of this violent crime on its victims, their families, and the community (Faller, 1988; Finkelhor & Brown, 1986; Sgroi, 1982).

Despite the various research studies completed, one fact was agreed upon: child sexual abuse is a complicated, harmful, and life-altering violent crime. A number of criminal offences are defined in the *Criminal Code of Canada* regarding sexual crimes against children. ("From the Pen of . . ." Box 7.3 in Chapter 7 describes the laws for children testifying in the Criminal Court.) What's more, in Canada each province/territory has unique legislation defining and describing its response to sexual abuse. With this in mind, we will begin our discussion with a broad definition of sexual abuse.

According the Department of Justice Canada, sexual abuse and exploitation of children and youth occurs when an older child, adolescent, or adult takes advantage of a younger child or youth for sexual purposes. Sexual activity includes all sexual contact ranging from sexual touching to intercourse. Sexual abuse can further include **fondling, intercourse, incest,** sodomy, exhibitionism, and commercial **exploitation** through prostitution or the production of pornographic materials. Sexual abuse and exploitation is perpetrated on children of all ages, from infancy to adolescence.

Sexual abuse also exists on a continuum that describes specific sexual behaviours (Sgroi, 1982). These behaviours include:

1. viewing a child in a state of undress
2. **fellatio** (oral contact with male genitalia)
3. **cunnilingus** (oral contact with female genitalia)

4. **interfemural intercourse** (often called dry intercourse: rubbing the penis between the legs or buttocks without penetrating a body opening)

5. inserting objects in a child's genitals; vaginal or anal intercourse

6. acts of mutilation; burning genitals

7. exhibitionism and commercial exploitation through prostitution or the production of pornographic materials.

All sexual activity with a child under the age of 16 is a criminal offence in Canada, regardless of the child's consent (see Box 7.2 in Chapter 7 for more on changes to Canada's age of sexual consent).

There are many overlapping dimensions to the sexual abuse and exploitation of children and youth. A child or youth may be sexually abused and exploited by one or more family members, by others outside the family, including those known to the child or youth (e.g., a priest or teacher), or by a stranger. Plus they may not be protected, despite the fact the other adults know the violence exists.

The perpetrator might be acting alone, or be part of an organized group or network. But many more victimizations take place in the privacy of a child's home, by those known to the child and their family. One such sexual predator of this magnitude was Father Charles Sylvestre, a Catholic priest who used his revered role to sexually abuse countless female girl children across southwestern Ontario during the 1950s through the 1970s (see "Canadian Headline News" Box 3.3).

3.3 Canadian Headline News: Charles Sylvestre— Sexual Predator, Catholic Priest

Cheers and sobs erupted in court when officers handcuffed retired priest Charles Sylvestre after a judge sentenced him to three years in prison for methodically sexually victimizing young girls for nearly 40 years in southwestern Ontario. The abuse occurred despite complaints by the victims to the police, school, and church officials throughout that time period.

Sylvestre *then* asked to be forgiven!

A joint sentence was submitted by the Crown attorney and Sylvestre's defence lawyer. For some victims, the three years was a compromise, which avoided a lengthy trial and the chance Sylvestre might die before being convicted and going to jail. He was 84 at the time of his sentencing.

Crown Attorney Paul Bailey agreed with the sentence, but made sure the judge knew what Sylvestre was capable of. "Consider the reason why the accused committed these hideous offences," Bailey said.

"His motive for each offence was nothing more or less than depraved lust. To satisfy his own lust he was prepared to destroy the lives of innocent children . . . [he] threatened his victims to shut them up. Father Sylvestre pointed to the crucifix on the wall and told her that if she said anything Christ would come down off the cross and strike her dead and she would burn in hell."

(continued)

In response, Ontario court Justice Bruce Thomas addressed Sylvestre's victims:

> "His perverted cravings, it appeared, were almost insatiable," he said. "Justice is at the best of times an elusive commodity. How does one do justice in a case like this? There is nothing I can say and nothing I can do to make matters right for you."

But the acts of violence by Sylvestre would be addressed not just in the criminal justice system. Many of the victims chose to hold Sylvestre and the Diocese of London responsible for the decades of violence. And just how many children were involved during those 40 years? When CBC reporter Hana Gartner directly asked lawyer Rob Talach, who represented many of the victims in civil litigation, to "Put the case of Father Sylvestre in context for me. How big is it, in scope and size?" Rob Talach responded: "I think the largest we've seen in Canada with respect to a single perpetrator and number of known victims."

"So, it's large," responded Gartner.

Reflection Question

Many adult victims of child sexual abuse are coming forward. You often hear divergent comments when it relates to civil litigation and victims receiving financial compensation for the harm done. What are your views?

Sources: CBC, 2006.

Despite the fact that statistics suggest the majority of perpetrators are male, sexual perpetrators may be the same sex as or the opposite sex of the victim. Regardless of where and how it occurs, who the perpetrator is, or whether the child or youth consents, the sexual abuse and exploitation of children and youth is a betrayal of trust, an abuse of power, and illegal. Figure 3.4 describes the types of abusive or exploitive non-contact behaviour that often are used.

Dynamics of Sexual Abuse and Exploitation Sexual exploitation and abuse involve a great amount of planning. These are not impulsive violent acts; they require

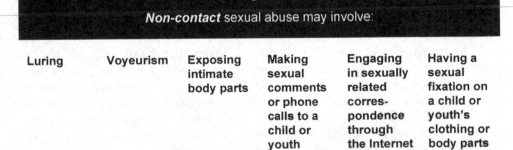

Figure 3.4 Types of Sexually Abusive or Exploitive Non-Contact Behaviour Often Used to Sexually Groom, Exploit, or Abuse Children and Youth

considerable thought and energy. A perpetrator may spend a great amount of care and time befriending and **grooming** the victim. Perpetrators need access to children and invent and use various methods to isolate, manipulate, and control their young victims. These dynamics are an important piece of theory to understand. There is almost always a power differential between the perpetrator and the victim. Perpetrators use bribery, trickery, and other forms of psychological coercion to gain access to children, make them compliant, and keep them silent (Finkelhor, 1986; Groth & Birnbaum, 1979; Russell, 1986).

Recently, retired NHL hockey player Theo Fleury came forward to describe the pain, shame, and unfolding nature of his sexual victimization. Fleury was the second NHL hockey player to publicly discuss his childhood sexual assault. Sheldon Kennedy was the first, when he took his complaint of sexual abuse to the Calgary police on September 3, 1996. After the subsequent conviction and sentencing of sexual offender Graham James, Kennedy spoke publicly in 1997 about the horror of his victimization. He stated that between the ages of 14 and 19, he was sexually abused more than 350 times by Graham James, his junior hockey coach. The abuse went on twice weekly between 1984 and 1990 (Kennedy, 2006). The anger, rage, guilt, shame, and stigmatization he felt cannot be overemphasized. Kennedy and Fleury were both sexually assaulted by the same perpetrator, Graham James (see "Canadian Headline News" Box 3.4).

3.4 Canadian Headline News: Canada and Hockey Go Hand in Glove

One could say Graham James was a gatekeeper to a Canadian boy's biggest dream—a junior hockey career followed by an NHL contract. Many of us, coast to coast, have watched the draft on television witnessing the exhilaration and delight on the faces of the players and their families and friends when they don their NHL jersey.

James, like many people with great prestige in society, could open doors AND slam them shut. For a sexual predator hockey coach it was the perfect hat trick: power, the stigma of abuse, and a homophobic sports culture created the ideal opportunity to exploit, violate, and silence young players.

It was Sheldon Kennedy who first went public about being abused by James. At the time of his disclosure Mr. Kennedy had indicated that he knew of one other NHL player who had also been abused; however, Kennedy intentionally did not name the player. That player would in time reveal himself. In October 2009, retired hockey player Theoren Fleury publicly confirmed that he had been sexually abused by his junior coach, Graham James. Mr. Fleury would write, "Graham recruited Theo at 13 from his minor hockey team in Russell, Manitoba. Graham was on me once or twice a week for the next two years . . . An absolute nightmare, every day of my life" (Fleury & McLellan Day, 2009, p. 1).

James required Fleury to sleep two nights a week at his coach's house, rather than at the home where he had been billeted. "He tried to fight off the coach at first, wrapping himself in blankets each night and pretending to sleep as James attempted to masturbate him and give

(continued)

him oral sex. But the fear of James's advances left him sleepless, and exhaustion broke him down" (Fleury & McLellan Day, 2009, p. 1). And so too did James's frequent warnings that, without his coach's support, he stood little chance of playing professional hockey (Fleury & McLellan Day, 2009).

Theo Fleury would also divulge the impact caused by years of violation and violence. "What took me down was rage. Rage fuelled by drugs, alcohol and relationships. I had two exes and three great kids back home in Canada, I lived in this fantastic mansion . . . yet I wanted to die. I went on a three month bender, just me and my mounds of cocaine. Nobody could handle all the guilt, self-hate and dark secrets I had" (Fleury & McLellan Day, 2009, p. 1).

Sheldon Kennedy would also write about the terror he felt at the hands of James. "He didn't have to say anymore. He knew the effect the gun would have on me. I was alone in a strange place with a strange man who held the keys to the world that I had wanted to be part of since I was a little kid. He was a man who I'd been told to look up to and obey. He knew all of this, and he knew that he would use his authority and my fear and ignorance to get me to do something that I didn't understand and didn't want to be a part of" (Kennedy, 2006, p. 37).

Following the release of Theo Fleury's book in 2009, which described the abuse he suffered, further criminal charges were laid against Graham James. On December 7, 2011, the formerly convicted sex offender James, who had previously been granted a pardon, pleaded guilty to sexual assaults involving two of his former players, including NHL star Theoren Fleury. Originally James faced nine charges of sexual assault involving three players spanning 1979 to 1994, but pleaded guilty to charges involving only two. The names of the two others were protected under a court-ordered publication ban. As mentioned earlier in this chapter, not all victims choose to be identified, nor are they legally obligated to do so.

On March 20, 2012, James was given a two-year sentence by Provincial Court Judge Catherine Carlson, which outraged many Canadians. This frustration was equal to the earlier public reaction when, in 2010, Canadians discovered James (as well as other sexual offenders) was granted a criminal pardon, clearing him of his previous sexual assault conviction. Two weeks later the Crown prosecutors in Manitoba stated the judge made errors in her sentence, and consequentially they were appealing the two-year prison sentence.

Reflection Question

Since 2010, the federal government has taken steps to enact legislation preventing convicted sexual offenders from having their crimes removed from the public record. However, this does not change earlier pardons. Although pardons and criminal sentencing are two separate entities in the Canadian criminal justice system, how well do you think the victimized are represented and respected? How are all Canadians protected in Canada's justice system?

Source: Fleury & McLellan Day, 2009; Kennedy, 2006.

The stories of Sheldon Kennedy and Theo Fleury demonstrate how the hope of an NHL career was exploited by a sexual predator. Yet they more profoundly demonstrate how those with power and privilege can exploit children. The sad fact is that Kennedy's and Fleury's stories are echoed by countless other nameless child victims who have also been left to fend privately by themselves, while trying to the best of their ability to manage and cope with the trauma caused by their victimization.

It is important to note that sexual abuse or exploitation may involve single or repeated acts. Additionally, these acts may become more serious, frequent, and intrusive over time. Many victims of sexual violence experience a lifetime of negative effects. This issue is further discussed later in this chapter.

Another population of Canadian child victims to consider is those who have been violently abused and abandoned by some of the most trusted people in society: the leaders of religious institutions. There are not enough pages in this textbook to outline the systemic historical cases of sexual child abuse perpetrated by clergy in religious institutions. However, the lid would be ratcheted open by key cases that eventually became known, ending the silence and shifting the shame by assigning blame.

One such case has earned the notoriety of being Canada's largest sexual abuse scandal—indeed, one of the largest in the world. The case involves a church-run orphanage called Mount Cashel and is described in "Canadian Headline News" Box 3.5. The abuse was revealed thanks to the courage of a victim and the integrity of a believer who chose to stand up to power and advocate for others. In "From the Pen of . . ." Box 3.6, you will read an account from Michael Harris, a Canadian truth teller—a person who had the integrity, courage, and the respect for the human dignity of others, to ask that the truth be told. Within his narrative Mr. Harris shares the process of his journey to ask that the past be revealed and acknowledged.

3.5 Canadian Headline News: Mount Cashel— A Canadian Story of Abuse and the Conspiracy of Silence

The year was 1989, and revolution was in the air. Germany's infamous Berlin Wall was being torn down, and democracy there was unfolding. At the same time another revolution of sorts was occurring in Canada. Canada's revolution, however, would soon require a different type of dismantling.

The events at Mount Cashel Orphanage in Newfoundland are considered one of Canada's largest sexual abuse scandals, and at the time were arguably one of the largest in the world. Once revered by many, by 1989 Mount Cashel had become synonymous with the terrible physical and sexual abuse inflicted on hundreds of orphanage residents for decades. But how did this occur? What had changed?

***

Mount Cashel was operated in Canada by the Christian Brothers of Ireland (CBIC). The CBIC was a branch of a lay Roman Catholic order that was founded in Ireland. They opened schools in many countries around the world, and one of those schools was Mount Cashel. Similar to many Canadian provinces, in Newfoundland the Roman Catholic clergy were highly respected by many. As discussed in Chapter 2, members of the church held a privileged position in society, and as such their behaviour was considered beyond criticism.

For generations there was an unwritten rule in Newfoundland that crimes involving the clergy were best dealt with in the backrooms of the justice system—a misplaced homage to the church's enormous prestige based on its innumerable good works. It was also testament to the immense political power of the pulpit in Newfoundland, a cultural reality dating from the island's earliest colonial beginnings (Harris,

(continued)

1990, pp. xxiii–xxiv). The provincial government and the police adopted a hands-off policy toward religious matters.

But things started to change. In December 1975 the Royal Newfoundland Constabulary (RNC) began an investigation into the first physical and sexual abuse allegations. This investigation resulted in five staff being implicated by 20 residents (victims). The investigation was curtailed by the Chief of the RNC on instruction from the Department of Justice, despite two members of the CBIC *admitting* to sexual wrongdoing. No further residents were interviewed, and the two staff members were placed in treatment centres outside the province and then transferred to other CBIC-operated institutions in Canada.

Later, in 1982, the RNC began a second investigation into more allegations of physical and sexual abuse. Thirteen separate reports were written (nine by the Department of Social Services and four by the RNC). One staff member, who was a member of the CBIC, was charged with sexual offences and convicted.

When the allegations of physical and sexual abuse began to surface *again* in the late 1980s, the government, police, and church cooperated in an unsuccessful cover-up.

The conspiracy of silence, suppression, and cover-ups could not hold indefinitely, however. On February 13, 1989, a caller to VOCM's radio call-in program *Open Line* mentioned suspicion of a cover-up by the Government of Newfoundland and Labrador into sexual and physical abuse at the orphanage. Listening to *Open Line* that day was a Justice of the Supreme Court of Newfoundland and Labrador, who would follow up on the issue with the provincial government's associate deputy attorney-general.

On Easter Sunday, March 26, 1989, the St. John's *Sunday Express,* under the direction of its publisher Michael Harris, began to publish the allegations of sexual and physical abuse perpetrated by staff at the orphanage dating back to the 1950s. The RNC investigation was reactivated.

What ensued were multiple criminal investigations and many charges and convictions. At the same time the provincial government commissioned a Royal Commission to investigate. It became known as the Hughes Inquiry/Commission.

The Archdiocese of St. John's also commissioned an inquiry, the Winter Commission Inquiry. Once completed, a report was issued: *The Archdiocesan Commission of Inquiry into Sexual Abuse of Children,* in 1990. Archbishop Alphonsus Penney of Newfoundland resigned after an internal investigative panel placed some of the blame for cover-ups of the abuse on him.

When the criminal court proceedings ended and the final commissions and inquiry reports were submitted the following was revealed:

- In 1992, four men in the Roman Catholic lay order were charged with the sexual and physical abuse of boys at the orphanage during the 1970s.
- In 1996, six additional members of the order were charged with sexually and physically abusing 17 boys at the same orphanage between 1950 and 1964.
- The total criminal conviction total was 14 staff members—nine members of the Christian Brothers of Ireland in Canada and five civilians—including 88 counts of physical and sexual abuse.
- In 2003, the Supreme Court of Canada ruled that the Roman Catholic Church was responsible—was (**vicariously liable**)—for sexual abuse by its priests in the diocese of Saint George's.
- In 2009, the Supreme Court of Newfoundland and Labrador ruled that the Roman Catholic Church in St. John's was responsible ("vicariously liable") for the sexual abuse of eight former altar boys by disgraced priest Reverend James Hickey.
- There have been millions of dollars in court-imposed financial settlements.

When all was said and done, it would be revealed that hundreds of former pupils alleged physical and sexual abuse at the orphanage. As a result of the investigation the last remaining residents were moved, and Mount Cashel was closed down permanently in 1989.

Reflection Question

Recently revealed in the news was a sexual abuse case involving Penn State, a prestigious university in the United States. Embroiled in this story are the world of sports, as well as the alleged offenders and institutions that the general public has held in high esteem for decades. The story is similar to many Canadian cases, which have involved power, prestige, and influence. Do you think Canadians have heard the last of our institutionalized child abuse cases, or will there be more to confront?

Sources: Harris, 1990; O'Brien, 1991.

3.6 From the Pen of Michael Harris, Author of *Unholy Orders*

The first inkling I had of a child abuse scandal that would rock my country, and then send dominoes tumbling around the world, was whispered into my telephone by a young waiter with a story to tell.

At the time, I was running a new, weekly newspaper called the *Sunday Express*. The call from Shane Earle had been prompted by an editorial I had written in 1989 under the headline "Justice for All."

Shane had a very simple question: why hadn't there been justice for the boys of Mount Cashel Orphanage back in 1975?

My coffee remained untouched that day at the Radisson Hotel in St. John's as I listened to Shane reprising the nightmare of sexual and physical abuse that had stolen his childhood. The details of the crimes against the boys of Mount Cashel were horrific; that they had been perpetrated by the people charged with caring for the children made them monstrous. I was left in front of the biggest challenge of my journalistic career. Was the story true, and if it was, how should I tell it given that every level of empowered society in Newfoundland was involved?

Every story of consequence poses dangers in the telling. But the tragedy at Mount Cashel was a minefield. Shane's account brought into criminal disrepute the reputation of a beloved institution, the Irish Christian Brothers. "The Brothers" as they were affectionately known in Newfoundland, were a renowned lay order of the Roman Catholic Church who had earned their fame as teachers from the early days of the colony.

Newfoundland in those days had a denominational education system, in which the Catholic and Protestant school boards divided the work of schooling generations of young students. Religion was in the bones of the place. I could already imagine what the Archbishop of St. John's, let alone our readers, would say if I told the story of Mount Cashel on the front page of the *Sunday Express*.

Since Shane was alleging that the police knew all about the crimes against the children at Mount Cashel back in 1975, publishing the story would also impugn the reputation of the Royal Newfoundland Constabulary. How could they have had written confessions from the clerical abusers at the time and yet done nothing about bringing them to justice?

Equally daunting, both the justice and the child welfare systems of Newfoundland had heavy responsibilities in this case, which they had utterly failed to discharge. Nor was the media of the day divorced from the cover-up.

(continued)

The province's only daily newspaper, *The Evening Telegram,* knew about the abuse when it happened, but the publisher decided not to print the Mount Cashel story because of the harm the news might cause to a revered institution.

Like a man standing at the edge of a cliff, I knew how far down a false step would take everyone. What would happen to Shane if the story could not be fully proven? What would happen to the young and talented staff of reporters I had recruited at our fledgling paper if they started their careers with an expose that was crushed by all the institutions that had been compromised by Mount Cashel—a real possibility since the story had already been suppressed once?

Yes, I was afraid. On that first day, listening to Shane, he and I had not yet appeared on *Oprah Winfrey.* A royal commission had not yet found that the boys of Mount Cashel had been failed by every institution in the establishment. There were as yet no compensation payments, no apologies, and no perpetrators had been sent to prison. There was just a young waiter and a newspaper editor sharing the gray cocoon of a late winter afternoon, talking in hushed tones of what had happened long ago and what might be done about it all these years later.

That night, I came home late and let myself into our house at Three Island Pond. I saw my youngest daughter Emily asleep on the couch. A book lay open on her chest, her hands folded over it. She was about the age of the children at Mount Cashel when their horror had begun.

I knew then that no person or power, no threat or fear, was greater than the need to protect this innocence—even if that protection were offered retroactively. Without knowing how this story would end, there was one thing that I did know: I believed Shane Earle. After intensive investigation, the *Sunday Express* published his story on March 19, 1989. It appeared beneath a picture of the five-year-old boy Shane had been when he entered Mount Cashel.

Years later, after the offending Christian brothers had been sent to jail, I stood outside the Mount Cashel Orphanage and watched as it was torn down. The wrecking ball was not made of steel and cable alone, but of the words and the courage of a diffident waiter speaking for a generation of child ghosts.

I have never been afraid since.

Review Question

Mr. Harris, like all of our "From the Pen Of . . ." contributors, each in their own way served others. This brings to mind the concept of altruism, which describes virtue—the opposite of selfishness. What qualities and attributes do you think are required to stand up for others, even at the risk of personal or professional harm?

Source: Submitted by Michael Harris, author of *Unholy Orders, Tragedy at Mount Cashel,* to Anastasia Bake.

To ensure an authentic presentation of violence against children in Canada, the historical record of the countless known and unknown victimizations of Aboriginal children that took place during the residential school system years must be honoured. Although many of these violent acts began before the conception of child protection legislation in Canada, they continued to occur after—and in spite of—the enactment of both provincial laws and the *Criminal Code*. It took many decades for the systems that perpetrated those crimes to publically assume responsibility and apologize.

Risk Assessments

When violence is reported it must be investigated, and a child's protection, needs, and safety must be assessed and guaranteed. The professionals ultimately held accountable to make these decisions are child protection workers and our courts: our Justices. To address these questions and the potential for ambiguity, risk assessments have been developed to approximate the likelihood that a particular negative event will occur. Risk assessments generally involve determining the likelihood of future maltreatment, and deciding whether action is needed to reduce the risk of future harm so that action can be taken to thwart it (Knoke & Trocmé, 2004).

Professionals, many of them social workers, have always used their clinical judgment to assess risk for future neglect and abuse. Structured risk assessments were developed, however, to improve accuracy and consistency in identifying children at high risk for future severe harm. Severe maltreatment typically refers to acts that endanger the physical health and safety of a child, including sexual abuse (Knoke & Trocmé, 2004). Structured risk assessments provide a standardized way to collect and organize case information relevant to risk. This also means information is collected, considered, and recorded in a consistent fashion.

Risk assessments do not, however, provide the information required to address broader aspects of child well-being. Nor do they provide information about the long-term needs of children and families. Risk assessments relate to safety to ensure short-term decisions can be made (Knoke & Trocmé, 2004).

Knoke and Trocmé (2004) identified several factors that are measured when assessing risk:

- nature and severity of previous maltreatment

- characteristics of the family environment (e.g., domestic violence)

- caregiver characteristics (e.g., mental health issues, substance abuse)

- child characteristics (e.g., age, problem behaviour)

Furthermore, age, gender, or disabilities may place some children at higher risk for maltreatment. Each risk factor is given a rating and social workers consider the combination of ratings to assess overall risk. This overall risk is generally classified into levels such as low, moderate, and high (Knoke & Trocmé, 2004).

As you consider the purpose of risk assessments it might be beneficial to reflect upon the following question: How would the lives of countless Aboriginal children who lived through the residential school era been affected had there been risk assessments that were universally mandated and applied to all populations of children to determine their safety and well being?

Conclusion

Child protection agencies and Justices must consider many variables when making decisions regarding how best to protect children. Providing support and help, imposing consequences, and perhaps making the ultimate judgment—the decision to remove a child from the care and custody of the parent—are all potential outcomes in fulfilling a child protection mandate.

3.2 IMPACT OF CHILD ABUSE AND NEGLECT

All violence consists in some people forcing others, under threat of suffering or death, to do what they do not want to do.

—Leo Tolstoy Novelist, playwright (1828 – 1910).

What are the consequences of childhood violence? So far in this textbook the historical and present-day descriptions of child abuse and neglect have been discussed. From the extreme and systemic acts of brutality committed against vulnerable and *isolated* Aboriginal children beginning before Confederation, to the relatively recent victimizations of our very *public* and *celebrated* elite male hockey players. The scope of harm done to Canadian children is broad and all-encompassing. Although the consequences of violence for children may vary according to its nature and severity, the short- and long-term repercussions are often grave and damaging (Felitti et al., 1998).

The visible effects of child abuse and neglect are only the tip of the iceberg when considering the impact of child maltreatment. Abusive experiences can shape child development and the effects can last years, even a lifetime. Research now shows that the physical, psychological, and behavioural consequences of child abuse and neglect impact the child and family, as well as the community as a whole. This principle is most profoundly illustrated by the effects of abuse on Aboriginal children, their communities, and ultimately their culture—their way of life. Similarly the violence committed by so many Catholic clergy has lead many people who were born into Catholic homes to question the church.

Child abuse is traumatic. Before we begin to examine the impact of the different forms of abuse, specific criteria are important to keep in mind. Apart from the violence, a child victim's eventual outcome also is modified by experiences they have within their family and the wider community. It has been noted in the literature that specific variables do have direct bearing on the eventual impact of child abuse. They include characteristics of the child, type of trauma, relationships, and validation.

Characteristics of the Child

The age, emotional, and cognitive development, gender, race/ethnicity, personality, and strengths or resiliency of the child all play a part in determining the effects of abuse. Resilience is key. **Resilience** is defined as the capacity to emerge intact from negative life experiences. According to Paris (1998), research on children at risk shows that resilience is the rule, not the exception. In general, only about 25 percent of children exposed to severe trauma develop demonstrable psychopathology as adults.

Type of Trauma

For the purpose of determining the impact of abuse, two types of trauma are identified. The first type is defined as a single incident. The second type involves chronic or repetitive abuse over time. This second type is usually more difficult for a child to overcome. All forms of abuse create the possibility of long-term effects on psychological and social adaptation. When multiple abuses occur at the same time (known as co-occurrence), the risk of maladaptive behaviour is heightened.

Relationships

An abused child's relationships greatly determine his or her level of resiliency and the extent of trauma. These relationships and the quality of the relationship can include the following:

- The perpetrator: was it a stranger, authority figure, friend, family member, parent?

- Reaction to the violence by parents and extended family members: were they protective, supportive, offering sanctuary, *or* uncaring, disbelieving, ridiculing and blaming?

- Peers: who knew? Did they rally, speak up, and support, *or* ostracize and embarrass?

- Child advocates: church leaders, police officers, government officials, and courts. How did they respond? Where they complicit, did they deny and cover up, *or* step up and do the right thing? Did they take legal action and apply the law despite the person's position, membership in a particular group or profession, status, or personal connections?

Validation

An abused child's relationships are extremely significant. Second to the actual victimization is the aftermath. Was the child believed and supported, or was their reality denied? Support and validation for a victimized child is vital for two important reasons. The first reason is to ensure immediate safety and a cessation of abuse, and the second reason is to provide a protective caring foundation, which is essential to healing (Erickson, Egeland, & Pianta, 1989; Garrett & Libbey, 1997).

The importance and necessity of support and **validation** has been noted and underscored by research and the testimonies of adult victims (Sgroi, 1982). For many child abuse victims not only were their pleas for help unanswered, but the aftermath of their disclosures led to systemic, and well planned and executed, cover-ups, collusion, and rejection. *Power protects power,* and families also pick and choose whom they will support. Consequently, when long-overdue personal and public apologies do take place, healing for many victims is finally possible.

Validation helps, and an apology is critical from those who knowingly remained silent, even years later, or who colluded, covered up, or consciously chose not to protect.

This was poignantly demonstrated when the Canadian government and various religious institutions eventually made public apologies to the Aboriginal victims of the residential school system. See "Canadian Headline News" Box 3.7 for details on the public apology and the reaction from some adult survivors.

3.7 Canadian Headline News: Three Little Words

Healing and Historical Words Uttered in a Hushed House of Commons

In 2008, Prime Minister of Canada Stephen Harper made an apology on behalf of the Canadian government.

In response to his apology, Assembly of First Nations Chief Phil Fontaine stated, "The memories of residential schools sometimes . . . cut like a knife at our souls. This day will help us to put that pain behind us."

In part Prime Minister Harper stated that:

The treatment of children in Indian Residential Schools is a sad chapter in our history. For more than a century, Indian Residential Schools separated over 150,000 Aboriginal children from their families and communities. In the 1870s, the federal government, partly in order to meet its obligation to educate Aboriginal children, began to play a role in the development and administration of these schools. Two primary objectives of the Residential Schools system were to remove and isolate children from the influence of their homes, families, traditions and cultures, and to assimilate them into the dominant culture. These objectives were based on the assumption Aboriginal cultures and spiritual beliefs were inferior and unequal. Indeed, some sought, as it was infamously said, "to kill the Indian in the child". . . .

Many were inadequately fed, clothed and housed. All were deprived of the care and nurturing of their parents, grandparents and communities. First Nations, Inuit and Métis languages and cultural practices were prohibited in these schools. Tragically, some of these children died while attending residential schools and others never returned home . . .

The government now recognizes that the consequences of the Indian Residential Schools policy were profoundly negative and that this policy has had a lasting and damaging impact on Aboriginal culture, heritage and language. While some former students have spoken positively about their experiences at residential schools, these stories are far overshadowed by tragic accounts of the emotional, physical and sexual abuse and neglect of helpless children, and their separation from powerless families and communities. The legacy of Indian Residential Schools has contributed to social problems that continue to exist in many communities today. It has taken extraordinary courage for the thousands of survivors that have come forward to speak publicly about the abuse they suffered.

He Is Sorry: The Catholic Church Apologizes

On Wednesday, April 29, 2009, at a meeting with representatives of Native Canadians, The Pontiff expressed his sorrow and emphasized that . . .

". . . acts of abuse cannot be tolerated" . . . "Given the sufferings that some indigenous children experienced in the Canadian residential school system, the Holy Father expressed his sorrow at the anguish caused by the deplorable conduct of some members of the church and he offered his sympathy and prayerful solidarity."

In response, Chief Phil Fontaine said he appreciated the apology from the Church. Fontaine is quoted as saying,

"I think His Holiness understands the pain that was endured by so many and I heard him say that it caused him great anguish . . . I also heard His Holiness say that the abuse of the nature that was inflicted on us has no place in the Church, it's intolerable and it caused him great anguish . . . What I heard, it gives me comfort."

Reflection Question

Is "sorry" ever enough? Or, because these words acknowledged a wrong, does it help victims heal?

Source: Indian and Northern Affairs Canada, www.ainc-inac. gc.ca. Courtesy Prime Minister Stephen Harper.

While there are as many outcomes from harm as there are types and circumstances, research in this area has attempted to create categories. The main areas to be examined are the physical and psychological impacts.

Physical Harm

The immediate physical consequences of abuse or neglect can be relatively minor, such as bruises or cuts, or they can be severe, such as broken bones, hemorrhage, or even death. While in some cases the physical effects are temporary, the pain and suffering they cause cannot be overestimated. Poor physical health is also a possible outcome. Several studies have shown a relationship between various forms of childhood abuse and poor health (Felitti, 1998; Flaherty et al., 2006). Adults who experience abuse or neglect during childhood are more likely to suffer from ailments such as allergies, arthritis, asthma, bronchitis, high blood pressure, and ulcers (Springer et al., 2007).

Furthermore, when physical abuse was the primary substantiated maltreatment the Canadian Incidence Study of Reported Child Abuse and Neglect (CIS, 2003) found the most common child functioning challenges were:

- emotional or behavioural problem, 36 percent of cases
- negative peer involvement, 19 percent of cases
- ADD/ADHD, 19 percent of cases
- violence toward others, 19 percent of cases
- depression or anxiety, 18 percent of cases
- learning disability, 18 percent of cases

Many other possible effects were noted in the literature specific to physical abuse (Briere, 1992; Kolko et al., 1992). They included:

- denial
- personality changes related to grief and rage
- trauma-specific fears

- **posttraumatic stress**
- repression
- **dissociation**

Dissociative disorder is a class of psychiatric disorder recognized in the *Diagnostic and Statistical Manual of Mental Disorders* (*DSM-IV-TR)* that involves dissociative processes. It can appear as any symptom in which the person prevents traumatic experiences, feelings, or thoughts from entering consciousness by cutting oneself off from traumatic experiences, thoughts, memories, or feelings.

Risk of Death The first year of a Canadian child's life places them most at risk of death. Shaken baby syndrome (SBS) is the ultimate tragic consequence (refer to Box 3.1 for a discussion of SBS). The injuries caused by shaking a baby may not be immediately noticeable, but the potential for harm is real. King et al. (2003) specifically state, "Presenting signs and symptoms are often nonspecific, which means that health care providers must have a high index of suspicion when infants and young children present with subtle neurological signs such as lethargy or decreased level of consciousness. Although a significant number of children had evidence of severe trauma with external bruising or fractures, or both, up to 40% of children had no external sign of injury" (p. 158). Further, children under the age of one year were the most likely to be investigated by child welfare agencies, with a rate of 51.81 investigations per 1000 children (Trocmé et al., 2010).

Psychological Harm

Psychological harm is an additional category. It can take place in conjunction with physical or sexual abuse as well as on its own. The consequences can include a damaged sense of self, distortion in thinking, and thinking of the self as bad; victims are often told this or, worse yet, they themselves think they are in some way deserving of the abuse (Briere, 1992; Briere & Runtz, 1993; De Bellis & Thomas, 2003; Dubowitz et al., 2002; Springer et al., 2007; Teicher, 2000).

Harm from Sexual Abuse Sexual abuse is considered one of the most complex and multifaceted forms of child victimization. A complete picture of this population of victims can never really be known, because not all sexually abused victims report and receive counselling. Compassion and understanding are necessary when studying the complexities and nature of child sexual abuse.

While it has been well documented that child sexual abuse can have profound impact, some survivors function at high levels, excelling in professions or other important areas. The professional success and perhaps their contribution to their community can be a way of compensating. Or, their personal levels of achievement can simply be a way of feeling, and being, competent (Paris, 1998).

The greater percentages of survivors, however, have severe personal adjustment problems. What is not known with any degree of certainty is why some individuals have less obvious problems and go on to lead productive and perhaps fulfilling lives while others experience crippling life difficulties.

Part of the explanation is due to the inconsistencies in our knowledge base. Statistics and research are also multifaceted. Much violence against children remains hidden for many reasons. Some are due to the fact that only extreme cases come to the attention of child welfare authorities. Research studies and clinical insights are gleaned from known cases, and from victims seeking counselling. The outcomes of victims who have not sought treatment and/or legal intervention may never be studied. That particular population of victim can, therefore, never be theoretically or statistically considered.

An abundance of clinical studies have acknowledged and addressed the serious difficulties experienced by sexual abuse victims. There have also been publicly shared, personal and painful accounts of how sexual trauma affected their lives. Further, with respect to long-term outcomes, researchers have pointed out that specific difficulties can occur later during adolescence as a result of childhood abuse and neglect. Studies indicate that abused and neglected children are at least 25 percent more likely to experience problems such as delinquency, low academic achievement, drug use, and mental health problems (Kelley, Thornberry, & Smith, 1997). Victimized children are also more likely to engage in sexual risk-taking as they reach adolescence, thereby increasing their chances of contracting a sexually transmitted disease and/or becoming pregnant (Garrett & Libbey, 1997; Johnson, Rew, & Sternglanz, 2006).

Additionally, one long-term study found that as many as 80 percent of young adults who had been abused met the *DSM-IV-TR* criteria for at least one **psychiatric disorder** at age 21. These young adults exhibited many problems, including depression, anxiety, eating disorders, and suicide attempts (Silverman, Reinherz, & Giaconia, 1996).

Physical Injuries Resulting from Child Sexual Abuse Although one might think that a sexual victimization has no visible physical injuries, there are in fact significant symptoms. The limitations lay in those who are able to observe and detect the physical indicators of harm, and what they do with that knowledge. Physical injuries are visible in the genital or buttocks area—simply stated, a child's "private" areas.

Medical professionals—that is, nurses and physicians—are the most capable of diagnosing these signs; however, many abused children are never seen. Suzanne Sgroi (1985) lists the following physical indicators of child sexual abuse: trauma to the genital or rectal area; foreign bodies in the genital, rectal, or urethral openings; abnormal dilation of the urethral, vaginal, or rectal openings; sperm in the vagina; trauma to breasts, buttocks, lower abdomen, or thighs; sexually transmitted diseases; and pregnancy.

Behavioural Symptoms Resulting from Child Sexual Abuse Behavioural symptoms of child sexual abuse are numerous. The spectrum of possible symptoms is as varied as the different victims and the forms of sexual victimizations (Berliner, 1991; Briere, 1992; Sgroi, 1985). Although there are no conclusive or exclusive indicators, Figure 3.5 provides a list of symptoms that have been reported in child sexual abuse studies.

1	Makes strong efforts to avoid a specific person, without an obvious reason
2	Runs away from home
3	Wetting or soiling (especially for young children)
4	Hypervigilence
5	Problems getting along with others
6	Personality changes: irritability, mood changes, withdrawal
7	Problems with concentration
8	Profound unhappiness
9	Heightened physiological arousal: jumpy
10	Sleep disturbances: nightmares
11	Distortion of thinking
12	Depression and anxiety
13	A sexually transmitted infection or pregnancy; especially under the age of 14
14	Sexualized behaviour: compulsive masturbating, precocious sex play, trouble walking or sitting
15	Posttraumatic stress disorder
16	Dissociative Disorder: Disassociation

Figure 3.5 Signs and Symptoms of Child Sexual Abuse

Sources: Berliner, 1991; Sgroi, 1982; Trocmé et al., 2005.

The immediate and lifelong impact of child sexual abuse is not simply a result of the violence. To try to explain outcome with a single-cause explanation does not work. Many factors determine a victim's ability to adapt and cope (Berliner, 1991; Briere, 1992).

Although most children and adult victims of childhood abuse require some level of support, research indicates there is potential for a positive prognosis. In 1998, psychiatrist Joel Paris examined the relationship between trauma in childhood and personality disorders in adulthood. Paris found that:

> Early childhood may be no more important than later childhood in personality formation, nor is there good evidence showing that traumatic events in childhood, by themselves, lead to disorders in adulthood. Rather, the literature shows that negative childhood events are one of many risk factors for psychopathology in adulthood; whether such events go on to produce long-term consequences depends on interactions with other risks and protective factors in development. (1998, p. 25)

Conclusion

Child abuse is complex. Numerous short-term and long-term outcomes are possible. Yet for countless victims, we know the horrifying result of child abuse has created devastating symptoms with profound life consequences. Children may experience similar symptoms to abuse as an adult would, but their ability to verbalize the sadness and fear they feel, and the thought of losing their caregiver, compounds their trauma.

3.3 THE STATISTICS AND PREVALENCE OF CHILD ABUSE AND NEGLECT

It is impossible to know exactly how many children are harmed each year. Violence against children takes a variety of forms and is influenced by a wide range of factors. It is not unusual for a victim of violence to suffer from more than one form of abuse. For instance, a child who is physically beaten also is emotionally harmed. How this information is recorded is one of the many legitimate variables that can make determining the frequency of child abuse difficult. To begin, we will define some specific statistical terms.

Statistics: Prevalence and Incidence

Prevalence and incidence are two related but different measures that describe the distribution of a particular issue being studied in a particular population. *Incidence* is the frequency with which an event occurs within a given time period (such as one year). The incidence is the number of *new cases* occurring in a population over a defined time interval.

By contrast, *prevalence* refers to how many people currently have that condition at a certain moment in time. In the case of sexual abuse, prevalence would include those who have already reported their abuse and are continuing to live with its impact from earlier years, *combined* with new cases.

Thus, it is possible in a one-year time frame to have a situation of high prevalence but low incidence and vice versa. For example, the incidence of new cases of child sexual abuse in a population may be only 1 per 1000 people per year (or 0.01 percent annually), but the prevalence of sexual abuse in a population could be 8 percent. The .01 percent incidence estimate includes only people who disclosed child sexual abuse in a one-year interval, whereas the prevalence estimate includes those people as well as those already living with child sexual abuse who had disclosed in the past.

Likewise, is it possible to have pockets of high incidence in settings with an overall lower rate of prevalence. This has happened in Canada when the known existence of a sexually abusive environment is exposed (Mount Cashel), or an individual perpetrator is revealed (Charles Sylvestre), and support and respect are publicly offered when police reach out to the public and encourage other victims contact them. It is then possible for new disclosures (incidents) to emerge in one area at one particular interval of time.

Canadian Statistical Sources of Child Violence and Maltreatment

In Canada there are no national representative data; in addition, challenges can be made to the accuracy, type, and quality of statistics. Therefore, how numbers and statistics are gathered and analyzed is both complicated and debatable. An additional challenge relates to the various data collection methods that are available. Unlike anonymous survey research that seeks feedback from adults regarding past victimizations, this method cannot be used with children. A child's experience often requires an adult to report their abuse.

The other factor to consider when examining the topic of child abuse is the population of adults who disclose their childhood victimizations. Additionally, some child victims did report their victimizations in childhood only to be harshly treated, blamed, and called a liar; thus, these facts were covered up. And some victims, young and old, have yet to tell their stories.

Violence as such remains hidden. Generally only the most extreme presenting cases come to the attention of child welfare authorities. A significant reason for the hidden nature of abuse is fear. Children are afraid to report. In many cases the abuser is their parent, the person they love and depend upon. Often the "non-abusing" parent, who should be protecting their child, may also remain silent if the violence is perpetrated by a spouse or another family member. Further, fear exists when the perpetrator is an influential member of society, such as a member of the clergy, a coach, an employer, a teacher, a police officer, or a community leader. The fear of not being believed is overwhelming, and Canadian history has proven that this is in fact a valid reality.

Another factor adding to the complexity of evaluating statistics is the disagreement regarding a definition of abuse in Canada's diverse society. (Nowhere is this more clearly demonstrated than in the debate and discussion regarding the "spanking law" in Canada; see Chapter 7.) And, although discussing numbers can depersonalize an issue as grave as child abuse, it is important so that public policies and prevention efforts can be evaluated. The need to provide effective intervention via child welfare services is consistently being noted in the professional and research literature (Flynn & Bouchard, 2005; Vandermeulen, Wekerle, & Ylagan, 2005). Yet research is done, so let's look at some of Canada's key sources for statistical data.

The Canadian Incidence Study of Reported Child Abuse and Neglect (CIS) As you will read in Chapter 7, child welfare in Canada requires mandatory services. The importance of government accountability also underscores the continued need to have information about the burden of child abuse in Canada. In an effort to draw an accurate picture of the number of Canadian children victimized each year, in 1995 the Family Violence Prevention Division of Health Canada funded the Child Welfare League of Canada. The purpose of this league was to bring together experts to conduct a Canadian study of reported child maltreatment. This group strongly recommended that a study be undertaken with a focus on the child maltreatment cases reported to child welfare agencies (Trocmé & Wolfe, 2001).

From this commitment grew the creation of the Canadian Incidence Study of Reported Child Abuse and Neglect (CIS). It became the first of three Canada-wide cycles to begin to fill the information gap using a common set of definitions with respect to child maltreatment and prevalence. Research was completed in 1998, 2003, and 2008 and involved child welfare service areas across Canada, excluding Quebec.

The CIS addressed the five principal forms of maltreatment: physical abuse, sexual abuse, neglect, emotional maltreatment, and witnessing family violence. This research captured information about children and their families as they came into contact with child welfare sites during a specified time period (interval) when the three research cycles were being conducted. These reports provide insight into the extent and scope of the problem (Trocmé & Wolfe, 2001). Before we examine the results it is important to note the limitations of this information. The CIS studied child maltreatment *reported to,* and *investigated by,* child welfare agencies in Canada (Trocmé & Wolfe, 2001). The following cases or occurrences (incidents) of victimized children would not have been included in the data:

- reports of child abuse and neglect that were screened out by child protection workers (i.e., not investigated)

- cases of child abuse and violence reported to the police

- cases of child abuse and neglect known to other professionals, or citizens, but not reported to child protection agencies

- unidentified child maltreatment; cases in which the child's situation is simply unknown (Trocmé et al., 2010).

The Uniform Crime Reporting Survey (UCR, UCR2) The second main source of statistical information to be presented represents information collected through the **Uniform Crime Reporting Survey (UCR)**. In 1961, Statistics Canada and the Canadian Association of Chiefs of Police entered into a joint effort to begin systematically collecting crime data at the national level (Schmalleger et al., 2004). (Chapter 4 includes a detailed explanation of these statistics.) Essentially, the UCR2 survey was designed to measure the incidence of crime and its characteristics, which were gathered by police departments in Canada. This data collection created a file for each criminal incident. Similar to the CIS data, the UCR statistics do not include crimes that are not brought to the attention of the police (Schmalleger et al., 2004).

Statistics and Their Results

As mentioned earlier in this chapter, three data collection cycles have been conducted through the Canadian Incidence Study of Reported Child Abuse and Neglect. The CIS 1998 used information from 51 child welfare service areas across Canada, the CIS 2003 used 63 child welfare service agencies, and the CIS 2008 investigation represented a sample drawn from 112 child welfare service agencies—23 sites were from Aboriginal organizations (Trocmé et al., 2010).

When a case is first referred to a child protection agency, an initial screening step is conducted to determine whether or not the referral will be investigated. Some cases are immediately closed because they do not warrant an investigation, but a number of cases do require an investigation. Following an investigation, if a child is found to have been the victim of abuse or neglect, the case is referred to as **substantiated abuse**. According

Table 3.2 Suspected Child Maltreatment Cases Investigated and Their Outcomes

Year	Total Number of Suspected Child Maltreatment Cases Investigated	Substantiated % and the Number		Suspected % and the Number		Unsubstantiated % and the Number		Risk of Future Maltreatment	
		%	#	%	#	%	#	%	#
1998	135 573	45%	61 201	22%	29 668	33%	44 704	n/a	n/a
2003	235 315	47%	103 297	13%	28 053	40%	85 969	n/a	n/a
2008	235 842	36%	85 440	8%	17 918	30%	71 053	26%	61 431

Sources: (Trocmé & Wolfe, 2001; Trocmé et al., 2005; Trocmé et al., 2010)

to the definition used by the CIS reports, a case is considered substantiated if the balance of evidence indicates abuse or neglect has occurred. The CIS outcomes are listed in Table 3.2 and highlight the results from 1998, 2003, and 2008.

One statistic that stands out is the total number of suspected child maltreatment cases between the 1998 and 2003 cycles: it almost doubled (Trocmé et al., 2005). This begs the question of whether there were more victimized children, or more reports. The accepted explanation behind these findings is that statistics increased due to the detection, reporting, and investigation practices and *not* because there were more victims (Trocmé et al., 2010). An additional explanation relates to the increase in reports made by professionals. This may have increased the actual number of reported cases. The last important explanation is based on the fact that a new category was introduced to the second cycle: exposure to intimate partner violence.

The statistical data for the third cycle (Trocmé et al., 2010) were also different due to changes made in child welfare investigative practices. Data collecting methodology changed, providing different statistics. The 2008 sample added a category referred to as *risk of future maltreatment* (Trocmé et al., 2010). This new category posed a particular challenge since these statistics were not identified in the 1998 and 2003 cycles. Not all statistical findings from the CIS 2008 cycle are therefore directly comparable to the results presented in the CIS 1998 and CIS 2003 reports; however, when possible equivalent data will be presented (Trocmé et al., 2010). The data from the 2008 cycle will be emphasized, because they represent the most current research. Table 3.3 outlines the number of cases investigated and their outcome.

Results: Witnessing Violence When examining the results of the 2008 data, the two highest categories of substantiated maltreatment recorded were exposure to intimate partner violence and neglect. Thirty-four percent, or 4.86 investigations per 1000 children, of all substantiated investigations, identified exposure to intimate partner violence as the primary category of maltreatment. Neglect also represented 34 percent of the substantiated investigations, or 4.81 investigations per 1000 children (Trocmé et al., 2010).

Table 3.3 Categories of Substantiated Maltreatment

Year	Total Number of Referred and % of Substantiated Physical Abuse Cases		Total Number of Referred and % of Substantiated Sexual Abuse Cases		Total Number of Referred and % of Substantiated Emotional Maltreatment Cases		Total Number of Referred and % of Substantiated Neglect Cases		Total Number of Referred and % of Substantiated Exposure to Domestic Violence	
	#	%	#	%	#	%	#	%	#	%
1998	41 551	34%	14 406	38%	25 694	54%	53 922	43%	n/a	n/a
2003	25 257	24%	2 935	3%	15 369	15%	30 366	30%	29 370	28%
2008	17 212	20%	2 607	3%	7 423	9%	28 939	34%	29 259	34%

Sources: (Trocmé & Wolfe, 2001; Trocmé et al., 2005; Trocmé et al., 2010)

Table 3.3 indicates the number and percentage of substantiated cases included in the various categories of child maltreatment (Trocmé et al., 2005).

The same study also investigated caretaker risk factors. Where applicable, when workers were investigating they were asked to identify within the previous six months whether or not one of nine possible caregiver risk factors existed. Seventy-eight percent of substantiated maltreatment investigations (an estimated 66 282 child investigations) indicated that at least one primary caregiver risk factor was identified. The most frequently noted risk factor (46 percent) was being a victim of domestic violence. This information elevated a concern of researchers: the significant overlap between children who witness family violence and children who experience direct violence (Jaffe et al., 1990). The statistical prevalence of children witnessing family violence in the home has also been studied in the General Social Survey on Victimization (GSS).

According to the 2004 GSS, a person other than the spouse was harmed or threatened in 11 percent of spousal assaults in the previous five years, of which 44 percent were children under the age of 15. Further, 394 000 victims of spousal violence reported that children saw or heard this violence, which represents one-third (33 percent) of all spousal violence cases. Table 3.4 highlights the data noted in the 2004 GSS. The 2004 results indicated that female victims of spousal violence reported a child saw or heard this violence 40 percent of the time, compared to 25 percent of the male victims who reported spousal violence.

Further, 49 percent of women victims who had a child who witnessed spousal violence reported that they feared for their life, compared to 22 percent of the male victims who had a child who witnessed spousal violence. Of the female victims of spousal assault who had a child who witnessed the assault, 52 percent sustained an injury compared to 28 percent of male victims (GSS, 2004).

Results: Child Physical Abuse Physical abuse was substantiated in 20 percent of investigations, or 2.86 investigations per 1000 children (Trocmé et al., 2010). In 21 percent of these cases, a physical injury was documented but was not severe enough to

Table 3.4 Factors Relating to Children Witnessing Violence

Type of Violence Recorded	Female Victim	Male Victim
Report that children saw or heard this violence	40%	25%
Victims with child witnesses to violence and reported they feared for their life	49%	22%
Victims with child witnesses who sustained injury as a result of the violence	52%	28%

Source: Statistics Canada, 2005.

require medical treatment. In five percent of cases, medical treatment was required. The fact that no physical harm was noted in 74 percent of physical abuse cases may seem surprising to some readers (Trocmé et al., 2010). It is important to note that in most jurisdictions physical abuse includes caregiver behaviours that could seriously endanger a child, as well as those that lead to injuries.

Data from the 2009 UCR indicated that the rate of family violence against children and youth has remained relatively stable since the 2004 data were published. Specifically, in 2009 the UCR reported that almost 55 000 children and youth victims (0 to 17 years) were victims of a physical or sexual assault. Of these, about 3 in 10, or close to 15 000 children and youth, were victimized by a member of their own family. Approximately two-thirds (67 percent) were physically assaulted. The majority of these offences (81 percent) were level 1 assault, the category of least physical harm to victims (this *Criminal Code* offence is discussed in Chapter 7). Serious assaults, aggravated assault, and assault with a weapon or causing bodily harm included approximately 18 percent of all physical assaults committed by family members against children and youth. The remaining 1 percent involved other assaults and firearm offences.

Similar to the CIS results, in 2009 the UCR found 57 percent of those who had been physically assaulted and 16 percent of those who had been sexually victimized required minor treatment, such as first aid (e.g., a bandage). Unlike the 2004 UCR, which found boys to be more likely (46 percent) than girls (36 percent) to be injured as a consequence of family-perpetrated violence, the 2009 results indicated the results were very similar for both boys and girls. For both, the rates of physical violence were highest during the teenage years, particularly between ages 12 to 17. These statistics were similar to the 2004 results (Statistics Canada, 2007).

For boys, the rate of physical assault by a family member peaked around 15 years; there were 200 incidents per 100 000 population. In comparison, the rate for girls was highest among 15- to 17-year-olds. This statistic represents the highest rate of family-related physical assault for all children and youth, regardless of sex (Statistics Canada, 2011).

Moreover, the presence of physical harm as a result of sexual abuse victimization was identified in 11 percent of investigations where sexual abuse was the primary substantiated concern, with 8 percent of cases requiring medical treatment (Statistics Canada, 2007).

A Canadian study reviewed the 364 cases of shaken baby syndrome (SBS) that had been reported over a 10-year period to the child protection teams of 11 tertiary care pediatric hospitals (King et al., 2003). When examining the SBS cases, it was discovered there was a past medical history of previous maltreatment in 220 children (60 percent), and 80 of the families (22 percent) had previous involvement with child welfare services. Further, of the 364 children, 69 died of SBS while only 65 were "well" at discharge.

Results: Child Sexual Abuse Overall, the 2009 UCR data indicated that girls under the age of 18 were more likely than boys of the same age to be victims. This statistic was the result of the large percentage of sexual offences committed against girls. In 2009, the rate of sexual offences by family members that came to the attention of police was four times higher for girls than boys (113 versus 28 per 100 000 children and youth population). Regardless of age, sexual victimization was greater for girls.

The age of the victim of a sexual offence committed by a family member differed between girls and boys. For girls, the rate of sexual victimization tended to increase throughout childhood and peaked at 14 years of age. For boys, the rates were highest between 5 and 8 years of age.

Aboriginal Children

Of the total cases of substantiated maltreatment reported in the CIS 2003 research, 15 percent (about 15 000 cases) involved children of Aboriginal heritage: 10 percent involved First Nations status children, 2 percent involved First Nations non-status children, 2 percent involved Métis children, and 1 percent involved Inuit children. Table 3.5 describes the type and percentage of the primary substantiated maltreatment case for neglect, physical abuse, and sexual abuse.

Child maltreatment investigations were four times higher in Aboriginal child investigations than non-Aboriginal child investigations (49.69 per 1000 Aboriginal children versus 11.85 per 1000 non-Aboriginal children). Twenty-two percent of substantiated cases (an estimated 18 510 investigations) involved children of Aboriginal heritage, as

Table 3.5 First Nations Child Maltreatment Category by Level of Substantiation in Canada, Excluding Quebec, 2003

Year: CIS 2003	Neglect: Primary Substantiated Case	Physical Abuse: Primary Substantiated Case	Sexual Abuse: Primary Substantiated Case
Percentage of cases	27% of total cases	6% of total cases	9 % of total cases
First Nations Status	20%	4%	7%
First Nations Non-Status children	3%	1%	N/A
Métis children	3%	1%	1%
Inuit children	1%	N/A	1%

Source: Trocmé et al., 2005.

Table 3.6 Police-Reported Rates of Physical and Sexual Assault by a Family Member

Child Gender	Physical Assault by Family Members	Sexual Assault by Family Members
Male child	4965	1010
Female child	5031	3827

*Rates are calculated on the basis of 100 000 children and youth population (0 to 17 years).

Source: Perreault & Brennan, 2010.

follows: 15 percent First Nations status, 3 percent First Nations non-status, 2 percent Métis, 1 percent Inuit, and 1 percent with other Aboriginal heritage.

In the CIS 2003 report, neglect was the most common primary category of substantiated maltreatment in First Nations child investigations, including more than half (56 percent) of all substantiated investigations. Specifically, neglect included an estimated 6833 investigations. Exposure to domestic violence was the second most frequently reported form of abuse in First Nations child investigations. By contrast, the most common primary category of substantiated maltreatment for non-Aboriginal child investigations was exposure to domestic violence, accounting for 30 percent of substantiated investigations.

Perpetrators of Violence against Children

Parents were responsible for more than half (59 percent) of all family-related sexual offences and physical assaults against children and youth victims in 2009 (Perreault & Brennan, 2010). Table 3.6 provides data regarding the description of the police-reported rates of physical and sexual assault by a family member.

The perpetrators of child abuse in the CIS reports are outlined in Table 3.7. As in previous years, children and youth were more likely to have been physically assaulted

Table 3.7 Perpetrators: Who Committed Child Maltreatment, Substantiated Cases

Year	Biological Mothers	Biological Fathers	Step-Mothers/ Common-Law Partners	Step-Fathers/ Common-Law Partners
1998	61%	38%	3%	9%
2003	54%	48%	2%	12%

*Extended family is defined to include persons related by blood, marriage, adoption or foster care (i.e., aunts, uncles, cousins, sisters/brothers-in-law, etc.).

Sources: (Trocmé & Wolfe, 2001; Trocmé et al., 2005; Trocmé et al., 2010)

than sexually assaulted by a parent. The rate of physical assault by a parent (92 victims per 100 000 population) was nearly four times higher than the rate of sexual assault (24 victims per 100 000 population) (Trocmé et al., 2005).

It should be noted that in many instances non-familial allegations of abuse are investigated by the police, not by a child welfare service.

The CIS indicated that physical abuse was committed largely by biological mothers and fathers. In particular, fathers were the alleged perpetrator in almost half (46 percent) of substantiated cases of physical abuse, closely followed by 43 percent of mothers (Trocmé & Wolfe, 2001). Yet, the distribution of physical abuse statistics is somewhat biased because 30 percent of physical abuse victims were living in lone female-parent households where 51 percent of substantiated physical abuse took place. The boyfriends and girlfriends of the parents were the non-familial figures most frequently reported as the perpetrators in cases of substantiated physical abuse (Trocmé et al., 2005).

Similar to the CIS results, police statistics indicated that fathers were involved in 44 percent of family-related physical assaults against children. Female family members, however, were identified as a perpetrator of physical violence 29 percent of the time. Yet, mothers were named as perpetrators in incidents of family-related violence against children in the youngest age categories (6 years and under) about 19 percent of the time (Perreault & Brennan, 2010).

It is noteworthy and concerning that most cases of the substantiated physical abuse referred to child protection agencies had stemmed from an escalation of child physical punishment (Durrant, 2006; Durrant & Ensom, 2004). One of the findings in the CIS 2003 indicated that 75 percent of substantiated incidents in which physical maltreatment was a primary category for investigation indicated they resulted from punishment (Trocmé et al., 2005).

Sexual Abuse Sexual abuse, according to the CIS reports, is quite different from the other categories of maltreatment because it was committed less often by the child's primary caregiver. Non-parental relatives represented the largest group of alleged perpetrators (28 percent), followed by biological fathers (15 percent), and step-fathers (9 percent) (Trocmé & Wolfe, 2001). Similarly in the CIS 2003 results, non-parental figures were most often the perpetrators in cases of substantiated sexual abuse. Non-parental relatives represented the largest group of perpetrators (35 percent), followed by the children's friends and peers (15 percent), stepfathers (13 percent), biological fathers (9 percent), other acquaintances (9 percent), and boyfriends and girlfriends of the parents (5 percent). Table 3.8 provides a description of who the sexual offenders were in the data generated from the CIS research.

Two facts must be highlighted. Child sexual abuse is a *Criminal Code* offence; police are generally informed when a child is a victim of a sexual offence. Plus, many sexual abuse allegations involving non-family members are investigated by the police alone, and child welfare services are involved only if there are concerns about the ongoing protection of the child or if other children may be at risk of abuse.

Table 3.8 Sexual Abuse Perpetrators		
Relationship	**CIS 1998**	**CIS 2003**
Non-parental relatives	28%	35%
Step-fathers	9%	13%
Biological fathers	15%	9%
Other acquaintances	n/a	9%
Boyfriends and girlfriends of the parents	n/a	5%
Children's friends and peers	n/a	15%

Sources: Trocmé & Wolfe, 2001; Trocmé et al., 2005.

Child Abuse Resulting in Death

When a child is murdered in Canada it's usually at the hands of a relative, not a stranger. Between 2000 and 2009 there were 326 homicides against children and youth (0 to 17 years) committed by a family member, accounting for 7 percent of all solved homicides and 21 percent of all family-related homicides (Statistics Canada, 2010).

The majority of family-related homicides against children and youth are committed by parents. During the most recent 10-year period, fathers and/or mothers were responsible for 84 percent of all family-related homicides against children and youth under 18 years of age (Statistics Canada, 2010).

Infanticide is still a problem in Canada. Children under the age of one year are at the highest risk of death due to abuse and neglect. Between 2000 and 2009, the rate of family-related homicide against infants was nearly triple the rate of 1- to 3-year-olds, the next highest age group (Statistics Canada, 2010).

Mandated Reporting Statistics

Mandated reporting refers to the legislative requirement that certain professionals report cases of suspected child abuse or neglect to a designated authority within a specified period of time (see Chapter 7 for details). In Canada, child welfare laws require that all cases of suspected child abuse be investigated to determine if a child is in need of protection. Being cognizant of these laws is important because it sheds light regarding who is reporting, and the substance of these reports.

When examining the results, CIS 1998 indicated that school personnel referred 35 percent of all of physical abuse investigations, and 39 percent of those cases were substantiated. Parents referred the second largest number (14 percent) of physical abuse cases.

By comparison, the sexual abuse referral statistics (Trocmé & Wolfe, 2001) found that parents were the most common source of referral for sexual abuse cases (29 percent). Of these referrals, 47 percent were substantiated. School personnel (16 percent) and the police (13 percent) accounted for most of the other sexual abuse referrals. Unlike physical and sexual abuse child neglect investigations, no particular source of referral stood out in cases of neglect.

Malicious Referrals With the opportunity to do harm to a parent, and more severely, a child, comes the question of how often false—or, more specifically, "malicious referrals"—are made to child protection agencies. The CIS reports from 1998 and 2003 found that most of the unsubstantiated reports were considered to have been made in good faith, and that only a small percentage, four percent and five percent, of allegations were judged to have been intentionally false (Trocmé et al., 2001; 2005).

Conclusion

In this module, an effort was made to provide Canadian research to assist in our understanding of the type and scope of child maltreatment in Canada. A complete and accurate picture may never be known, though the CIS cycles demonstrate significant changes. Noteworthy was the increase in the number of reported cases of suspected child maltreatment between 1998 and 2008. Some explanations have been discussed, yet it is important to end on this note. As pointed out by Trocmé and colleagues (2010), the overall actual number of maltreated children in Canada may not be increasing. What might be increasing is the *visibility* of cases of abuse and neglect, and this is a good thing. The sooner a child's harm is known and acted upon, the sooner that help is possible and the greater the chance of healing. The first goal is always immediate protection. Helping a child immediately often involves disruption and the introduction of many new people. But the long-term benefits that can evolve from support and curative intervention have lasting effects. Therefore, educating society and intervening in the lives children is essential.

The statistics don't lie; many children in Canada have been harmed. Yet the numbers do not even begin to define the pain, or the resultant loss of innocence and childhood. Nor do these numbers reflect the loss of trust and respect for the many people and the professionals who work within those systems when they don't respond ethically and legally.

CHAPTER CONCLUSION

The topic of child abuse in Canada has been presented using academic knowledge, government data, and stories from the Canadian media. For years, the media helped ensure these stories were unearthed and told. As a consequence, numerous in-depth cases have been reported, and the unthinkable nature of these crimes committed against children, and the circumstances surrounding them, have been shared with Canadians.

Thoughtful, compassionate advocacy first began with J. J. Kelso in the 1800s and later continued with publisher Michael Harris of the St. John's *Sunday Express*. These individuals pushed the agenda to ensure that the hidden and unimaginable child abuse stories were investigated and exposed. It took courage and a commitment to stand up and advocate for children simply because it was the right thing to do.

In large measure, however, the occurrence of child abuse and neglect was authenticated when the problem was revealed in human terms through the personal narratives of survivors. Survivors of abuse have created two important outcomes:

1. They raised awareness of abuse, and the abusers.

2. They created the sense of safety and support that allowed others to start talking about their own abuse history.

The public awareness that was generated through survivors' individual truth-telling has helped our nation. It would be the hope of any civilized society that the reaction to these stories would invoke public outrage and compassion. Although these personal stories are tragic, unplanned, and unfocused mechanisms for reform, a great deal of social, clinical, and positive government and legal initiative has been undertaken in response to these personal tragedies.

Multiple Choice Questions

1. Under Canadian law, which of the following describes when physical punishment of children is deemed reasonable:

   a. only parents and teachers are permitted to use corporal punishment
   b. the child is between the ages of 2 and 12, inclusive
   c. the child is capable of learning from correction
   d. it does not involve the use of objects or blows or slaps to the head

2. Which of the following best describes Jordan Heikamp?

   a. He was an adolescent boy who was sexually abused by his junior hockey coach.
   b. He successfully sued the Catholic Church for the years of abuse by a priest.
   c. He was a 35-day-old baby who died of starvation.
   d. He was the newspaper reporter who exposed the Mount Cashel story.

3. Being detached and uninvolved and interacting with a child only when necessary is:

   a. emotional neglect
   b. emotional abuse
   c. psychological abuse
   d. not serious enough to be considered a form of maltreatment

4. Child sexual abuse began to receive academic attention only in the 1980s. According to Benjamin Schlesinger's review of the literature, written in 1980, from the period of 1937 to 1974 there were:

   a. 16 published articles relating to child sexual abuse
   b. 32 published articles relating to child sexual abuse
   c. 86 published articles relating to child sexual abuse
   d. 153 published articles relating to child sexual abuse

5. All sexual activity with a child under what age, is a criminal offence in Canada regardless of the child's consent.

   a. 12   b. 14
   c. 16   d. 18

6. Box 3.3 described sexual predator Father Charles Sylvestre. For almost how many decades did he sexually abuse female children?

    a. one decade
    b. two decades
    c. three decades
    d. four decades

7. The sexual abuse and exploitation of children and youth involve a range of behaviours. Which of the following is NOT considered a form of non-contact sexual abuse?

    a. luring
    b. making sexual comments about a child
    c. making child and youth participate in pornographic acts
    d. exposing sexual body parts

8. Who was the author of *Unholy Orders,* and one of the people credited for exposing the Mount Cashel sexual abuse story?

    a. Rob Talach
    b. Michael Harris
    c. Sheldon Kennedy
    d. Graham James

9. Knoke and Trocmé list specific factors that are used when conducting a child abuse risk assessment. Which of the following is NOT one of those factors?

    a. nature and severity of previous maltreatment
    b. family's socioeconomic situation
    c. caregiver characteristics
    d. child characteristics

10. Many factors potentially impact how an abused child will be affected. Specific variables do have direct bearing on the eventual impact of child abuse. Which of the following was NOT indicated?

    a. the characteristics of the child and their relationships
    b. type of trauma
    c. validation
    d. quality of treatment

Discussion Questions

1. Identify and describe the five categories of child abuse and neglect.

2. What are the psychological effects of child abuse and neglect?

3. Choose one of the Canadian Headline News stories from this chapter and discuss it in relation to what you have learned about the past and present existence of child abuse knowledge.

4. What is meant by the term "mandated reporting"?

Key Terms

battered child syndrome: a syndrome or clustering of signs and symptoms proposed by family abuse pioneer C. Henry Kempe to describe characteristics of children who have been severely physically abused.

cunnilingus: oral-genital contact involving the female sexual organ.

dissociation: a psychological process whereby a person cuts the self off from traumatic experiences, thoughts, memories, or feelings.

exploitation: occurs when a child is used to meet the needs or desires of a caretaker. In extreme cases this could involve making the child sexually available to others for monetary gain.

fellatio: oral-genital sexual act that involves oral contact with the male sex organ.

fondling: touching a child sexually, often including sexual parts but not involving any type of oral-genital contact or intercourse.

grooming: in the study of child molestation, the process whereby the perpetrator gradually introduces more and more sexually explicit activity and prepares the child for the intended sexual activity.

infanticide: occurs when a female person by a willful act or omission causes the death of her newly born child, if at the time of the act or omission she is not fully recovered from the effects of giving birth to the child and by reason thereof or of the effect of lactation consequent on the birth of the child her mind is then disturbed (R.S., c. C-34, s. 216).

incest: child sexual abuse perpetrated by a blood relative.

intercourse: sexual contact that involves the insertion of the male sex organ into an orifice of another person's body, for example the anus or vagina.

interfemural intercourse: sometimes referred to as simulated intercourse or dry intercourse because the active party inserts his penis between the legs. Some perpetrators engage in interfemural intercourse to prevent injuring the vagina so they do not leave evidence.

mandated reporting: the requirement that suspected abuse be reported to the appropriate child protection agency.

posttraumatic stress: a disorder recognized in the *DSM-IV* that is characterized by the presence of a trauma-inducing experience, intrusive symptoms, avoidance of situations that trigger intrusive symptoms, and hyperarousal.

psychiatric disorder: in the mental health field, a disturbance characterized by specific psychological signs and symptoms.

resilience: a term used in developmental psychology and the human services to refer to the ability of individuals to do well despite difficult life experiences.

substantiated abuse: when the balance of evidence indicates that abuse or neglect has occurred; the abuse is valid and this has been determined by the appropriated investigating authority.

Uniform Crime Reporting Survey (UCR): a summation of crime statistics tallied annually by the Canadian Centre for Justice Statistics (CCJS) and consisting primarily of data on crimes reported to the police.

vicariously liable: based on the rationale that the person who puts a risky enterprise into the community may fairly be held responsible when those risks emerge and cause loss or injury to members of the public. Effective compensation is a goal. Deterrence is also a consideration. The hope is that holding the employer or principal liable will encourage such persons to take steps to reduce the risk of harm in the future.

validation: process by which a child protection worker or other appropriate personnel attempts to assess whether claims of maltreatment are true.

Chapter 4
Violence Against Women

The good we secure for ourselves is precarious and uncertain until it is secured for all of us and incorporated into our common life.

Jane Addams. Social worker, social and political activist, community organizer (1860–1935).

Chapter Objectives

1 Identify the different forms of violence against women and explain their significance.

2 Describe the consequences and impact of violence against women.

3 Interpret the statistics regarding the prevalence of violence against women.

4.1 DEFINING VIOLENCE AGAINST WOMEN

In this chapter we will examine the key forms of violence against women. Only specific forms of violence will be covered in this chapter; others are described in greater detail in Chapter 5. The main types of violence against women to be discussed are sexual harassment, stalking or criminal harassment, and sexual assault; issues specific to the adolescent female are also examined. The language used to define these violent acts is determined based on how the term is being used.

Sexual Harassment

Sexual harassment is a form of discrimination in Canada; it is, therefore, illegal. There are two types of sexual harassment. The first is **quid pro quo**, which occurs in workplaces or educational institutions when a higher-status person (e.g., a boss or professor) demands some type of sexual conduct in exchange for a job promotion or other benefit. It can adversely affect or threaten—directly or indirectly—a person's job security (livelihood), working conditions, or prospects for promotion or education, and even their career hopes and aspirations.

The second category of sexual harassment occurs when someone is subjected to a hostile work or school environment that interferes with everyday life (Larkin, 1994). In very broad terms it includes anything from jokes to sexual advances, a "friendly" pat, an "accidental" brush on a person's arm, or unwanted sexual attention. Because of the variety of actions that can fall under this term, many people are confused about what exactly constitutes sexual harassment; however, it is a problem that has many manifestations.

While put-downs and negative comments about one's gender are among the more common forms of sexual harassment, it also includes any unwelcome behaviour that is sexual in nature, such as:

- suggestive remarks, sexual jokes, or compromising invitations
- verbal abuse
- visual display of suggestive images
- whistling
- leering, or eyeing someone in a suggestive way
- commenting on someone's sexual attractiveness or sexual unattractiveness
- persistently asking for a date after having been refused

Sexual harassment is an expression of sexism that reflects and reinforces the unequal power that exists between men and women in our society. What is also known is that sexually harassing behaviour can foreshadow the potential for further forms of violence—or, more specifically, an escalation of violent actions. In cases of harassment, employers can be held legally responsible, not to mention having the legacy or the memory of knowing that what occurred was because protection was not provided.

A Canadian tragedy that exemplifies how an escalation of violence can take place occurred in November 2005. Lori Dupont was a victim of sexual harassment and stalking, and it ultimately led to her death. The highly respected lawyer Greg Monforton represented Ms. Dupont's family following the event, and in the process of acting on their behalf—and despite their irreplaceable loss—some significant outcomes transpired.

What followed from Mr. Monforton's advocacy exemplifies what is possible in our Canadian legal system when a lawyer is committed to uphold the rights of injured victims and is also determined to challenge the existing laws, or to advocate for legislation that will ultimately enhance lives and better serve and protect all Canadians.

Indeed, new legislation resulted from the legal process and the exposure and examination of the facts. This achievement provided the family some comfort in knowing that meaningful, positive change came from their grief. Part 1 of the story is told by Mr. Monforton here in "From the Pen of . . ." Box 4.1; part 2 is presented in Chapter 8.

Stalking (Criminal Harassment)

Stalking is a more common term used to describe criminal harassment. This crime can happen in *any* relationship. It involves a pattern of behaviour that is meant to harass, annoy, or frighten. This is a relatively new area of study, but those who have examined stalking within the context of intimate partner relationships have found strong associations between physical and sexual violence by intimate partners and stalking (Palarea et al., 1999; Tjaden & Thoennes 1998). Criminal harassment is a *Criminal Code of Canada* offence. Simply stated, stalking is serious.

4.1 From the Pen of Lawyer Greg Monforton: The Lori Dupont Story, Part 1

What follows is not a detailed account of the story of the tragic and senseless murder of Lori Dupont. Nor is it a comprehensive chronicle of the **coroner's inquest** held in the aftermath of her murder, or a scholarly analysis of the resulting legislation passed to prevent the occurrence of similar deaths in the future. To do any of these things would require an entire book; a book that my present circumstances do not allow me the opportunity to write. And no doubt those personally familiar with the events in question will feel that critical events that should have been brought to light have been left out. In a sense, they will be correct. But what follows instead is a personal and brief retelling of my encounter with one of the most inspiring families I have had the privilege to represent over the course of my career.

My story will discuss the aftermath of the cold-blooded, horrific, and premeditated stabbing death of Windsor, Ontario nurse Lori Dupont by Windsor anesthesiologist Dr. Marc Daniel in the early morning hours of November 12, 2005, while they were both at work at Hotel-Dieu Grace Hospital.

Lori's death rocked the community at large and the health care community in particular. And it set in motion a series of events which culminated in the passage by the Province of Ontario of the *Ontario Occupational Health and Safety Amendment Act*, the first legislation in Canada to recognize the dangers of domestic violence in the workplace.

Lori was just over a week shy of her 37th birthday when she was murdered by Marc Daniel. She was the divorced mother of an 8-year-old daughter. Everyone who knew Lori described her as a loving mother, caring sister and daughter, devoted friend, and dedicated and hardworking professional. Having obtained her nursing diploma in 1989, Lori had an impressive resume, including stints at Whitehorse General Hospital in the Yukon Territory and St. John Hospital in Detroit, Michigan, prior to starting her work at Hotel-Dieu Grace Hospital as a recovery room nurse in Windsor in 2000.

My personal involvement in the aftermath of this tragedy began on the day of Lori's death. I can remember it as if it were yesterday. November 12, 2005 was a cool, sunny, and pleasant Saturday. I was driving home from my office at around one o'clock in the afternoon when I happened to notice a silver-coloured sports car parked in one of the small municipal parking lots overlooking the Detroit River. What made the scene noteworthy were the car's open driver's door and the presence of a number of police officers milling about the car. I naively assumed that someone, perhaps after having too much to drink, had left their car parked in the city lot overnight, and possibly wandered away to sleep it off.

Later on that day I learned from a friend that a local nurse had been murdered by a local doctor while working at Hotel-Dieu Grace Hospital in Windsor. It was not until the next day that the grisly details of the murder, as reported in the local media, began to come to light. It was then that I realized the deserted sports car I had observed the day before in fact belonged to Marc Daniel, and that he had driven to that spot after attempting to kill himself by self-injecting massive amounts of surgical anesthetics after fleeing from Hotel-Dieu Hospital in the moments immediately following the stabbing.

In the days and months that followed, the circumstances surrounding the troubled relationship between Lori Dupont and Marc Daniel came to light. Their relationship began in early 2004. At that time Daniel was separated from his wife, although divorce proceedings had not yet been commenced. Their relationship was anything but stable. Tired of Daniel's steadily worsening abusive and controlling behaviour, Lori told Daniel early in 2005 of her wish to end their relationship. On February 27, 2005, Daniel, in an effort to prevent Lori from ending their relationship, attempted suicide by over-dosing on surgical anesthetics. He was in res-piratory arrest when discovered by Lori. Lori, with her mother's help, immediately called an ambulance and almost certainly by so doing saved Daniel's life. Daniel was released from hospital in March of 2005, after agreeing to take a medical leave and enroll in the Ontario Medical Association's Physician Health Pro-gram. Meanwhile, Lori had had enough. She immediately terminated their relationship and asked him to move out of the house they had been sharing.

At no time after Daniel's suicide attempt did anyone from the hospital ever attempt to determine where or how Daniel, an anesthesi-ologist with privileges at Hotel-Dieu Hospital, obtained the surgical anesthetics he used to try to end his own life.

What also came to light was the troubled working relationship Daniel had had with a number of the hospital's nurses for at number of months prior to his February 2005 suicide attempt. In fact, as of February of 2005 there were already two pending formal complaints by hospital nursing staff regarding Daniel's past conduct. One of these complaints had already culminated in Daniel being required to sign a "memorandum and agreement" in January of 2005, in which he agreed to provide a written apology to the nurse in question, be placed on probation for one year from the signing of the agreement, and acknowledge the hospital's entitlement to invoke a mid-term review of his privileges if he failed to abide by the agreement.

Shortly after Daniel's suicide attempt, Lori changed the locks on her home and got an unlisted telephone number. Daniel called her cell phone repeatedly, wanting to reconcile. He would also stop by the hospital unan-nounced and attempt to intimidate Lori by staring her down and generally behaving in a hostile manner. Daniel even went so far in early April of 2005 as to place compromising photographs he had taken of Lori on the windshield of her car in the hospital's parking lot, threatening to distribute them throughout the hospital if she did not give in to his demands. In response, Lori asked to meet with hospital officials, further to which she was offered a parking spot closer to the hospital entrance, an escort to and from her car, and the assistance of someone from the hospital's security department when she attended with police officials a few days later to lay criminal charges against Daniel.

Despite the seriousness of Daniel's actions (and the fact that he remained on probation further to the complaint lodged by another hospital nurse), at no time did anyone from the hospital confront Daniel regarding his posting of the photographs on the windshield of Lori's car.

Without any notice to Lori or even the head of the hospital's department of anesthesiology, Daniel was permitted to return to work at the end of May of 2005. He was to be monitored by two staff physicians, and continue to attend counselling with a psychiatrist.

Almost immediately, Daniel's harassment of Lori resumed: staring Lori down, displaying his intensely hostile gaze, and generally doing everything within his power to make Lori feel uneasy and unsafe.

The weekend of November 12 was the first time that Daniel and Lori were scheduled to work together. Daniel purposely scheduled himself to work that day, knowing that Lori would be working as well and knowing that, because it was a Saturday, there would be only a skeleton staff on hand.

(continued)

It was on that Saturday morning, prior to the commencement of the surgery that he was scheduled to attend as its anesthesiologist, that Daniel mercilessly stabbed Lori to death with a 12-inch-long military knife that he had smuggled into the hospital in one of his boots.

Daniel immediately fled the scene and was found in his car 45 minutes later after taking a massive drug overdose. He died three days later.

At the time of her death I knew neither Lori Duport nor her family. But like everyone else in our city, I was sickened to learn that such a tragedy could occur right in the midst of our otherwise relatively peaceful city. The fact that it took place in one of our public hospitals made the whole thing seem even more macabre.

Nevertheless, once the shock of the initial news somewhat passed I didn't give the tragedy a great deal of further thought until the following month, when Lori's parents John and Barbara asked to see me.

I am a lawyer. I restrict my practice to the representation of people who have been injured (as well as to the families of people who have lost their lives). At the time of Lori's death I had been practicing law in Windsor for approximately 25 years. And so while I was honoured to have been contacted by John and Barbara Dupont in their time of need, it did not, given my line of work, come as a complete surprise.

My initial meeting with the Duponts took place in December of 2005. What struck me most during my first meeting with Lori's parents (and her sister Christine) was their dignity, courage, unquestionable decency, and palpable sadness. They wanted to know what I could do to hold responsible those who had empowered Marc Daniel to take their daughter's life. But more importantly, they wanted to know if I could in any way help them prevent this from ever happening to someone else again.

During our initial conversation we discussed the good that might come from the implementation of recommendations made by a coroner's jury upon the holding of a coroner's inquest. In fact, by that time a number of volunteers with the Chatham-Kent Sexual Assault Centre had already started a petition (which was ultimately signed by over 50 000 people) calling on the chief coroner for the Province of Ontario to convene a coroner's inquest into the death of Lori Dupont.

The petition drive and the media scrutiny of the story ultimately resulted in a decision by the Chief Coroner's Office to convene a coroner's inquest. It began in September of 2007.

It is every lawyer's dream to represent people they admire and whose cause they truly embrace. And it is every lawyer's goal to play a role in helping create actual changes in the law for the better. Although I never had the pleasure of meeting Lori Dupont, I do feel that in some small way I did come to know her during my representation of her family during the coroner's inquest.

I believe that Lori would have been extremely proud of her family. And I believe she would have been immensely grateful to them for all they have done to celebrate her life, protect and preserve her legacy, and give positive meaning to her tragic death.

Lori Dupont and her family will always have a very special place in my mind and heart. To represent them was a privilege I will always be grateful for and never forget.

How this case unfolded is highlighted in Part 2 of this "From the Pen of . . ." feature in Chapter 8.

Review Question
What is your reaction to this story? Does the fact that it took place in an institution committed to healing compound the impact of this tragedy?

Source: Provided to Anastasia Bake by Greg Monforton, www.gregmonforton.com.

Stalking does not include just one act but generally involves repeated actions by a person that causes another person to fear for his or her safety. If the behaviour is overtly threatening, a single incident may be considered criminal harassment. A stalker cannot excuse the behaviour by stating there was no intention to frighten: no excuse is acceptable. Stalking is not flirting, and is not part of a developing consensual relationship. The intimidation is real. It is frightening.

In fact, the General Social Survey (GSS) has confirmed a strong link between stalking and partner violence. The GSS found that three-quarters of women who were stalked by an ex-partner within the previous five years also had been physically or sexually assaulted by an ex-partner. Some research suggests that intimate partner stalkers may be the most dangerous of all (Palarea et al., 1999). Stalkers are most likely to be violent toward those individuals with whom they have had an intimate relationship (Melton, 2007; Mohandie et al., 1998; Mohandie et al., 2006). Following a breakup, unable to accept or cope with rejection, an angered stalker may want to "take revenge" on the person who is seen as causing their painful feelings. Becoming obsessed with the victim is also common.

Stalkers are predominantly male. Hackett (2002) specifically reported that males accounted for 84 percent of accused in 1999. Further, most are described as having an exaggerated sense of entitlement, being unable to handle rejection, possessing a vengeful attitude, being obsessional, and having a history of taking very little or no responsibility in their lives (Hackett, 2000; Mohandie et al., 2006; Mullen et al., 1999).

How does stalking appear in a woman's day-to-day life? Is stalking behaviour crystal clear, or could it be misunderstood as harmless attention from a "smitten other"? What's the harm in sending flowers ~ repeatedly ~ to a woman's home or work, and waiting for her outside her classroom or workplace? Couldn't these actions be considered charming and flattering? This question may offend some readers, and it should. This type of thinking is unfortunately widespread. Now add to the equation the fact that the stalker might be a "privileged person"; a famous or successful person, or an individual whom others hold in high esteem: a famous athlete, a teacher, doctor, or judge. What additional challenges might a victim face? They would be numerous, if not insurmountable.

The reality is that **victim blaming** is widespread. Often it is the woman or her behaviour that is used to explain the stalker's attention or fixation. The opinion that deep down she *wanted* attention has fuelled the flames of mythical and sexist thinking. For the victim, the fear and worry about when it will happen next is real. The stalker's actions may not be criminal, but these behaviours, coupled with the intent to instill fear or injury, constitute a behaviour that is now illegal.

The idea that a woman might bring about and therefore be responsible for a man's obsessive behaviour was illustrated in *There's Something about Mary*, a 1998 movie classified as a "romantic comedy." This movie describes how a beautiful and friendly woman ultimately caused the pathological behaviours (stalking) of her stalkers. She—her very essence—created the men's infliction, rendering them at her mercy. Mary is held accountable for the stalkers' behaviours. As the name of the movie states, *There is something about Mary*.

4.2 Are You Being Stalked? Are You a Stalker?
What Stalkers Do

- Follow you and unexpectedly show up at places and events where you are
- Repeatedly request a date
- Send unwanted flowers, gifts, letters, emails
- Call/text repeatedly, trying to speak to you, leaving messages, and/or hanging up
- Spy on you, lurk around your home, school, work, or places you regularly go (e.g., a health club)
- Deliberately leave signs that you are being watched
- Hire a private investigator or pay people you work with to gather personal information
- Befriend or hang around your friends, coworkers, neighbours, or family to gain information about you and your activities
- Access information about you and your activities through Facebook, public records, online search services

- Disclose damaging or embarrassing personal information about you to friends, co-workers, employers, neighbours, or family members
- Spread rumours about you that negatively affect your reputation or relationships
- Vandalize your property, your car, your home
- Burglarize your home or otherwise steal from you, including your mail
- Threaten to hurt you or your family, friends, or pets
- Attempt to control, track, or frighten you

Review Question
Read the Lori Dupont story in Box 4.1 and this list of "red flags" or warnings, then identify indicators or behaviours that were demonstrated by her killer.
Source: Compiled by author.

Researchers Anderson and Accomando (1999) noted three underlying assumptions in this movie: (1) the normalization of stalking; pursuit and deception as appropriate heterosexual rituals; (2) the undermining of the woman's resistance to stalking; and (3) the assignment of blame to the target of stalking. Unfortunately, this subtle and not so subtle information is disseminated into the public domain each day, through movies and other forms of entertainment. It is therefore critical to know that stalking is not a welcomed whimsical act: it is a criminal offence. Plus, prior stalking behaviour has been identified as one of the primary risk factors for attempted and actual murder of an ex, or an existing female partner (McFarlane, Campbell, & Watson, 2002). Women need to be informed. Box 4.2 outlines questions to help you determine whether you recognize stalking behaviour.

Sexual Assault

A victim of sexual assault can be either a man or woman, and the attacker can be of the opposite or the same sex as the victim. In Canada, women constitute by far the greatest percentage of sexual assault victims. A common myth is "stranger danger"—the belief that sexual assaults are perpetrated by men lurking in bushes or by intruders breaking into our homes. The reality is that most women are assaulted by men they recognize, know, or have come to trust. Therefore, separate categories have emerged for discussing sexual assault: stranger sexual assault, acquaintance sexual assault, and **date rape**. Regardless of the terminology, the tremendous trauma resulting from a sexual assault, the social **stigma**, and the shame surrounding the crime can leave a victim feeling overwhelmed, confused and violated.

According to the Department of Justice Canada (2005), sexual assault includes any form of sexual activity without a person's consent. This may include:

- any kissing, fondling, touching
- oral/anal sex or sexual intercourse without voluntary consent
- not stopping sexual contact when asked
- forcing someone to engage in sexual intercourse or any other sexual act

It is important to note that consent obtained through pressure, coercion, or threats of force is not voluntary consent.

The Supreme Court of Canada also ruled in 1987 that the act of sexual assault does not depend solely on contact with any specific part of the human anatomy but rather the act of a sexual nature that violates the *sexual integrity* of the victim (*R. v. Chase*, 1987). When investigating a sexual assault, certain relevant factors are considered:

- the part of the body touched
- the nature of the contact; words and gestures accompanying the act
- the situation in which the contact occurred
- all other circumstances surrounding the act
- any threats that may or may not be accompanied by force

Numerous complex thoughts and feelings might lead many victims to downplay or minimize their experiences. What constitutes a sexual assault, however, is clear for those who work with victims and for those responsible for the administration of justice.

What Is Consent? The central issue in cases of sexual assault is that of sexual consent. The issue of consent is extremely important to the investigative process and the prosecution of sexual assault crimes. Over the years sexual perpetrators have developed various methods of coercion to help force a sexual offence. Consent defined by section 273.1 of the *Criminal Code* refers to the voluntary agreement of the complainant (victim) to engage in the sexual activity in question. Consent is NOT given if:

- it is given by someone else
- the person is unconscious, drunk, drugged, or sleeping
- it is an abuse of power, trust, or authority

- the person does not say yes, says no, or through words or behaviour implies no
- the person changes her or his mind

The Adolescent Female

It is important to include an examination of a specific population of women—adolescent females—because of this group's developmental vulnerability. Internally, adolescence is a time marked by conflict, self-doubt, and an exaggerated need for approval. Acceptance by peers is paramount, and it is often sought at the expense of self-respect. Developmentally, adolescents are searching for an identity, struggling with sexuality and sex-role identification, and developing a value system that will determine their lives. Acts of violence experienced by adolescents must also be understood in the context of the adolescent's place within the human life cycle. An adolescent girl's experience and exposure to violence is unique. Let's look at some types of violence specific to her.

Sexual Harassment Sexual harassment has been identified as an insidious yet pervasive form of violence that affects all girls. Although harassment in the workplace has been the focus of considerable attention during the last decade, there is a growing recognition that girls experience varied forms of sexual harassment, and that this behaviour begins at a surprisingly early age.

Sexual harassment is an action stemming from prejudicial or stereotypical views regarding all women; it is an action; a form of discrimination. Although the impact of gender discrimination on girls has been acknowledged for many years, it was not until the 1980s that girls were specifically placed on the international agenda. This occurred when UNICEF adopted the phrase "the girl child." After girls were identified as a vulnerable population by UNICEF, several international organizations followed suit.

The United Nations declared 1990 "The Year of the Girl Child," and the 1990s "The Decade of the Girl Child." This initiative was also motivated by the 1989 murder of 14 women engineering students in Montreal, Canada. This violent act of hatred grew out of a deeply felt prejudice against women; for a discussion of these events, see "Canadian Headline News" Box 4.3. Later, at the United Nations Fourth World Conference on Women in Beijing in 1995, the plight of girl children was on the platform as a significant topic for discussion.

Adolescent Physical and Sexual Violence When we look at adolescent dating or courtship, what is noteworthy are the changes in our culture. In many ways, adolescence is a new social construct. As Makepeace (1997) noted when describing adolescence, "adolescence was rare or nonexistent; the process of courtship generally took place later in life with marriage not long after . . . Adolescence is a time when teens learn how to make decisions about relationships with their family, friends, and dating partners. Today, heterosexual recreations, such as dances, parties, and sporting events, typically begin during junior high school and continue throughout adolescence and early adulthood" (p. 29).

4.3 Canadian Headline News: The Montreal Massacre

The year 1940 was a great year for Quebec women. They had won the right to vote in their provincial elections, making them the *last* province in Canada to be granted the vote. All other white Canadian women had earned this right by 1925. In that historic **feminist** struggle and victory, no woman was physically harmed or murdered. But in 1989, on the eve of the provincial vote's golden anniversary, nearly 50 years later, the events of the Montreal massacre were unleashed. And, one could say, it was fuelled by one person's opinion of what rights women should be allowed.

Acting on his beliefs—his views of women—on December 6, 1989, shortly after five o'clock, a 25-year-old male, Marc Lépine, carried a concealed semi-automatic rifle into École Polytechnique in Montreal. Angry and determined, he encountered in a school hallway the first women he killed. He then proceeded to a classroom that held 10 female students and 48 male students, and a professor. He fired two shots into the ceiling and shouted, *"I want the women. I hate feminists!"* Sorting out the men from the women, he expelled the men at gunpoint, lined up the remaining women students against the wall, and began to fire. Six women died; the others were injured but survived.

Continuing to fire, Lépine went down to the first floor and entered the cafeteria, where he killed three more female students. Still on the hunt, Lépine returned to the third floor and strode into another classroom. Unaware of the unfolding tragedy, students were there delivering presentations. He then opened fire sending two professors and 26 students scrambling for cover beneath their desks. Four more women were killed. Roughly 20 minutes after his rampage began Lépine took his own life. Thirteen students were injured, nine women and four men, and 14 women lay dead.

This bold, brazen, and deadly act is unfortunately part of Canadian history. December 6 now marks the anniversary of one of the worst unprecedented single-day massacres in Canadian history, a day that has since been termed the Montreal Massacre. The name underscores the horrific nature of the crime and Lépine's belief system that culminated in this tragedy.

Upon hearing of these stories, we inevitably ask why. Who was this person, and why did this happen? Prior to December 6, Lépine had sought to join the Canadian Armed Forces but was rejected. He had also applied to École Polytechnique, his application denied. He blamed these decisions on "affirmative action" policies, promoted by feminists and their sympathizers.

Quebeckers, Canadians, and many others around the world rallied to commemorate the victims and denounce the anti-feminist wrath of the attacker. Candlelight vigils were held across Canada. The Canadian flag flew at half mast. Since 1989, December 6 has been officially designated a National Day of Commemoration. The murdered women were Geneviève Bergeron, 21; Hélène Colgan, 23; Nathalie Croteau, 23; Barbara Daigneault, 22; Anne-Marie Edward, 21; Maud Haviernick, 29; Barbara Maria Klucznik, 31; Maryse Leclair, 23; Annie St.-Arneault, 23; Michèle Richard, 21; Maryse Laganière, 25; Anne-Marie Lemay, 22; Sonia Pelletier, 28; and Annie Turcotte, 21.

Reflection Question

Since 1989, there have been other school shootings in the United States and Canada. Have any of those tragic events been a gender-motivated killing?

Sources: CBC News, 2009a, 2009b.

Further, dating has become an extended process because Canadians are marrying later in life. These two factors have created a new population. Statistics Canada has indicated that single people are getting married at an older age. In 2003 (excluding Ontario), the average age of a first marriage (to someone of the opposite sex) was 28.5 years for women and 30.6 years for men, in comparison to first marriages in 1973 when the average age for a woman was 22.8 years and men 25.2 years (Statistics Canada, 2004).

Increased dating is likely; therefore, so too are more relationships. What adolescent girls learn in those relationships may affect the types of relationships they go on to develop. Early injurious or unhealthy relationships could last a lifetime, leaving young women vulnerable to dating violence (Becky & Farren, 1997).

Theoretically, conceptualizing adolescent victimization began to emerge in the mid 1980s to help professionals understand and identify the indicators unique to youth (Becky & Farren, 1997; Malik, Sorenson, & Aneshensel, 1997). Over time various definitions have been presented. Today, dating violence would be classified as physical, emotional and/or psychological, and sexual (Baker, 1995). Violence can occur in an established dating relationship or after a first date with someone slightly known by the victim. These categories can be broken down and understood by the following behaviours.

Physical

- Occurs when a partner is pinched, squeezed, shaken, shoved, thrown, bitten, choked, kicked, punched, or hit with an object

Emotional

- Harm to self-worth through name-calling, humiliation, withdrawing attention, deliberately doing something to make a dating partner feel diminished or embarrassed, blackmail, threats to divulge personal information
- Bullying can take on many forms: embarrassing on purpose, withholding information, making insults, starting rumours
- Controlling behaviour such as demanding an unrealistic amount of time be given to the relationship, which limits things like time with friends and family or participation in activities that were once enjoyed such as sports, school activities, or clubs. Over time it creates isolations and separation from previous sources of support and enjoyment.

Sexual Assault (sometimes called date rape or acquaintance rape)

- Forcing a partner to engage in a sex act; any form of sexual contact; putting something into the vagina when consent has not been given or when consent cannot be given. This could include unwanted touching, fondling, or groping, and forced sexual activity.

Technology: The New Violence Frontier

Technology has added a new dimension and opportunity for dating violence. Adolescents are well connected through cell phones and the Internet. These media have become tools of dating violence through which emotional abuse and sexual violence can occur. More than 80 percent of adolescents own at least one form of new media technology, for example a computer or a cell phone (David-Herndon & Hertz, 2007, 2009). They also use this technology with increased frequency to text, instant message, email, blog, and access social networking websites. "Canadian Headline News" Box 4.4 illustrates ways that technology is now being used to humiliate and violate. The scope of trauma and the **secondary victimization** is unimaginable.

Date Rape Drugs: A New Act of Violence In recent years new weapons have surfaced to create "drug-facilitated sexual assault." These weapons are commonly called date rape drugs and are used to commit sexual assaults. According to Levinthal (2010), "at one time rohypnol was odourless, colourless, and tasteless, so it could be easily combined with an alcoholic beverage without detection. Recently in response to instances of abuse . . . steps to reformulate the drug so that it turns blue when dissolved in a clear liquid have been made" (p. 368). Despite these changes, the drugs can still be concealed and remains dangerous. Remember, sexual assault is any type of sexual activity that a person does not consent to.

4.4 Canadian Headline News: When Viral Is Vile

In September 2010, police alleged a 16-year-old girl was drugged and repeatedly raped at a rave at a rural property in Pitt Meadows, east of Vancouver, British Columbia. During the incident a 16-year-old teen took cell phone photos of the incident and then posted them on Facebook. The gang rape was viewed over and over again.

Later, in December 2011, one teenager pleaded guilty to making and distributing obscene material in connection with the alleged gang rape. The 16-year-old could not be named because of his age at the time of the offence. Although he was initially charged with production and distribution of child pornography, he pleaded guilty to the lesser charge in B.C. Provincial Court in Coquitlam.

There are two more trials pending in this case: Colton Ashton McMorris was charged with sexual assault, and Dennis John Allen Warrington was charged with making and distributing child pornography. Police have said that as many as 12 people saw the incident, but investigators complained a code of silence among witnesses prevented them from coming forward.

The victim of the sex assault also allegedly was drugged with the date-rape drug Rohypnol or GHB.

Reflection Question

This victimization is disturbing on many levels—the alleged sexual assault, and the realization that others knowingly watched and recorded and then used social media to "share" the violation of a human soul. Do you think these unfolding behaviours (all of them) are random, or has today's society become so desensitized to violence that given the same set of circumstance in another part of Canada the same events would unfold? Are those who remain silent complicit? How many "others" located and sent the image of this victimization to facebook or another social networking site, so "others" could view and distribute? Is this distributing child pornography? The victim was younger than 18. Albert Einstein once said, "The world is a dangerous place not because of those who do evil but because of those who look on and do nothing."

Sources: CBC, 2010, 2011.

Table 4.1 Common Types of Date Rape Drugs and Their Effects	
Drug Name	**Effects and Facts**
Rohypnol, also known as roofies, "forget pill"	Felt within 30 minutes of being drugged. Muscle relaxation or loss of muscle control; difficulty with motor movements. If drugged, a person looks and acts like someone who is drunk; speech might be slurred, and the person might pass out.
GHB, also known as liquid ecstasy, bedtime scoop	Takes effect in about 15 minutes and can last three or four hours. Relaxation, drowsiness, dizziness, nausea, problems seeing, loss of consciousness (blackout).
Ketamine, also known as special K, black hole	Very fast-acting. The person might be aware of what is happening but unable to move. Causes memory problems; a person might not be able to remember what happened while drugged; an out of body experience, a dream-like feeling, lost sense of time and identity.

Source: Developed by author.

In 2002, a British Columbia study concluded that 27 percent of sexual assaults involved drugs such as GHB and Rohypnol (McGregor et al., 2004). See Table 4.1 for a description of the three most common date rape drugs. Although it is a common belief that these drugs are used in conjunction with alcohol, they also have been put in other drinks, including water. With an effect more profound than alcohol, these drugs make a person unable to resist assault. They cause weakness and confusion; some even cause a victim to pass out. Amnesia is another result, causing a high degree of vagueness about what has occurred. Once the unknowing victim consumes the drug, she is left to deal not only with the trauma of the sexual assault, but also with the uncertainty of knowing the horror of her victimization—what happened, who was there, and who knew. The emotional distress caused is incalculable.

Conclusion

In this section we have examined the key forms of violence against women. In an attempt to shine a light on violence within an authentic human framework, Canadian stories were told. These stories provide the reader with an opportunity to understand academic theory in a truthful, human context.

4.2 IMPACT OF VIOLENCE AGAINST WOMEN

Impact of Sexual Assault

Aggression, power, anger, and exerting control over someone else are the instigating factors of sexual violence. A sexual victimization is an extremely traumatic experience for anyone, despite the theoretical legal definition or the age or gender of the victim.

Sexual assault is a crime that is destructive on many levels—body, mind, and spirit. Moreover, many victims who have survived sexual assault fear for their lives during the attack (Polusny & Arbisi, 2006). It profoundly affects health and well-being. In describing the impact of sexual assault we will discuss two categories: physical impact and psychological impact.

Physical Impact Serious physical consequences often become known and usually are attended to before the emotional consequences begin. Internal and external injuries are some of the more common physical aftereffects. Women may suffer physical injuries such as chipped or broken teeth, cuts and bruises, and vaginal pain and bleeding. Women who have been forced to have oral sex may suffer damage or irritations to the throat. Rectal bleeding and pain are reported by women forced to have anal intercourse. An additional consequence is the fear of contracting a sexually transmitted infection such as HIV/AIDS, herpes, or hepatitis. Pregnancy can also result, which forces a woman to confront the decision whether to have an abortion (Hampton, 1995; Koss & Harvey, 1991).

Psychological Impact Numerous studies have been conducted to examine the psychological impact of sexual assault. In fact, as early as 1974 Burgess and Holmstrom (1974) coined the term rape trauma syndrome (RTS) to describe the impact of rape. Research shows that sexual assault is a time of crisis for a woman, and the effects can be immediate and potentially persist for months, a year, or more regardless of whether the perpetrator was a stranger, an acquaintance, or a date (Campbell, 2006; Burgess & Holmstrom, 1974; Dickinson et al., 1999; Koss, Figueredo, & Prince, 2002; Macy, Nurius, & Norris, 2006).

Self-Blame Victims commonly ask themselves why the sexual assault happened. The offender may have been someone they knew or trusted. Self-blame can prevent disclosure. Victims expend endless hours agonizing over what they might have done to cause the assault and what they could have done to prevent it. Self-blame is also linked to the worst long-term psychological outcome for victims (Dickinson et al., 1999; Koss et al., 2002). Further, the general public is particularly likely to blame the victim if alcohol or drugs were part of the environment in which the sexual assault took place (Wakelin, 2003).

Even when a victim believes she is not responsible for the sexual assault there is often accompanying guilt about not seeing the assault coming. Her belief is often directly or indirectly reinforced by the reactions of family or friends in the form of questioning her past sexual behaviour, the type of clothes she wore, or her decisions to drink alcohol during a date or to invite the perpetrator into her home. Even the people a victim may choose to turn to for help are not immune to subtle and overt victim blaming.

Many other psychological consequences have been noted in the research. Table 4.2 describes the consequences noted in the literature.

Posttraumatic Stress Disorder (PTSD) One of the most serious psychological outcomes that can develop is posttraumatic stress disorder (PTSD). Sexual assault is the

Table 4.2 Potential Harm to a Sexually Victimized Woman's Psychological and Physiological Well-Being

Psychological	Physiological
Depression, loss of motivation	Anxiety and/or panic attacks
Shame and guilt, self-blame	Dissociation
Withdrawal and isolation	Headaches, stomach problems, gastrointestinal disorders
Erosion of self-confidence and self-esteem	Fatigue and difficulty concentrating
Feeling powerless, helpless, out of control	Sleep disturbances including nightmares
Suicidal thoughts or attempts, suicide	Increased blood pressure

Sources: Burgess & Holmstrom, 1974; Campbell, 2006; Dickinson et al., 1999; Frazier, 2000; Gutek & Koss, 1993; Koss & Dinero, 1988; Koss et al., 2002; Larkin, 1994; Loy & Stewart, 1984; Macy et al., 2006; Smith, 1995.

most common cause of PTSD in women (Frazier, 2000; Resnick et al., 1999). PTSD is defined in the *Diagnostic and Statistical Manual of Mental Disorders (DSM-IV-TR)* as "the development of characteristic symptoms following exposure to an extreme traumatic stressor involving direct personal experience of an event that involves actual or threatened death or serious injury, or other threat to one's physical integrity" (American Psychiatric Association, 1994). For a full description of PTSD, see Box 4.5.

4.5 Posttraumatic Stress Disorder

Posttraumatic stress disorder (PTSD) is a type of anxiety disorder that is triggered by a traumatic event. PTSD has also been called shell shock or battle fatigue. The exact cause of PTSD is unknown. PTSD is triggered by experiencing or witnessing a traumatic event that creates feelings of intense helplessness, fear, or horror. Afterwards a victim can re-experience the event through memories and nightmares. When memories suddenly occur the victims will find themselves reliving the event; they will experience flashbacks. Victims often avoid (even unknowingly) anything that might remind them of their trauma. They often display a numbing of emotional responsiveness, which may be very disruptive to interpersonal relationships.

Those suffering from PTSD are sometimes unable to remember certain aspects of the event. It is possible that victims unconsciously attempt to avoid emotion, because intense emotions could bring back memories of the trauma. Finally, victims are typically over-aroused, easily startled, and quick to anger. Most people who experience a traumatic event have a difficult period of adjustment. But with support, time, and healthy coping methods such traumatic reactions usually get better. In some cases, however, the symptoms can worsen or last for months or even years. Sometimes they may completely disrupt a person's life. Each person who experiences trauma will not necessarily develop PTSD. Symptoms of PTSD are more likely to occur if the person has:

- previous traumatic experiences
- a history of being physically abused
- poor coping skills
- lack of social support

- existing ongoing stress
- a social environment that produces shame, guilt, stigmatization, or self-hatred
- alcohol abuse
- family psychiatric history

PTSD symptoms can change over time. They can increase during times of high stress or when a victim experiences a similar event. Hearing a news story about a sexual assault case may bring about the feelings or the terror of their assault. Experiencing various feelings is normal after a traumatic event.

Sources: Adapted from *DSM-IV-TR*, American Psychiatric Association, 2000.

There are many ways a victim might respond. Some victims have very strong reactions after being sexually assaulted, while others remain calm. Some victims may become very withdrawn and uncommunicative; others may act out sexually and become promiscuous. Mistrust, fear, and doubt can be triggered by simple encounters and communication with men. From the victim's perspective, prior to the assault the rapist had been impossible to tell apart from non-rapists. Now all men may be seen as potential rapists. For many victims, hypervigilance toward most men becomes permanent.

It is also important to note that some feelings and reactions might be experienced directly after the assault, while others can occur days, weeks, or even months later. Research has indicated that the victims of acquaintance or date rape report similar levels of depression, anxiety, and difficulty attaining pre-rape levels of sexual satisfaction to what victims of stranger sexual assault report (Gutek & Koss, 1993; Koss & Dinero, 1988). The research has also addressed specific characteristics that can influence impact.

Unique Characteristics Affecting Impact Because every person and situation is unique, victims of sexual assault will respond to an assault differently. Many factors can influence an individual's response to, and recovery from sexual assault. These factors may include:

- age, cognitive ability, and maturity of the victim
- frequency, severity, and duration of the assault(s)
- level of violence and injury inflicted (physical as well as sexual violence)
- setting of the attack
- social support system available to the victim
- victim's relationship to the offender
- response to the attack by police and medical personnel
- response to the attack by the victim's loved ones and friends
- victim's experience with the criminal justice system
- victim's workplace and community's attitudes and values

Apart from the known traumatic consequences, new research in psychology indicates that not everyone who experiences a serious traumatic event experiences long-term psychological harm. Some, in fact, display posttraumatic growth—positive life changes and psychological development following exposure to trauma. Research has confirmed that sexual assault victims—or, more precisely, sexual assault *survivors*—do report positive life changes such as an increased ability to take care of themselves, a greater sense of purpose in life, and greater empathy for others in similar situations (Burt & Katz, 1987; Frazier, 2000, 2003). The meaning and the understanding the victim is able to put together as she attempts to organize her traumatic event is critical to her capacity to go forward and heal (Koss & Harvey, 1991). With time and support healing it is possible for women who have been sexually assaulted.

Impact of Stalking

Stalking is another form of violence that can cause devastating consequences. Specifics regarding the impact of being a victim of stalking were addressed in the 2004 General Social Survey. According to the GSS, almost one-third of stalking victims feared their lives were in danger (AuCoin, 2005). Stalking victims also change their daily habits as a means of coping with the stress brought about by the stalking and to better protect themselves from their stalkers. They include:

- avoiding certain places or people as a direct result of being stalked

- getting an unlisted phone number, call display, call screening, or call blocking

- choosing to not go out alone

- changing their residence

In addition to changing their personal behaviours, stalking victims also reported turning to others for emotional, legal, and/or medical support.

Impact of Sexual Harassment

The impact of sexual harassment varies from person to person, depending on the seriousness and frequency of the harassment. Sexual harassment is probably best understood as existing on a continuum of sexual violence. With that in mind, it is easier to understand that a sexual harassment victim could potentially suffer psychological and physiological effects that are similar to those experienced by a victim of sexual assault; see Table 4.4.

Unlike stalking and sexual assault, in cases of sexual harassment the victim often works or attends school with their harasser. Deciding to report a case of sexual harassment can potentially lead to a further set of consequences.

The Aftermath from Reporting Sexual Harassment The consequences for those who choose to file a sexual harassment complaint, compared to those who do not, creates a vital concern (Schneider, Swan, & Fitzgerald, 1997). A victim of sexual harassment's social environment may be entirely altered, thereby creating a secondary victimization. She may become the subject of gossip, misinformation, and speculation. She will be judged by all who know about it, whether positively or negatively. Those whom she might ordinarily rely on for support may have mixed loyalties, or turn against her altogether. Depending on the work or school environment, peers may not feel safe to support due to their own fears and vulnerabilities. The following potential effects are specific to the aftermath of filing a sexual harassment grievance:

- Fear of:
  - retaliation from the harasser, or colleagues/friends of the harasser
  - revenge along with more sexual harassment, and the possibility of the violence accelerating—for instance, stalking or worse
- Exposure of one's personal life:
  - the victim becomes the accused; her lifestyle will often come under attack
  - being objectified and humiliated by scrutiny and gossip
  - defamation of character and reputation
- Increased absenteeism to avoid harassment
- Illness from stress
- Decreased work or school performance as the victim must focus on dealing with the harassment and the surrounding dynamics and/or effects
- The need to relocate to another city, job, or school
- Loss of:
  - job and income
  - trust in environments similar to where the harassment occurred
  - trust in the types of people who occupy similar positions as the harasser or their colleagues
  - references/recommendations
  - career
- Weakening of support network: colleagues, friends, and even family may distance themselves from the victim or abandon them altogether

Sexual harassment research is still relatively new, and much remains to be learned. Research concerning the health effects of sexual harassment on adolescent girls and young women is, for the most part, an under-researched area that would benefit from more investigation. Depending on the situation, the impact of sexual harassment can vary.

A Specific Note Regarding the Effect on Adolescent Girls It is not uncommon for girls to experience a decrease in their confidence during adolescence. In a 1990 poll involving more than 3000 girls between the ages of 9 and 15, researchers concluded that girls who had previously displayed confidence and enthusiasm about themselves and the world around them suddenly experienced self-doubt and insecurity

(AAUW, 1991). Specifically, those who had once enjoyed considerable success in academic performance unexpectedly found themselves struggling for recognition and achievement in the classroom.

Adolescent girls are vulnerable (Pipher, 1994). *Any* harm done to an adolescent girl during this development stage, therefore, could exacerbate these emotional challenges. If an adolescent girl is traumatized—which includes being sexually harassed—further problems could unfold. Several writers have observed a tendency among girls to drop out of school, or to suffer from diminished self-worth, depression, eating disorders, and suicidal thoughts and suicide attempts (Larkin, 1994; Orenstein, 1997; Reimer, 1999).

Conclusion

The impact of sexual harassment is individual and multifaceted. Continuous study of the problems associated with violent crimes is vital if we want to ameliorate trauma. It is essential that victims receive immediate and appropriate help and care. Clinical wisdom and treatment are crucial, but so too are policies and laws to eradicate violence and protect. The next section examines the prevalence of violence against women in Canadian society.

4.3 STATISTICS AND PREVALENCE OF VIOLENCE AGAINST WOMEN

Introductory Thoughts Regarding Statistics

Statistics are essential. They assist in describing the nature and extent of victimizations (crime), which supports the development of victim services and effective crime prevention policies. Data that describe the extent and type of violent crimes occurring in society also help to paint a picture of risk. For instance, knowing whether certain populations of people are more vulnerable to specific victimizations based on age, gender, and geographic location is essential. Statistics help this process, and are used as a basis for developing social policy and the crucial step that follows: evaluation.

Sources of Canadian Statistics

Statistics regarding victimizations or crimes are reported using two major surveys: the Uniform Crime Reporting Survey (UCR) and the Victimization Survey that is conducted through the General Social Survey. Both fall under the auspices of Canada's national statistics department, Statistics Canada. In 1981 the Canadian Centre for Justice Statistics was created as a satellite of Statistics Canada, through the cooperation of the federal and provincial governments. Soon it became the administrative arm of Canada's National Justice Statistic Initiative (NJSI). Its mandate was to supply information to the justice community and the public on the nature and extent of crime and the administration of justice in Canada (Canadian Centre for Justice Statistics, 1999, p. 5). Information generated through this office is provided to the public through a service bulletin known as *Juristat,* which is published periodically throughout the year (Schmalleger & Volk, 2004).

The Uniform Crime Reporting Survey The **Uniform Crime Reporting Survey (UCR)** was first introduced in 1961 to measure the incidence of crime in Canadian society and its characteristics. Over time, changes would unfold regarding the manner in which data were collected. The most recent system is based on a 2004 revision known as UCR2.2. The various changes that took place during the past 40 years were designed to provide certain efficiencies in reporting for police services.

The crime rate used in the UCR is based on a population of 100 000. By taking populations into account, the crime picture is standardized across the country in any given year. For example, in 2007 the murder rate was 594, and based on the 2007 Canadian population of 32 649 482 this crime rate would be calculated as follows:

$$\frac{594 \text{ homicides reported}}{32\,649\,482} \times 100\,000 = 1.8$$

This number indicates that in 2007 there were fewer than two homicides for every 100 000 Canadians.

It is also essential to underscore the quality and scope of the UCR data. The *Criminal Code* is applied nationwide. Therefore, the uniform data are beneficial because the categories of offences remain consistent regardless of the jurisdiction collecting the data (Schmalleger & Volk, 2004). These statistics have assisted the federal government in its policy development and in the creation of new legislative initiatives. In addition, the data provide critical information that allows Canada's violent crimes to be compared to those of other countries. This information is publicly shared and available to all Canadians, the media, academics, and students.

Victim Survey Data Taking hold in Canada separate from the statistics being generated by Canada's policing professionals was the gathering of other forms of statistics. In 1981, the first survey in Canada was conducted that specifically asked Canadians to share their personal victimization histories. Called the Canadian Urban Victimization Survey (CUVS), it used a telephone survey data collection method, which randomly sampled roughly 60 000 Canadians over the age of 16 in seven major cities. The respondents were asked to describe any victimization they experienced in the prior calendar year. Eight categories were identified. The data revealed 700 000 personal victimizations and 900 000 household victimizations. Noteworthy was the fact that fewer than 42 percent of these victimizations were reported to the police (Ministry of Solicitor General, 1982). Later, the General Social Survey was introduced in an attempt to reduce the gaps left by its regular method of generating statistical information.

General Social Survey (GSS) The General Social Survey (GSS) is conducted annually; however, the core content varies and examines different issues affecting Canadians. The issue of personal risk is one area that has been singularly examined (Schmalleger & Volk, 2004). The first year the category of personal risk was researched was in 1988, and four cycles have since followed: 1993, 1999, 2004, and 2009. No attempt has ever been made to survey the entire Canadian population.

Since the introduction of the CUVS and the subsequent GSS data, a picture of the quantity and types of crimes committed in Canada has been developed. Other surveys have also been conducted to examine crime. Most significant among these was the first-ever national Violence Against Women Survey (VAWS), undertaken by Statistics Canada in 1993.

Violence Against Women Survey (VAWS) Implemented in 1993, the VAWS interviewed more than 12 000 women 18 years and older by telephone regarding any physical and sexual violence experiences they might have had since the age of 16. They were also asked questions that related to their perception of personal safety. The findings of the survey found that there were substantially more acts of violence against women than had ever been formerly indicated in the UCR numbers. In fact, 50 percent reported having had experienced at least one incident of violence since the age of 16, and almost one-half reported that the violence had been perpetrated by men they knew.

Criticism of the UCR and Victimization Surveys While based on the same categories of victimizations (crimes), the data generated by the UCR and victimization surveys reveal very different pictures. Findings from the UCR are generated from the crimes *reported* to the policed by victims. Reporting rates can significantly vary due to numerous variables: age, type of crime, perception of police and the systems that administer justice. Thus, these numbers are based completely on reporting; or, crime known to the police.

On the other hand, a criticism of victimization surveys relates to the issue of *over-reporting*. This is due in large part to the fact that it is beyond the purview of most victimization surveys to authenticate the actual occurrences of any crime being reported during telephone survey interview/research. Over-reporting presents a legitimate concern and potential limitations when analyzing victim research and statistics. Conversely, the UCR has been criticized for not encapsulating all victimizations. Despite their difference these two statistical sources can complement one another.

Self-Reporting Studies Apart from the governmental statistical sources mentioned, numerous academic research studies exist. Many academic studies have examined specific areas of violence in an attempt to chisel out facts that help define a particular problem, its prevalence, and impact. All studies add to our understanding. A **self-report** is any method that involves asking a participant about his or her experiences, feelings, attitudes, and beliefs. This type of data collection method can be administered using a number of formats: survey, phone, online, or a written questionnaire (mail or in person) in which respondents read questions and select responses by themselves without researcher interference. Often these forms are completed anonymously. Another data collection method takes place within a face-to-face interview. Regardless of the format in which the information is being provided, questions can be presented as a set of highly structured written questions or as open-ended questions that allow participants to record their own answers.

Self-report studies also have limitations, including validity problems. Participants may exaggerate in order to make their situation seem worse, or they may under-report the severity or frequency in order to minimize.

Statistics are not perfect, yet statistics are vital. And even with the different data sources, we must be mindful of the fact that many victims continue to perceive intimate personal violence, especially sexual victimization, as a private matter and many do not disclose their victimization to any formal source (Sable et al., 2006). This would certainly include the police and a stranger at the other end of a telephone. The exact prevalence of sexual assault in Canada has been difficult to quantify. But Canada does generate two major statistics sources: the Uniform Crime Reporting Survey (UCR) and the Victimization Survey, conducted through the General Social Survey.

Sexual Assault Offences in Canada: The National Picture

It is impossible to know exactly how many women are victims of violent crime. Violence remains hidden for many reasons. Fear is a powerful deterrent to reporting. Fear of the offender, fear of the unknown—what will happen if they go forward? For some, it is fear of law enforcement or the government. Uncertainties abound, valid questions are asked. Fear also relates to stigma and shame. Will they be believed, judged, or ostracized? Sexual offences in Canada account for only a small portion of all reported crimes. According to Brennan and Taylor-Butts (2008), "sexual assault continues to be a challenge, since the largest majority (91%) of these crimes is not reported to police" (p. 8).

It is imperative to know the scope and types of intimate violent acts committed against women. Through statistical data we are able to begin to paint a picture of who, what, where, when, how, how much, and by whom acts of violence transpire. Understanding the nature of the crime is essential to the development of effective prevention policies. Schmalleger & Volk (2011) wrote, "These policies, in turn, are usually responsive to public pressure. Since it is the public that is the major player in reporting crime, the types of crime it reports reflects those issues most concerning it" (p. 45). Statistics assist in our understanding of the extent and forms of violence directed at women.

The following statistics are generated from the GSS and the UCR.

Victimization Survey (GSS, 2009) The General Social Survey (GSS, 2009) collected information on violent crime, theft of personal property, and household crime. These categories were also based on *Criminal Code* definitions. Incidents involving more than one type of offence (e.g., a robbery and an assault) were classified according to the most serious offence. The rank of violent offences from most to least serious is sexual assault, robbery, and physical assault.

In 2009, close to 1.6 million Canadians, or 6 percent of the population aged 15 years and over in the 10 provinces, reported having been the victim of a sexual assault, a robbery, or a physical assault in the preceding 12 months; this proportion is similar to that in 2004.

Just under one-third of Canadians (31 percent) who had been victimized reported their victimization to police, down slightly from 34 percent in 2004. The self-reported incidence of violent incidents included physical assault (19 percent), sexual assault (8 percent), and robbery (4 percent) (Perreault & Brennan, 2010).

Overall, rates of violent victimization remained stable between 2004 and 2009, as did the rates of sexual assault, physical assault, and robbery. Specifically, the following *self-reported* violent sexual assault victimizations were reported for the following three years:

- 2009   67 700   24 per 1000 population age 15 years and older
- 2004   54 600   21 per 1000 population age 15 years and older
- 1999   50 200   21 per 1000 population age 15 years and older

The data reported in 2004 also indicated that women were more likely to have been victims of sexual assault than were men. For every 1000 women, there were 34 incidents of sexual assault compared with 15 for every 1000 men (Perreault & Brennan, 2010).

Victimization and police-reported data both indicated that the least severe form of sexual assault was the most common, level 1 sexual assaults (s. 271) (see Chapter 7). The *Criminal Code* distinguished among three levels of sexual assault, according to the seriousness of the incident.

Uniform Crime Reporting Survey (UCR) The 2007 police-reported data estimated that 24 200 sexual offences were brought to police attention. This accounted for eight percent of all police-reported violent crime in 2007 (Brennan & Taylor-Butts, 2008). Police also report that the least serious types of sexual assault (level 1) comprised the majority (86 percent) of sexual offences. The more serious forms of sexual assault and other sexual offences, such as invitation to sexual touching and sexual exploitation, made up the remaining 14 percent.

A year later, in 2008, police-reported data indicate that an estimated 21 472 sexual offences were brought to police attention; of those cases, 20 982 were level 1; 351 were level 2; and 139 were level 3. In 2009, an estimated 20 931 sexual offences were brought to police attention; of those cases, 20 460 were level 1; 349 were level 2; and 122 were level 3 (see Table 4.5).

What is distinguishable after reviewing the past 25 years of police-reported data is that the prevalence of sexual offences has fluctuated. Brennan and Taylor-Butts (2008) pointed out that following the 1983 *Criminal Code* amendments there was a steady rise in the overall rate of sexual offences, which peaked in 1993. During this time period, rates for police-reported sexual offences nearly doubled, rising from 59 per 100 000 Canadians to 136 per 100 000.

Table 4.3 Police-Reported Crime, Selected Offences, Canada				
	2008		**2009**	
Total Crime	**Number**	**Rate**	**Number**	**Rate**
Type of Offence: Violent Crime				
Sexual assault—level 3—aggravated	139	0	122	0
Sexual assault—level 2—weapon or bodily harm	351	1	349	1
Sexual assault—level 1	20 982	63	20 460	61
Total sexual assault cases	21 472	64	20 931	63
Criminal harassment	18 550	56	20 007	59
Uttering threats	79 036	237	78 407	232
Threatening or harassing phone calls	24 306	73	23 203	69
Total	**443 608**	**1 331**	**443 284**	**1 314**

Source: Adapted from the police-reported crime for selected offences, Canada, 2008 and 2009: Statistics Canada, Canadian Centre for Justice Statistics, Uniform Crime Reporting Survey.

After peaking in 1993, the overall rate for sexual offences reported to police declined, paralleling the downward trend for violent offences in general (Kong et al., 2003). This trend was largely influenced by level 1 sexual assaults (the category with the least physical injury to the victim), as they account for the majority of sexual offence incidents reported to the police. Compared to level 1 sexual assault rates, rates for level 2 and level 3 sexual assaults, as well as other sexual offences, were relatively stable throughout the period from 1983 to 2007. Table 4.3 provides sexual crime statistics generated from the Uniform Crime Reporting Survey during 2008 and 2009. All statistics are based on a rate per 100 000 population.

Reporting Trends of Sexual Assault According to Geography According to police-reported data, in 2007 there were significant differences in the overall rates of sexual offences reported to the police across Canada. All statistics are based on a rate per 100 000 population. For an overview of those differences, see Table 4.4. As you will note, sexual offences were highest in Nunavut (746), followed by Northwest Territories (518) and Yukon (203). Canada's national average was 73 sexual offences per 100 000 population (UCR, 2007).

Among the provinces, Saskatchewan (138) and Manitoba (113) had the highest rates, while Ontario (61) and Prince Edward Island (58) had the lowest. Total sexual offence rates for Quebec (69) and Alberta (70) were also below the national average of 73 sexual offences per 100 000 population (UCR, 2007).

Level 1 sexual assault was overall the most frequently reported sexual assault across Canada. It was highest in Saskatchewan (119) and lowest in Prince Edward Island (51). In comparison, rates of sexual assault with a weapon (level 2) and aggravated sexual assault (level 3) were relatively low across all provinces, ranging from 1 to 3 per 100 000 population.

Table 4.4 Number of Cases of Sexual Assault Reported to Police across Canada

Canadian view of sexual assault cases reported to the police

National average: 73 sexual offences per 100 000 population

Province	Numbers per 100 000
Nunavut	746
Northwest Territories	518
Yukon	203
Saskatchewan	138
Manitoba	113
Newfoundland	89
New Brunswick	87
Nova Scotia	82
British Columbia	79
Alberta	70
Quebec	69
Newfoundland	89
Ontario	61
Prince Edward Island	58

Source: Adapted from Statistics Canada, Canadian Centre for Justice Statistics, Uniform Crime Reporting Survey, 2007.

Sexual assaults differed across the country (Brennan & Taylor-Butts, 2008); however, there are probable explanations for the differences in police-reported sexual assault rates. Explanations include differences in age, demographics, availability of victim services, variations in public attitudes toward sexual assault that would potentially influence reporting among victims, or police training (Kong et al., 2003).

It is also likely that these numbers are an *undercount* of the actual number of sexual assaults committed. According to self-reported victimization data from the General Social Survey, fewer than one in ten sexual assaults were reported to police. There are many reasons to not report to police: fear of the police, or the belief that the incident was not important enough or that it was dealt with in some other way (Brennan and Taylor-Butts, 2008).

Most at Risk for Sexual Assault Being young, attending school, and frequently participating in evening activities have been identified as the variables most associated with risk of victimization (Gannon & Mihorean, 2005; Perreault & Brennan, 2010). Youth and students may have higher rates of sexual assault because of their lifestyle. These individuals tend to go out more, engage more frequently in social activities, and are in close proximity to many different individuals at any given time (Cass, 2007).

Moreover, victimization surveys of students also found that those who frequently engaged in evening activities, such as going out to restaurants, bars or the movies, or visiting friends, reported higher rates of sexual assault. The 2004 GSS also found that those who participated in 30 or more evening activities per month had rates of sexual victimization that were 4.5 times higher than those who engaged in fewer than 10 evening activities in a month.

Age is also a risk factor for sexual victimization according to data from victimization surveys and police-reported data. For example, the findings from the 2004 GSS indicate that the rate of sexual assault for Canadians aged 15 to 24 was almost 18 times greater than the rate recorded for Canadians aged 55 years and older (5563 versus 315 per 100 000 population).

The Accused While females are unduly the victims of sexual offences, males are disproportionately the accused. According to 2007 police-reported data, 97 percent of persons accused of sexual offences were male. Compare that number with the 78 percent of males being accused of all other types of violent crime.

Both police-reported and victimization survey data suggested that sexual assault incidents are most likely to occur when a victim and offender are known to each other. Over half (55 percent) of the sexual assaults reported involved an offender who was a friend or acquaintance of the victim, while stranger assaults accounted for 35 percent of incidents (GSS, 2004).

In the case of police-reported data (when the relationship could be determined), the 2007 data showed that the victim and accused were known to each other in 82 percent of sexual assault incidents. In approximately 18 percent of incidents the accused was a stranger to the victim. In 19 percent of the cases of police-reported data the relationship between the victim and accused was unknown.

Dating Violence

Victims of police-reported dating violence indicated that more than 8 in 10 were female, but this number narrowed with age. From the age range of 15 to 19 years rates of dating violence were higher for female than male victims at a margin of nearly 10 to 1. As the age of victim increased, the range declined with near parity in rates for individuals 55 years of age and older (Hotton Mahony, 2010).

Common assault (the form of assault resulting in the least physical injury to victims) was the most frequent type of violent offence committed in dating violence incidents. The statistical outcomes of the different forms of violence within a dating relationship are outlined in Figure 4.1. This study likely represents only a portion of incidents of violence committed in dating relationships. Data from the 2004 General Social Survey on Victimization found that many victims of violence do not report their victimizations to police.

Stalking (Criminal Harassment)

Though stalking is not new behaviour, it has only recently been documented as a distinct *criminal* behaviour. In 1993, the offence of criminal harassment, also known as "stalking," was introduced in the *Criminal Code*. Similar to the measurement of crime in general, the prevalence of stalking can be measured either through police or victimization data.

To date, Canadian research focusing on stalking/criminal harassment has been limited to studies of police data that describe incident, victim, and accused characteristics of

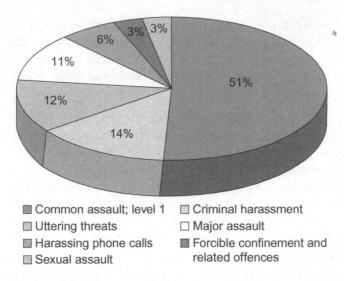

Figure 4.1 Forms of Violence within a Dating Relationship Source: Adapted from Hotton Mahony, 2010

police-reported criminal harassment cases (Beattie, 2003; Hackett, 2000; Kong, 1996; Pottie Bunge, 2002).

In 2004, Statistics Canada measured stalking for the first time through the General Social Survey on Victimization (GSS). The following discussion provides a picture of the prevalence of stalking in Canada. The categories that will be reported are victim characteristics, victim–offender relationships, forms of stalking experienced, and violent stalking relationships (AuCoin, 2005).

The incidence and prevalence of stalking was measured through the 2004 General Social Survey using a series of questions describing various stalking behaviours. The results indicated that women are more likely to be victims of stalking than are men. Overall, in Canada, it is estimated that 9 percent of people 15 years of age and over had been stalked in the five years prior to the survey. This represents more than 2.3 million Canadians. More than one in 10 females (11 percent), or more than 1.4 million women, reported being stalked in the preceding five years to such a degree that it caused them to fear for their safety or the safety of someone known to them.

Just under 900 000 men experienced stalking and the resulting fear during the same time period, which represents 7 percent of the male population. While the majority of female and male stalking victims reported that they had been stalked by only one person, just over one-quarter of victims (28 percent) reported that they had been stalked by more than one person in the previous five years (AuCoin, 2005).

Forms of Stalking More than half of female stalking victims reported that their stalker phoned them repeatedly or made silent or obscene phone calls (52 percent), while one-third reported being spied on (34 percent) and/or being intimidated or threatened (34 percent).

Table 4.5 Forms of Stalking Behaviour

Type of Stalking Behaviour	Phoned repeatedly or made silent or obscene phone calls	Reported being spied on	Reported being intimidated or threatened	Threatened to hurt their pets or damage property
Females	52%	34%	34%	n/a
Males	39%	n/a	56%	24%

Source: Adapted by author; AuCoin, 2005

In contrast, more than half of male stalking victims (56 percent) reported being intimidated or threatened, while more than one-third reported being phoned repeatedly (39 percent) and one-quarter reported being intimidated or threatened by the stalker by having pets hurt or property damaged (24 percent). Table 4.5 shows forms of stalking behaviour.

The Stalker Results from the 2004 GSS clearly indicate that stalking victims know their stalkers. Victims most frequently indicated that they were stalked by:

- people classified as friends (23 percent)
- current or ex intimate partners (17 percent)
- persons known by sight only (14 percent)
- co-workers, neighbours, and other relatives (18 percent)

Fewer than one-quarter of stalking victims were harassed by a stranger (AuCoin, 2005).

When examining the results of the intimate partner stalker, it appears that ex-spouses pose the greatest threat: eight percent of female stalking victims. This is not surprising, as research has consistently shown that the level of violence and conflict between couples is heightened during the initial period of separation following the end of an intimate relationship. Men represent the largest majority of stalkers at 80 percent, regardless of the sex of the victim.

Results indicate that the degree of familiarity between the stalker and their victim had an impact on whether multiple forms of stalking are employed by the stalker. Two-thirds (67 percent) of female stalking victims who were stalked by an intimate partner were more likely to experience multiple forms of stalking; for example, receiving obscene phone calls in addition to being spied on (AuCoin, 2005).

In contrast, female stalking victims pursued by a stranger were the least likely to experience more than one form of stalking (38 percent of female victims and 27 percent of male victims). These results might point to the reality that the more familiar the stalker is with the day-to-day habits of their victims, the more likely the victim will experience more than one form of harassing behaviour (AuCoin, 2005).

Aboriginal women were also more likely to be victims of stalking. The 2004 GSS results show that 11 percent of the northern residents were victims of some form of stalking. This finding was consistent with the proportion of provincial residents who reported having been stalked. As was the case in the provinces, northern women were almost twice as likely as men to have been stalked (15 percent compared with 7 percent) (AuCoin, 2005).

Sexual Harassment

Sexual harassment statistics are not generated by the GSS or the UCR. One Canadian survey (Bagley, Bolitho, & Bertrand, 1997) found that 23 percent of its sample of 1025 adolescent women from western Canada had experienced sexual assault, including harassment. A limitation of this research was that the questionnaire used in the study asked about "more serious" dimensions of sexual harassment, including sexual assault. Thus, the more subtle forms of harassment were unlikely to capture sexual harassment.

A survey involving 1990 Canadian women between the ages of 18 and 65 found that 56 percent had experienced sexual harassment in the previous year; the overall lifetime rate was 77 percent (Crocker & Kalemba, 1999). The preponderance of harassers were male.

Sexual harassment on campus also occurs. A 1989 survey at the University of Prince Edward Island found that 29 percent of the female students reported that they had been personally sexually harassed by a faculty member (Mazar & Percival, 1989). Harassment ranged from sexual teasing and jokes to unwanted touching and offers of favours for sex.

The significance of these results was also reported in an Ontario study of 1213 youth in grades six to eight in which 36 percent of boys and 21 percent of girls reported having been a perpetrator of sexual harassment. The two most common sexually harassing behaviours were homophobic name-calling, and sexual comments, jokes, gestures, and looks (McMaster et al., 2002). (We discuss the impact of creating a homophobic environment in Chapter 6.)

Sexual Assault and Aboriginal Women

I would say countless, countless atrocities that have never been counted. The trouble is if they were documented what a hurt it would impose on those who are still living. Death's breath consistently in our presence, the unrecognizing of the destruction lain all around us, and us not knowing we are locked, still and immobile in this continuous traumatic cycle.

—*Pacific Association of First Nations Women et al., 2005, p. 3*

In 2004, Amnesty International Canada published a report called *Stolen Sisters: A Human Rights Response to Discrimination and Violence against Indigenous Women in Canada.* The report highlighted the 1996 Canadian government statistic that stated indigenous women between the ages of 25 and 44 with status under the federal *Indian Act* were five times more likely than other women of the same age to die as the result of violence (Indian and Northern Affairs Canada, 1996).

A number of advocacy organizations, especially the Native Women's Association of Canada (NWAC), have forced attention to the fact that the violence perpetrated against Indigenous women is done predominantly in non-Indigenous communities. Their efforts, coupled with media reports that highlight high-profile cases of assaulted, missing, or murdered Indigenous women and girls, have shone a spotlight garnering greater public attention. Unfortunately, in most instances this awareness has been too late, especially in specific cities in Canada. The following list provides examples of some of those cases (Amnesty International, 2004):

- 1994—In two separate instances, 15-year-old Indigenous girls, Roxanna Thiara and Alishia Germaine, were found murdered in Prince George in eastern British Columbia. The body of a third 15-year-old Indigenous girl, Ramona Wilson, who disappeared that same year, was found in Smithers in central British Columbia in April 1995.

- 2002—While hitchhiking along a road that connects Prince George and Smithers, 26-year-old non-Indigenous woman Nicola Hoar went missing. Only after her disappearance did media attention focus on the unsolved murders and other disappearances along what has been dubbed the "Highway of Tears."

- 1996—John Martin Crawford was convicted of murder in the killings of three Indigenous women, Eva Taysup, Shelley Napope, and Calinda Waterhen, in Saskatoon, Saskatchewan.

- 2004—A former British Columbia provincial court judge, David William Ramsey, pleaded guilty to buying sex from and assaulting four Indigenous girls, ages 12, 14, 15, and 16, who had appeared before him in court. The crimes were committed between 1992 and 2001. In June 2004, the former judge was sentenced to seven years in prison.

An important case of immeasurable consequence is the story of the heinous murders of at least 26 women by pig farmer Robert Pickton. For details, see "Canadian Headline News" Box 4.6.

4.6 Canadian Headline News: Murderer Robert Pickton

Robert Pickton was elevated to infamy in February 2002, after police began dissecting his British Columbia pig farm where they would eventually find DNA remains and other evidence that tied him to the slaughtering deaths of 27 women. He is also suspected of being involved in several other murders of women from an impoverished Vancouver neighbourhood and elsewhere. Vancouver's Downtown Eastside is the poorest neighbourhood in British Columbia, and possibly in all of Canada. It has been called Vancouver's Skid Row.

For years, complaints to police about the disappearance of dozens of women were

(continued)

mishandled. During the investigation that eventually took place, which included the excavation of the pig farm, the daunting and horrifying facts unfolded. After he picked up these women and brought them to his farm, Pickton killed and butchered them, and in some cases fed their remains to pigs. Twenty-seven murder charges were laid.

One of the murder charges was thrown out by a judge before trial. The remaining counts were split into two groups; one comprised 20 charges, the other six. The prosecution began with the smaller group.

On December 9, 2007, Pickton was convicted of second-degree murder in the deaths of the following six women:

Sereena Abotsway, age 29 when she disappeared in August 2001

Mona Lee Wilson, age 26 when she was last seen on November 23, 2001

Andrea Joesbury, age 22 when last seen in June 2001

Brenda Ann Wolfe, age 32 when last seen in February 1999; reported missing in April 2000

Marnie Lee Frey, last seen August 1997

Georgina Faith Papin, last seen in 1999

Pickton appealed the conviction. Prosecutors indicated at the time that if his appeal to Canada's top court for a new trial was rejected he would not be tried on the remaining 20 charges.

On July 30, 2010, the Supreme Court decision denied Pickton a new trial, and indicated that he received a fair trial and there was no miscarriage of justice. At that point, the Crown decided to end the prosecution. As such, Pickton's confirmed death toll may never be known.

Following the Supreme Court decision in August 2010, the Vancouver Police Department provided the following statement by Deputy Doug LePard, when he released to the Canadian public the *Missing Women Investigation Review* report:

Before I begin I would like to reemphasize what I said on the day that the Supreme Court of Canada made its final decision about the fate of Robert Pickton.

While slamming the door forever on this vile killer might seem like the end of the road for some, I'm sure that for the families of his victims the nightmare will never end.

Some of the families may feel that they received justice with his convictions and I'm aware that others feel robbed of their day in court. What they all share, however, is a terrible loss and a right to know not just what happened to their loved ones but how he got away with it for so long.

I have said it before and I know I will think about it every day for the rest of my career, as I have every day since I started my review: I wish we could have caught this monster quicker and saved more lives . . . THIS CAN NEVER HAPPEN AGAIN!

The families and the public have a right to know why police didn't stop him sooner, what went wrong and what we have done since to ensure this type of tragedy will never happen again. The Vancouver Police Department is very dedicated and committed to answering those questions. For several years, I investigated and assembled the information necessary. I pored over about 20,000 pages of documents, interviewed every key VPD member from clerks to Chief Constables along with examining other documents, literature and media reports. I also had the benefit of interviewing a key RCMP officer, who had been the lead investigator in the Coquitlam RCMP into the Pickton information.

The report I am giving you today contains hundreds of pages of facts, portions of statements, analysis and a chronology that outlines every step and misstep along the way from the time there was a significant increase in women going missing from the Downtown Eastside in 1997, until Pickton was arrested in 2002 . . .

My report focuses primarily on the problems in the VPD Missing Women investigation overall, but also looks at the parallel investigation that was conducted by the Coquitlam RCMP into information the VPD received about Pickton in 1998 and 1999.

I'm not going to sugar coat this; I owe it to the families and the public to be open and forthright. They will likely find the contents of this report to be shocking and sad. But I hope they will find some consolation in the fact that the lessons we have learned leave us much better equipped to safeguard the vulnerable and those who have been marginalized.

I also want to be clear: there was only one villain in this story and that is Robert Pickton . . . .

Reflection Question
What variables do you think led to this horrific Canadian story? What types of system and/or legal changes could be implemented to ensure this form of violence never occurs again?

Source: Vancouver Police Department.

Following the Supreme Court decision in the Pickton case and the release of the Vancouver Police Department's *Missing Women Investigation Review* in September 2010 (LePard, 2010), the Lieutenant Governor in Council issued an Order in Council establishing the Missing Women Commission of Inquiry. Wally Oppal, QC, was named Commissioner. Under the terms of reference the Missing Women Commission of Inquiry would:

a) inquire into and make findings of fact respecting the conduct of the investigations conducted between January 23, 1997 and February 5, 2002, by police forces in British Columbia respecting women reported missing from the Downtown Eastside of the city of Vancouver;

b) inquire into and make findings of fact respecting the decision of the Criminal Justice Branch on January 27, 1998, to enter a stay of proceedings on charges against Robert William Pickton of attempted murder, assault with a weapon, forcible confinement and aggravated assault;

c) recommend changes considered necessary respecting the initiation and conduct of investigations in British Columbia of missing women and suspected multiple homicides; and

d) recommend changes considered necessary respecting homicide investigations in British Columbia by more than one investigating organization, including the co-ordination of those investigations.

At the time of writing this textbook, Commissioner Oppal's report had not been submitted (Missing Women Commission of Inquiry, http://www.missingwomeninquiry.ca/n.d.).

The Native Women's Association of Canada (NWAC) believes that the number of cases that have come to light represent only a small percentage of the number of Indigenous women across Canada who have been violently harmed. The organization has estimated that over the past 20 years more than 500 Indigenous women may have been murdered or gone missing in circumstances suggesting violence (NWAC, n.d.).

Aboriginal Statistics In 2006, statistics indicated that Aboriginal peoples made up 4 percent of Canada's population, among whom 60 percent identified as First Nations, 33 percent as Métis, and 4 percent as Inuit. This population is young compared to the rest of Canada, with a median age of 27 compared to the Canadian median age of 40. Almost half (48 percent) of the Aboriginal population in Canada is under the age of 25 (Johnson, 2006).

The information indicated that Aboriginal women were 3.5 times more likely than non-Aboriginal women to be victims of violence (343/1000 versus 96/1000, respectively). Aboriginal people were nearly twice as likely as non-Aboriginal people to be repeat victims of crime. Approximately 75 percent of survivors of sexual assault in Aboriginal communities are young women under 18 years of age. A further 50 percent of these girls are under the age of 14, and approximately 25 percent are under the age of 7.

Sexual assault against women was particularly prevalent in Northern Canada, where there is a much higher proportion of Aboriginal people in each of the territories than in the provinces (Johnson, 2006).

In 2002, the rate of sexual assault in Nunavut was 96.1 for every 10 000 people compared to the overall rate in Canada of 7.8 in every 10 000 people (Levan, 2003). In one study of the Vancouver sex trade, 52 of 101 women interviewed were Aboriginal (Farley, Lynne, & Cotton, 2005). The overwhelming majority of these women reported both a history of childhood sexual abuse by multiple perpetrators, and a history of rape and other assaults while working as prostitutes. Aboriginal women have also been found to be greatly overrepresented as sex trade workers compared to non-Aboriginal women (Oxman-Martinez, Lacroix, & Hanley, 2005).

As noted earlier in this chapter, being a youth in Canada places one at a greater risk of being a victim of sexual assault. This fact is also true for Aboriginal youth. In 2004, the rate for northern Canadians aged 15 to 24 years was 860 per 1000, more than three times greater than the rate for those aged 25 to 34 (276 per 1000), four times greater than the rate for those aged 35 to 44 (209 per 1000), and more than 15 times greater than the rate for those aged 45 and over (56 per 1000).

The GSS (2004) further revealed that Aboriginal people were three times more likely than non-Aboriginal people to experience a violent victimization such as an assault, sexual assault, or robbery (319 versus 101 incidents per 1000 population). These data are similar to findings from the previous GSS cycle completed in 1999.

An initial concern in gathering Canadian statistics relates to how violent crimes are reported and recorded. As you have just read, the GSS statistics grouped both genders; therefore, the breakdown of specific violent crimes and a victim's gender was not available. However the goal of reporting these facts was to present the statistical reality of an Aboriginal person's life in Canada, and to make it quite clear that Aboriginal women are by far the most vulnerable to violence in our society.

Conclusion

Statistics, although far from perfect, help to enhance our understanding. Statistics provide the tools required to react intelligently to information. In this sense, statistics represent one of the most important pieces of knowledge that we can use to study, analyze, debate, and learn. If the government that creates our laws and policy cannot distinguish good from faulty reasoning, then we are vulnerable to bad information and manipulation. Erroneous decisions will be made, and the best interests of all Canadians will suffer.

CHAPTER CONCLUSION

Violence takes place! Violent acts left unchecked can escalate. Every victim matters regardless of their perceived worth in society, or their worth compared to that of their offender. In this chapter, the pain and trauma experienced by victims was examined. Statistics were also presented that described the scope of the types of victimizations. Without comprehensive data, it is impossible to put together an authentic picture of the actual scale of violence against women. Data further help to answer important questions: are our laws working, do we have programs in place to help prevent crime, are they culturally sensitive, and if so, how efficient are they? Appropriate programming therefore cannot be developed and assessed without statistical proof.

Multiple Choice Questions

1. Based on the GSS 2009 self-reported victimization results, which of the following represents the most accurate number of those Canadians who indicated they had been a victim and reported their victimization to the police?

   a. 10 percent　　　　　　　　　**b.** 20 percent
   c. 30 percent　　　　　　　　　**d.** 40 percent

2. In Box 4.1, Greg Monforton wrote about the killing of a woman named Lori Dupont. Which of the following statements describes her killer and where this violent act took place?

   a. he was anesthesiologist and it took place in a hospital operating room
   b. he was an emergency room doctor and it took place in the emergency room
   c. he was a police officer and she was killed in her car driving home
   d. he was an educator and he killed her when she was arriving to her home

3. In the GSS 2009 self-reported victimization results, which percentage of the Canadian population aged 15 years reported having been the victim of a sexual assault, a robbery, or a physical assault in the preceding 12 months?

   a. 1 percent　　　　　　　　　**b.** 6 percent
   c. 12 percent　　　　　　　　　**d.** 18 percent

4. According to the GSS self-reported victimization survey, the overall rates of violent victimization between 2004 and 2009 did what?

   a. increased dramatically　　　　**b.** increased slightly
   c. remained stable　　　　　　　**d.** decreased significantly

5. The *Criminal Code of Canada* distinguishes among three levels of sexual assault according to the seriousness of the incident: level 1 is the least serious type of assault and level 3 is the most extreme. According to the police-reported data, which of the following statements is true?

   a. level 1 sexual assault was the most common
   b. level 2 sexual assault was the most common
   c. level 3 sexual assault was the most common
   d. All three levels were evenly reported.

6. Based on the entire population of Canada, which group has been identified as being most at risk to become a victim of sexual assault?

    a. females of all ages 30 to 45
    b. all youth ages 15 to 24
    c. Aboriginal youth ages 15 to 24
    d. No group has been identified to be more at risk than others in Canada.

7. According to statistics regarding various forms of dating violence, which of the following was reported to be the most frequently occurring?

    a. common assault; level 1
    b. sexual assault; level 1
    c. criminal harassment/stalking
    d. uttering threats

8. According to police statistics from 2007 and the reporting trends of sexual assault according to geography, which of the following answers correctly represents the province/territory with the highest and lowest levels of reporting?

    a. Nunavut; Nova Scotia
    b. Northwest Territories
    c. Yukon; Newfoundland
    d. Nunavut; Prince Edward Island

9. A number of common types of date rape drugs and their effects were noted in this chapter. Which of the following is not a street name of one of the drugs listed?

    a. roofies
    b. forget pill
    c. sleepytime
    d. special K

10. In memory of the attack on female engineering students in 1989, December 6 has been officially designated as a National Day of Commemoration in Canada. In what Canadian city did this tragedy take place?

    a. Montreal
    b. Toronto
    c. Quebec City
    d. Vancouver

Discussion Questions

1. Compare and contrast some key differences among sexual assault, stalking, and sexual harassment.

2. From a historical perspective, significant changes have been noted in police data with respect to sexual assault reporting. What distinguishable factors are noted?

3. Lori Dupont's tragic death set in motion a series of events that culminated in the enactment of an important piece of legislation for Canadians living on Ontario. What was this called, and what makes it significant?

Key Terms

coroner's inquest: a hearing that investigates a human death; does not determine civil or criminal responsibility, but instead makes and offers recommendations to improve public safety and prevention of death in similar circumstances.

Criminal Code: first enacted in 1892, the most important source of criminal law in Canada; divided into 28 parts and contains the full listing and explanation of criminal offences and procedure in Canada.

date rape: a sexual assault that occurs within the context of a dating relationship.

feminist: someone who supports feminism, which focuses on women's issues, and seeks gender equality.

Posttraumatic stress disorder (PTSD): a type of stress reaction brought on by a traumatic event and characterized by flashbacks of the experience in the form of disturbing dreams or intrusive recollections, a sense of emotional numbing or restricted range of feelings and heightened body arousal.

quid pro quo: in the area of sexual harassment, a form of sexual blackmail; the conditioning of employment benefits on an employee's sub-mission to unwelcome sexual conduct.

secondary victimization: the act of blaming the victim of a crime rather than the person who committed the crime.

self-report: research investigation of a subject in order to record and report the subject's behaviours.

stigma: social disapproval of action or beliefs that are against cultural norms.

Uniform Crime Reporting Survey (UCR): national crime statistics maintained by the RCMP in Ottawa; offences are grouped into three categories: crimes against the person, crimes against property, and "other" crimes.

victim blaming: attributing responsibility to victims for the bad things that happen to them.

Chapter 5
Family Violence

We fatuously hoped that we might pluck from the human tragedy itself a consciousness of a common destiny which should bring its own healing, that we might extract from life's very misfortunes a power of cooperation which should be effective against them.

Jane Addams. Social worker, social and political activist, community organizer (1860 – 1935).

Chapter Objectives

1   Identify the different forms of family violence and explain their significance.

2   Describe the consequences and impact of family violence.

3   Interpret the statistics regarding the prevalence of family violence.

INTRODUCTION

Today, at the beginning of the second decade of a new millennium, the way in which society views domestic violence has changed dramatically. At one time a married woman had no other refuge but to conform herself entirely to the temper of her husband, because the husband ruled: she was his possession. These attitudes, although ancient, continued for hundreds of years until the women's movement sounded an alarm.

Unfortunately, there still are times when these ancient sentiments regarding women are expressed. They are heard in public and political dialogue, in our courts, through personal opinions, and in current violent relationships. Despite the great victories gained over the years, or the way in which society views or defines spousal abuse and family violence, the overarching problem—and the pain experienced by many—require Canadians to continually confront the changing needs in society.

5.1 DEFINING FAMILY VIOLENCE

A significant challenge was faced by this author in determining what title to give this chapter. It is about violence in the home—sometimes called domestic violence, sometimes family violence. Family violence could be researched and introduced from a gender standpoint and, from the perspective of human development, age: child, adolescent, young adult, adult and elder.

The importance of words and definitions has been extensively debated in the literature on intimate violence. Words paint an immediate picture, and they provide important knowledge. For this writer, it is the victims and their stories that have left unforgettable imprints. Clinical experience has taught that violence exists everywhere. Victims and their victimizers represent every socioeconomic level, profession, education, age, sexual orientation and gender. Violence does not discriminate—in fact, it is quite inclusive.

Recognizing all victims of family violence is not meant to minimize the work that has brought domestic violence onto the political and social agenda. Feminists would argue that not being gender-specific is an inaccurate way to present the realities of family violence. In some cases the reaction is understandable, since the stakes are very high. Statistics don't lie: women are more frequently and more severely injured in intimate relationships. Plus, feminist theory has been influential if not dominant in guiding the domestic violence field. It brought violence to the table for discussion, debate, and resolution.

Naming all victims in a family system is not meant to undermine the enormous problem faced by millions of females. Yet for those who clinically intervene in the lives of families the fact is known that many boys are victimized, and many more wait and disclose their childhood victimization once they are adults. Moreover, adult men are also victimized in their homes. They too have been harmed by those we assumed would provide respect and love. This parallel discovery, although much more muted, has been finding its way slowly into academic studies and the public sphere: male victims exist (Archer, 2000; Fiebert & Gonzalez, 1997; Straus & Gelles, 1986).

The last point to make—and one that is often overlooked—is the role men play when helping and supporting their wives and children. Abusive women, mothers, also exist. Treating violence in the family one-dimensionally, therefore, does not work. Lastly, many men and many male students reading this text are not violent and never will be.

Family violence includes many different forms of abuse that adults or children may experience in their intimate, kinship, or dependent relationships. Family violence also includes being mistreated or neglected by these members. As a result, this module will focus on the sub-categories of spousal abuse (including abuse to women and men) and elder abuse. Separate chapters in this text have been devoted to violence against children and violence in same-sex intimate relationships.

Spousal Violence

The Department of Justice Canada defines spousal abuse as "the violence or mistreatment that a woman or a man may experience at the hands of a marital, common-law or same-sex partner. Spousal abuse may happen at any time during a relationship, and especially when it is breaking down, or after it has ended (Department of Justice, 2007).

Spousal violence is multifaceted. There are different types of violence and an individual could be subjected to more than one. It includes physical and sexual violence; however, many nonviolent but highly injurious behaviours also are noteworthy. They too cause harm, for example emotional, psychological, and economic abuse. Destruction of property or isolation from friends, family, and other potential sources of support can also be added to this definition.

Statistics reveal that the majority of people who are abused are women. Consequently, the term "spousal violence" has been criticized because it is not gender-specific; it does not precisely identify the victim and the abuser. But other labels exist to emphasize gender differences: wife battering, battered wives, wife abuse. Moreover, the term "patriarchal terrorism" has been used to describe a woman who is repeatedly beaten by her violent husband (Johnson, 1995); this was later labelled "intimate terrorism" (Johnson & Ferraro, 2000).

Regardless of the label, at the core of violence is the element of power and control. The intention of all actions is to dominate regardless of the method of violence (Pence & Paymar, 1993; Straus, 1993a; Walker, 1979). Whether it is physical or emotional, it remains a serious concern. Figure 5.1 lists the four major types of abuse: physical, emotional/ psychological, sexual, and economic. This figure also helps to concretely identify what is considered abuse. We will at this point examine wife assault, followed by husband assault.

Wife Assault

A respected and frequently used theoretical approach in understanding wife assault that emerged in the early 1980s was the **Duluth model**, with the conception of the **power and control wheel** (Pence & Paymar, 1993). This theoretical curriculum was developed to illustrate the elements of a battering relationship. Each spoke in the wheel represents a form of behaviour that in total makes up the abusive conduct. (For more information on the Duluth model, refer to Chapter 2.)

The Duluth model helped expand our understanding of spousal violence beyond physical harm. Spousal abuse precisely described as physical violence does not encompass other harmful actions, such as emotional or verbal abuse. These acts themselves are not illegal; however, they are part of a battering pattern, and warn of a potential violent relationship or the existence of one. Verbal indignities are indicators. Verbally deprecating another person is a strategy used to break a person's strength and self-worth, which can eventually overtake the spirit.

We will examine the four types of spousal abuse, beginning with emotional or psychological abuse.

Emotional Abuse Emotional abuse leaves no physical marks, no bruises, no lacerations, no scars; no one can see or notice. It attacks self-worth—one's humanity. Adults are also emotionally neglected. An intimate relationship requires intimacy, and intimacy requires empathy. If one partner withholds information and feelings, then intimacy is weakened. When a partner is ignored they deny their experience and create isolation (Carden, 1994; Holtzworth-Monroe & Stuart, 1994). The following points are examples of emotional abuse.

Physical	Emotional or Psychological	Sexual	Economic
Squeezing	Ignoring	Treating as sex object	Not allowing outside employment
Grabbing	Discounting	Minimizing sexual needs	Interfering with the victim's work performance through harassing activities, such as frequent phone calls or unannounced visits
Pushing, shoving	Demeaning	Criticizing sexuality	Stealing from the victim
Cornering	Countering and correcting everything	Obsessive jealousy	Making the victim's paycheque the abuser's paycheque
Restraining	Making putdowns disguised as jokes	Touching that is unwanted	Putting all the bills in the victim's name
Pulling hair	Forgetting—from promises to dates (birthday, Mother's Day, anniversary)	Calling the victim names during sex	Refusing to pay bills/creditors
Choking	Withholding affection	Demanding sex	Destroying victim's personal belongings
Kicking	Minimizing feelings	Forcing to strip	Placing own wishes before family needs
Throwing things	Ridiculing/insulting	Inflicting sexual humiliation	Controlling the chequebook
Biting	Yelling	Forcing prostitution	Requiring spouse to account for every penny
Harassing	Accusing	Forcing to observe sex	Leaving family's basic needs unmet; family lacking adequate clothing and money for groceries and medication
Stalking	Humiliating	Forcing unwanted acts	Accumulating debt without partner's awareness or deliberately ruining spouse's credit rating
Punching	Destroying valued things	Forcing sex after beatings	Selling family possessions
Striking with a weapon	Threatening to injure pets	Using weapons to force sex	Spending family funds on alcohol/drugs
Denying medical care	Threatening to abandon	Forcing prostitution	Refusing to give spouse personal money
Disfiguring and maiming	Threatening to have spouse declared an unfit mother/parent	Injuring during sex	Cancelling insurance or credit cards without spouse's knowledge
Murdering	Threatening violence		Providing no knowledge of assets/finances

Figure 5.1 Continuum of Harm in Spousal Abuse

Sources: Frieze, 1983; Frieze & Browne, 1989; Frieze et al., 1987; Gannon & Mihorean, 2005; Johnson & Ferraro, 2000; Pence & Paymar, 1993; Straus, 1993a; Walker, 1979.

1. *Discounting* the ideas and thoughts of a spouse is abusive. Discounting denies the authenticity and experience of a person. For example, abusers might cut off a discussion in mid-sentence before their spouse can finish their thought; this is disallowing self-expression.

2. *Forgetting* is a more devious form of emotional abuse. This may involve both overt and covert behaviour. From time to time everyone forgets, but the abuser consistently does so. Some abusers consistently forget important promises they made to their partners, or special dates and celebrations; for instance, their partner's birthday, or Mother's Day (Carden, 1994; Holtzworth-Monroe & Stuart, 1994).

3. *Threatening* is a classic form of emotional abuse. An abuser manipulates his spouse by bringing up her fears. This may include threatening to expose personal information, or threatening to take her children by alleging erroneously she is an unfit parent.

4. *Verbal abuse* includes using words to demean, blame, or unfairly criticize. This form of abuse attacks a person's abilities; self-esteem gradually diminishes, often without her realization. It can include overt angry outbursts and name-calling or blaming and accusations.

When one spouse repeatedly speaks disrespectfully to the other, it might be only a matter of time before retaliation occurs and verbal abuse escalates into yelling, screaming, and name calling. Physical abuse may follow, starting with "accidental" shoves and pushes.

The scope of emotional and verbal abuse is broad. Some types may even go unrecognized or normalized because of the regularity of their occurrence. Over time, victims become acclimatized and lose sight of their worth. They can no longer conceptualize a healthy relationship.

Physical Assault The spectrum of physically abusive behaviours is extensive. Some examples include pushing, shaking, choking, and striking a person with a fist or a weapon causing injury, for example a chipped tooth. Figure 5.1 defines other examples.

Relationship violence often intensifies during a breakup of a marriage or long-term relationship. Stress is heightened. Physical aggression may also increase. Toews, McKenry, and Catlett (2003) found that some men became violent for the first time during the separation period. And a further and more grave form of physical violence exclusive to women is physical violence during pregnancy.

Physical Violence During Pregnancy Violence during pregnancy is generally a topic that no one wants to explore; the harm done to countless women is enough to digest. Unfortunately, women who are in abusive relationships are at greater risk of continued violence during pregnancy. One would hope the opposite would be true, that an abused woman would enjoy a reprieve from violence and experience a peaceful and safe pregnancy. Regrettably, this is not the case (McFarlane, 1992, 1993; Parker, McFarlane, & Soeken, 1994).

Precise occurrences of physical violence during pregnancy are difficult to determine, because women might hesitate to report experiences of violence to survey interviewers due to shame or embarrassment. Yet Canada and other countries have studied this issue which consequently illuminated a serious problem. Studies have shown that physical violence may take place for the first time or become more severe over the course of a pregnancy (Campbell et al., 1992; Campbell, Oliver, & Bullock, 1993; Huth-Bocks, Levendosky, & Bogat, 2002).

The most extreme act of violence leads to death: in extreme cases, men kill their pregnant wives and their unborn children. For example, in 2000 Ganeshram Raghunauth from Pickering, Ontario, poisoned Hemoutie Raghunauth, his 28-year-old pregnant wife, on Mother's Day (*Toronto Star,* 2000), killing her and the baby. Information presented during the murder trial in 2003 indicated that police emergency crews responded to a phone call and later found her unconscious at her home. She was pronounced dead on arrival to the hospital. Toxicology tests showed she had 64 times the lethal amount of cyanide in her blood. The toxicology tests also found that Mrs. Raghunauth was 8 to 10 weeks pregnant when she died.

Abuse During and After Labour and Delivery
Abuse is not just physical violence; emotional harm can transpire during and following the birth of a child. An abusive spouse might try to control a woman's decision to have an epidural, pain medication, or other medically permissible type of interventions. He might attempt to control who is and is not present for the birth. An abusive partner might even choose to not be present for the birth, or leave shortly after.

Since abuse undermines a victim's sense of capability and confidence, the **World Health Organization** believes abused women may not be able to breastfeed successfully, which could further diminish her feeling of competency as a women and a mother. Abuse specific to her role as mother can continue after birth. Examples include the following:

- blaming her because the infant is not the desired gender
- sharing publicly the intimate details that took place during labour and delivery, including her behaviour, fears, changes to her body
- making negative comments about her sexuality, attractiveness, and appearance
- putting her down when she spends time with the baby
- demanding sex soon after birth
- making her stay at home with the baby
- insulting her parenting ability
- threatening to abduct or actually abducting the baby
- telling her she will never get custody of the baby
- preventing her from taking a job or returning to work

Because some abusers maintain control of their victims through socially isolating them, abused women are often unable to access the support of family, friends, local services, and public health agencies.

Economic Abuse The Department of Justice Canada (2009) considers economic or financial abuse any act done without consent in a way that financially benefits one person at the expense of another. Being in command of the household finances is a method used to have authority over a spouse. Economic abuse is a methodical manipulative tactic of power and control. Abusers control the finances by preventing their spouse from working, thereby preventing them from achieving self-sufficiency and financial independence. For those who do work, every dollar is accounted for. Moreover, victims frequently cite income as the strongest and most immediate deterrent to leaving abusive situations.

Sexual Assault The first study on rape in a marriage was conducted in 1982, which revealed that rape in marriage existed (Russell, 1982). As you might remember from Chapter 1, laws protecting women from marital rape did not exist in Canada until 1983. Further, as the research indicated, sexual assaults are perpetrated by current or former male partners significantly more often than by strangers.

Rape by male partners seems to occur most frequently as a form of physical domination in relationships when other forms of physical aggression are ongoing (Basile, 2008; Frieze & Browne, 1989; Frieze, Hymer, & Greenberg, 1987; Russell, 1982). An American study done by Pagelow (1984) found that in relationships in which physical violence occurred, 35 to 59 percent of the female partners experienced sexual as well as nonsexual attacks. Further studies on sexual assault against their spouses indicated that women who have sexually aggressive partners had a higher risk of experiencing more injurious nonsexual aggression than women with male partners who were physically but not sexually violent (Browne, 1993; Frieze & Browne, 1989; Frieze & McHugh; 1992; Shields & Hanneke, 1983).

Violence Overtime: Walker's Cycle of Violence

Onset, type, and frequency of abuse can vary across relationships. Even violent physical aggression is often preceded by nonviolent verbal abuse and can be accompanied by attentive and loving behaviour. Violent relationships do not involve continuous abuse. Episodes are uneven. While no two abused women share the identical experience, some experts have documented that abuse usually follows a cycle made up of three phases. The first to write about the cyclical or phase component of abusive relationships was Lenore Walker in 1979 when she proposed a *cycle theory of violence*. Dr. Walker based her theory on interviews conducted with women who had survived abusive relationships. The goal of the **cycle of violence** theory was to describe and predict the pattern that violent relationships often fall into. Walker identified three phases that

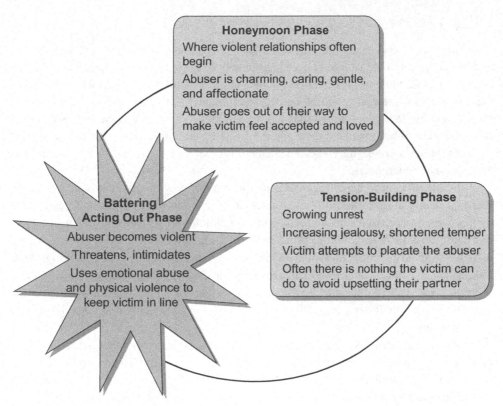

Figure 5.2 Walker's Cycle of Violence

these relationships tended to cycle through: the tension-building phase, the acute battering phase, and the tranquil or loving phase (Walker, 1979). This theory is discussed in detail in Chapter 2.

Walker's theory has been criticized over the years. Some think her sample size was too small and not diverse enough. Others do not believe that domestic violence is as predictable as Walker first made it out to be. Abusers can vary widely in their behaviours, motivations, and tactics. There are numerous ways abusers manipulate and control, many using emotional or verbal abuse. Additionally, some rarely use physical attacks, and some do not cycle through the three phases.

Whether Walker's cycle of violence precisely defines every abusive couple or not, it was and continues to be an important study that accurately describes countless abusive relationships. It also shed a light on abusive behaviour and suggested *why* some victims do not leave their abusers. For many women, throughout these stages exists a continued hope that the violence and abuse will not happen again. Regrettably, this is rarely the case. Violence escalates; it does not end without intervention. Descriptions of spousal violence often raise the question: Why does she stay?

Why Women Stay

Why do women stay in abusive relationships? Why choose to endure such humiliation and brutality; why not just leave? This is a commonly asked question when discussing the issue of spousal violence. It is a question that simplifies a problem that is incredibly complex. It is also somewhat provocative, because it blames the victim. A more fitting statement might be, Why does a man hurt the woman he loves; why does he beat her? These same men are able to manage their anger outside of the home. They are not acting out violently when a colleague makes a statement they don't like, or their boss reprimands them for incomplete work.

The other point to make regarding the question of why a woman would stay is the fact that it might be a question based on an invalid assumption. Research clearly tells us that women do leave abusive relationships, get help, move forward, and heal. Without being able to poll the entire population of women subjected to violence, it seems difficult to even estimate how many victims stay, and if they do, for how long. And, although it might not be apparent to outsiders looking in, many women learn to cope with the violence while they are secretly seeking out the necessary information required to plan their departure—their escape. Leaving an abusive relationship requires serious planning.

Yet, women do stay. Concrete reasons exist to explain why they remain (Frieze et al., 1987). One of the reasons is a woman's fear. Very often the abuser will tell her that if she leaves he will find her and kill her. Studies have shown that one of the most dangerous things a woman can do is leave an abusive spouse (Wilson & Daly, 1993). The severity of spousal violence frequently increases after a relationship is over, or when a woman informs her spouse she is leaving.

Many professionals and advocates tell us that victims are at the greatest danger when trying to get out of an abusive relationship, or just after separation (Browne, 1987; Edleson & Tolman, 1992; Hotton, 1991; Schecter & Ganley, 1995; Wilson & Daly, 1993, 1994). Statistically, this fact was noted as the *most consistent* predictor in Canada's coroner's *Domestic Violence Death Review Reports* (Marra, 2002, 2004, 2005). Violent men might kill or nearly kill their partners because they do not want to lose them. In addition to a recent separation, two other common predictors were noted that existed prior to a domestic homicide: previous domestic violence, and the offender having mental health problems (Marra, 2002, 2004, 2005).

The story of Sandra Clark (surname Atkin at the time of her assault) is a disturbing example of spousal violence. The background to this crime is described in "Canadian Headline News" Box 5.1. Later in this chapter, you will read "From the Pen of . . ." Box 5.7, where Clark herself describes her experiences. What you will notice is that although her story is tragic, Ms. Clark is an exceptionally courageous woman. Her ability to carry on, fight for justice, and make a difference for other victims is nothing short of remarkable. Regrettably, similar acts of intimate violence continue to occur in our society.

5.1 Canadian Headline News: Sandra Clark, Survivor of Attempted Murder

The good life! For Bill and Sandy Atkin it was one long party—expensive furs and cars, winter Caribbean cruises, frequent trips to Florida and Mexico. Summers were spent at the family cottage in Muskoka, sailing and swimming with a house full of friends, barbecues and parties, and months of fun in the sun.

When Bill Atkin's father died, he and one of his brothers inherited the family business; the Leamington-based Atkin-Flowers, which at the time was one of Canada's largest producers of flowers and plants. A partnership soon followed and the family business became known as Yoder-Atkin after a joint venture with the American Yoder seed company. Later, the entire business was sold to Yoder. Their price at the time was estimated to be between a quarter-million and a million dollars. Mr. Atkin became a very wealthy man, and this occurred around the time he met Sandy. Within a year of meeting they would marry. Bill Atkin had been previously widowed, and Sandy was divorced. They blended their two families and became a family of seven. Sandy was a loving wife and mother. Bill was attentive, generous, and fun. For the next 10 years they lived the good life.

Mr. Atkin liked his get-rich-quick schemes, but after many bad financial decisions things began to catch up; loss followed loss. In the midst of all this Sandy had some serious health problems that led to several surgeries and brief hospital stays. Bill became insensitive to her needs. Things started to change. He began to drink more heavily after he sold the family business. Later he began to work out of town during the week, then return on the weekend when he would drink incessantly.

He kept the family finances a secret, never sharing financial information. Accidentally one day Sandy found out from a family friend that they were bankrupt. Despite this, Bill continued to hit the bottle. Sandy took charge, sought employment and began to work. In November of 1986, Sandy told her husband she was leaving the marriage. But she told him she would stay until the children finished their school year in June.

Then, on January 1, 1987, Mr. Atkin entered the bedroom where Sandy was sleeping. What followed was an unimaginable and unthinkable act of violence. Please see "From the Pen of . . ." Box 5.7 to read, in Sandra Clark's own words, the description of this horrendous crime and the injuries she experienced.

During the trial that followed, Mr. Atkin's attorney put forward the defense that his client had been drinking all day; he was drunk, therefore he had no memory of the events that transpired. The Crown Attorney did not call any witnesses. People who had been with Mr. Atkin during the day were never called to give testimony. They might have indicated that in fact he had not been drinking.

Later, an Ontario Supreme Court jury found 53-year-old William Atkin not guilty of attempted murder because he was drunk. He was convicted of aggravated assault. At the time of this crime, the maximum sentence for aggravated assault was 14 years. The Supreme Court Justice sentenced Atkin to the minimum term allowed: two years. The Justice imposed an additional one year for the use of a firearm during the commission of an indictable offence (after all, he did use a gun to shoot his wife in the head). Incidentally, at the time the maximum time for this offence was also 14 years. Mr. Atkin was sentence to three years in total for his crime, committed against his sleeping wife. Sandy continues to cope with her injuries in 2012.

The court's decision left Sandy Atkin devastated, and so too were many within the community. She and countless others began to organize.

(continued)

Sandy wrote a letter to the Crown Attorney who had handled the case, Mr. Denis Harrison. Mr. Harrison had told her earlier that he would not seek an appeal because he did not think it would be successful. She did not accept his position. The media became involved—print, television, and radio took hold of this issue to expose a gross injustice. A public outcry ensued. Mr. Harrison then filed with the Ontario Court of Appeal.

Success followed. In 1988, the Ontario Court of Appeal increased Mr. Atkin's penitentiary term to five years from the original two years, six years in total.

Sandy was unable to support herself during her recovery, but her friends stepped up and took care of Sandy and her children. In Ms. Atkin's words, their children's lives were scattered in the wind. Ms. Atkin went on welfare. She suffered numerous injuries including the development of posttraumatic stress disorder. Her life was forever changed.

Mr. Atkin claimed to have had the loaded gun in his house because he had contemplated suicide. Mr. Atkin stated he had blacked out, and had no memories of the injuries he inflicted upon his wife. He also stated that he would never harm his wife—he loved her, and he still did. Later, after his trial, Mr. Atkin admitted that alcohol affected his life.

But who was Mr. Atkin? What type of man attempts to kill his wife? Many would say he was "privileged." He had money and the social connections that most people could only hope for. He was the nephew of a former Ontario Premier, and his first cousin was the Treasurer of Ontario at the time. He was educated in Leamington, Ontario. He attended private schools in Pickering before entering McMaster University in Hamilton, where he had earned a degree in business administration and economics. He later earned a degree in chartered accounting. After his release from prison he re-married.

The brutal crime that Mr. Atkin committed against his wife changed her life forever. Any sense of safety Sandy Atkin had worked to restore in her life swiftly vanished after Mr. Atkin's release from prison. Fearing for her life, she left the province of Ontario. She did not have enough time to complete the degree she was working on at the University of Windsor, so after moving to Alberta she would continue her classes as a visiting student at the University of Calgary. In time, she earned an honours degree in criminology from the University of Windsor. On the day of her graduation she received the President's Medal for her academic achievement and her contribution to the community. She fought the system for her *own* justice and continues today to seek out justice for innumerable victims.

For an explanation of the levels of courts, appeals, and the criminal justice sentencing process, see Chapter 8.

Reflection Questions

1. Do you think that if this case took place today the judicial decision would have been different? Explain your position.

2. Do you think most people consider spousal violence to be associated with a specific demographic in our society?

Source: Interviews with Sandra Clark and her personal records and letters.

Another chief reason why a woman may stay with or return to an abusive partner is based on resources: housing and money. It is easy to say she should leave, but it is extremely difficult if she does not have the financial means to support herself and her children.

Moreover, if she recently immigrated to Canada, does not speak English, and has no money or a place to go, her situation becomes even more dire. Immigrant women may be particularly vulnerable since they may not have established social support systems (Dasgupta, 1998). Getting out of the abusive relationship is critical, but for many victims money and shelter create realistic roadblocks. And, despite the fact that many women in abusive relationships do work, often this income is not substantial enough to provide the finances necessary to support herself and her children. When there are children involved the concerns are more complex. Children often will be uprooted from their neighbourhood, school, friends, and their other parent.

Although emergency shelters are available in many Canadian cities, they often provide only an immediate emergency solution. Length of stay allowed is problematic; most shelters do not provide a long-term residential solution. Plus, shelters have many rules, and depending on a women's situation (age, culture, and mental health) her ability to adapt to her new situation may be difficult, thereby preventing her from complying with all the expectations. Women in rural areas have even more problems than those in the cities because they are more isolated. Some women have lived on the streets after leaving an abusive partner. Yet they do so even with the more serious fear and reality that those who find themselves living on the streets may lose their children to a child protection agency or to the abusive partner (OAITH, 1996, 1998).

We all know that tackling change requires motivation and energy. An abused woman's emotional state can be debilitated, making it more difficult to take action. Abused women often suffer from depression or anxiety (for details, see the next section in this chapter). Energy loss is a symptom of depression. Imagine the amount of energy required to make and implement a plan of this magnitude. The burden is enormous. Additional reasons have been noted in the literature to explain why abused women remain in abusive relationships (Frieze et al., 1987; Schecter & Ganley, 1995):

- being psychologically immobilized
- cultural/family/religious beliefs that encourage the person to stay
- belief that the abuser might change
- belief that it is her fault, that she somehow provokes his violence
- love for their partner; willingness to do anything to make the relationship work
- fear of loneliness
- fear she cannot make it on her own

The myth that women stay "because they like it" is preposterous and blaming. The violence is the abuser's responsibility, and only his, never the victim's. Women do not take pleasure in being berated or beaten, especially by the men who are supposed to love and support them. He may promise it will never happen again, but without intervention, research tells us that if he did it once chances are he will do it again.

A Violent End to a Violent Relationship

Women are murdered by men. But a topic that also must be addressed is the reality that battered women have killed. Often when a woman finally retaliates it happens after months or years of abuse. They do so out of fear for their lives, or the lives of their children; often it grows from a response to a protracted cycle of victimization—a last resort to end the abuse. Some women kill their husbands as a reaction to a beating, for instance when she stabs him during the violence (Browne, 1987, 1993; Hotton, 2001). The courts might recognize this action as a valid defence, since it could be argued that her life was in imminent danger; she acted in self-defence. Some women, however, do not kill their spouses "in the heat of the moment." Some women have killed their abusive partner while he slept (*R. v. Whynot*) or when he walked away (*R. v. Lavallee*).

Jane Whynot shot and killed her husband Billy Stafford as he slept in their truck. She was acquitted at her original trial, but after the Crown appealed she pleaded guilty to manslaughter and served six months in prison. At her original trial, Jane Whynot used the defence of "self-defence." Her husband had been brutally violent to her throughout their marriage. The night of his death he had made threats about killing her son. She believed him, and she killed him to protect her child. In 1983, the appeal court said that self-defence should not have been considered as she was not being assaulted at the time of the offence—that is, there was no immediate danger (*R. v. Whynot*, [1983] N.S.J. No. 544, 9 C.C.C. (3d) 449 (N.S.C.A.)).

In sharp contrast, almost a decade later, in 1990, a judgment was written by Bertha Wilson, the first woman appointed to the Supreme Court of Canada (see Photo 5.1). This judgment is considered one of her most famous, and the acquittal was the Supreme Court of Canada's first use of the "battered woman's defence." In this case, *R. v. Lavallee,* Ms. Lavallee was acquitted of murder at her original trial, but the Manitoba court of appeal overturned the acquittal. The case was then appealed to the Supreme Court, which restored it, signifying the Court's recognition of the battered woman's defence (*R. v. Lavallee*, [1990] 1 S.C.R. 852 (1990)). For a full description of this story, see "Canadian Headline News" Box 5.2.

5.2 Canadian Headline News: The Supreme Court of Canada's First Use of the Battered Woman Defence

On August 30, 1986, following the scene of a boisterous party, 22-year-old Angelique Lavallee shot her partner, Kevin Rust, in the back of the head as he was walking away from her. They had been living together for three years, and he had a history of beating her. The relationship between Lavallee and Rust was volatile and punctuated by frequent arguments and violence. They would apparently fight for two or three days at a time or several times a week. During the trial, facts were presented to document the years between 1983 and 1986.

Ms. Lavallee also went to the hospital; her injuries included severe bruises, a fractured nose, multiple contusions, and a black eye. Dr. Dirks, a physician who treated Ms. Lavallee, testified that he didn't believe Ms. Lavallee's explanation, on one such occasion, that she had sustained her injuries by falling from a horse. Many other witnesses provided similar testimony. The following facts were recorded:

- A friend of the deceased admitted to seeing or hearing Mr. Rust, beat up Ms. Lavallee on several occasions and, during the preliminary inquiry, described her screaming during one such incident like "a pig being butchered."
- He also stated he saw Ms. Lavallee with a black eye on one occasion and doubted that it was the result of an accident as she and the deceased stated at the time.
- Another acquaintance of the couple recalled seeing Ms. Lavallee with a split lip.

During the altercation on August 30, Mr. Rust slapped, pushed, and hit Ms. Lavallee twice on the head. That night he had threatened to kill her after their guests were gone. When the altercation began he handed Ms. Lavallee a gun and told her that if she did not kill him, he would kill her. She believed him. At first Ms. Lavallee contemplated shooting herself; however, when Mr. Rust turned around to leave she shot him in the back of the head and killed him.

At trial, Ms. Lavallee argued self-defence. An expert witness testified as to her state of mind. The evidence was provided by psychiatrist Dr. Fred Shane, who had extensive experience in treating battered women. Dr. Shane prepared a psychiatric assessment of Ms. Lavallee. The essence of Dr. Shane's opinion was that Ms. Lavallee had been terrorized by Rust to the point of feeling trapped, vulnerable, worthless, and unable to escape the relationship despite the violence. Using Walker's battered woman syndrome, the witness explained that because of the continued abuse she honestly and reasonably believed that her partner was going to kill her later that night. It was a desperate act of survival.

Angelique Lavallee was acquitted at her original trial. The Manitoba Court of Appeal overturned the acquittal, and the Supreme Court restored it in recognition of the "battered woman defence" (*R. v. Lavallee*, [1990] 1 S.C.R. 852 (1990) Docket Number: 21022).

Reflection Question

Justifying murder is a difficult thought for many people to consider. What is your opinion regarding the battered woman defence?

The Honourable Madam Justice Bertha Wilson.
www.scc-csc.gc.ca/court-cour/ju/wilson/index-eng.asp

The 1990 Supreme Court decision in *R. v. Lavallee* was a significant step in society's understanding of wife abuse, and a victory for those involved in the battered woman's movement. However, the *first* Canadian case that asked the courts to assess a woman's life—that is, to examine the life of a battered woman—took place 80 years earlier, in 1911, and is Canada's first recorded case of the battered woman defence. Her name was Angelina Napolitano; she was born in 1882. She was pregnant and the mother of four children when she killed her husband on Easter Sunday while he slept. Angelina struck him four times on the neck and head with an axe. To read the details of Canada's first battered woman defence, see "Canadian Headline News" Box 5.3.

5.3 Canadian Headline News: Canada's First Battered Woman Defence

On May 9, 1911, Angelina Napolitano (1882–1924), a pregnant mother of four children, was convicted in Kingston, Ontario, of murdering her abusive husband and sentenced to hang. This verdict created a massive protest from Britain and North America that ultimately caused a reduction in Angelina's sentence. But what happened?

Angelina Napolitano was born March 12, 1882, in a rural town near Naples, Italy. She married Pietro Napolitano in 1898, and then immigrated with him to New York in 1901. Later, in 1902, they moved to Thessalon, Ontario, eventually settling in Sault Ste. Marie where they lived in the rented upper flat of a house in the section of town called "the little Italy." Pietro worked as a labourer. Together they had four children; at the time of the murder Angelina was pregnant with their fifth child.

The evidence presented at her murder trial painted a picture of women who had been brutally beaten by her husband. Her husband was also forcing her into prostitution, to earn money so he could build a house. (Remember, married women had few legal rights). Angelina however, refused to "be a bad woman," as she stated during the trial.

At the trial it was also discovered that Mrs. Napolitano's face, neck, and shoulder had previously been disfigured when he knifed her nine times. She was hospitalized for two weeks. He was charged with assault and received a suspended sentence. The abuse and Pietro's alcohol consumption continued, and on the fateful day he again told Mrs. Napolitano to prostitute, but this time he added if she did not have money when he awoke he would beat or kill her.

Terrified that he would kill her or take her children away, while he slept Mrs. Napolitano struck him four times on the neck and head with an axe. She then called a neighbour, told him what she had done, and waited for the police to come. Their four children were removed by the Children's Aid Society. It is reported that Angelina Napolitano killed her husband on Easter Sunday, 1911.

On the first day of her trial on May 8, 1911, it was discovered that Mrs. Napolitano had no counsel, therefore the proceedings were adjourned to the next day. Her court-appointed lawyer had no witnesses other than the defendant, who did not fully understand the English language. The Crown attorney had nine witnesses. Justice Byron Moffatt Britton presided over Mrs. Napolitano's trial. Despite the fact that scars from the knife attack were visible, Justice Britton ruled that evidence of her husband's violence against her was inadmissible. It was also reported that elements of racism entered into some public discussions and newspaper reports.

Although the jury had suggested clemency after a three-hour trial, Mrs. Napolitano, who was 29 years old at the time, was convicted and sentenced to hang on August 9, 1911. Her execution date was set to allow her time to give birth to her fifth child. Mrs. Napolitano is considered the first woman in Canada to use the battered woman syndrome defence in a murder case.

Perhaps one could say this is when societal moral justice began. News of the verdict and sentence caused a media frenzy; again the media played a role in pointing out a blatant injustice. An overwhelming number of letters and petitions were sent to the federal justice minister's office. Supporters asked that Mrs. Napolitano's history of abuse be acknowledged and that her life be spared. Correspondence from supporters arrived from Sault Ste. Marie, Toronto, New York, Chicago, and Montreal, and from Austria and Poland.

Further, Canadian, British, and American feminists were instrumental in keeping her case in the forefront. Supporters asked the government to acknowledge Mrs. Napolitano's history of abuse and spare her life; a few even demanded a pardon. Some of the loudest voices were those of feminists who were becoming seasoned lobbyists. Indeed, the presence of an international women's movement helped account for the sustained publicity the case received. Various feminists stressed that Mrs. Napolitano's beatings had constituted sufficient provocation and that she had acted in self-defence. The judge's rejection of this argument, they added, revealed sexist codes.

Also quoted was Dr. Alexander Aalto of Cleveland, Ohio, who in the June 23 issue of *The New York Times* stated he would be willing to hang in place of Mrs. Napolitano. He stated "it would only be fair to Mrs. Napolitano for a man to give his life for her, inasmuch as her life is in peril on account of a man's persecution of her, and because men condemned her" (Airdrie, 2008). At the time, Dr. Aalto had a large practice among Finnish and Swedish citizens.

On July 14, 1911, the federal cabinet commuted her sentence to life imprisonment.

Initially, a member of the Toronto Council of Women offered to pay the Children's Aid Society for care of the four children so that they could remain together, but they were broken up and placed in separate foster homes in Ontario. Newspaper stories kept the public informed of Angelina's children, who remained in the care of the Children's Aid Society. Angelina's fifth child died a few weeks after birth.

Mrs. Napolitano wrote regularly to the Justice Department asking for her freedom. Over time only the Salvation Army continued the efforts on her behalf, and offered to care for her if she were released on parole. On December 30, 1922, Ms. Napolitano left the Kingston prison. All she wanted was to be reunited with her children. She was led to believe that she had to stay in the city until authorized to move, so she worked as a domestic servant. Finally, she wrote to the governor general for permission to go to her children; only then did she learn that she could have left Kingston after her release. There are no records of Mrs. Napolitano ever reuniting with her children.

Reflection Questions

1. Reflect back to Chapter 1 and 2 and the theory regarding a woman's place in society, and the theoretical explanation of oppression. Do you think racism and sexism played a part in her treatment?

2. Do you think Ms. Napolitano's fate would have been different had she been a white women of British descent?

Sources: Airdrie, 2008; *Dictionary of Canadian Biography:* her story in the on line vol. XV www.biographi.ca/009004-119.01-e. php?&id_nbr=7952; *Looking for Angelina, the Movie,* 2004; *New York Times,* June 24, 1911.

Abused Male Spouses

As mentioned at the beginning of this chapter, men are abused in their intimate relationships, yet their situation is different. Males experience shame and embarrassment when disclosing their victimization. In many ways their stigma is comparable to the experience women faced when society was beginning to unearth the issue of violence against women. Fearing they will not be believed and supported, many are reluctant to report or seek help (Straus, 1993b, 2004). Part of this belief stems from the fact that stereotypically men are the abusers (which, *statistically,* they usually are). Another difference is the fact that often the form of violence experienced by men is not as physically dangerous as those suffered by women.

The General Social Survey (GSS) 2004 findings indicated that seven percent of both males and females either in a current or previous marital or common-law union had experienced spousal violence in the five years prior to the survey. The consequences of violence, however, were disproportionally more severe for women. Similar to the previous GSS victimization cycles, in 2009 women were found to be three times more likely than males to report more serious forms of spousal violence (Brennan, 2011). When looking at the most serious types of violence reported, it was found that a larger proportion of women reported being beaten, choked, or threatened or had a gun or knife used against them by their intimate partner than were men. The physical abuse men suffered from a woman consisted of slaps, pushes, and kicks. While these actions are intolerable, they are not as injurious as being physically beaten (Brennan, 2011).

A last point to mention is the fact that abused men generally do not have the same financial vulnerability as women. Most men work outside of the home; many are the major income provider. And generally men are not the primary care giver for children.

Elder Abuse

The mistreatment of seniors has probably received less academic, professional, and public attention compared to the other forms of intimate personal violence. The problem of elder abuse was first introduced in 1975 in British scientific journals under the term "granny-battering" (Baker, 1975; Burston, 1975). Much later, on December 16, 1991, the **United Nations (UN)** passed resolution 46/91 to encourage the governments of the world to incorporate principles of independence, participation, care, self-fulfillment, and dignity for their aging citizens. The goal was to *add life* to the years that have been added due to improved hygiene, control of infectious diseases, and reduction of premature deaths (Seniors Resource, 2005).

In Canada, the ethos of the United Nations declaration is also guaranteed under the *Canadian Charter of Rights and Freedoms*. Violations to the *Charter* might include withholding information, denying privacy, restricting liberty, censoring mail, and not informing the person of her or his rights. Even with the *Charter* and the UN's call for dignity, violence against elder persons is one of the most pressing issues of our time. As this textbook has already documented, people at any position in the human life cycle may be subjected to violence, but the elderly (and very young children) are exceptionally vulnerable.

Before we head into further discussion of this topic, let's pause and determine whether there is an exact number that signifies "old age." When does the notion of being an elder person in our society actually start? What number applies? For the purpose of establishing a definition, when discussing an elderly person in this textbook the terms *senior, older person,* and *elderly person* will be used interchangeably to refer to those aged 65 or over. The age of 65 has also been used statistically around the world to define old age and, more concerning, to denote a time when the global population will see a significant population alteration.

Canada is no exception to this encroaching population shift. According to the 2004 Census, one out of seven Canadians is 65 years or older. The fastest growing group of seniors is those 80 and over. Experts forecast that if the current aging trend continues, more than one in four Canadians will be over age 65 by 2031 (McLachlin, 2008). Furthermore, Canadians over 65 years of age will outnumber those less than 15 years of age by 2015.

So, despite the fact that senior abuse was first reported in 1975, and this societal problem has been around for many decades, the concern is heightened because in the coming decades in Canada and many countries of the world there will be a dramatic increase in the population of elder individuals—those 65 or older (Statistics Canada, 2007). For Canadians in particular, because of our country's commitment to universal health care we have been fortunate to have free access to medical technology and improved healthcare knowledge. Our overall lives and well-being have been enhanced and our chances for longevity have increased. Today the average woman can expect to live to be 83 and the average man 78 years of age. A significant strain will consequently be placed on society and families to care for their parents; as such, a growing concern is the abuse of the elderly person (McLachlin, 2008).

As is the case with other forms of violence, elder maltreatment is complex. No single definition can encompass its many aspects. Also, the question of how to precisely label it is problematic. Lack of agreement about definition has therefore been a hindrance to evaluating research (Bobyk-Krumins & Holosko, 2004). Different terms have been used to indicate abuse or violence against an older person. Most researchers do agree, for the purpose of study and research, that an acceptable starting point is to divide elder abuse into two broad categories, which also include different types. The two broad categories are institutional elder abuse and domestic elder abuse.

Institutional elder abuse occurs in a nursing home or another facility that is paid to care for the elderly person. They usually have a legal or contractual obligation to provide care and protection. Elder abuse may involve both the purposeful or active abuse and the passive abuse that results in negligence due to the ignorance or an inability to provide proper care. In this textbook, the focus will be on domestic elder abuse.

Domestic elder abuse differs from institutional abuse in that the harm is committed by a caregiver who has a special relationship with the elder person, such as an adult child, spouse, friend, or acquaintance. Within this category are various forms of acts of violence similar to those studied in spousal and child abuse: sexual abuse, physical abuse, emotional or psychological abuse, neglect, and financial or material exploitations (Tatara, 1996; Wolf, 1992).

Sexual Abuse of the Elderly Person For most people, sexuality in the later years of life is a challenging topic to discuss, even when it is in the context of a consensual, loving, sexual relationship between two elder people. The sexual victimization of a senior is a topic most people don't want to explore or envision. It causes great discomfort. But remember, sexual violence is about power and control, not sex. Sexual victimizations do take place in Canada. They may take the form of sexual assault, sexual harassment, or sexual exploitation (Department of Justice, 2007). Specifically, a provincial government (Newfoundland & Labrador) publication in Canada states that about 10 percent of seniors who are 65 or over with dementia are sexually abused (Violence Prevention Initiative, 2005). The Department of Justice found, when researching the topic of seniors as victims of crime, that similar to other groups of females, senior females had higher rates of sexual assault than their male counterparts; six versus less than one per 100 000 (Ogrodnik, 2007). The problem of sexual violence is real.

Physical Abuse of the Elderly Person Physical abuse consists of intentional acts to cause pain or injury. Figure 5.1 lists the many forms of physical violence that could also be inflicted upon an elderly person. But an elder person's health is even more compromised. Many are frail; as such, any injury would be exacerbated. For example, a younger person might be able to maintain their balance when forcefully pushed. But an elder person would generally fall and may even break a bone, and a broken bone could cause serious injury or even death.

Two additional forms of physical violence are unique to the elder person: constraints and confinement. Examples would include controlling their environment so their ability to move is restricted, possibly by taking away medically required equipment, medical aids, and assistive devices that allow mobility. Confining an elder person to a room, by locking them up or forcing them to remain in their bed or tying them to furniture, and forcibly restraining them are other examples of physical abuse (Department of Justice, 2007). (These also are *Criminal Code* offences, a topic which is discussed further in Chapter 7.)

Emotional or Psychological Abuse of the Elderly Person Emotional or psychological abuse includes words or behaviours that demean, dehumanize, intimidate, or threaten an older adult. At the most extreme end would be counselling an individual to commit suicide. This action, if taken, would be considered a *Criminal Code* offence in Canada. It is also a type of emotional harm that is specific to this population (Department of Justice, 2007).

Socially isolating, forcing an individual to stop participating in their chosen spiritual or religious faith and ceremonies, or forcing them to participate in ceremonies they do not believe in are considered abusive actions. In the long run, psychological abuse reduces self-worth, and robs individuals of enjoyment of life and a will to live.

Neglect of the Elderly Person Neglect can be defined as the intentional or unintentional failure of the caregiver to fulfill the caregiving obligations (Tatara, 1996; Wolf & Pillemer, 1989). The occurrence of neglect must be chronic, usually involving repeated incidents. Neglect is somewhat difficult to identify or even define, because the person inflicting harm is failing to act rather than overtly abuse. This can be done by failure to provide a clean and safe living environment, adequate nutrition, personal hygiene, medication, physical aids and prostheses, and human contact. Intentional neglect is a way of controlling and influencing the elder person; this form of abuse also has been called active neglect (McDonald & Collins, 2000; Tatara, 1996; Wolf, 1992; Wolf & Pillemer, 1989).

Elderly people who are abused are more often isolated from friends, neighbours, and family than those who are not abused. It is unclear whether this isolation is the product of the abuse, or if it is a necessary condition that provokes the abuse. It is also difficult to know who is being abused since they rarely report the abuse to the police. They may love their abuser; the abuser might be their own child, and this causes immense shame. It is vital that the elderly know they are not responsible for the crime committed against them. Reaching out is essential.

Conclusion

Each type of abuse previously mentioned can exist on its own or in combination with other forms. The abuse can occur once or over a protracted period of time. The nature and consequences of elder abuse will also vary depending on the physical, cognitive, and emotional health of each person.

Family Homicide

Family homicide is not a distinct crime in Canada. These types of incidents involve first-degree murder, second-degree murder, manslaughter, or infanticide committed by family members related by blood, marriage, or adoption (Taylor-Butts, 2010). Just how common is this crime? According to statistics, homicide in Canada, particularly involving family members, is a relatively rare occurrence, accounting for less than one percent of all violent crimes reported to police each year (GSS). Most family homicides involve one spouse killing the other, usually fuelled by a man's attempt to control female sexual and reproductive behaviour (Taylor-Butts, 2010). But what happens when the killing is done by a child, and the victims are their parents and siblings? These forms of killings do not happen often in Canada, but they do occur. To illustrate, we will discuss two family tragedies referred to as the Mandin murders and the Shafia murders.

The first took place in Alberta in 1991. Fifteen-year-old Gavin Mandin was determined to kill his family, and he did. He murdered his mother, Susan; his stepfather, Maurice; and his sisters, 12-year-old Islay and 10-year-old Janelle. To read the details of this story, see "Canadian Headline News" Box 5.4.

5.4 Canadian Headline News: 15-Year-Old Murders Four Family Members

On August 6, 1991, 15-year-old Gavin Mandin fired 10 shots from a lever-action .22-calibre rifle and shot his mother, Susan; his stepfather, Maurice; and his sisters, Islay, 12, and Janelle, 10, outside their hobby farm near Valleyview, Alberta. He shot his sisters at close range, less than five centimetres from their faces, and defiled his mother by cutting open her clothing. He then moved the car his mother and sisters were in and parked it in the woods. He dragged his stepfather's body behind an all-terrain vehicle to hide him in tall grass. He left them all there, in 30-degree heat, to perish. Three adult siblings were not present and survived. On that August day, those siblings lost their parents, their home, and three step-siblings.

Mandin was apprehended by police, and in 1994 he pleaded guilty in adult court to second-degree murder. Sentenced under the *Young Offenders Act,* he received the most severe punishment allowed, a life sentence with no chance of parole for 10 years.

Ten years after the murders, in 2001, the first parole hearing was held at the Bowden Institution in Alberta to determine if Gavin Mandin was ready to be released from prison. If parole were granted, he would be released within the month.

Several members of the victims' family were present at the parole hearing, including two of the three remaining siblings. His grandfather, Dr. Louis Mandin, was also present. Dr. Mandin and Gavin Mandin's aunt, Colette Mandin, were scheduled to speak at the hearing. At the time Colette Mandin had not seen any of the reports prepared for Gavin Mandin's hearing; therefore, she did not know if her step-nephew was about to be released. "I think what's going to be the most difficult is I don't expect him to fully understand or comprehend the impact of his crime on the family and his community," said Mandin. The Mandin family members were the first victims of crime in Canada to present an *oral victim impact* statement at a parole hearing.

Gavin appeared before a three-member panel of the National Parole Board. They learned that day that Gavin contravened prison rules by having pornography on his computer. He also continued to show little concern regarding the impact if his crime. At 25 years of age, he told a parole board that remorse had always been a challenge for him: "I still see myself as a victim." He said that his anger over having to do household chores and his all-consuming hatred of his controlling mother drove him to kill his family. He said he felt trapped: "I remember the feeling of helplessness . . . feeling there was no way out," he told the board. There has never been any evidence that Gavin was abused by his mother or any other member of the family, nor did he specifically state this.

On Thursday, July 19, 2001, Gavin Mandin was denied parole after admitting that he felt justified for murdering his family 10 years prior. His parole eligibility would automatically be reviewed every two years.

Update

Since Gavin Mandin's first parole hearing many more have been scheduled. Each time the family was contacted; many hearings were scheduled and cancelled at the last minute. At the time of writing this textbook, he had changed his name and was transferred to a prison in Ontario, and is slowly receiving escorted and unescorted temporary absences to help prepare for his inevitable release.

Reflection Question

Each time a parole hearing was scheduled the family would be contacted and offered an opportunity to attend. This involved arranging the time (leave from their work), the cost of travel (family must pay). Sometimes the hearing was cancelled at the last minute. What type of system could be implemented to help the surviving victims who want to be part of the parole hearing?

Source: Interviews with Colette Mandin, and her personal documents.

Gavin Mandin's surviving family, like many others, became motivated by their life-altering tragic event. In time, they would challenge the criminal justice system and ask it to examine the needs of the "other" victims—the loved ones who are left behind to grieve and make sense of their loss and their altered life. In "From the Pen of . . ." Box 8.4 in Chapter 8, you will read an account from Colette Mandin. Because of the timing of legislative changes, Colette Mandin and her father would become the first Canadians to provide an oral victim impact statements at a parole hearing in Canada; they did so in response to the murder of their family by Colette's nephew Gavin Mandin.

The next case to discuss occurred more recently, 20 years after the Mandin case. And although much had changed in Canadian society, a particular belief or set of values regarding the roles and rights of women would strongly define this type of murder, referred to as an "honour killing." Despite the motive, in the end four females were killed by not only their brother but also by involving the father and the mother of three of the victims: see "Canadian Headline News" Box 5.5.

5.5 Canadian Headline News: The Shafia Murders

Four counts of guilty in the first degree.

"You have each been convicted of the planned and deliberate murder of four members of your family . . . (a verdict) clearly supported by the evidence presented at this trial, . . . It is difficult to conceive of a more despicable, more heinous crime . . . the apparent reason behind these cold-blooded, shameful murders was that the four completely innocent victims offended your completely twisted concept of honour . . . that has absolutely no place in any civilized society." Judge Robert Maranger.

In January 2012, outside the old Frontenac County courthouse in Kingston, prosecutor Gerard Laarhuis stated it was a good day for Canadian justice but also a sad day given it involved the death of four women.

Two and a half years earlier, on June 30, 2009, four women were discovered submerged in a shallow canal in Kingston, Ontario. According to the coroner's report the victims had all drowned; three of them had bruises on their heads that remain unexplained. The victims

(continued)

were sisters Zainab, 19; Sahar, 17; Geeti, 13; and Rona Amir Mohammad, 52, who was their polygamist father's first wife and a woman the sisters loved like a mother.

Later charged with four counts of first-degree murder of their family members were Montreal Afghan businessman Mohammad Shafia and his wife Tooba Mohammad Yahya, 41, and their son Hamed, 20. They all pleaded not guilty to the killings.

The murder of the four family members had been called an honour killing. "Honour is men's need to control women's sexuality," and is at the core of what is known as "honour killing," expert Dr. Shahrzad Mojab stated during the Shafia murder trial. In some cultures, women are considered the property of men; men are responsible for controlling their behaviour, particularly their sexuality. A woman who is even perceived to be out of control reflects on the man's honour, and "the way to deal with the dishonouring is through the shedding of blood . . . It's a way of purifying the honour of the family and the community" (Blatchford 2011b).

Prosecutors alleged Mohammad Shafia was angry that his daughters defied him, took boyfriends, and dressed in revealing clothes. Additionally, in the trial it was revealed that Rona Amir Mohammad had asked for a divorce, however, Shafia denied the claim. Shafia acknowledged during questioning by Prosecutor Laurie Lacelle that he had called his daughters Zainab and Sahar "whores" and "prostitutes" after he saw photos of them posing in bikinis or underwear or hugging boyfriends; however, he also stated he did not see the photos until after their deaths.

Ontario Superior Court Justice Robert Maranger and a jury had heard that the Shafia daughters were so desperate for more freedom that Zainab ran away, Sahar tried to kill herself, Geeti begged to be taken into foster care, and Ms. Amir was so deeply unhappy she had raised the possibility of a divorce. The older girls also had boyfriends they tried to keep secret.

Dr. Shahrzad Mojab also stated during the trial that, "Often mothers are in the middle . . . They have to negotiate between the power of the male members and the protection of the female members" (Blatchford 2011b). She also said in most of the cases she's studied, "mothers have participated" by either "creating [the environment that supports honour killing] or not preventing the killing."

But as you will read in Chapter 8, Canada's systems of protection are made up of people. Police, child protection, members of the justice system are all sworn to administer justice. They can and do make a difference, however professional knowledge, skills and commitment levels can vary.

So, it should also be fitting to honour in this text, those who demonstrate professional excellence. Staff Sgt. Chris Scott, who led the Shafia investigation, did an outstanding job, and so too did the prosecutors; Assistant Crown Attorney Gerard Laarhuis and Laurie Lacelle. And the Canadian jury was best summed up by Laarhuis when he stated "Four counts of guilty in the first degree verdict sends a very clear message about our Canadian values and the core principles of a free and democratic society that all Canadians enjoy and even visitors to Canada enjoy."

Also added to this list should be freedom from violence, at home in and society!

Reflection Question

In Chapter 8 you will discover when, how, and why a coroner's inquest unfolds. Although a positive prosecution was obtained for these victims, should we as society be asking the following question: With so many supportive and protective services involved in this family's life, how did it escalate to such a point that four women were murdered? Is a coroner's inquest needed to prevent other tragedies like this?

Sources: Blatchford 2011a, 2011b.

Figure 5.3 *The Canadian Leaf,* by Emily Trajkovski

Numerous Canadians each year are left to cope with the physical and emotional pain, plus the shame and fear that follows their victimization.

5.2 IMPACT OF FAMILY VIOLENCE

Being victimized will impact virtually every aspect of a person's life; it seeps in every-where. But how does the impact reveal itself? To begin, let's reflect upon two previous "Canadian Headline News" features, Box 5.2 about Angelique Lavallee and Box 5.3 about Angelina Napolitano. These stories described two women who, after unsuccess-fully trying to cope within their violent relationships, killed their husbands. From their perspectives, they had exhausted all other options. Such cases are controversial, perhaps because in our society we define criminals by *what* they do, not by *why* they do it. What they did was wrong, but it was not part of their normal repertoire of behav-iour. And so we could consider these killings to be the *extreme culminating impact of domestic violence.*

Impact of Spousal Abuse

Impact is multidimensional and uniquely individual. The first theorist to write about the severe impact of being a battered woman was Lenore Walker, who published *The Battered Woman* in 1979 (Browne, 1987; Walker, 1984). Similar to individuals caught in hostage situations or concentration camps, women with violent spouses learn to weigh all alternatives against the perceptions of their assailant's ability to control or to harm them (Browne, 1993). As the violence escalates their alternatives become restricted, and any alternative they might consider may seem too dangerous to try (Browne, 1987, 1993). For these women, from their perspective, their choices evaporate.

Cumulative Effects of Spousal Violence

Even one singular assault can have permanent negative effects. However, severe and repeated violence is destructive. Women who are assaulted frequently sustain physical injuries, and women are more likely than men to be physically injured. Specifically, the GSS 2004 data indicate that 44 percent of female victims of spousal violence suffered a physical injury, compared to 19 percent of men. The GSS 2004 data also reported on the nature, prevalence, and types of physical violence experienced. They found female victims suffered numerous bruises (92 percent), cuts (40 percent), and fractures (7 percent). The physical consequences of domestic violence can be quite severe, up to and including loss of life. The literature is replete with research and discussions about physical injuries.

Emotional Impact Women who are abused frequently talk about the emotional impact, which can be worse than the physical violence. Common sense would lead one to think that living in a domestic combat zone could produce the kind of signs and symptoms associated with terror. First and foremost, victims of spousal violence experience shame, embarrassment, humiliation, abandonment, and an enhanced sense of vulnerability (Browne, 1987, 1993; Walker, 1984). Moreover, many suffer from self-doubt, a sense of worthlessness, and a feeling of failure accompanied by extreme guilt. This is especially true when children must be uprooted because to save herself the family system must be drastically altered. Instead, many women in an effort to regain perspective and avoid embarrassment will deny or minimize the abuse. In order to expand our understanding and sensitivity regarding abused women, Lenore Walker in 1984 coined the term **battered woman syndrome**. This syndrome was discussed in Chapter 1. Box 5.6 provides a description of battered woman syndrome.

5.6 Battered Woman Syndrome

When we hear about emotional trauma, we might think about psychological problems or mental illness. In the mental health field, the clinician's bible is known as the *Diagnostic and Statistical Manual of Mental Disorders (DSM-IV)*. To date, it does not recognize battered woman syndrome (BWS) as a distinct mental disorder. In fact, Dr. Lenore Walker,

the author who conceptualized the theory of BWS, clarified that the syndrome is not an illness but a theory that draws upon the principles of learned helplessness to explain why some women are unable to leave their abusers.

The theory of learned helplessness was developed in the late 1960s and early 1970s by

Martin Seligman, a famous researcher in the field of psychology. The classical battered woman syndrome theory is best regarded as a consequence of the theory of learned helplessness and not a mental illness that afflicts abused women.

Dr. Walker also entered the legal realm when she began giving expert testimony about battered woman syndrome at trials of women accused of killing their abusers. Combining the theories of the "cycle of violence" and learned helplessness, she explained the psychological outcome to women who were repeatedly abused by their husbands.

Source: Walker, 1979.

The psychological impact of trauma does not go away. Repeated abuse has long-lasting traumatic effects. Typical reactions to ongoing violence and aggression include:

- chronic fatigue and tension
- eating disorders
- hypervigilance
- disturbed sleeping; nightmares
- flashbacks; intrusive memories
- anxiety, panic attacks, startle reactions
- depression
- suicidal ideation

These are serious outcomes. From a mental health point of view, many of these problems are consistent with mental health disorders recognized in the *Diagnostic and Statistical Manual of Mental Disorders* (*DSM-IV-TR*). Acute stress disorder or reaction and depression is but one of many possibilities (APA, 2001).

Some victims' lives or bodies have been unequivocally threatened by abusive spouses and many become clinically depressed, neglecting their health and personal appearance. Some succumb to rage.

Imagine facing your own, or someone else's, looming death, violation, personal injury, or overwhelming pain. Many victims feel as if their "life is over" and expect to have no career, family, or otherwise meaningful future. Some victims feel they could never be safe if they lived in close proximity to their abuser. For a personal account of this, see "From the Pen of . . ." Box 5.7 by Sandra Clark. Despite the fear and harm done, you will discover a woman of great strength who somehow found the courage not only to heal, but also to go forward and fight for the rights of other victims. (For additional information regarding Ms. Clark's story, see "Canadian Headline News" Box 5.1.)

A victim's experiences and profound emotions are sufficient to provoke the behaviours, cognitions, and emotions that together are known as posttraumatic stress disorder (PTSD), which is described in detail in Chapter 4 in Box 4.4.

5.7 From the Pen of Sandra Clark, a Survivor of Attempted Murder

When I speak about violence against women, I speak from experience. I am going to tell you my story and I will continue to tell it because telling my story is part of my healing process. It is also my way of working toward breaking the silence and myths regarding domestic violence. Most importantly, if you are reading this textbook, or sitting in a class studying the topic of intimate personal violent crimes, and you are in an abusive relationship, and you learn something from my traumatic story, then my experience will have value.

At the time my story begins, I had been married for 10 years to my now ex-husband, the convicted felon. Over the years his drinking habit had escalated into full-blown alcoholism. I was never physically abused, but the ongoing emotional and verbal abuse took a great toll on me. Then in November of 1986, I gathered up enough courage and I told my husband that I was leaving him. Up until that point I thought I could make it work for our children. Since he worked out of town and was only home on weekends, I thought we could live together, as civilized adults, until the kids finished their school year in June 1987. THAT WAS MY MISTAKE! At least, for quite some time I *thought* it was my mistake. I always used to say "that was my mistake" but now I realize I made no mistake as I was not at fault and the statement blames me, the victim.

As the title of this feature states, I am a survivor of attempted murder. I survived a savage attack that began when my husband stood over me as I slept, and said, "you're not going to leave me you fucking bitch, I'm going to kill you." He then fired a .22 rifle, and shot me through the head at point-blank range. The bullet travelled through my face, shattering my cheekbones, smashing teeth and jawbone, sending bone and metal fragments into my sinus cavities, destroying my left eye, and finally coming to rest one centimetre from my brain.

I got up from bed looking for help. My husband saw me standing in the kitchen, and knowing he had but one bullet found the next best weapon, a butcher knife—which he plunged into my body with such force that part of the blade broke off in my intestines. My stomach and bowels were ripped open, my spleen was torn, and my left lung collapsed. I sustained 37 separate internal injuries.

I have lost my senses of taste and smell and suffer minimal brain damage, which has affected my memory. It has been over two decades since the attack, yet I still live with constant pain and I still face future surgery. Posttraumatic stress has left me with a legacy of horrific nightmares, a sleep disorder, and terrifying memories.

Before the attack, my daughter had come into the bedroom as my ex and I were arguing and I told her I was fine and she should go back to her room as she had a friend sleeping over. He left the room and I went to sleep. Twenty minutes later he was back with the .22 rifle. My daughter heard something and came back to my room. He was leaving the room, and she said to him, "did you hit my mother?" And he said "no, I shot and killed her."

My daughter entered the bedroom and saw me covered in blood and the rifle on the bed. She did not use the bedroom phone because the rifle was there and she feared he would return. She left to use the kitchen phone.

After I was shot I had an out of body experience where I was in a tunnel filled with light and peace. My grandmother was at the end of the tunnel and I was walking toward her. That peace was shattered when I heard my daughter's voice and at that moment I was catapulted from my bed. I walked down the hall and a flight of stairs to the kitchen where my daughter was on the phone with 911. My ex had gone out to start his car, but returned for his briefcase. He saw me standing there, and found the butcher knife.

As he repeatedly stabbed me, all I could think about was not to get my hands near the blade because I used to own a hair salon and needed to work again. I backed out of the kitchen door to the landing and his 15-year-old son came and pushed him down the stairs, grabbed the knife, threw it in the bushes, and ran into the house. He took the entire knife drawer, hid it, and ran out into the yard using a door on the other side of the house. My daughter and I then walked to the neighbour's house and waited for the ambulance.

The police came as he was exiting the house. He put his hands up and said I shot her and I don't know where she is. Both the knife and .22 rifle were admitted as evidence.

As these facts were all laid out, they were difficult to disprove during the criminal justice process. Yes, the "Canadian Criminal Justice System" . . . which leads me to the next part of my story, or should I say my second assault, my second victimization, or the never-ending victimization. Theoretically, it's called secondary victimization.

Review Question

Numerous consequences resulted from the attack on Ms. Clark's life. Consider the description you have read of spousal violence and the personal violent victimization Ms. Clark endured, plus the background information described in Box 5.1. What key universal spousal violence facts exist?

Source: Submitted to Anastasia Bake by Sandra Clark.

As survivors of trauma began to tell their stories in more detail, service providers began to realize not only was there impact from the assault, but emotional injuries were also part of the aftermath. The emotional trauma that often follows the actual violence is sometimes called the second wave of victimization, or the secondary victimization. Further, the violence affected not only the victims, but also their friends, families, and communities as a whole. Many people are victimized when an act of violence takes place, and this is particularly profound when the victim and the victimizer are part of the same family system and community.

Impact on the Children When an Abused Woman Leaves an Abusive Relationship

Ending spousal abuse and thereby the exposure of children to violence in the home is the single best decision to make (Lehmann, 1997). If, however, that exposure has been lengthy the challenges do not disappear; in fact, new difficulties often unfold. On the surface an abusive parent can appear to effectively maintain control and keep the children "in line." When he leaves and this "parenting style" is gone, the children might misbehave because they have not developed internal controls; consequently, they have not learned how to self-regulate their behaviour and impulses. Some might become angry and out of control. Difficulties can arise both at home and school. Conflict and tension between siblings is also possible. Mothers will struggle to establish parental authority within the family.

Added to those issues is the very real stress children face when adjusting to the changes from the family breakup. Examples include:

- leaving their home and moving to a shelter
- decline in standard of living
- residential move, or many moves
- changing schools
- disruption in a child's peer relations

Although it might be very clear to an adult that an abusive man is an unfit parent, he still can be loved and respected by his children. In some abusive homes, over time some children will grow closer to and identify more with him than their mother. Some even go as far as to believe his rationalizations about the abuse being their mother's fault. Therefore, once gone from the family, children may grieve his absence as in any parental separation. For children too young to comprehend the dynamics of violence, the separation, from their perspective, seems to be caused by the mother who leaves the relationship, rather than the father whose behaviour made the relationship dangerous (Huth-Bocks, Levendosky, & Semel, 2001; Krane & Davies, 2007; Levendosky & Graham-Bermann, 2001). Many, consequently, will blame their mothers.

Impact of Violence on Pregnancy

As noted earlier, partner abuse continues to take place when a woman is pregnant. The emotional impact is real, and so too are the serious consequences to the mother's and child's physical well-being. In Statistics Canada's 1993 Canadian study *Violence Against Women Survey*, injuries reported by abused women during their pregnancy included the following:

- they were four times as likely as other abused women to report having experienced very serious violence, including being beaten up, choked, and threatened with a gun/knife or sexually assaulted (Johnson, 1996a).
- of the women who were abused during pregnancy, approximately 18 percent reported that they had suffered a miscarriage or other internal injuries as a result of the abuse (Johnson, 1996a).

Further studies revealed that the most common body parts affected by physical abuse during pregnancy appear to be the head, neck, and abdominal region (McFarlane, 1993; Purwar et al., 1999; Stewart & Cecutti, 1993). Abuse directed at the abdominal region can lead to serious consequences for the mother, fetus, and newborn. It can cause injuries to or rupture the woman's uterus, liver, or spleen. It can cause premature labour, low-birth-weight babies, fetal injury, and more health problems for infants after birth. It is also linked to an increased risk of miscarriage (Torres et al., 2000).

Embarrassment and fear deter women from disclosing their abusive relationship, which may prevent many women from seeking medical attention or attending a prenatal class or postnatal care. Government intervention is also an authentic deterrent; this is especially true for Aboriginal women. Their fear is deeply rooted due to years of legalized oppression.

Impact of Elder Abuse

The impact of elder abuse has not been assessed to the same extent as other types of victimizations. Moreover, the impact would vary according to age, severity, frequency, and the health of the senior. All these variables can influence the outcome.

According to Bobyk-Krumins and Holosko (2004), signs of abuse are not always visible. Whereas a black eye is likely to generate specific questions, a friend or neighbour who comes into contact with an unresponsive elderly person may consider a number of other factors before abuse is even suspected. Furthermore, they write, "in light of the persistent ageist attitudes present in North American society, agitation and unexplained fears, for example, may even be interpreted as part of the aging process or as a sign of dementia" (p. 3). Ageism can be defined as discrimination based on age, especially prejudice against older people (Edwards & Mawani, 2006).

Seniors are also placed at a disadvantaged due to their lifestyle. Unlike children who legally must attend school, an elderly person can be isolated and hidden from view. Yet, the consequences of elder victimization have been studied and they are serious. Figure 5.4 provides various indicators that might be detectable under the various categories of elder abuse (Byers & Hendricks, 1993; Pillemer & Finkelhor, 1988; Quinn & Tomita, 1997). An important cautionary note is that confusing abuse indicators with what may or may not be in fact maltreatment is serious. Proof is needed. Some of the same signs and symptoms can have different causes and might simply indicate something is wrong. Similar to child abuse, determining the cause of symptoms requires an assessment which involves knowledge and skills. In fact, a significant amount of abuse perpetrated against the elderly requires a qualified professional to look beyond initial presenting problems. Recognizing the indicators of abuse is a critical step.

Health Implications for Abused Seniors Stress is a real concern for all victims of abuse and neglect, but for a vulnerable elderly individual the impact is greater; it can cause long-term effects on health and well-being. The stress of abuse creates physical health issues. High blood pressure, breathing problems, stomach problems (e.g., ulcers), and panic attacks are common symptoms among older people who experience abuse. It may set off chest pain or angina, and may be a factor in other serious heart problems. Furthermore, age exacerbates vulnerability. Compared to younger people, in general elder adults have diminished physical resilience and strength. An injury or the amassing of injuries over time can lead to serious harm or death (McDonald & Collins, 2000; Wolf, 1988).

Type	Possible Indicators
Physical abuse	Skin discolouration Burns, especially if they leave a pattern Fractures, sprains, lacerations
Sexual abuse	Visual signs are noticed or indicated: genital cuts, venereal disease, pain, vaginal or anal bleeding, overt sexual behaviour There might also be a hesitation to speak openly (shame)
Emotional or psychological	Disturbance of sleep, eating Loss of energy and lethargy Loss of interest in things the person normally enjoys Isolation and withdrawal Unusual agitation or trembling
Financial abuse or material exploitation	Sudden inability to pay bills Unusual bank activity Bank statements stop arriving at elder's home Given documents to sign that the elder does not understand Quality of care is less than elderly person can afford Forgery of signature on personal cheques or legal documents Forcing or tricking an older adult to sell a home or possessions, or to pay for unnecessary services
Intentional neglect	Severe malnutrition or dehydration Blood levels that are inconsistent with medication compliance reported by primary caretaker Skin rashes Lack of eyeglasses and hearing aids, if required Untreated injuries

Figure 5.4 Indicators of Elder Abuse

Sources: Bobyk-Krumins & Holosko, 2004; Byers & Hendricks, 1993; Pillemer & Finkelhor, 1988; Quinn & Tomita, 1997; Wolf, 1988.

Some elder victims may simply give up, become withdrawn, or lose interest in life. This might be manifested in their self-car, including poor eating habits, refusing to eat, and not taking their medication or following the proper schedule. Some may even begin to drink alcohol, or drink more, to cope with their emotional and physical pain. Some have suicidal thoughts.

Professionals who study human development would agree that we are all constantly learning, adapting, and developing. Change never stops, and old age is no exception. Erik Erikson, a human developmental theorist, proposed that our social and psychological development involves eight stages that span our human life cycle. At each of these stages we face a specific conflict. Two options are always presented: one positive, one negative. The last stage, integrity versus despair, is the conflict we will all confront in old age. Integrity refers to whether or not all the aspects of a person's life add up to have significance and worth. If the older individual is unable to imagine life as having overall meaning, Erikson suggests, they may fall into despair.

Responding to elder abuse, therfore, is critical. So too is identifying the indicators that bring about the stressors that create the incubator encouraging the growth of abuse.

Most importantly, elder abuse must be placed front and centre on society's agenda. Our elderly Canadian citizens deserve to know their lives are valued and meaningful.

Impact of Family Violence Specific to Aboriginal People

The legacy of the residential school system is the direct result of the Canadian laws that created the residential school system and the subsequent government policies that conceptualized the Sixties Scoop (see Chapter 1). Intergenerational or multi-generational trauma happens when the effects of trauma are not resolved in one generation. When trauma is ignored and there is no support for dealing with it, the trauma will be passed from one generation to the next. Wesley-Esquimaux and Smolewski (1999) specifically described this in their report for the Aboriginal Healing Foundation.

> Intolerable, unresolved and cumulative stress and grief experienced by communities and nations became translated, in time, into a collective experience of cultural disruption and a collective memory of powerlessness and loss. In turn, this was passed on to successive generations as a collective contagion, manifesting itself in a variety of social problems that Aboriginal people across the continent continue to experience today. . . .
>
> These examples, which include Indigenous nations of South and Central Americas, help explain how First Nation people were traumatized in a global context and that this global context of trauma and suffering produces similar psychological and social reactions in trauma victims, regardless of their cultural background or direct experience with the original source of the trauma. (p. 5)

For decades, adult survivors of residential school abuse found themselves struggling alone with the pain, rage, and grief of unresolved trauma. Like most people in society they sought and hoped for peace, love, and life's meaning through marriage and having their own children. However, many found themselves unprepared for, and often overwhelmed by the complex demands of parenting and intimacy. They had no positive role models. Some were re-victimized in their spousal relationships or they became abusers of their partners, children, or parents. Survivors, as well as their culture and communities, have faced inconceivable difficulties and hardships (Aboriginal Healing Foundation, 1999).

Conclusion

All forms of family violence affect victims and their families, friends, and communities. When one family member seriously harms or kills another, the grief and confusion is even more unimaginable. In some cases, depending on the nature of the family dynamics, relationships with the abuser or killer create schisms within a family, community, or city. Some people feel sadness, shame, and guilt, while others become enraged at their inability to know and consequently protect the victim or stop the violence. At a time when people need to come together, many are left shocked and searching to find the best way to cope. Family and friends who are left in the wake of violence are in their own right victimized.

5.3 STATISTICS AND PREVALENCE OF FAMILY VIOLENCE

Home at last, safe and sound. . . . Wait, not so fast!

In order to describe the statistical prevalence of the various forms of family violence, we will use primary data sources to analyze spousal violence. These are the incident-based Uniform Crime Reports (UCR2) and the General Social Survey reports (GSS). These statistical sources are discussed in detail in Chapter 4.

An additional research study that will be highlighted is the Violence Against Women Survey (VAWS), which was conducted in 1993. It randomly selected and interviewed by telephone 12 300 Canadian women, 18 years of age and older, about their experiences of violence. The primary objective of the survey was to provide reliable estimates of the nature and extent of male violence against women in Canada. These data will be discussed primarily in the section on violence in pregnancy.

Violence experienced by a spouse or common-law partner is measured in the General Social Survey on Victimization (GSS) by a module of 10 questions. This questionnaire consisted of asking respondents about *unambiguous* types of actions instead of simply asking about "violence" or "assaults." This approach was used to minimize differing interpretations of what constitutes violent behaviour.

Spousal Violence

The first statistics to present are based on the outcome of the 1993 Violence Against Women Survey (Statistics Canada/VAWS, 1993). The survey found that 29 percent of women who had ever been married or had lived with a man in a common-law relationship reported having been physically or sexually abused by their partner at some point during the relationship.

Interestingly, according to the General Social Survey on Victimization, statistics indicated that 12 percent of women had been assaulted by a spousal partner in the preceding five years. A slight but significant decline also occurred for women in 1999, when it dropped to eight percent. Recently, an estimated seven percent of women in a current or previous spousal relationship (i.e., living in a common-law or marital relationship) encountered spousal violence during the five years up to and including 2004 (GSS, 2004). These figures for women represent approximately 690 000 women in 1999 and 653 000 in 2004. Men also saw a decline; the figures for men were 7 percent in 1999 and 6 percent in 2004.

According to Brennan (2011), the incidence of spousal violence reported in the GSS 2009 cycle indicated that the numbers remained stable, at about six percent of the Canadian adult population.

An important variable to underscore is that fewer than 3 in 10 (28 percent) victims of spousal violence reported their victimization to the police. That would specifically include 36 percent of female victims, and 17 percent of male spousal victims (Mihorean, 2005). Despite the lack of reporting, the following data were generated by the 2007 incident-based Uniform Crime Reporting Survey (UCR2). There were nearly 335 700 reported incidents of violent crime across Canada (UCR2, 2007). About one-third of reported violent crimes were committed by

- friends or acquaintances of the victim: 38 percent

- family members: 23 percent

- strangers: 23 percent

Of the nearly 75 800 incidents of police-reported family violence in 2007, nearly 40 200 were violent incidents perpetrated by a current spouse, common-law partner, or ex-spouse. Spousal violence represented more than half (53 percent) of family violence in 2007, and about 12 percent of all police-reported violent crime in Canada (Taylor-Butts & Porter, 2011).

Of these reports, female victims were overwhelmingly the majority of those who reported to the police. In 2007, more than 8 in 10 victims of police-reported spousal violence were female, while 17 percent were male (Mihorean, 2005). Specifically, they were:

- 305 per 100 000 for female spousal victims

- 67 per 100 000 for male spousal victims

Spousal violence was more likely to occur between current spouses or common-law partners (71 percent) than between former spouses or partners (29 percent). These findings were consistent for every province and territory.

Nationally, the police-reported spousal violence rate stood at 188 per 100 000 in 2007. While police-reported data are not completely geographically representative, among those provinces where there was full coverage rates of spousal violence were highest in Saskatchewan and lowest in New Brunswick. In Canada, the rates of spousal violence per 100 000 population were

- Saskatchewan: 329

- Alberta: 249

- Quebec: 241

- Manitoba: 215

- Prince Edward Island: 128

- Newfoundland and Labrador: 123

- New Brunswick: 84

Rates of spousal violence against women have remained relatively unchanged in all provinces. The largest change was recorded in Prince Edward Island, where the rates dropped by half. Newfoundland and Labrador was the only jurisdiction to show a rise in spousal violence over this five-year period.

Severity and Type of Spousal Violence

Emotional Violence Spousal violence involves various actions. Emotional abuse is a salient component of the cycle of violence. The following information describes the type and prevalence of emotional abuse that was reported in the 1999 and 2004 General Social Survey. A summary of those data is presented in Table 5.1.

Physical Violence When analyzing the most serious types of violence reported in the GSS (2004), women experienced more serious forms of violence than men in the previous five years. Specifically, women overall were two-and-a-half times as likely as men to report forms of violence such as being beaten, choked, threatened with a gun or knife, and sexually assaulted. The estimated number of women and men who experienced these types of assaults over the five-year period was 254 000 for women and 89 000 for men.

Specifically, 39 percent of women reported being beaten, choked, or threatened with or had a gun or knife used against them by their intimate partner compared to 16 percent of the men. Men, on the other hand, were most likely to self-report being pushed, shoved, or slapped (34 percent), and being kicked, bitten, hit, or hit with something (34 percent) (see Table 5.2) (Brennan, 2011). One limitation of the GSS 2004 data is that they do not indicate the level of force used in each of these violent acts.

Although the types of criminal offences committed against female and male victims of spousal violence were generally similar, a few exceptions were noted in the police-reported data. Specifically, in cases of spousal violence, 23 percent of men were victims of major assault, compared to 13 percent of female victims of spousal violence. One possible reason for this difference may be due to the fact that male victims of spousal violence were more likely to have had a weapon used against them (15 percent of male victims versus 5 percent of female victims), while physical force was more likely used against female victims (46 percent of female victims versus 38 percent of male victims).

When examining the issue of injuries resulting from spousal assaults, the 2009 GSS found that 3 in 10 spousal violence victims had been injured during the abusive act, with females being twice as likely as males to report an injury (42 percent versus 18 percent). Among those who stated that they had been injured, bruises were the most common form of injury reported by both female (95 percent) and male (75 percent) victims. Male victims were more likely than female victims to report suffering cuts, scratches, or burns (59 percent versus 30 percent). Fewer than 1 in 10 females reported bone fractures as an injury. Among victims of spousal violence who reported an injury, 13 percent stated that they were hospitalized as a result of the violence (Brennan, 2011).

Table 5.1 Number and Percentage of Women and Men Reporting Emotional Abuse by Type of Abuse, Past 5 Years, 1999 and 2004

Type of Emotional Abuse	Female 1999		Female 2004		Male 1999		Male 2004	
	No. (000s)	%	No. (000s)	%	No. (000s)	%	No. (000s)	%
Total population 15 years and older with current or previous spouse	8356	100	9048	100	8346	100	9006	100
Any emotional/ financial abuse	1552	19	1616	18	1487	18	1492	17
He/she tried to limit contact with family and friends	606	7	588	6	447	5	451	5
He/she put you down or called you names to make you feel bad	1006	12	1153	13	554	7	646	7
He/she was jealous and did not want you to talk to other men/women	888	11	829	9	885	11	858	10
He/she harmed, or threatened to harm, someone close to you	320	4	316	3	84	1	120	1
He/she demanded to know who you were with and where you were at all times	750	9	712	8	727	9	732	8
He/she damaged or destroyed your possessions or property	456	5	457	5	198	2	246	3
He/she prevented you from knowing about or having access to the family income, even if you asked	322	4	367	4	124	1	186	2

Source: Adapted from Statistics Canada, General Social Survey, 2005 data.

Table 5.2 Women Experience More Serious Violence Than Men

Type of Violence	Female Victims	Male Victims
Threatened, threw something	11%	15%
Pushed, shoved, slapped	40%	34%
Kicked, bitten, hit, hit with something	10%	34%
Beaten, choked, used a gun/knife, sexually assaulted	39%	16%

Source: Adapted from Mihorean, 2005.

Table 5.3 Changes in the Severity of Spousal Assaults Against Women Over Time, 1993, 1999, and 2004

Type of Violence	1993	1999	2004
Threatened, threw something	6%	10%	11%
Pushed, shoved, slapped	35%	35%	40%
Kicked, bitten, hit, hit with something	9%	11%	10%
Beaten, choked, used a gun/knife, sexually assaulted	50%	43%	39%

Source: Mihorean, 2005.

Females were also more likely than males to report multiple victimizations, at 57 percent and 40 percent, respectively. This finding suggests that despite similar prevalence rates reported by women and men, assaults on women were more frequent and more serious (Brennan, 2011).

The bright side of these dark facts is that when comparing the most recent data with previous statistics (1993, 1999, and 2004) a slight reduction in the *severity* of the assaults occurred. Specifically, there has been a drop across all three time periods with respect to the percentage of female victims of spousal violence who were subjected to the most severe types of assault (being beaten, choked, threatened with a gun or knife, or sexually assaulted), from 50 percent of all victims in 1993, to 43 percent in 1999, to 39 percent in 2004. The change from 43 percent to 39 percent is arguably not very significant, but it is a decrease in the right direction. Table 5.3 provides an outline.

An important point to make when examining the statistics is that 16 percent of women who had experienced spousal violence in the past five years indicated that the most serious was being sexually assaulted by their partner (Mihorean, 2005). Improvements have been noted. These statistical changes may be an outcome of better societal interventions, which helps reduce the opportunity for violence to escalate. The decline noted in violence in spousal relationships is also consistent with the decline in spousal homicides. Yet, these facts have not resulted in a decrease in the use of shelters for abused women (see Chapter 8).

Who Are Spousal Abuse Victims?

Income and education had little effect on risk. Victims of spousal violence similarly reported all levels of income. Whether one earned a household income of less than $30 000 or more than $60 000, rates of spousal violence held constant. Likewise, the level of educational achievement had little impact on the level of violence overall, with respect to both the victim's education and the abusive partner's education (Mihorean, 2005).

Moreover, whether one lives in an urban or rural area also had little impact on their risk of becoming the victim of spousal violence. No statistical variation was found for both men and women with respect to living in either an urban or rural area.

But some differences did exist. For female victims, the rate of spousal violence was highest among women aged 25 to 34 (632 per 100 000 population). For men, the rate was highest among those aged 35 to 44 (125 per 100 000 population). However, for both male and female victims, the police-reported rate of spousal violence was lowest among adults aged 55 or older (46 per 100 000 for women, and 20 per 100 000 for men) (Brennan, 2011).

Family type also creates vulnerability. Research suggests that family composition can impact the level of violence in a household. Those living in a step-family were at increased risk of violence (Brzozowski, Taylor-Butts, & Johnson, 2006; Daly et al., 1993; Klymchuk et al., 2002). Police information also supported these findings.

Violence During Pregnancy

The *Maternity Experiences Survey* (MES) was conducted in 2006 by Statistics Canada on behalf of the Public Health Agency of Canada, and was the first national survey devoted to this topic (Public Health Agency of Canada, 2009). Its purpose was to collect data on important perinatal health indicators from mothers who had recently given birth. Telephone interviews were conducted with more than 6000 new mothers aged 15 years and over and covered a range of health issues related to pregnancy; questions concerning physical and sexual abuse were also included.

Of the mothers who had recently given birth, 74 percent reported that partner abuse occurred before they were pregnant. Further, this sample of women indicated that:

- 32 percent were abused during their pregnancy

- 47.6 percent stated the level of violence during their pregnancy stayed the same

- 5.4 percent experienced an increase

- 16.3 percent experienced an increase in violence after the birth of the baby

- 32.2 percent experienced the same level of violence after the birth

- 82.2 percent of these women stated that the person perpetrating the abuse knew she was pregnant (Public Health Agency of Canada, 2009, p. 95)

Earlier Canadian studies in 1993 and 1999 yielded similar results. Specifically, they estimated the prevalence of physical abuse during pregnancy to be 5.7 percent (Muhajarine & D'Arcy, 1999) and 6.6 percent (Stewart & Cecutti, 1993). The sample in the first study consisted of pregnant women attending a publicly funded, community-based health program in Saskatoon. In the second study, done by Stewart and Cecutti (1993), the women surveyed were receiving prenatal care from family physicians and obstetricians working in either community settings or university teaching hospitals in Toronto. Their results showed that:

- among those physically abused during pregnancy, the first episode of physical abuse occurred during the pregnancy in 14 percent of cases; 86 percent reported previous abuse

- 64 percent of the abused women reported an increase in abuse during pregnancy
- 95 percent of women who were physically abused in the first trimester of their pregnancy stated they had also been physically abused in the three-month period after delivery (Stewart, 1994).

Moreover, when analyzing the 29 percent of women who had acknowledged they were physically or sexually abused by their partner, the 1993 Violence Against Women Survey revealed the following statistics regarding the violence and their pregnancies:

- 21 percent had been assaulted by their partners during pregnancy
- 40 percent of the women who were abused during pregnancy reported that the abuse began during pregnancy

Aboriginal Spousal Violence

The under-reporting of victimization, particularly for domestic violence, is a serious concern in Canada, but it is believed that in many Aboriginal communities the problem is far more severe (Chartrand & McKay, 2006; LaPrairie, 1995). LaPrairie (1995) reported in her study of Aboriginal victimization in urban centres that 74 percent of respondents who experienced family violence did not report their victimization.

Changes made to the 2004 GSS made it possible to look at spousal violence rates among Aboriginal people because of the addition of a question to the survey that was adapted from the Census that asked respondents to self-identify their race/ethnicity, including whether they were Aboriginal (that is, North American Indian, Métis, or Inuit).

Through this question, 2 percent of respondents aged 15 years of age and older living in the 10 provinces identified themselves as Aboriginal. This figure is consistent with the proportion of Aboriginal people living in the 10 provinces according to the 2001 Census.

The GSS 2004 found that Aboriginal people were three times more likely to be a victim of spousal violence than those who were non-Aboriginal (21 percent versus 7 percent). Unlike non-Aboriginal women and men, where the difference in the rate of spousal violence was found to be statistically significant, there was no statistical difference between the rate of spousal violence experienced by Aboriginal women (24 percent) and Aboriginal men (18 percent). And, unlike the non-Aboriginal population, the rates of self-reported spousal violence against Aboriginal women and men between 1999 and 2004 have not changed significantly. Table 5.4 provides information regarding the percentage of Aboriginal and non-Aboriginal men and women who self-reported being a victim of spousal violence.

Further research reveals that Aboriginal women experience dramatically higher rates of violent victimization than non-Aboriginal women (Brzozowski, Taylor-Butts, & Johnson, 2006; de Léséleuc & Brzozowski, 2004; Proulx & Perrault, 2000). Table 5.5 specifically illustrates the comparison between Aboriginal women and non-Aboriginal women.

Table 5.4 Aboriginal and Non-Aboriginal Men and Women, Self-Reported Spousal Violence in the Previous Five Years

	Female	Male
Aboriginal: 1999	25%	13%
Aboriginal: 2004	24%	18%
Non-Aboriginal: 1999	8%	7%
Non-Aboriginal: 2004	7%	6%

Sources: Adapted from Statistics Canada; General Social Survey, 1999 and 2004.

Violence within the domestic context is the most pervasive form of victimization experienced by Aboriginal women. Nearly one-quarter (24 percent) of Aboriginal women in Canada reported having been assaulted by a current or former spouse, compared to 7 percent of non-Aboriginal women (Brzozowski et al., 2006).

Additionally, Aboriginal victims of spousal violence experience more serious forms of violence at the hands of their intimate partners than do non-Aboriginal spousal violence victims (Johnson & Hotton, 2001). Overall, Aboriginal victims of spousal violence were more likely than non-Aboriginal victims to state that they were beaten, choked, threatened with or had a gun or knife used against them, or were sexually assaulted (41 percent versus 27 percent).

When considering only female victims of spousal violence, differences in the level of serious violence emerge more strongly between Aboriginal and non-Aboriginal populations. While 37 percent of non-Aboriginal women reported severe and potentially life threatening violence, including being beaten, choked, threatened with or having a gun or knife used against them, or were sexually assaulted, this figure increased to 54 percent for Aboriginal women (Table 5.5). The numbers of Aboriginal men who experienced being beaten, choked, threatened with or had a gun or knife used against them, or were sexually assaulted were too small to produce reliable estimates (Mihorean, 2005).

Table 5.5 Aboriginal Women More Vulnerable to Violence Than Non-Aboriginal Women

	Aboriginal Women	Non-Aboriginal Women
Been assaulted by a current or former spouse	24%	7%
Reported having been assaulted by a current or former spouse	24%	7%
Experienced emotional abuse	36%	17%
Reported being beaten, choked, threatened with or had a gun or knife used	54%	37%
Experienced injury resulting from violence	43%	31%
Feared for their life as a result of the violence	33%	22%

Source: Mihorean, 2005

Similar differences existed for emotional abuse. In the previous five-year period, 36 percent of Aboriginal people experienced emotional abuse from either a current or previous marital or common-law partner compared to 17 percent of the non-Aboriginal people. This was true in the case of both genders (37 percent versus 17 percent for women, and 36 percent versus 16 percent for men).

Given that the level of violence experienced by Aboriginal people was generally more serious than that experienced by non-Aboriginal victims of spousal violence, it is not surprising that the injuries reported by these two populations are different (43 percent Aboriginal versus 31 percent non-Aboriginal). Also, a greater proportion of Aboriginal victims than non-Aboriginal victims stated that they feared for their life as a result of the violence (33 percent versus 22 percent) (Mihorean, 2005).

It is important to consider that the results of the survey described rates of violence committed against those who self-identified as Aboriginal, but does not distinguish the identity of the *perpetrator*. In addition, this analysis does not include the Northwest Territories, Yukon, or Nunavut, where high concentrations of Aboriginal people live.

Elder Abuse

It is difficult to know exactly how many seniors in Canada are harmed each year. Violence against seniors takes many forms and is influenced by a wide range of factors. Problems in reporting and the differences in definitions also make elder abuse mostly a hidden crime, making the real extent of elder abuse anyone's guess. What's more, it is impossible to be physically violated and not be emotionally harmed, so there is overlap.

Yet effective intervention and treatment requires statistical data. Once in a while, we do get a glimpse of the problem from large surveys that are conducted in Canada or the United States.

The pioneers who systematically studied elderly abuse in North America were Pillemer and Finkelhor (Bobyk-Krumins & Holosko, 2004). Pillemer and Finkelhor conducted a landmark study in the greater Boston area in 1985–86, designed to determine the level of physical and verbal abuse and neglect experienced in the elderly population. They found from their sample of 2020 seniors that 3.2 percent had been maltreated.

Since that time, Canada has made a national effort to begin to study the pervasiveness of violence against elder Canadians. A comparable study to Pillemer & Finkelhor (1988) was done in Canada, using a national telephone survey in 1990. It revealed that four percent or 100 000 elderly persons living in dwellings had recently suffered from one or more events of abuse (Podnieks et al., 1990).

An additional study was completed by the Canadian government through the national General Social Survey on Victimization (GSS, 1999). Of those adults over the age of 65 who responded, seven percent reported experiencing either emotional or economic abuse by an adult child, spouse, or caregiver within the last five years. It is believed that as many as 10 percent of the elderly living in the community and using community-based services are subjected to abuse.

Research studies also show that only one in four cases of elder abuse are reported (Besserer et al., 2001). Psychological and financial abuses are listed as the most common types of abuse, both reported and unreported. Physical abuse is the third most prevalent type of abuse, generally perpetrated by spouses. Moreover, elder abuse shows an escalating pattern: from 1986 to 1998 elder abuse has increased by almost 20 percent nationwide (Besserer et al., 2001). However, this may be the tip of an iceberg.

Elder abuse, similar to child and spousal abuse, is under-reported. The reasons behind under-reporting vary, but many are similar to why individuals who witness or suspect child abuse may not report. People don't want to get involved, and many people do not want to interfere in the personal matters of other people. But comparable to cases of child abuse, if someone does witness abuse it is critical to come forward on the elder person's behalf, rather than stay silent.

Why report? Self-reporting their own victimization is a difficult task for an elder person, as it is for all victims. Feelings of shame and stigma exist, but unique to the elderly person is the fact that often their mental or cognitive abilities might have become impaired, or they may have physical disabilities (Health Canada, 2002). Or, like children, they may be totally dependent on the abuser for care, and therefore fear they will be removed from their home. For a senior this might lead to a forced institutionalization (Health Canada, 2002).

Conclusion

In many ways elder abuse is positioned to be the next area of national concern. As chapter 1 described, we have seen tremendous examples of social activism so there is no doubt positive substantive progress is possible. Interestingly, if we consider time and space, many of the members of this new population of Canadians may well be those who 30 or 40 years earlier were advocating for the rights of children and women.

Family Homicide

The last theme required to complete this section of statistics relates to the most extreme act of violence: murder. Homicides are relatively rare in Canada, and in 2007 they made up less than one percent of all violent crime.

Spousal Homicide Spousal homicides accounted for 16 percent of all solved homicides in 2007, and represented nearly half of all homicides committed by family members. Women in Canada are only about half as likely as men to be murdered; however, one in five homicides in Canada involves the killing of an intimate partner (Orgrodnik, 2009).

Consistent with other forms of victimization, women are much more likely than male victims to be killed by someone they know, particularly a family member. Rates of spousal homicide against both female and male victims have fluctuated over the past 30 years but have showed an overall decline. Between 1974 and 2003, the rate of spousal homicide against females has typically been four to five times higher than the rate of male spousal homicide. The rate of spousal homicide declined:

Female victims

- 1974: 16.5 per million spouses
- 2003: 7.5 per million spouses

Male victims

- 1974: 4.4 per million spouses
- 2003: 1.7 per million spouses

Common-Law Couples Most Often Victims of Spousal Homicide The GSS further indicated that 37 percent of all female homicide victims in 2004 were killed by a spouse or former spouse. Common-law spouses and those separated from a spouse were overrepresented as victims of spousal homicide in Canada. Noteworthy is the fact that a larger proportion of separated women were killed by a spouse than men who were separated (26 percent compared to 11 percent). A larger proportion of males (54 percent), however, were killed by their common-law partner compared to females (35 percent).

Young Adults Are Most Vulnerable to Spousal Homicide Age matters. Rates of spousal violence were found to be highest among certain segments of the population. Specifically, young adults are at greater risk of spousal homicide, but as is in the case of all forms of violence toward women, young women were at greater risk of being a victim of spousal homicide.

Between 1994 and 2003, females aged 15 to 24 had the highest rate of spousal homicide (22.5 per million female spouses). This rate is nearly three times the overall rate of spousal homicide for other female victims during the same period (7.7 per million female spouses) and nearly three times the rate of males in the same age range of 15 to 24 (8.5 per million male spouses) (Orgrodnik, 2009). And while the total of young male spouses was lower than that of their female counterparts, their risk was more than four times the rate for all other male spouses (8.5 for males aged 15 to 24 compared to 2.0 for all male victims) (Orgrodnik, 2009).

Homicides of Seniors The rate of family-related homicides against seniors has gradually declined over the past 30 years. In 2009, the rate of family-related homicide against seniors was 61 percent lower than in 1980 (Taylor-Butts & Porter, 2011). There were 160 family-related homicides against seniors (65 years and older) between 2000 and 2009, accounting for 4 percent of all solved homicides and 10 percent of all family-related homicides.

Data from the homicide survey indicate that the rate of homicide was lower among older adults compared to those less than 65 years of age. This is consistent with overall police-reported crime rates, which showed that older Canadians were the least likely age group to be victimized (Taylor-Butts & Porter, 2011).

Table 5.6 Spousal Homicide Rates per Million Spouses Based on Age and Gender from 1998–2007

Age	15–24	25–34	35–44	45–54	55 Years and Over
Female	21	11	9	6	3
Male	8	3	2	2	1

Source: Adapted from Statistics Canada, 2011: Canadian Centre for Justice Statistics, Homicide Survey.

Senior women were most likely to be killed by a spouse (41 percent) or son (36 percent), while the majority of senior men were killed by a son (72 percent).

In 2006, a total of 30 homicides were committed against seniors (18 males and 12 females). One-half of the homicides against seniors were committed by a family member, one-quarter (26 percent) were killed by an acquaintance, and 13 percent by a stranger. The remaining killings were unsolved (Taylor-Butts & Porter, 2011).

CHAPTER CONCLUSION

Since the second-wave women's movement in the 1970s, when domestic violence first began to receive public attention, until the recent guilty finding on four counts of first-degree murder in the Shafia murder trial, when Judge Robert Maranger stated in a Kingston courtroom that "it is difficult to conceive of a more despicable, more heinous crime," violence continues. And although there are many public and horrifying cases that insult our sensibilities, the greatest percentage of intimate personal and "secretive" violence unfolds in homes daily. The belittling, berating, and the often hidden bruises and broken spirits impact Canadians coast to coast. Canadians—*not* Canada, but its *people*—must always be better than its enacted laws and policies, and the systems we create and fund. Awareness of the hidden nature of violence is necessary. So, too, is a universal commitment that violence in any form, directed at any person, is intolerable—for "The hottest places in hell are reserved for those who in times of moral outrage retain their neutrality" (Dante, *Inferno*).

Multiple Choice Questions

1. Which of the following cases was the Supreme Court of Canada's first battered woman defence?

    a. *R. v. Lavallee*   **b.** *R. v. Atkin*
    c. *R. v. Whynot*   **d.** *R. v. Napolitano*

2. Which of the following statements reflects the outcome for a woman once she decides to leave an abusive relationship, according to the theory put forward by professionals?

    a. she will be protected and supported due to the various women's shelters that exist
    b. she is in the greatest danger when trying to get out of an abusive relationship
    c. she will struggle to find housing but she will be protected
    d. she will endure many changes whether she works or not, but her physical safety will be secure

3. All of the following phases are included in the cycle of violence EXCEPT which one?
   a. tension-building phase
   b. acute battering phase
   c. debriefing phase
   d. tranquil or loving phase

4. If spousal violence existed prior to pregnancy, according to research, which of the following statements describes what will generally unfold?
   a. physical violence generally stops
   b. physical violence stops but emotional abuse escalates
   c. All forms of violence generally continue and or escalate.
   d. Pregnancy is a time when the loving phase of the cycle theory of violence is extended.

5. Which of the following statements is true regarding rape in a Canadian marriage?
   a. it is rare
   b. it is a form of sexual violence
   c. it became illegal after 1948
   d. it is the most frequently reported sexual crime

6. Which form of family violence has probably received the least amount of academic, professional, and public attention?
   a. spousal sexual assault
   b. elder abuse
   c. infanticide
   d. child neglect

7. Compared to child and spousal abuse, which type of elder abuse is more common?
   a. physical abuse
   b. emotional or psychological abuse
   c. neglect
   d. financial or material exploitation

8. According to statistics, homicides in Canada, particularly those involving family members, account for:
   a. less than 1 percent of all violent crimes reported to police each year
   b. 10 percent of all violent crimes reported to police each year
   c. 20 percent of all violent crimes reported to police each year
   d. more than half of all violent crimes reported to police each year

9. How old was Gavin Mandin when he murdered his mother, stepfather, and his two sisters?
   a. 15
   b. 20
   c. 25
   d. 30

10. When quality of care is significantly less than an elderly person can afford, it is a symptom of which of the following forms of violence?
    a. emotional or psychological abuse
    b. physical abuse
    c. financial abuse or material exploitation
    d. intentional neglect

Discussion Questions

1. The battered woman syndrome as an "understanding of why someone kills" continues to be controversial. Even within the justice system, many think there is enough public and personal support for spousal abuse victims to get help, and not feel trapped. Do you think it should continue to be a legal reason, or should this defence be challenged again in the courts?

2. List and describe some of the consequences for the elder person who is physically abused.

3. Describe the battered woman syndrome. Who developed this theoretical framework?

Key Terms

battered woman syndrome: a set of specific psychological and behavioural symptoms that are caused by protracted exposure to situations of intimate partner violence.

Canadian Charter of Rights and Freedoms: the constitutional document that sets out the rights and freedoms affecting the people of Canada.

cycle of violence: a theory developed by Dr. Lenore Walker to explain that violence in intimate relationships is not even, but waxes and wanes. The three stages are tension-building, explosion or acute phase, and the calm loving respite phase.

Duluth model: a batterer group treatment model based upon a pro-feminist philosophy, which incorporates principles form social learning theory and cognitive-behavioural psychology. Developed by the Duluth Abuse Intervention project, it is regarded as one of the best-articulated perpetrator treatment programs.

power and control wheel: A diagram used in the Duluth program that depicts the coercive strategies used by batterers against their intimate partners.

United Nations (UN): formed in 1945; international organization of independent states, with headquarters in New York City, that promotes peace and international cooperation and security.

World Health Organization (WHO): an agency of the United Nations that monitors outbreaks of infectious disease and sponsors efforts to prevent and treat diseases.

Chapter 6
Violence in Same-Sex Relationships

The worst loneliness is not to be comfortable with yourself.

Mark Twain, American writer (1835–1910)

Chapter Objectives

1   Identify the different forms of violence in same-sex intimate relationships.

2   Describe the consequences and impact of violence in same-sex intimate relationships.

3   Interpret the statistics regarding the prevalence of violence in same-sex intimate relationships.

INTRODUCTION

Embracing and accepting oneself is necessary for healthy growth and development. The historical treatment of homosexual persons has been for the most part oppressive, and at its worst, violent. Acknowledging, honouring, or celebrating oneself, for many homosexual people and particularly gay men, has been historically perilous and continues for many to be fraught with uncertainty.

Gay and lesbian citizens have suffered an extensive period of **oppression** at the hands of society's most powerful and prestigious social institutions: religion, medicine, government and the justice system. Over time, to address overt inequalities corrective measures have evolved. Oppression and the structures that create and enforce its existence are discussed in Chapter 2. Let's now begin to examine intimate violence in same-sex relationships.

6.1 SAME-SEX INTIMATE VIOLENCE

In order to begin our exploration of violence in same-sex relationships, a very salient point will be reiterated. When the right to choose the person one loves and how and when to express intimacy can lead to disdain, a discriminatory reaction, or even legislated violence, it will be difficult to seek out help when an intimate partner becomes abusive. Yet, as you will soon read, similar to heterosexual spousal violence, same-sex intimate violence also exists.

Domestic violence in heterosexual relationships began to be identified in the late 1960s, which led to the opening of the first shelter for battered women, the Chiswick Women's Aid, in London, England, in 1972. As noted in Chapter 1, the UK women's movement was at the forefront of developing services for women experiencing violence in their intimate heterosexual relationships. In the wake of these activities an increased effort was made to study the incidence of domestic violence.

The initial focus of domestic violence was mainly directed at heterosexual men as the perpetrators and heterosexual women as the victims (Dutton, 1995; Ellis & DeKeseredy, 1997; Johnson & Ferraro, 2000; Kurz, 1989). Today, an extensive body of literature and research on heterosexual domestic violence exists (Hester et al., 2007; Hester & Donovan, 2009; Puzone et al., 2000). Yet, even in the United Kingdom, where the lid covering domestic violence was first ratcheted off, there have been only a small number of local and national surveys and little qualitative research exploring same-sex domestic violence and their services.

The strides that have been made for female victims of intimate partner abuse within heterosexual relationships have not translated to a comparable body of research, social services, or policy responses for victims of same-sex intimate violence.

Eventually, during the late 1980s and 1990s, an increased awareness about domestic violence in lesbian relationships and, to a lesser extent, gay male relationships, began to emerge. An unwillingness to acknowledge intimate partner abuse has come from outsiders as well as from within the gay community. Recent literature has identified a number of factors that may have contributed to the invisibility of same-sex domestic abuse. In fact, Hester and Donovan (2009) noted that there has been a strong tendency to minimize, hide, and deny the existence of such abuse.

As Canada's history has revealed, gay and lesbian populations have been victimized and vulnerable. And although in Canada GLBT (gay, lesbian, bisexual, transgender) persons are no longer criminally and medically targeted groups, the resultant belief systems of individuals and some religious faiths continue to perpetuate a perspective that devalues and shows a lack of acceptance and respect. Therefore, one of the underlying variables creating this deficiency of research stems from the fear of reporting or disclosing these problems within communities where widespread **heterosexism** existed. This heterosexist point of view has existed in the fields of social sciences as well as society in general. Heterosexism can be defined as a form of oppression whereby heterosexuality is considered to be the only acceptable and viable life option. It is considered natural, the norm, by society, and all other alternatives are considered unnatural (Mullay, 2010).

Heterosexism oppresses. Some theorists argue that "it also oppresses anyone who exhibits gender behaviour that does not fit the traditional one-man, one-woman monogamous marriage or union with children" (Mullay, 2010, p. 212). As such, all too often identifying oneself as GLBT carries with it a burden of stigma or societal disapproval. Heterosexism can be witnessed every day through subtle negative messages directed toward sexual minority groups. They are also heard across North America in gratuitous humour in sitcoms and commercials that comes at the expense of the gay person. More blatant anti-gay statements are uttered within the contents of sermons by leaders of major religious dominations and even political candidates.

For example, in 2012 during Alberta's provincial election, it was reported that Allan Hunsperger, the Wildrose Party candidate for Edmonton-South-West, stated in a blog post that gays "will suffer the rest of eternity in the lake of fire, hell, a place of eternal suffering." He went on to write that others shouldn't accept homosexuals for the way they are because "accepting people the way they are is cruel and not loving" (CBC News, 2012). Perhaps it should be noted that Hunsperger did not win his seat in the April 2012 election.

An even more critical and concerning element is the undeniable existence of overt negative societal attitudes referred to as homophobia. **Homophobia** refers to the condemnation, loathing, fear, societal disdain, and religious rejection of all things homosexual and of those who practise it (Herek, 2004). Further, unlike other intimate personal crimes of violence, forms of violence provoked by homophobia tend to be perpetrated by strangers rather than by acquaintances.

A point to underscore is that some theorists and clinicians dislike the term *homophobia* because, although some people unquestionably have anti-gay feelings strong enough to identify them as a phobia, what is actually more common are negative attitudes and prejudicial behaviours. The preferred terms for these situations are homo-negativity, anti-gay prejudice, sexual prejudice, or **heterocentrism** (Berkeman & Zinberg, 1997).

Despite the term used, or the intensity of the emotion felt or expressed, a victim of intimate same-gender violence may legitimately fear a very real internal conflict and additional judgment when attempting to seek protection and help. Moreover, even if a couple mutually agreed to seek out professional intervention to address their relationship struggles, they may be dissuaded. For gay couples, the more urgent concern might be to whom they should (or should not) disclose their sexual orientation. Let's now begin to explore domestic violence in same-sex relationships.

Same-Sex Intimate Violence Defined

For the purpose of clarity, the Department of Justice Canada defines spousal abuse as "the violence or mistreatment that a woman or a man may experience at the hands of a marital, common-law or same-sex partner. Spousal abuse may happen at any time during a relationship, including while it is breaking down, or after it has ended" (Department of Justice website). Academics who have studied same-sex violence have similarly defined intimate partner abuse (Island & Letellier, 1991).

What was true for heterosexual violence is also true for same-sex domestic violence. Spousal violence is multifaceted. There are different types of violence, and an individual could be subjected to more than one. Partners in same-gender intimate relationships are no more or less susceptible to the range of violent or harmful acts than heterosexuals.

Forms of Same-Sex Intimate Violence

Same-sex intimate violence includes physical and sexual violence; however, many non-violent but highly injurious behaviours are noteworthy. They too cause harm—for example, emotional or psychological, verbal, and economic. Destruction of property and isolation from friends, family, and other potential sources of support can also be added to this definition.

Wise and Bowman (1997) found the similarities between heterosexual and homosexual abusive relationships are greater than the differences. When same-gender couples experience problems within the context of their relationships, the issues of conflict are also similar to those faced by heterosexual couples (Harris & Cook, 1994; Lockhart et al., 1994; Patterson, 2000).

The types of intimate violence in same-sex relationships are included in Figure 6.1, which includes the four overarching forms of violence: physical, emotional/psychological, sexual, and economic. These behaviours could occur on a continuum, but they can also take place without any prior action or behaviour. Figure 6.1 also helps to concretely identify what actions are considered abusive.

Abuse also occurs in a cyclical style, where there appears to be a violent episode eventually followed by the "honeymoon period" (Bernstein & Kostelac, 2002; Elliot, 1996). (This cycle was discussed in Chapter 2 and Chapter 5; refer to Figure 5.2.)

In addition, a correlation with intergenerational transmission of domestic violence exists in both homosexual and heterosexual couples (Tjaden, Thoennes, & Allison, 1999); see Chapter 2. Findings from Tjaden and colleagues (1999) corroborated other studies in that participants who reported experiencing domestic violence in their romantic relationships were more likely to report forcible rape both in childhood and in later adulthood, physical violence in childhood from caretakers, and physical violence from all types of aggressors, including intimate partners (Farley, 1996; Merrill & Wolfe, 2000; Schilit et al., 1991; Wise & Bowman, 1997).

Issues Unique to Same-Sex Intimate Violence

While there are similarities between heterosexual and homosexual couples with regard to intimate personal violence, there also are several very distinct differences. To define these unique differences, Rod and Jogodinsky adapted the power and control wheel developed by Domestic Abuse Intervention Programs in Duluth, Minnesota (see Chapter 2) to create a wheel entitled the Gay, Lesbian, Bisexual, and Trans power and control wheel (see Figure 6.2). It was then updated by the Texas Council on Family Violence. Much like the original power and control wheel, it depicts behaviours that batterers use to dominate their intimate partners and/or children. Violent acts are not driven from a place of aggression; rather, the central needs are control and domination, and they are commonly perpetrated by the stronger against the weaker.

#	PHYSICAL	EMOTIONAL OR PSYCHOLOGICAL	SEXUAL	ECONOMIC
1	Squeezing	Ignoring	Treating as sex object	Not allowing outside employment
2	Grabbing	Discounting	Minimizing sexual needs	Interfering with the victim's work performance through harassing activities, such as frequent phone calls or unannounced visits
3	Pushing	Demeaning	Criticizing sexuality	Stealing from the victim
4	Shoving	Countering and correcting everything	Acting obsessively jealous	Making the victim's paycheque the abuser's paycheque
5	Shaking	Making put-downs disguised as jokes	Touching that is unwanted	Putting all the bills in the victim's name
6	Cornering	Forgetting—from promises to dates (birthday, Mother's Day, anniversary)	Calling the victim names during sex	Refusing to pay bills/creditors
7	Restraining	Withholding affection	Demanding sex	Destroying partner's personal belongings
8	Pulling hair	Minimizing feelings	Forcing to strip	Placing own wishes before family needs
9	Choking	Ridiculing	Inflicting sexual humiliation	Controlling the chequebook
10	Kicking	Yelling	Forcing prostitution	Requiring partner to account for every penny
11	Throwing things	Isolating	Forcing to observe sex	Leaving family's basic needs unmet; family lacking adequate clothing and money for groceries and medication
12	Biting	Insulting	Forcing unwanted acts	Accumulating debt without partner's awareness or deliberately ruining partner's credit rating
13	Harassing	Accusing/not gay enough	Forcing sex after beatings	Selling family possessions
14	Stalking	Humiliating	Using weapons to force sex	Spending family funds on alcohol/drugs
15	Punching	Destroying valued things	Injuring during sex	Refusing to give spouse personal money
16	Striking with a weapon	Questioning sanity		Cancelling insurance or credit cards without partner's knowledge
17	Denying medical care	Threatening to "out their partner"		Providing no knowledge of assets/finances
18	Disabling	Threatening to abandon		
19	Disfiguring and maiming	Threatening to have spouse declared an unfit/parent		
20	Murdering	Threatening violence		

Figure 6.1 Types of Intimate Violence in Same-Sex Intimate Relationships

Sources: Harris & Cook, 1994; Lobel, 1986; Lockhart et al., 1994; Patterson, 2000; Tully, 2000; Wise & Bowman, 1997.

Figure 6.2 Power and Control Wheel for Lesbian, Gay, Bisexual, and Transgender People

Source: Rod and Jogodinsky adapted the power and control wheel developed by Domestic Abuse Intervention Program, Duluth Minnesota

Fear of discrimination was a main theme in the domestic violence literature regarding same-gender couples, often preventing them from reporting partner abuse (Klinger, 1995; Lie & Gentlewarrier, 1991; Patterson, 2000; Renzetti, 1992; Turrel, 2000). Reporting the abuse would not only expose their sexual orientation as well as their partner's, but would place them in a potentially homophobic legal system with a lack of resources and services. As noted in Chapter 1, historically the lives and experiences of gay people have been overtly **pathologized** and/or criminalized (Allen & Leventhal, 1999). This shared cultural and historical experience, together with the context of police and community violence, may account for that fear.

In fact, this belief was substantiated by a Canadian study that reported that gays, lesbians, and bisexuals expressed lower levels of satisfaction with police performance than their heterosexual counterparts. For example, fewer gays, lesbians, and bisexuals felt that the police were doing a good job of treating people fairly compared to heterosexuals (42 percent of gays/lesbians and 47 percent of bisexuals versus 60 percent of heterosexuals) (Hotton Mahony, 2010).

The same study also revealed that the proportion of gays, lesbians, and bisexuals who felt they had experienced discrimination was about three times higher than that of heterosexuals. And of the 78 percent of gays and lesbians who experienced discrimination, they believed it was because of their sexual orientation, compared to 29 percent of bisexuals and 2 percent of heterosexuals (Hotton Mahony, 2010).

Gays are also concerned about revealing the issue of domestic violence because it could jeopardize the positive steps taken to overcome homophobia in the larger community (Klinger, 1995). The unfortunate result is a veil of silence that leads to even more alienation, isolation, lack of protection, and the potential for an increase in violence (Merrill & Wolfe, 2000).

There have been studies that focused specifically on either the lesbian or gay man who is a victim of intimate personal violence. We will now examine the abused gay male followed by the abused lesbian.

Gay Male Intimate Violence

Existing studies published by various researchers and clinicians that have examined domestic violence among gay male couples note the dearth of information and encourage continued research. Merrill and Wolfe (2000) postulated that the lack of research might result either from the mistaken assumption that battering is an exclusively heterosexual phenomenon or from the fear that investigating this issue may result in increased negative stereotyping. The lack of available research could, however, lead to the assumption that domestic violence is not an issue of concern among gay male couples. But the available data clearly indicate that intimate abuse does exist in gay male relationships (Klinger, 1995; Landolt & Dutton, 1997; Merrill & Wolfe, 2000). The facts that have emerged have evolved from the research done on gay men's health (Island & Letellier, 1991). Regardless of their inception, the encouraging news is that studies do take place.

In their research on gay men's health, Island and Letellier (1991) cited domestic violence as the third largest health problem that gay males face, after AIDS and substance abuse. Further, Merrill and Wolfe (2000) cited several studies that suggested that the prevalence of gay domestic violence is comparable to that in heterosexual and lesbian relationships.

While studies on domestic violence in lesbian relationships have included both inter-view samples as well as surveys, studies of domestic violence in gay male relationships have tended to be more survey format, relating to "overall" health-related questionnaires (McClennen, 2005). Few studies directly compare lesbian and gay male domestic abuse, or attempt to compare abuse in same-sex and heterosexual relationships (Tjaden & Thoennes, 2000; Turrell, 2000).

Similar to female victims, battered gay men did not initiate the battering and indi-cated feeling trapped and helpless. In terms of types of abuse experienced, 87 percent reported severe recurrent physical abuse, 85 percent reported some form of emotional abuse, 90 percent identified financial abuse, and 73 percent recounted one or more forms of sexual abuse.

Some studies also noted that the existence of a **cycle of violence** in gay domestic abuse is similar to heterosexual relationship violence. More than two-thirds of the partici-pants reported no incidents of physical violence within the first three months of their relationship. The first incidence of violence occurred between three months and a year for 54 percent of respondents, and after a year for 23 percent. Seventy-three percent acknowl-edged a "honeymoon" period after violent incidents in which the partner was attentive, caring, and apologetic (McClennen, 2005). Similarly, Klinger's (1995) review of the existing literature concluded that gay male domestic violence occurred most often when there was an imbalance of power.

Overall, the occurrence of domestic violence has typically been viewed as either a feminist issue or as a power and control issue (Klinger, 1995). Although some research-ers have attempted to apply a patriarchal, gender-based model to gay domestic abuse, most of the research indicates that male–female role-playing in gay male relationships is not the norm. Rather, some research points to the fact that most gay male relationships follow a pattern of egalitarian friendship (Landolt & Dutton, 1997). Landolt and Dutton (1997) suggested that gay males are at high risk for domestic violence because both partners are biologically male and conditioned to assert dominance and control, not because of the roles assumed within the relationship. Landolt and Dutton's (1997) study also noted that abuse was not necessarily related to power dominance; rather, it was most often in divided-power relationships, indicating that abuse may occur in relationships that are roughly equal.

Several research studies have reported that between 80 percent and 90 percent of men in treatment for heterosexual domestic violence have diagnosable personality disor-ders, contributing to a belief that there is an abusive personality type (Elliot, 1996; Klinger, 1995; Landolt & Dutton, 1997). Landolt and Dutton's (1997) study of 52 gay male couples also supported this notion of the existence of an abusive personality in gay domestic violence. Some of the characteristics noted include *borderline personality organization*, which includes many of the diagnostic criteria of borderline personality disorder: anger, fearful or preoccupied attachment, and the recollection of a poor child–parent relationship (see Chapter 2). In those relationships where the men are mutually abusive, Landolt and Dutton (1997) noted that the abusive tendencies were higher than in relationships where only one partner was the identified victim. The abusive personality was particularly evident when both partners were abusive.

Lesbian Intimate Violence

Most studies pertaining to same-gender partner abuse examine lesbian relationships more often than gay male couples. This might relate back to the role the women's movement played in giving voice to women and generating attention to domestic violence issues (Dobash & Dobash, 1992; Renzetti, 1992). In the case of lesbian same-gender violence the initial belief that women were not aggressive and do not batter other women was false. This hypothesis became an obstacle during the early domestic violence movement. Feminist theorists wanted to focus on the heterosexual violence, emphasizing the patriarchal structure as the leading cause. And while this is one of the key underpinnings, the existence of abusive women was real. Although this presented an early obstacle to research, studies would slowly reveal violence in intimate same-gender lesbian relationships exists.

Early analysis of lesbian domestic violence recognized that the dynamics of domestic violence in lesbian relationships were similar to those in heterosexual relationships. But an important factor in shaping the particular experience of domestic violence in same-sex relationships was homophobia (Lobel, 1986; Tully, 2000).

Homophobia and heterosexism, as mentioned earlier, must be considered in order to understand the experience of battered lesbians. Pharr (1986) stated that the battered non-lesbian experiences violence within the context of a misogynist world. **Misogyny** was defined by Mullaly (2010) as an extreme form of sexism, "which refers to the hatred, fear, and mistreatment of women by individuals" (p. 211). Consequently, the lesbian victim experiences violence within the context of a world that is not only misogynistic but also homophobic (Pharr, 1986). This is a significant difference. Moreover, these consequences shape a lesbian's experience of domestic violence (Pharr, 1986). Internalized homophobia has serious consequences that affect both gay men and lesbians. This will be discussed in greater detail.

Lesbians and gays are often reluctant to report their abuse because they believe it is a private concern—as do heterosexual couples, but for different reasons. Thus, domestic violence is often under-reported because gays and lesbians fear coming out and do not want to bring added subjugation and discrimination upon the gay and lesbian community (Tully, 2000).

Based on research regarding intimate violence in lesbian relationships, a similar prevailing model of power and control over a partner also exists (Pence & Paymar, 1993). Hart (1986) specifically noted that lesbian battering included a pattern of violence and coercive behaviours whereby a lesbian seeks to control the thoughts, beliefs, or conduct of her intimate partner, or to punish the intimate for resisting the perpetrator's control over her. Similarly, Renzetti (1988) found in her study that jealousy, power, and control functioned as major sources of conflict within lesbian relationships. She also found that abusive lesbian partners appeared to be greatly threatened by a partner's attempt to secure independent friendships.

Sources of conflict in lesbian relationships revolve around social fusion and power imbalances, and violence is often used as a means of resolving this friction. **Fusion** is defined as an unhealthy collapse of boundaries between partners that results in the loss of individuality, and was more likely in lesbian relationships due to their isolated nature (Lockhart et al., 1994). As such, it would spur codependency and conflict would arise from miscommunication regarding rules and roles.

Role conflict was particularly intense for lesbian couples. According to Renzetti (1988), most lesbian relationships do not receive affirmation and support outside of the lesbian and gay community; thus, lesbian couples tend to isolate themselves from the larger society. This isolation may facilitate insecurities where one or both partners view separateness and autonomy as threatening to the relationship.

A further struggle for lesbian partners was a fear of rejection. These emotions would take hold if their partner made any attempt to have separate friends, to hold different views, or to go places by themselves. Lesbian batterers also displayed an excessive neediness and used violence as a way to stymie their partner's autonomy (Lockhart et al., 1994; Renzetti, 1988, 1992). We will now address the specific forms of violence in lesbian relationships.

Verbal Abuse and Psychological Abuse in Lesbian Relationships The current literature demonstrates that abuse in lesbian relationships is more often verbal than physical (Lie & Gentlewarrier, 1991; Osier, 2001; Renzetti, 1988, 1992). Lesbians who report verbal abuse and aggression claim their conflict stems from disagreements over their partner's job, their partner's emotional dependency, housekeeping/cooking duties, sexual activities, and drug or alcohol use (Carlson, 1992; Johnson & Ferraro, 2000). There were some overarching themes to the types of verbal and psychological abuse used.

Humiliation Part of the verbal abuse involves humiliation. For instance, in one study, many participants reported a shared experience of abusers questioning or challenging the victim's "gay" identities as a tactic of control (Bornstein et al., 2006). For example, many participants reported that they were accused of being straight, or not "good enough" at their chosen gender identity.

Challenges to a person's authenticity or "realness" served to make survivors feel unsure of themselves or "inauthentic." Research participants reported that these assertions served as a means of coercion, which was sometimes connected to sexual violence. For example, several victims reported being pressured into sex in order to prove they were "really a lesbian" (Bornstein et al., 2006).

Isolation Isolation was almost universally identified as central to participants' experiences of abuse, and a variety of isolation tactics were described. The abusive person would try to cut the partner off from personal relationships. If one non-abusing partner had or was attempting to have same-sex friends, statements such as "you are a whore," a "slut," or a "cheater" would be used. If they had close family relationships this would be framed as a negative, such as, "you're tied to the apron strings." Victims reported that these abusive tactics were threatening and intimidating enough to prevent them from making connections within the community (Freedner et al., 2002; Bornstein et al., 2006).

There is a unique point worth mentioning within the literature that was not indicated in any previous heterosexual or homosexual research or clinical writings (Bornstein, 2006). Some victims observed that because their abusive partner was also female, she would access all the same supports and resources. This made it difficult for victims to truly feel safe, because they did not have a system separate and apart from their abusive partner. Many also noted that their abusers were often well-liked by friends, and were able to take advantage of the small size of the gay community and the fact that both knew the same people as a method to cut survivors off from their friends (Bornstein et al., 2006).

Some survivors also noted that their partner's tactics of emotional control were elusive enough to confuse them. Bornstein and colleagues (2006), for example, noted that one participant reported being controlled by a constant fear that her partner would commit suicide; however, at the time she had trouble identifying her partner's suicide threats as a mechanism of control.

"Outing" a partner to their family, employer, and friends can be a common form of emotional or psychological abuse unique to same-gender couples (Elliot, 1996; Johnson & Ferraro, 2000). Again, these types of challenges supported and reinforced isolation, making it difficult to get support.

Physical Violence in Lesbian Relationships In addition to verbal abuse, various levels of physical violence also exist among lesbian couples as a means for resolving conflicts emerging from issues related both to power imbalances and to autonomy/fusion (Johnson & Ferraro, 2000; Schilit et al., 1991; Tully, 2000). Lesbian domestic violence may also include coercion, where one partner seeks to control the behaviours, actions, or beliefs of the other (Tully, 2000). In relationships where one partner had a greater need for fusion than the other partner, higher levels of severe physical abuse were reported (Renzetti, 1988). Participants in the Bornstein (2006) study described what would be considered *Criminal Code* offences, experiences including physical and sexual violence, threats of homicide, stalking, and destruction of property. Although these experiences were shared by many, most participants focused the majority of their attention on or described emotional abuse, which encompassed a wide range of abusive tactics.

Lesbians who reported victimization in childhood were more likely to report physical violence in their relationships (Lockhart et al., 1994; Margolies & Leeder, 1995; Schilit et al., 1991). Unlike gay male couples, the relationship between victimization in childhood and violence in lesbian relationships is still open for questioning since research findings have posed a host of non-definitive conclusions. For example, the fact that a woman was abused as a child did not increase her likelihood of becoming a batterer, but it did increase her chances of finding a partner who would batter her (Girshick, 2001; Lockhart et al., 1994).

Violence Over Time: Why They Stay

For both lesbian and gay male victims of violence (Bornstein et al., 2006), research studies found that the invisibility of gay relationships may impede a victim's ability to distinguish abusive behaviour from "normal" relationship dynamics. Specific challenges exist, including the following:

- the gay socialization process often includes secrecy, isolation, and fear of abandonment, which compounds community silence
- the lack of positive, public role models for healthy gay relationships
- the prevailing model of domestic violence in which men are perpetrators, women are victims (for example, survivors believed that an abusive partner must be male, or physically bigger)
- limited awareness of intimate personal violence in gay communities
- the lack of language to describe abusive relationships in terms of domestic violence or abuse

Moreover, gay community leaders have also stated emphatically there is "no problem." Thus, it is not surprising that support services remain virtually non-existent for gay men. However, the gay community as well as the greater society has accepted that gay men are victims of hate crimes (which occur with less frequency than gay domestics).

Isolation Isolation serves to keep survivors in abusive relationships. Gay and lesbian people are often estranged to some extent from family support and many might not have access to institutional supports that are generally available to heterosexual couples (that is, churches, workplaces, and schools). Further, many people in same-sex relationships place greater value on their families of choice, because they have often been rejected, misunderstood, or alienated from their families of origin. In isolation, these partnerships can sometimes take on an insular us-against-the-world quality (Allen & Leventhal, 1999; Bornstein et al., 2006; Freedner et al., 2002; Renzetti, 1992).

Isolation from the larger community, along with the small interconnected nature of gay communities, creates an environment of intense vulnerability that has a tremendous impact on victims (Allen & Leventhal, 1999; Bornstein et al., 2006; Renzetti, 1992). Victims and their abusive partners often have the same friends and community connections. For example, if every friendship network a victim has access to includes one person who also knows her batterer, the survivor's isolation may considerably intensify. At a time when they would require help finding housing and planning for safety this process could be compromised, particularly if they were from a small community.

Last, participants in the Bornstein study overwhelmingly reported the need for support and education in identifying their relationships as abusive. Similar to all victims of crime, especially intimate personal violence, gays and lesbians need to have their victimization validated, but their added obstacles makes this very difficult (Bornstein et al., 2006).

Gay Men Who Stay in Abusive Relationships

Research was also conducted to determine why gay men remain in an abusive intimate relationship. With respect to gay men, one study found that gay and bisexual men who experience violence from a male partner remained in the relationship because, similar to heterosexual couples, they hoped the violent partner would change and in fact loved their partner (Merrill & Wolf, 2000). Merrill and Wolfe (2000) specifically found that the most frequently cited reasons for remaining in an abusive relationship were "hope for change" and "love of partner." About one-third indicated "fear of harm," "lack of assistance," "fear of loneliness," "partner pursuit," and "loyalty/commitment" as further reasons for staying. However, more than half of the respondents indicated "lack of knowledge about domestic violence" as a major reason. This appears to be more of a concern for gay males since there were few agencies that specifically provide assistance to gay male victims of domestic violence.

The AIDS Issue Dependency keeps victims silent, which forces them to stay. This fact arises, for example, when discussing child and elder abuse. They don't tell due to the dependency they have on their abuser, who is often their primary caregiver. One reason for remaining that appears to be unique to gay men is related to their own or their partner's HIV status (Merrill & Wolfe, 2000).

The gay man who is HIV-positive, or has AIDS, and who is the victim might remain with his partner simply because he fears the alternative is worse. When the batterer is the caregiver, his opportunity to abuse becomes staggering. First, there is the threat of outing their sexual orientation. But that worry is quickly dashed with the crushing fear that their HIV/AIDS status could be disclosed. The impact could drastically affect a person's status at work or with his friends and family.

Health and economic fallout is also a danger. As such, financial dependence and health insurance could play a part in the choice of a victim who has HIV/AIDS—or his perceived lack of choice—to remain in the relationship.

Conversely, victims may remain with their abuser who has HIV/AIDS out of a sense of guilt or moral obligation. Also, when the perpetrators have fully developed AIDS, the victim might simply see the abusive behaviour as a consequence of the illness rather than what it really is. Merrill & Wolfe (2000) reported the following facts when they researched the topic of HIV/AIDS and intimate partner violence:

- of the 20 respondents who reported being HIV-positive, 60 percent said that fear of getting sick or dying greatly affected their decision to remain in the relationship

- of the 14 respondents who reported that their partners were HIV-positive, half indicated that not wanting to abandon their partner played a major part in remaining

- another consideration for 30 percent of the HIV-positive respondents was the fear of dating in the context of the HIV epidemic

The last but most profoundly devastating emotional expression given by both gay men and lesbian victims of same-sex violence to explain why they remain in the abuse is the relief from loneliness.

6.2 IMPACT OF SAME-SEX INTIMATE VIOLENCE

Marginalized Status

The added impact of belonging to an oppressed or marginalized group in comparison to the experience of other victimized citizens is a significant point to remember. According to Tully (2000), it is extremely important for practitioners to be cognizant of the fact that gays and lesbians are members of a marginalized group; a form of oppression. Studies of attitudes toward sexuality suggest that anti-homosexual perspectives remain common, but such views may vary among most people. Moreover, the general consensus was that negative attitudes would not escalate into a significant threat or actual physical attacks on others (Kite 2002; Tomsen & Markwell, 2009).

Marginality for a homosexual's status in society does exist, and gays and lesbians must confront numerous common stressors that other groups of people do not. These stressors include the following:

- societal discrimination; prevailing myths and stereotypes, legal proscriptions, hate crimes, institutional homophobia

- conflict with families of origin; lack of understanding or acceptance about coming out, lack of familial support, emotional distancing or rejection

- stressors from families of choice regarding **coming out**; creating, maintaining, and terminating relationships; monogamy vs. non-monogamy; having children or not, or adoption (Tully, 2000).

In addition to these stressors, it is also important for clinicians to be aware that many gays and lesbians who look for therapy, especially those who come as a couple, may not initially disclose the actual motive for seeking help. Rather than labelling their presenting problem as intimate violence, they are likely to couch the reason in terms of "relationship problems." Therefore, during the assessment process the clinician's job is to establish whether violence is a problem (Istar, 1996). Further, a client may not define "violence" using the same political or clinical language used by a clinician, making it more difficult to determine whether or not abuse has taken place. Consequently, when clinicians ask the right questions they give comfort by bearing witness to the person's fear, suffering, and human dignity.

One such therapist lives and works in Calgary. Jane Oxenbury generously provided a personal recollection of the past and present, which underscores the importance of having specific knowledge and sensitivity when providing support to victims of same-sex intimate violence. You will read her professional insights in "From the Pen of . . ." Box 6.1. She runs a private practice where she works with individuals, couples, and families, specializing in the areas of family violence, sexual abuse, depression, and anxiety. She works extensively with the gay/lesbian/bisexual/transgender communities, specializing in the areas of same-sex domestic violence, the bullying and harassment of GLBT youth, and gender identity disorder. She consults with and trains groups and professionals regarding the issues members of the GLBT population face, and serves on many committees working to increase the knowledge and services for these communities.

6.1 From the Pen of Jane Oxenbury, M.Ed., R.Psych

In 1988 the lack of domestic violence services for the lesbian, gay, bisexual, and trans-identified (LGBT) community came to my attention and I began my work in this area. After much research and discussion with others, I started the first psychoeducational group for lesbian women who had been victims of same-sex domestic violence. It was difficult to get individuals to admit this, and the shelters didn't think women would batter one another.

Social Context

- Homophobia and heterosexism in society denies the reality of gay, lesbian, bisexual, and transgender lives, including the existence of their relationships, and in particular abusive ones, while an average of 25 to 33 percent of all same-sex relationships involve domestic violence.
- Services for abused and abusive lesbian individuals and families are limited and are not specialized for this community's unique need. It not unusual for persons in these communities to experience a lack of understanding of the seriousness of the abuse when reporting to a therapist, social worker, medical personnel, or police officer. Also, many are very reluctant to come forward

due to homophobia, and the fear that they will neither be believed by the service providers nor have confidentiality within their own community.

The root of such violence, as in heterosexual relationships, is the need for power and control; however, the amount of physical violence is less among lesbian couples and more verbal and emotional in nature. For gay couples there is more physical violence. There are other important similarities and differences.

Facts

- Lesbian partner violence leads to short- and long-term physical and emotional health problems similar to those in heterosexual domestic violence.
- Partner violence includes physical, sexual, verbal, emotional, economic, and spiritual abuse.
- Partner violence occurs in all segments of the gay community.
- Partner violence has nothing to do with sex roles or physical appearance.
- This is not "mutual battering"; one partner is controlling through abuse and the other is defending her/himself.

- Homophobia and heterosexism increase isolation in partner violence. Threats of being "outed" to family, friends, or work, threats to "out" the children in their school/community, and the lack of a legal position for the non-biological parent are used as a means to control a partner.
- The fear of having to "out" yourself if you talk about the abuse often keeps lesbian individuals in silence.

The secrecy and isolation occurs even within the LGBT community itself. The myths that women don't abuse women and that gay men are just having a fair fight reinforce the silence. Homophobia keeps both from talking about the issue out of fear that they will not be believed or supported or will be discriminated against.

Lesbians and gay men often find themselves blamed by medical, police, and legal personnel for an assault because of their sexual orientation and face the risks of public exposure if they report the assault. In addition, violence often occurs after a sexual encounter. This may be a reaction to the level of vulnerability involved. Rates of domestic violence are directly related to experiences of internalized homophobia. If one partner is struggling with her/his own internalized homophobia, she/he may find it more difficult to maintain her/his own level of denial when she/he has just been sexual with someone of the same gender. This insecurity, self-doubt, and fear may lead to violent acts designed to reestablish control.

In order to address these unique abuse issues we first developed our programs that would train students, front-line workers, and professionals about same-sex domestic and how to work with it. We started by creating a day-long workshop on this problem in the lesbian and bisexual women's communities, and then established the additional half-day workshop that dealt with this in the gay and bisexual men's communities.

This included the development of a website presence, posters, and resource information cards. Now the two workshops are combined into a day-long workshop called Same-Sex Domestic Violence. After about 10 years, we have trained hundreds of individuals and agencies. Now we are entering a phase where our program will be tailored to each organization that requests the training.

Screening and Risk Assessment

- Ask for the names of the last four partners, including the most recent abusive one. This ensures that safety and confidentiality can be upheld in counselling, groups, and housing.
- Be aware of legal, custody, and access limitations and issues for lesbian individuals.
- Be aware that individuals may be victims in one relationship and abusers in another.
- Make sure your space is gay-friendly and accessible for the lesbian community.
- Be aware of your own homophobic, discriminatory, or stereotyped attitudes and views.

As time went on, research began to tell us that those who bully others in their childhood are at a greater risk to go on to be abusers in their adult years, and those who are bullied are at risk for further victimization. This included both heterosexual and LGBT individuals. We addressed this by developing a day-long professional training around the issue of bullying and harassing LGBT children and youth, which we named YouthSafe. This program has gone on to spawn a 50-minute school-based training for junior and senior high school students to teach them anti-homophobia views of the LGBT peers in their midst.

Both these focuses are now two streams under the name of Safety Under the Rainbow (SUTR).

Source: Provided to Anastasia Bake by Jane M. Oxenbury, M.Ed., R.Psych.

Internalized Homophobia

Internalized homophobia is a struggle confronting many GLBT individuals. The simple definition is that **internalized homophobia** refers to negative feelings that a gay person has toward themselves because of their homosexuality (Carroll, 2010). The severe consequence of internalized homophobia has been highlighted as a chief source of suffering for victims of intimate partner violence in same-sex relationships. Among GLBT, internalized homophobia has also been called internalized sexual stigma. This refers to the personal acceptance and endorsement of sexual stigma as part of the individual's value system and self-concept.

These feelings begin to develop in childhood for two main reasons. First, most children are generally exposed to heterosexist norms. Negative homosexual stereotypes and misinformation exist in families, schools, and society. Even if an individual is from a supportive family and community, and they do not speak disrespectfully about homosexuality or even actively support it, messages from the larger society are still heard and absorbed (Renzetti & Miley, 1996; Szymanski, 2004).

For gay children these negative attitudes become "internalized" because *they* are the subject—the target of these prejudices. Whether realized or not, its impact is hurt. As a result of being a socially stigmatized person, overwhelming negative feelings can develop. The forms it may take can vary from diminished self-worth to outright shame, denial, or self-hatred. Sue and Sue (2008) point out that the internal battle can also cause high-risk sexual behaviours, substance abuse and suicidal thoughts or attempts.

Feelings of hatred toward other gay people can also develop. These feelings and thoughts do not happen overnight or in a few weeks. As such, they take time to overcome. It's never a conscious choice to have internalized homophobia, but it must be a conscious choice to change. Dealing with internalized homophobia is often an ongoing process (Herek, Gillis, & Cogan, 2009).

Identity Abuse

A consequence unique to same-sex partnerships for both gay men and lesbian women is **identity abuse**. It consists of the threat of outing and exposing someone to homophobia (Freedner et al., 2002). Outing is the act of exposing someone as a homosexual. Anticipated rejection by society frequently leads to concealing one's identity. Telling family, neighbours, or a boss may jeopardize a person's relationships and even job security. Threatening to "out" someone is a manipulative form of emotional abuse; it can cause anxiety and increase the victim's isolation.

Outing is an extremely cruel and precarious action to take. One of the most important tasks of adolescence is to develop and integrate a positive adult self (Carroll, 2010). This task is an even larger undertaking for gay and lesbian youths, because they have learned from a young age the stigma of not being heterosexual; they grew up hearing the jokes and the public commentary.

Canadian society past and present has not helped, and no more clearly was this exemplified than when 17-year-old Marc Hall would catapult the same-sex relationships issue into the Canadian collective consciousness. In 2002, the Durham Catholic School Board (in Ontario) refused to grant Hall's request to take his boyfriend to his high school prom. And although Marc Hall's case occurred three years before the *Civil Marriage Act* made same-sex marriage legal nationwide, the school board's decision was made in spite of the fact that in 1999 the Ontario Supreme Court stated that the *Canadian Charter of Rights and Freedoms* must be interpreted in favour of prohibiting discrimination based on sexual orientation (*M. v. H.*, 1999).

Although denied the right to choose his prom date, which was an entitlement of "the norm" (that is, his heterosexual peers), Mr. Hall was not deterred, and challenged his school board's decision in court. The public's response was instant. For a full account of this case, see *"Canadian Headline News"* Box 6.2. Marc Hall led the daily news with his personal story of courage and perseverance and success eventually came—but certainly not without "outing" himself to the world.

6.2 Canadian Headline News: Ontario Court Rules Student Can Take His Same-Sex Date to the Prom

One might begin this Headline News story with the image of David versus Goliath: the 17-year-old adolescent gay male versus the Durham Catholic School Board. The story first began in February 2002, when Marc Hall informed his school principal, Michael Powers, that he planned to bring his boyfriend to the school prom. Mr. Powers sought advice from his superiors at the provincially publicly funded Durham Catholic School Board. A meeting followed on February 25, 2002, at which time the principal, Mr. Powers, informed Marc and his parents that he would not be allowed to attend the event with his boyfriend.

Mr. Hall's situation was reported in numerous newspapers and aired on two of Canada's national stations, CBC and CTV. On March 19, 2002, the Durham Catholic School Board publicly supported Mr. Powers' decision in a press release that proclaimed its constitutional right to administer its schools in a manner consistent with Church teachings (CBC News, 2002).

When the matter became public, there was a tremendous outpouring of support for Mr. Hall in Canada and abroad.

However, Marc Hall, although shy, wouldn't take no for an answer. He then went to court to appeal the Board's decision. In responding to the legal challenge, the school board's strategy was to use the provision of denominational education, which is guaranteed in sec. 93 of the Constitution Act of 1867, to override sec. 15(1) of the *Canadian Charter of Rights and Freedoms,* which protects against discrimination on the basis of sexual orientation.

But, in a full and clear decision, Mr. Justice Robert MacKinnon of the Superior Court of Justice (Ontario) said a ban on same-sex dates at the prom was a clear violation of Mr. Hall's constitutional rights. The judge stated in his decision that he could find no evidence of a single position on homosexuality in the "Catholic faith community" among the materials that had been presented during the hearing. The Catholic

(continued)

catechism says homosexuality is contrary to "natural law" and cannot be tolerated. He went on to say that homosexuals should be accepted with "respect compassion and sensitivity, and also that every sign of discrimination should be avoided."

David Corbett, a human rights lawyer acting on Mr. Hall's behalf, noted that while extramarital sex is also contrary to Catholic teaching, the school board had previously allowed pregnant, unmarried students to attend the prom.

Marc Hall won a momentous court victory for Catholic students in May 2002 when the judge ordered the Durham Catholic school board to allow Hall and his date, Jean-Paul Dumond, 21, to attend the dance. The Ontario

Supreme Court ruled that Hall could go to the prom because the school board had violated his constitutional rights to equality.

Reflection Questions

1. What type of impact do you think this event had for not only Marc Hall but also all gay youth who were struggling with their own sexual identity and the fears of coming out?

2. This event took place in 2002; do you think these thoughts are still present in Canada?

Sources: CBC News, 2002; [2002] O.J. No. 1803. Court File No. 02-CV-227705CM3. *Hall vs. Michael Powers and the Durham Catholic School Board,* defendants. www.samesexmarriage.ca/docs/MacKinnon_Hall.pdf

Many youth plan and build up their courage to disclose their sexual identity. This is a difficult and anxiety-ridden process. The Marc Hall case unfortunately underscores the undeniable truth that special challenges do confront GLBT youth. Disclosing identity plays an important role in identity development and psychological adjustment for gay, lesbian, and bisexual men and women (Carroll, 2010). Abusive individuals—abusive partners, regardless of their sexual identity—will seek out the best way to expose or use their fears, possibly leading gay and lesbian people to publicly face their sexual identity prematurely.

Gay Male Victims of Same-Sex Intimate Violence

Many significant differences exist for same-sex victims of intimate violence, but perhaps the most considerable difference is the community's invalidation. Unlike the eventual awakening of mainstream society's recognition and response to battered women, the gay community has responded, especially to its battered gay men, with denial and silence.

Although claims of mutual abuse exist in heterosexual spousal violence, gay male batterers who respond to their victims' charges build upon the myth that abuse or violence between two men is "just fighting," or that it was actively initiated by or participated in by both parties. As a result, it is difficult for men to identify themselves as victims. The combination of community silence, isolative gay socialization, and competitive/aggressive male socialization creates an emotional hurdle hindering recognition of one's abuse, or of one's violence.

If this were not enough, gay men also face re-victimization due to homophobia. Perpetrators are the first to point out the likelihood of re-victimization in an attempt to undermine their partner's escape. A re-victimization (or secondary victimization) has been discussed in other chapters of this book. men and women, and the elderly all fear the unknown aftermath when reporting their victimization.

Reporting includes involving police, courts, and service providers whose responses could be prejudicial or apathetic and, as such, invalidate the victim. As upsetting as the fear of rejection from community professionals might be, a victim's anxiety may be greater with the impending potential of a rejection or invalidation from those closer to home. Family, friends, and community might refuse to accept the reality of the situation because of their feelings regarding homosexuality or the gender bias or **gender stereotyping** that the victim should just be a man and fight back.

Social (and possibly family) stigmatization, community denial, and lack of support and services reinforce the victim's feelings of low self-worth. An internalized homophobia (manifesting as self-hate) is frequently one more factor in the perpetrator's motivations.

Conclusion

Until recently, domestic violence among gays and lesbians has remained unacknowledged; a taboo subject (Kulkin et al., 2007). Of all the significant differences between heterosexual and homosexual abuse, this hushed denial of the community is the most injurious factor as it perpetuates abuse; suffocates prospective policies, funding, and services; and removes support, protection, and validation from the victim.

6.3 STATISTICS AND PREVALENCE OF SAME-SEX INTIMATE VIOLENCE

Estimates vary regarding the incidence of same-sex intimate violence. It was noted at the outset that some studies have found that partner abuse occurs among homosexual couples at the same rate as it does among heterosexual couples (Harris & Cook, 1994; Johnson & Ferraro, 2000; Puzone et al., 2000; Turrell, 2000).

One major limitation of past attempts to study domestic violence among same-gender couples is that research has had to rely on small, opportunistic samples producing results that cannot be generalized. A likely explanation for this lack of representativeness may be the isolation of gays and lesbians from society. Statistics that are presented should nevertheless be interpreted cautiously. For one thing, most reports are based on anecdotal evidence. Even in empirical studies, samples are self-selected, not random. In addition, the majority of studies have focused on lesbian relationships. Partner abuse in gay male relationships has been less studied.

In 2004, Statistics Canada conducted the fourth victimization cycle of the General Social Survey (GSS). The survey's objective was to provide estimates of the extent to which people experienced an incidence of eight possible offences, which included assault, sexual assault, robbery, theft of personal property, break and enter, motor vehicle theft, theft of household property, and vandalism. The study also examined risk factors associated with victimization; to examine rates of reporting victimization to police; and to measure fear of crime and public perceptions of crime and the criminal justice system (Beauchamp, 2004).

For the first time, the General Social Survey on Victimization asked Canadians to identify their sexual orientation. This profile examined:

- victimization rates
- perceptions of discrimination
- fear of crime
- attitudes toward the justice system

According to this research, just over 362 000 Canadians aged 18 years and older (1.5 percent) identified themselves as being gay, lesbian, or bisexual (Beauchamp, 2004). When examining those who identified themselves as being gay, lesbian, or bisexual, it was found that these individuals experienced higher rates of spousal violence compared to heterosexuals. Fifteen percent of gays or lesbians and 28 percent of bisexuals reported being victims of spousal abuse in comparison to 7 percent of heterosexuals (Beauchamp, 2004).

A further study published by Tina Hotton Mahony entitled *Police-Reported Dating Violence in Canada, 2008–Statistics Canada* provided additional data regarding same-sex intimate violence. Hotton Mahony (2010) specifically examined dating violence in same-sex relationships, and used the data generated by the Incident-Based Uniform Crime Reporting (UCR2) Survey. These data were generated from the 2008 UCR2 survey, which included information collected from 155 police services covering 98 percent of the Canadian population.

This study analyzed a smaller subset of incidents from the UCR2 by examining only one victim and one accused. This statistical strategy was necessary to establish the sex of both the accused and the victim of the offence. Consequently, the results for this section do not necessarily match those in the main 2008 police-reported data analysis, which included incidents involving multiple victims. Further, statistics including cohabitating same-sex dating relationships were removed from the analysis because it could not be determined if these were current or former common-law unions (Hotton Mahony, 2010).

Nevertheless, according to 2008 police-reported data (UCR2), approximately 10 percent of male victims (265) and 1 percent of female victims (179) of dating violence had taken place within a same-sex relationship. Male victims accounted for 60 percent of these incidents, and female victims 40 percent.

The types and frequencies of offences perpetrated in same-sex and opposite-sex dating relationships were similar, predominantly involving common assault (representing 49 percent and 54 percent of incidents, respectively); uttering threats (16 percent and 10 percent); major assault (14 percent and 11 percent); and criminal harassment (12 percent and 14 percent). Table 6.1 presents the types and frequencies of offences perpetrated in same-sex and opposite-sex dating relationships.

Table 6.1 Types and Frequencies of Offences Perpetrated in Same-Sex and Opposite-Sex Dating Relationships

Violent action	Same-Sex Dating Relationships	Heterosexual Relationships
Common assault	49%	54%
Uttering threats	16%	10%
Major assault	14%	11%
Criminal harassment	12%	14%
Charges laid by the police in violent incidents	65%	81%

Source: Hotton Mahony, 2010.

Police charging rates were lower on average for incidents involving same-sex compared to heterosexual dating relationships. Approximately 65 percent of violent incidents involving same-sex dating relationships and 81 percent involving heterosexual dating relationships resulted in charges being laid or recommended by police. This difference was statistically significant after controlling for other factors known to be associated with the probability of police charging, such as the severity of the offence, use of weapons, and sex of the victim among other factors (Hotton Mahony, 2010).

One of the largest same-sex partner violence studies completed was conducted in the United States (Tjaden et al., 1999). They analyzed data from the one percent of a national random sample who indicated that they had lived in a same-sex-couple relationship at some point in their lives. These data were then compared with the results of heterosexual couples.

They found that the male same-sex partners were more likely to have been assaulted by their partner than the men who lived with women (15 percent versus 8 percent). For the women studied in this sample, 11 percent of those living with women were assaulted by their female partner, compared to 20 percent of those who reported being assaulted by their male partner. But, again, all data should be interpreted cautiously.

Lesbian Studies

With respect to quantitative studies of lesbian or bisexual domestic violence several surveys have estimated the incidence and prevalence in LBT communities based on self-reported incidents of violence or abuse (Brand & Kidd, 1986; Lie et al., 1991; Loulan, 1987; Scherzer 1998). Prevalence estimates in these surveys vary widely (Waldner-Haugrud et al., 1997). Rates of intimate violence range from 17 percent (Loulan, 1987) to 75 percent (Lie et al., 1991).

An additional study done by Brand and Kidd (1986) compared 75 heterosexual women and 55 lesbians who had reported they had experienced intimate partner victimization. This study examined four categories of physical violence and rape. Overall, male partners of heterosexual women perpetrated the greatest number of acts of physical aggression compared to the violent acts perpetrated within a lesbian relationship. However, the following percentages were comparable in both the lesbian and heterosexual relationships:

- victim of physical abuse: 25 percent of lesbian and 27 percent of heterosexual
- victim of rape: 7 percent of lesbian and 9 percent of heterosexual

It is important to note that none the previous studies are true prevalence studies because of the non-random nature of the samples. However, regardless of these shortcomings the information does raise and underscore some vital issues. First, these data show quite convincingly that partner abuse does exist in same-sex relationships, and not as infrequently as to be anomalous. Moreover, given these frequencies, it is unlikely that most violence in same-sex relationships is a one-time event.

CHAPTER CONCLUSION

Various studies have been reported within the literature beginning in the late 1980s, and many yielded very different outcomes. Reasons for this variation could include the use of non-representative samples and the lack of a standard definition of domestic violence across surveys (Renzetti, 1992; Waldner-Haugrud et al., 1997). In Chapters 1 and 2, the issue of developing a precise and mutually agreed upon definition for violence and the population being studied was discussed. The crisper the definition the better statistical reporting and analysis can be and the more meaningfully policy development can unfold. More research must be conducted before a complete picture emerges. Yet enough data are available to encourage further research and analysis and treatment strategies.

Multiple Choice Questions

1. An irrational fear or hatred of or discomfort with homosexual people that is often manifested in individual violence or structural discrimination is referred to as:
   a. heterocentrism   b. homophobia
   c. heterosexism   d. misogynism

2. All of the following are correct statements EXZCEPT which one?
   a. Researchers found that the similarities between heterosexual and homosexual abusive relationships are greater than the differences.
   b. The dynamics surrounding same-gender abuse also mimic heterosexual domestic violence.
   c. A correlation with intergenerational transmission of domestic violence did not exist in homosexual and heterosexual couples.
   d. Lesbians who reported experiencing domestic violence in their romantic relationships were more likely to report forcible rape both in childhood and in later adulthood.

3. Research on gay men's health cited domestic violence as the _____ health problem that gay males face.

   a. largest
   b. second largest
   c. third largest
   d. fifth largest

4. Which of the following defines a form of oppression whereby heterosexuality is considered the only acceptable and viable life option?

   a. heterocentrism
   b. homophobia
   c. heterosexism
   d. misogynism

5. Which of the following terms describes the implicit assumption that everyone is heterosexual?

   a. heterocentrism
   b. homophobia
   c. heterosexism
   d. misogynism

6. Marc Hall won a momentous court victory in May 2002. Who was he and what did he achieve?

   a. He was a 17-year-old student who was allowed to take his same-sex date to his high school prom.
   b. He was a teacher who was allowed to discuss same-sex relationships in religion class.
   c. He was a school librarian who fought to have textbooks that described all forms of families (same-sex) allowed in school libraries.
   d. He was a 6-year-old boy who was allowed to bring both his lesbian mothers to a Father's Day celebration.

7. What statement has NOT been cited as a reason gay men remain in abusive relationships?

   a. it's a problem that they can solve
   b. they hope for change
   c. fear of being "outed"
   d. guilt or moral obligation

8. According to Jane Oxenbury, services for abused and abusive lesbian individuals and families are:

   a. limited but specialized for this community
   b. limited and specialized for this community's unique need
   c. not limited but situated within heterosexual agencies
   d. not specialized because violence is violence

9. According to a research study involving a sample of just over 362 000 Canadians aged 18 years and older, when examining those who identified themselves as being gay, lesbian, or bisexual in comparison to heterosexuals, which of the following statistics were revealed?

   a. 7 percent of gay or lesbians and 28 percent of bisexual and 15 percent of heterosexuals reported being a victim of spousal abuse
   b. 15 percent of gay or lesbians and 28 percent of bisexual and 7 percent of heterosexuals reported being a victim of spousal abuse
   c. 28 percent of gay or lesbians and 7 percent of bisexual and 15 percent of heterosexuals reported being a victim of spousal abuse
   d. No statistical difference was recorded.

10. Marginality for a homosexual's status in society does exist, and gay men must confront numerous common stressors that other groups of people do not. All of the following statements are true EXCEPT which one?

    a. societal discrimination
    b. internalized homophobia
    c. misogynistic society
    d. non-monogamy; having children or not, or adoption

Discussion Questions

1. This chapter presents the added burden GLBT citizens face to seek out support if they are a victim of intimate personal violence. What societal factors do you think add to their burden?
2. What efforts should be made to address these issues?

Key Terms

coming out: the process of establishing a personal self-identity and communicating it to others.

cycle of violence: a theory developed by Dr. Lenore Walker to explain that violence in intimate relationship is not even, but waxes and wanes. Three stages were identified: tension-building; explosion or acute phase; and the calm, loving respite phase.

fusion: an unhealthy collapse of boundaries between partners that results in the loss of individuality.

gender stereotypes: the application of the belief or attitude that certain characteristics are specific to one's gender that indirectly affect one's abilities; such attitudes are based on beliefs of traditional stereotypes.

heterocentrism: the implicit assumption that everyone is heterosexual.

heterosexism: a form of oppression whereby heterosexuality is considered to be the only acceptable and viable life option. It is considered natural by society, and all other alternatives are considered unnatural.

homophobia: an irrational fear or hatred of or discomfort with homosexual people or homosexuality; often manifested in individual violence or structural discrimination.

identity abuse: the threat of outing and exposing someone to homophobia.

internalized homophobia: negative feelings that a gay person has toward themselves because of their homosexuality.

misogyny: an extreme form of sexism, which refers to the fear, hatred, and mistreatment of women.

oppression: the exercise of authority or power in a cruel or unjust manner.

pathologizing: interpreting a victim's reaction to their victimization as an "illness," sickness, or pathology.

Chapter 7
Laws

Nothing is more destructive of respect for the government and the law of the land than passing laws which cannot be enforced.

Albert Einstein, German physicist (1879–1955)

Chapter Objectives

1 Identify and explain the Canadian legislation that protects children from violence and harm.

2 Identify and explain the Canadian legislation that protects adults from violence and harm.

3 Identify and explain the Canadian legislation concerning intimate personal violence and domestic violence.

4 Identify and explain the Canadian legislation specific to the elderly.

5 Identify and explain the Canadian legislation specific to those in same-sex relationships.

7.1 LAWS PROTECTING CHILDREN FROM VIOLENT CRIMES AND MALTREATMENT

Over the years, national concern regarding the welfare and well-being of abused and neglected children has led to the creation of several federal and provincial/territorial laws. Now that you have read Chapter 3, you will have a greater understanding of the extent of child abuse in Canada, its complexity, and the processes involved in responding to a child victim. Supports and services are essential and require ongoing commitment and community collaboration.

International attention to the issue of child protection and children's rights led to the creation of the United Nations *Convention on the Rights of the Child* in 1991. It is the most ratified of all the United Nations Human Rights treaties. It forms the most comprehensive and well-established international standard for children's rights, and provides the framework for the actions of UNICEF, the UN children's agency. When a country ratifies the Convention it incurs the obligation to submit regular reports to the Committee on how children's rights are being implemented. This system of human rights monitoring is common to all United Nations Human Rights treaties.

In Canada legislation protecting children fall under the jurisdictions of two forms of law, the *Criminal Code of Canada* and child protection legislation. Let's begin with child protection legislation.

Child Protection Legislation

At the provincial/territorial level, child protection legislation permits intervention to ensure a child's protection. Every province, with the exception of federally funded services to First Nations peoples' living on reserves, has unique legislation defining and describing appropriate responses to neglect and abuse. Some jurisdictions do not use the term "child protection"; instead, they prefer the term "child welfare." That said, the overarching intent of all child welfare legislation is to protect children from violence and maltreatment. There are five major categories of child abuse: physical abuse, sexual abuse, physical neglect, emotional/psychological abuse or maltreatment, and witnessing family violence.

Child abuse and neglect includes acts of commission or **omission** by a parent or other caregiver that result in harm, potential for harm, or threat of harm to a child. An omission is a failure to protect or act in a child's best interest. Another essential component to child protection legislation is mandated reporting.

Mandated Reporting Laws to Protect Children

The term **mandated reporting** refers to the legislative requirement that certain professionals report cases of suspected child abuse or neglect to a designated authority for investigation. In turn, child welfare laws require that all cases of suspected child abuse be investigated to determine if a child is in need of protection. This requirement underscores the ethos that we all share a mutual responsibility to protect children from harm, and that includes situations where children suffer abuse and neglect in the privacy of their own homes.

Legislation also addresses the definition of reasonable grounds. The legislation clearly states that it is not necessary for a person *to be certain* that a child is or may be in need of protection to make a report. The term reasonable grounds itself refers to the information that an average person, exercising normal and honest judgment, would need in order to make a decision to report (*CFSA s.72. (1)*).

After a report of suspected abuse is made an investigation will follow. Figure 7.1 outlines a brief overview of the general steps that occur once a case is reported. If a child is determined to be in need of protection the child welfare authorities respond. The investigator will assess the level of risk to the child in his or her present living arrangement. If abuse is present, protection options could include the removal of the suspected offender from the home if he or she lives with the child.

During an investigation great concern and planning unfolds to prevent the child from feeling punished for having divulged their abuse. Removal of the child from

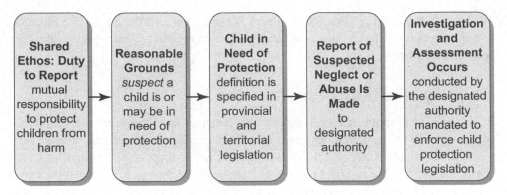

Figure 7.1 Steps That Follow Suspected Child Abuse

his/her home to a safe living environment is an option that is exercised only if a non-offending parent or guardian is unwilling or unable to protect the child from the suspected abuser. Additional supports are also provided according to the available community resources.

An investigation to determine whether a *Criminal Code* offence has been committed is conducted independently by law enforcement, or may be done jointly with a child protection agency. Although the initial concern of any investigation involves a child's safety, law enforcement and child protection agencies have different mandates for investigative procedures.

Who Must Report? All citizens have a responsibility to report their suspicion. Child protection legislation does differentiate between the public and the professional person. This position recognizes that people who work with children have more contact, therefore have a special awareness of the signs of child abuse and neglect. In fact, if a professional or official fails to report a suspicion that a child is or may be in need of protection they could be fined if they obtained information in the course of their professional or official duties (see Table 7.1).

So who has a greater duty to report? In Ontario, for instance, those who perform professional or official duties with respect to children include "health care professionals, physicians, nurses, dentists, pharmacists and psychologists; teachers and school principals; social workers and family counselors, priests, rabbis and other members of the clergy; operators or employees of day nurseries; youth and recreation workers (not volunteers); peace officers and coroners; solicitors; service providers and employees of service providers; and any other person who performs professional or official duties with respect to a child" (*CFSA s.72(5)*).

A child is defined by a specific age in child welfare legislation; this age varies across Canada. For instance, a child is a person less than 19 years of age in British Columbia, while in Ontario a child is under 16 years. Table 7.1 provides an overview of the various Canadian child welfare legislations.

Table 7.1 Child Protection Legislation in Canada

Province or Territory	Child Protection Legislation	Responsibility for Child Welfare/Protection	Definition of Child	Legal Consequences for Not Reporting
Alberta	Child, Youth, and Family Enhancement Act, 2000	Ministry of Children's Services, Child and Family Services Authorities	Under the age of 18	Maximum fine of $2000 (or six months jail for defaulting on fine). Reports must be made to professional body.
British Columbia	Child, Family and Community Service Act, 1996	Ministry of Children and Families, Child Protection Division.	Under the age of 19	Maximum fine of $10 000 and six months in jail
Manitoba	Child and Family Services Act, 1985	Ministry of Family Services and Housing, Department of Child and Family Services.	Under age of 18 can be extended to 21 in special circumstances	Reports may be made to professional body regarding violation of statutory duty.
New Brunswick	Family Services Act, 1983	Family and Community Services Division	Under the age of 18, or 19 if disabled	Minister may require professional body to investigate
Newfoundland and Labrador	Child, Youth and Family Services Act, 1998	Department of Health and Community Services, Children's Services Division	Under the age of 16	Maximum fine of $10 000 and six months in jail.
Northwest Territories	Child and Family Services Act, S.N.W.T. 1997, c. 1	Ministry of Health and Social Services, Department of Child and Family Services.	Under the age of 16, or 18 if already incare	Maximum fine of $5000 and/or six months in jail.

(continued)

Province/Territory	Act	Authority	Age	Penalty
Nova Scotia	Children and Family Services, amended 2002	Ministry of Community Services and Independent Children's Aid Societies	Under the age of 16	Maximum fine of $5000 and/or six months in jail.
Nunavut	Child and Family Services Act, S.N.W.T. (Nu.) 1997, c. 13	The Department of Health and Social Services	Under the age of 16. There is a framework of support for youth to extend services up to age 19.	Failure to report is punishable by a prison term of not more than six months, a maximum fine of $5000, or both.
Ontario	Child and Family Services Act R.R.O. 1990, as of July 30, 2002	Ministry of Community and Social Services authorizes services by independent Children's Aid Societies	Under the age of 16, or 18 if already incare	Minimum fine of $1000
Prince Edward Island	Child Protection Act, 2003	Ministry of Health and Social Services, Child and Family services Division	Under the age of 18	Maximum fine of $1000
Quebec	Youth Protection Act, R.S.Q. 1991	Department of Health and Social Services	Under the age of 18	Maximum fine of $250–$2500.00
Saskatchewan	Child and Family Services Act 1989–1990	Department of Social Services	Under the age of 16, 18 for adoption	Maximum fine of $5000 and six months in jail.
Yukon	Children's Act, R.S.Y. 2002, c. 31	Department of Health and Social Services	Under the age of 18	For reports of malicious information, maximum fine of $5000 and/or six months in jail

Sources: Information compiled through sourcing information posted on provincial/territorial websites; www.cecw-cepb.ca/legislation; www.ontariodivorces.com/child-protection.html.

Are Mandated Reporting Laws Necessary? The need for mandated reporting has raised significant debate. A major criticism is that it produces many unsubstantiated reports that can increase the workload of child protective services, wasting resources and reducing the quality of service given to known deserving children and families (Ainsworth, 2002). Some critics have gone even further (Melton, 2005) and claimed mandated reporting is a policy without reason. Melton (2005) states, "the primary problem is no longer case-finding" (p. 10), and argues that "common sense and empirical research show mandated reporting is "a bankrupt policy" (p. 15). Yet, Benjamin Mathews and Donald Bross (2008) challenged this point. They addressed Melton's position, and stated the following:

1. The problem with mandated reporting lies not in the reporting, but in how reports are responded to by the child protection agencies.

2. Without a system of mandated reporting a society will be far less able to protect children and assist parents and families, because many cases of abuse and neglect will not come to the attention of authorities and helping agencies.

3. Parents who inflict most abuse and neglect do not usually seek out voluntary assistance. Additionally, professionals who are the mandated reporter contributed the largest percentage of referrals, accounting for 75 percent of all substantiated cases in Canada in 2003 (Trocmé et al., 2005).

Mathews emphasized his perspective by stating: "A just society must include measures to address the vulnerability of children to abuse and neglect. Notions of parental liberty should not be unduly privileged over children's rights to personal security" (Mathews & Bross, 2008, p. 10).

Yet, the question regarding the legality of mandatory reporting has also been raised in the Canadian judicial system. The fact is that mandatory reporting creates child protection investigations; parents *will* be investigated. The constitutionality of this law was brought to the highest level of the Canadian justice system, the Supreme Court of Canada. A legal challenge was made to determine whether or not a parent's *Charter* rights were being violated over the right to protect their children. In 2007, the Supreme Court of Canada re-affirmed that it was not unconstitutional, and that the mandate of the Children's Aid Societies (CAS) under the *Child and Family Services Act* was in fact to:

- proceed in the best interests of the child

- protect children and youth from abuse and neglect

- ensure children's well-being

With the prevalence of publicly documented cases, why then would people still remain silent and not report a suspected case of child abuse? The Department of Justice through its Family Violence Initiative project provided a number of reasons to explain why individuals who witness or suspect a child is being abused might not report. Among the many reasons included were not wanting the demands of becoming "involved," having personal views that condone the use of physical punishment, and the often held belief that they did not think it "serious" enough because they could not see any visible injuries.

Child Victims and Canadian Criminal Law

The Government of Canada has the constitutional authority to make laws in relation to criminal law and procedure. As a result, the *Criminal Code* applies to all Canadians. Canada's *Criminal Code* has several provisions that prohibit certain contacts dangerous to a child. Amongst those offences is the catchall sec. 215:

> Everyone is under a legal duty as a parent, foster parent, guardian or head of a family, to provide necessaries of life for a child under the age of sixteen years, to provide necessaries of life to their spouse or common-law partner, and to provide necessaries of life to a person under his charge if that person is unable, by reason of detention, age, illness, mental disorder or other cause, to withdraw himself from that charge, and is unable to provide himself with necessaries of life. (*Criminal Code of Canada*)

The following discussion presents *Criminal Code* provisions including the duty to provide necessaries of life; criminal **negligence**, manslaughter, failure to act, and infanticide; sexual offences that pertain to children; and laws for children testifying in criminal court.

Duty to Provide Necessaries of Life

A number of laws impose a legal duty to act in a variety of situations in Canada. The *Criminal Code* does address serious and extreme cases of neglect. The "duty to provide necessaries of life to a person under [one's] charge" is covered in section 215. This section specifically speaks to those who are in one way or another responsible for the welfare of others. "Necessaries" describes not only food and drink, but also includes medical care and other goods or services that safeguard and preserve life.

The critical question to determine is whether an **accused** person was aware of the fact that a person to whom he or she owed a duty was actually in need of the unmet assistance. For example, if a parent knew their child was diabetic and with that knowledge chose not to provide the essential medication, then the parent could be held criminally responsible. If, however, a parent did not know their child had a particular illness that required a specific medical intervention, then failure to provide care is not present.

Criminal Negligence, Manslaughter, Failure to Act, and Infanticide

If a failure to provide a legal duty results in death or bodily harm to the person to whom the duty is owed, then an accused person may be liable for a more serious offence of causing death or bodily harm by criminal negligence. Specifically, in section 219(1)(b) of the *Criminal Code,* if an accused person fails to perform a legal duty and by this failure shows "wanton or reckless disregard for the lives or safely of other persons," then they would be guilty of criminal negligence causing bodily harm or death (as the case may be). If you reflect upon "Canadian Headline News" Box 3.2, which told the story of Jordan Heikamp's starvation death, you will recall that in this case, despite a coroner's inquest's determination that the child died of starvation, Madam Justice Mary Hogan of the Ontario Court of Justice ruled that case would not proceed to a criminal trial because there was a lack of evidence to support the legal requirement of wanton and reckless disregard for the life or safety of another person.

Infanticide The legal definition of murder is complex in Canada. Later in this chapter you will read the *Criminal Code* descriptions. The killing of a child, particularly a very young child, is a distressing crime. In Canada, their numbers are few and their stories vary, but women *specifically* who deliberately kill their newborn children could potentially be charged with infanticide. **Infanticide**, covered in section 233 of the *Criminal Code,* occurs when a female is considered disturbed from the effects of giving birth such that she causes the death of her newborn child under the age of one. As such, infanticide could operate as a partial defence to a murder charge. In a criminal court process this act of violence could possibly lead to more leniency.

One such case that took place in September 2011 involved Albertan Katrina Effert, who, in 2005 at the age of 19, strangled her child after giving birth in her parents' basement. Court of Queen's Bench Justice Joanne Veit called Effert's actions "a classic infanticide case—the killing of a newborn after a hidden pregnancy by a mother who was alone and unsupported" (Zabjek, 2011). She was sentenced to a three-year suspended sentence, to be served in the community. The sentencing hearing did not mark the end of the case. The Crown has sought leave to **appeal** the case to the Supreme Court of Canada.

Sexual Offences That Relate Specifically to Children

Progressive changes to the *Criminal Code* specifically involved the implementation of new sexual offences against children and youth. Many concerns had been raised prior to the 1988 changes. One of the most cited criticisms was the perceived unequal treatment of boys and girls, since the earlier sexual offences related strictly to female victims. Furthermore, the offences of unlawful sexual intercourse did nothing to protect young women from other forms of sexual contact short of intercourse.

It is important to note that, unlike the provincial child protection legislation, the *Criminal Code* defines a child as a person who is or appears to be under the age of 18 years. The sexual offences that relate specifically to children in Canada are described in Table 7.2.

Table 7.2 *Criminal Code* Sexual Offences That Relate Specifically to Children

1	Every one commits incest who, knowing that another person is by blood relationship his or her parent, child, brother, sister, grandparent or grandchild, as the case may be, has sexual intercourse with that person.	Incest	s. 155(1)
2	Every person who, for a sexual purpose, touches, directly or indirectly, with a part of the body or with an object, any part of the body of a person under the age of 16 years	Sexual interference	s. 151
3	Every person who, for a sexual purpose, invites, counsels or incites a person under the age of 16 years to touch: directly or indirectly, with a part of the body or with an object, the body of any person, including the body of the person who so invites, counsels or incites and the body of the person under the age of 16 years.	Invitation to sexual touching	s. 152
	A Person: ■ in a position of trust or authority towards a young person, ■ with whom the young person is in a relationship of dependency or ■ who is in a relationship with a young person that is exploitative of the young person, and who: (a) for a sexual purpose, touches, directly or indirectly, with a part of the body or with an object, any part of the body of the young person; or	Sexual exploitation	s.153. a
4	(b) for a sexual purpose, invites, counsels or incites a young person to touch, directly or indirectly, with a part of the body or with an object, the body of any person, including the body of the person who so invites, counsels or incites and the body of the young person.	Invitation to sexual touching	s. 153 (1)(b),
	**This offence prohibits adults from engaging in virtually any type of sexual contact with either boys or girls under the age of 14, *irrespective* of consent.		
5	Every parent or guardian of a person under the age of eighteen years who procures the person for the purpose of engaging in any sexual activity prohibited by this *Act* with a person other than the parent or guardian	Parent or guardian procuring sexual activity	s. 170
	*Procuring includes behaviours such as: offering, selling, or providing an underage child to another person for sexual purposes.		
6	Everyone who, in the home of a child, participates in adultery or sexual immorality or indulges in habitual drunkenness or any other form of vice, and thereby endangers the morals of the child or renders the home an unfit place for the child to be.	Corrupting children	s. 172. (1)

The Criminal Code contains several offences in relation to child prostitution:	Procuring – child prostitution	s. 212
Soliciting: Purchasing or offering to purchase sexual services from a person under 18 years of age. The services may be purchased with anything (e.g. drugs, food, the promise of a ride home, etc.)		s. 212 .1
Procuring: Encouraging or forcing a person under 18 years of age to become a prostitute; selling the sexual services of		s. 212 .2
Every person who uses the *Internet* (referred to as a "computer system") to communicate with a person under 18 years of age for the purposes of facilitating the offences of sexual exploitation (153(1)), incest (155), corrupting morals (163.1) , procuring sexual intercourse (212), sexual assault (271), or the abduction of a person under the age of 14 or 16 (280 and 281) or, as to a person under 14, sexual interference (151), invitation to sexual touching (152), bestiality (160), indecent acts (173).	Luring a "child" on the Internet	s. 172.1

Source: Criminal Code of Canada

Canada's Age of Sexual Consent

A progressive legal change occurred in May 2008, when Canada raised its age of sexual consent from 14 to 16 years (see Box 7.1). Until that point, Canada's age of consent was among the lowest of Western nations, where it varies between 16 and 18. Despite the age increase to 16 years, it is still not in line with the UN *Convention on the Rights of the Child,* which explicitly states that every child, who is a person under the age of 18 years, must be protected from sexual abuse.

7.1 Canada's Age of Sexual Consent Increases to 16

On May 1, 2008, Canada's age of sexual consent increased to 16; this was the first time in 116 years that Canada's age of sexual consent changed. The change means adults who have sex with boys or girls aged 14 and 15 years old could now face criminal charges.

The intent of the new law was not to criminalize teenage sex. The *Criminal Code* contains a "close-in-age" exemption of less than five years, added so that teens who engage in sex are not breaking the law. For instance, an 18-year-old could have relations with a 15-year-old without being criminally charged, as long as the older partner is not is a position of trust or authority over the younger teen and the relationship is not exploitive.

The age of consent legislation was brought in by the Conservative government in part to deal with older Internet predators who troll the Web looking for younger individuals. The age of consent at 14 had been a bone of contention for many Canadians who believe that having the world's lowest age of consent allowed Canada to be a target destination for pedophiles.

Figure 7.2 Repeal 43 Committee Logo

Permission granted by Corinne Robertshaw: Founder/Coordinator, Repeal 43 Committee

Spanking Law

Despite some legislative progress in the Senate, child advocates suffered a significant blow on January 30, 2004, when the Supreme Court of Canada upheld, in a 6–3 decision, section 43 of the *Criminal Code,* commonly known as the "spanking law." The issue was whether section 43 was constitutional. Advocates argued that section 43 violated the *Canadian Charter of Rights and Freedoms* and should be struck down as unconstitutional. The majority of Canada's Supreme Court, however, upheld section 43, stating that spanking does not violate a child's rights to security of the person or the right to equal treatment under the law without discrimination, and is not cruel and unusual punishment.

This section became part of the *Criminal Code* in 1892, and has allowed severe spanking, slapping, and striking with belts and other objects to be used against children in the name of "correction." The aim of the Repeal 43 Committee is to persuade Parliament to end this harmful and unjust defence to assaults against children; it has no place in a democratic society that values children and should be **repealed**.

The process leading up to this Supreme Court ruling involved many Canadian professional perspectives and expertise. Corinne Robertshaw, founder of the Repeal 43 Committee and a retired lawyer and federal public servant who had authored a federal study on child protection, assisted counsel for one of the interveners. In "From the Pen of . . ." Box 7.2, she describes how and why the Repeal Committee was formed and why the Supreme Court decision has left the law in an unsatisfactory position. The goal of repeal is shared by many Canadian organizations, and they all will continue to advocate for the repeal of section 43 until this relic of a bygone age is ended.

Internet Luring Law

Despite the spanking law setback, the pursuit for legislation to protect children continued, this time it related to section 172.1 of the *Criminal Code.* Added in 2002, this new law criminalized electronic communication with a person believed to be a child for the purpose of facilitating the commission of sexual offences. Depending on the offence, the requisite age (real or believed) of the intended victim varied from 14 to 18.

7.2 From the Pen of Corinne Robertshaw: Founder/Coordinator, Repeal 43 Committee

Campaign to End Legal Approval of Corporal Punishment of Children

Section 43, Criminal Code of Canada: *"Protection of Persons in Authority; Correction of Child by Force: Every schoolteacher, parent or person standing in the place of a parent is justified in using force by way of correction toward a pupil or child, as the case may be, who is under his care, if the force does not exceed what is reasonable under the circumstances" (R.S.C., 1985, c. C-46).*

In 1951, the Quebec Court of Appeal explained the kind of force justified by s. 43: "That the punishment naturally may cause pain hardly needs to be stated; otherwise its whole purpose would be lost. The mere fact that the children disciplined suffered contusions and bruises is not in itself proof of exercise of undue force" (*Campeau v. The King* 1951, *103 C.C.C. 355 at p. 361.)*

The defence of "reasonable" correctional assaults on children by teachers and parents in Canada's *Criminal Code* came from English common law in 1892. Judicial acquittals under s. 43 have included spanking, strapping, hitting with belts or sticks, causing bruises, welts, slapping the face, and kicking with stocking feet. Acquittals for such assaults basically continued until the Supreme Court of Canada reinterpreted section 43 in its 2004 decision on the section's constitutionality.

In 1984, Dickson J., speaking for the Supreme Court of Canada, stated:

Section 43 is, "in other words, a justification. It exculpates a parent, schoolteacher or person standing in the place of a parent who uses force in the correction of a child, because it considers such an action not a wrongful, but a rightful, one" (*Ogg-Moss v. The Queen,*

[1984] 2 S.C.R. 173, Dickson J. at p. 193 [court's emphasis]).

Eight Private Members' Bills to repeal s. 43 were introduced in the House of Commons between 1989 and 2001, and five in the Senate between 1996 and 2010. Because of the limited amount of time allowed for private bills, none made it to a final vote.

In 1994, I suggested that a non-government committee of lawyers, pediatricians, social workers, and educators be established to advocate repeal of s. 43. A small, voluntary committee was formed and we began our campaign with a 30-page brief I wrote to the Minister of Justice and other federal ministers. It set out the reasons for advocating repeal of this section: arguing that the law's justification of corporal punishment can lead to physical and psychological injury (and even death), contributes to violence in society, is contrary to both *Canada's Charter of Rights and Freedoms* and the United Nations *Convention on the Rights of the Child,* and has no place in a democratic society that values children.

Thanks to a grant from the Laidlaw Foundation, we had funds to print and mail the brief to various organizations and individuals asking them to write federal ministers to advocate repeal. We issued press releases, and as the issue was new to the media, were interviewed on radio and television and invited to submit articles to newspapers. We sent information to MPs, spoke at conferences, encouraged petitions to Parliament, and organized press conferences for Private Members' bills in 1997 and 2001. Over the next few years, more than 200 organizations wrote letters to ministers stating their reasons for supporting repeal.

(continued)

In 1998, the Canadian Foundation for Children, Youth and the Law launched a constitutional challenge to s. 43 in the Ontario Superior Court of Justice on the grounds that s. 43 was vague, overbroad, infringed sections 7, 12, and 15 of the *Charter*, was not saved by s. 1, and was inconsistent with the UN *Convention on the Rights of the Child,* to which Canada is a signatory. Mr. Justice McCombs delivered judgment in July 2000 and dismissed the application, holding that s. 43 did not violate any provision of the *Charter.* The Foundation appealed to the Ontario Court of Appeal, and in January 2002 the appeal was rejected on the basis that sections 7 and 12 of the Charter were not violated, and although s. 43 does violate s. 15 of the *Charter*, this violation was "clearly justified" under *Charter* s.1.

In 2002, we launched the Repeal 43 Committee website as a more efficient way to make information on the issue available to a wider audience. I update it every two months or so with developments in Canada and, where relevant, in the international community. From 2003 to 2008, we accessed funds for publishing an Open Letter in *The Globe and Mail* on Canada's National Child Day, which commemorates ratification of the UN *Convention on the Rights of the Child* in 1991. The letters urged the Prime Minister and MPs to respect the Convention by ending our law's licence to hit children for discipline.

In 2002, the Foundation applied to the Supreme Court of Canada for leave to appeal. Leave was granted and a number of organizations for and against repeal were granted intervener status to present argument. The Ontario Association of Social Workers was one of the organizations that intervened to support repeal and we assisted counsel with background information on the issue.

The Supreme Court heard the appeal in June 2003 and delivered its 30-page judgment January 30, 2004. In a split decision, Chief Justice Beverley McLachlin wrote that s. 43 does not infringe the *Charter* and is therefore constitutional. Justices Louise Arbour, Marie Deschamps, and William Binnie wrote dissenting opinions, Justices Arbour and Deschamps holding that s. 43 infringes the *Charter* and should be struck down, and Justice Binnie holding that s. 43 infringes the *Charter* but is justified under *Charter* s. 1.

In order to find s. 43 constitutional, the majority substantially reinterpreted the section. It held that s. 43 was not a defence of corporal punishment by teachers; a defence for parents only if the force was used against children age 2 to 12 years; the force was no more than "trifling" and "symbolic"; and accorded with several other guidelines set out in the judgment. The Court upheld the power of parents and teachers to use reasonable force to restrain a child (of any age), provided the force is used for restraint and not as corporal punishment for correction.

The Supreme Court decision dismayed child advocates and was strongly criticized for its uncertain, confusing, and potentially dangerous message. Critics wrote that the notion of a safe level of physical punishment was fundamentally flawed because there is always a risk of escalation inherent in using any physical force to punish a child. As Professor Joan Durrant wrote: "The court's criteria for defining reasonable force do not protect children adequately because they perpetuate the belief that some level of physical punishment is safe and harmless." Stephen Lewis, United Nations special envoy on HIV/AIDS in Africa, commenting on the decision at a 2006 child welfare forum in Victoria, B.C., said: "I've always had some reverence for the Supreme Court, but when the decision came down on section 43, I wondered what had happened to the judges."

A 2006 national survey showed that the Supreme Court's judicial changes to s. 43 are virtually unknown by the general public. As a result, witnesses and children are unaware that many correctional assaults are now criminal offences and parents are unaware they risk prosecution for such assaults.

Because many of the Court's guidelines are subjective, uncertain, and pose a risk to young children, they cannot be a fitting basis for public education. Our task now is to convince a member of the House of Commons to introduce a bill to repeal s. 43, as this is the only appropriate and realistic way to end the confusion and clarify the law. As Schopenhauer said: *All truth passes through three stages. First it is ridiculed. Second, it is violently opposed. Third,* *it is accepted as being self-evident.* We have not yet reached the third stage but will continue our efforts until we do. Readers wishing further information are invited to visit our website at www.repeal43.org.

Review Question

This advocacy movement, like so many, relies on Canadian support. Can you think of how your school might provide an awareness campaign illuminating the goals of the Repeal 43 Campaign?

Source: Provided to Anastasia Bake from Corinne Robertshaw, B.A.(Hons), LL.B. Retired lawyer and federal public servant.

On July 15, 2010, a significant victory was achieved when, in a unanimous 9–0 ruling, the Supreme Court of Canada upheld the conviction of an Edmonton man. Despite the fact that it was a police officer who had baited him, 50-year-old Michell Rayal Levigne was charged with luring a 13-year-old boy on the Internet. Levigne was initially found not guilty of Internet luring, but was later convicted by the Alberta Court of Appeal. At issue was the extent to which Internet users must go to confirm the age of the person they're chatting with, *when* an online conversation turns to sex.

Writing for the Supreme Court, Justice Morris J. Fish said that under the law Levigne is presumed to have believed that a police officer (who baited him) on the Internet was a 13-year-old boy calling himself Jessy G. "He is presumed by law to have believed that he was communicating with an underage sexual target," Fish wrote. "The constitutional validity of that presumption is not in issue" (*R. v. Levigne*, 2010, SCC 25).

Justice Fish said in the ruling that Levigne did not take the "reasonable steps" required by law to determine whether the person he was communicating with was, in fact, 13 before arranging a sexual liaison. Levigne had arranged a meeting online, and was arrested at a fast-food restaurant in an Edmonton shopping mall in 2006; he testified he "would have walked out" had a 13-year-old showed up. Levigne also contended he didn't believe the person he was chatting with was 13, even though the undercover officer said repeatedly that he was 13 and in Grade 7. The Supreme Court agreed with this decision by the Alberta Court of Appeal that had reversed Levigne's **acquittal**, and didn't accept Levigne's argument. Fish wrote that the "decisive question is whether the trial judge was bound by two provisions of the *Criminal Code* to find that Levigne believed he was communicating by computer with an underage boy for the purposes of sex."

Justice Fish wrote, "The 'reasonable steps' invoked by the accused were in fact neither 'reasonable' nor 'steps to ascertain the age' of the person with whom he was communicating by computer for the avowed purpose of his own sexual gratification. . . . Rather, they were circumstances which explain why he in fact took no steps to ascertain the actual age of JG. And this despite the latter's repeated assertion that he was only 13" (*R. v. Levigne*, 2010, SCC 25).

In structuring the *Criminal Code* provision on Internet luring as it did, Justice Fish said Parliament "recognized that the anonymity of an assumed online profile acts as both a shield for the predator and a sword for the police" (*R. v. Levigne*, 2010, SCC 25). "As a shield, because it permits predators to mask their true identities as they pursue their nefarious intentions; as a sword...because it permits investigators, posing as children, to cast their lines in Internet chat rooms, where lurking predators can be expected to take the bait—as the appellant did here" (*R. v. Levigne*, 2010, SCC 25).

With the advent of technology parents have something new to fear. Sexual predators have always been cunning and calculating, and online predators are no different. They often have an easily accessible audience and can capture the attention of a vulnerable child.

This Supreme Court decision wiped out a grey zone in Canada's Internet luring law, and it sent a strong message that children are off-limits. Moreover, if a person engages in this type of behaviour there will be legal consequences.

Laws for Children Testifying in Criminal Court

Testifying in any court process can cause fear and vulnerability for adults, so image the impact on a child. Yet, children are required to testify about their own victimization or about violent acts they have witnessed. A courtroom is a frightening environment for a child, and children are placed under an enormous emotional burden and responsibility when they are testifying. In "From the Pen of . . ." Box 7.3, Wendy van Tongeren Harvey describes the laws that support children in the Canadian criminal court system. Ms. van Tongeren Harvey is a nationally and internationally acclaimed Canadian lawyer, author, lecturer, trainer, consultant, and reformer. For more than 30 years, she has specialized in the prosecution of sex crimes against society's most vulnerable people—children and persons with disabilities. She has also prosecuted crimes against humanity through her participation in the legal team appointed to try war crimes at the Special Court of Sierra Leone, in Sierra Leone, Africa. Wendy van Tongeren Harvey has used her multiple roles, expertise, and passion to ultimately tell the story of victims. She has influenced public awareness, legislation, and practice standards both here and abroad. Ms. Harvey currently practises law as a prosecutor with the British Columbia Ministry of the Attorney General in New Westminster.

7.3 From the Pen of Wendy van Tongeren Harvey, Crown Counsel: Laws for Children Testifying in the Criminal Courts

Significant numbers of children are required to testify in our Canadian criminal courts each year. The system demands that, in a trial, they describe illegal, unsavory, and sometimes frightening acts surrounding their own victimization or what they have witnessed inflicted upon others. That Canada's is an **adversarial system**, with its emphasis on public access, potentially makes the experience all the more intimidating, placing a huge emotional responsibility on the children.

The fears articulated by child witnesses—which interfere not only in a child's willingness and ability to participate in the process at the outset, but also later in providing a full and candidate account in the courtroom—have been studied and documented by well-known and highly respected researchers in Canada. This research has informed judges and Parliament alike, resulting in sorely needed important and meaningful changes in our laws. The Supreme Court of Canada has played a role in acknowledging the failings to children of our justice system in the past while upholding newly enacted laws designed to protect them.

Since 1983, 1988, and forward, significant changes to the *Criminal Code (Code)* and the *Canada Evidence Act (CEA)* incrementally enacted, have resulted in a dramatic shift not only in the procedures but also the atmosphere sustained in a courtroom where child witnesses are present. The innovations have encouraged justice personnel to become more aware of children's needs and, perhaps more importantly, have allowed lawyers, judges, and supporters of child witnesses who are already sensitized the freedom to bring their awareness into the courtroom. The result is a child integrative approach involving compassion and age-appropriate questioning befitting the reality that a child on the stand presents quite differently than an adult.

Where the legislators and judges, guided by research and the past experiences of children in court, intended to bring about more convictions in the right cases, and therefore better protection for children with fewer traumatic court experiences for children, the effort has paid off. There are obvious signs that the court experience for children has improved and the innovative legal reforms have improved the handling of cases involving child victims generally and even increased the likelihood of convictions in cases of child sexual abuse. Examples of the changes behind these results include:

1. *Closed courtroom:* In cases involving a witness under 18, there is an inference in law allowing judges to close the courtroom during a child witness's testimony (s. 486(1) *Criminal Code*). In 2006, Parliament amended the *Code* and in a separate section (s. 486.2 *Code*) created a presumption that a child under 18 is entitled to testify without having to enter the courtroom in person. The testimony is transmitted by vidconferencing or closed-circuit television technology. Therefore, a child witness would already be separated from those court watchers who would be asked to leave the courtroom if it were closed to the public under s. 486(1). In practice, therefore, this means that there is a lesser need to resort to this section of the *Code* closing the court to the public.

(continued)

2. *Privacy protection:* The *Criminal Code* protects the privacy of a witness under 18 in a sexual crime or child pornography trial. Where an application for a ban of publication is made by the prosecutor, complainant, or witness, and the judge shall prohibit the publication or broadcast of any information that would identify a complainant or witness in a case involving the offences listed in the section which are sexual offences (subsection 486.4 *Code*). Similar bans are available upon application in writing under s. 486.5 of the *Criminal Code*. In addition, s. 111 of the *Youth Criminal Justice Act* (YCJA) protects the privacy of all complainants and witnesses in a youth criminal trial by prohibiting the publication of their identify no matter what the alleged offence.

The Crown normally asks for a ban of publication at the early stages of court appearances on a routine basis.

3. *Pre-recorded audio/visual statements:* The prosecution may tender an audio and visual recording of the child's pre-recorded statement(s) if the recorded statement(s) was made "within a reasonable time after the alleged offence" and the child testifies and adopts the contents of the recording (section 715.1 of the *Code*). This normally means acknowledging that s/he was trying his/her best to tell the truth during the telling of their version of events in the previously recorded statement. The recording, usually a DVD and corresponding transcript, becomes part of the testimony of the child to be considered by the Trier of Fact in the trial. The recording is not corroborative of what is said on the stand, and does not bolster the reliability of the witness merely because both versions are consistent. The recording is admitted even in circumstances when the child no longer fully recalls the details of the offence, although the lack of recall will be taken into consideration by the Trier of Fact when weighing the evidence later in the trial

(see *R. v. F. (C.)* [1997] S.C.J. No. 89 (S.C.C.)).

The Crown will likely ask the child further questions on matters not covered in the forensic interview. The direct examination structure is quite different from the free narrative, or stepwise interview structure at the investigative stage.

Although the underlying assumption behind s. 715.1 is that a report given shortly after the alleged offence is likely to be more complete and accurate than a report given (in court) several months or even years later, courts have demonstrated a trend to look to all the circumstances in determining "within a reasonable time after the alleged offence" and have admitted recordings from statements taken years after the offence. This arises particularly where there is a delay in reporting. There is a body of jurisprudence (see, for example, *R. v. D.D.* [2000] 2 S.C.R. 275) which reiterates the abrogation of the rule of recent complaint (1983 Bill c.127) to say that a delayed report is but one circumstance to be taken into consideration in weighing a complaint, and is never deemed to invalidate a complaint on its face. Courts have shown a growing acknowledgment that delayed reporting is more likely than an immediate one, and have therefore shown a willingness to accept delayed recorded statements under s. 715.1 resulting from a complainant's reluctance to report.

A number of factors will determine whether the trial Crown lawyer will decide to enter the statement DVD rather than rely on the child to retell the evidence in whole. The recording must be of acceptable quality. The courts have shown flexibility and at times— where the audio is not of sufficient volume, for example—have allowed the audio CD to be played simultaneously. Equally, the quality of the interview must be acceptable. Factors which may contribute to not using the pre-recorded interview include excessive leading, or an interfering third party being in the room, to a degree that the integrity of the interview process is compromised beyond repair.

Most police agencies appreciate, firstly, how critical an excellent interview is to the success of a prosecution, and secondly, the necessity of assigning trained, skilled interviewers to an investigation if one is to achieve excellent results in a child's forensic interview. In 2012, the RCMP in E Division adopted the stepwise interview guidelines as the standard practice for their officers when interviewing children. The same approach will expand to RCMP in the rest of Canada in 2012.

In addition, child advocacy centres are opening across the country encouraged by funding opportunities from the federal government as well as private funders. Sophie's Place in Surrey and the ORCA Centre in Victoria are but two examples in British Columbia of the budding trend. These centres embody a coordinated approach in investigating and prosecuting crimes against children.

4. *Competence:* Until recently, all persons younger than 14 were required to be questioned, usually by the judge but sometimes by the Crown, before testifying, to allow the judge to determine if the child was competent to testify. The old threshold for competency was "sufficiently intelligent," which became "ability to communicate the evidence" in 1988. The questioner framed the questions to demonstrate that the child possessed the cognitive skills and moral understanding required to provide accurate and honest testimony. As a result of research that indicates there is no relevant connection between such an inquiry and a child's true ability to communicate their evidence, the *CEA* was amended in 2005 and now all

witnesses, including children, are deemed competent to testify unless otherwise challenged. A difference still exists between children and adults at the preliminary stage of testifying, where children are asked to "promise to tell the truth" whereas adults either swear an oath or affirm to tell the truth.

Testimonial Aids

There are special courtroom procedures set out in the *Code* designed to assist children in testifying (Bala, 1990 Jaffe et al., 1986 Child Witness Project, 2002). The provisions are sensitive to the needs of children in the court process and are presumed to be available to any witness under 18 at the time of testifying. These include the right to:

1. Have a support person of the witness's choice be present and close to the witness when testifying;

2. Testify outside of the courtroom or behind a screen, the method being the choice of the witness, so not to see the person accused of the offence;

3. Being cross-examined by an appointed lawyer rather than directly by the person accused of the offence where she or he is without counsel.

The availability of these testimonial aids was an important addition to the criminal justice process. But how are these services utilized, who requests them, and who prepares the child who needs them?

An important place to start in this discussion is with a clear statement on the necessity of the children/adolescents and their supporters being aware of their rights to these accommodations in order to encourage their use. To this end, both levels of government have published and funded the creation and distribution of user-friendly material describing their availability. Two clear examples (beyond the Canada

(continued)

Justice published material, including the website www.justice.gc.ca) is the website www.courtchoices.ca, created in B.C. with funding from Ottawa as an initiative of the Bill C-2 interministry committee whose mandate was to implement the Bill in 2005 and 2006. The website has two components: "Let's Go to Court," designed for children 7–13 describing their anticipated court experience, and the interactive presentation designed for adolescents 13–17 which takes the user through the stages of the system. The title "Court Choices" communicates the ideology of choice for the witness in the court process; the number of choices having been expanded by the recent law reform. In addition, the London *Centre for Children and Families in the Justice System* has published a series of booklets that individually describe the accommodations available. This material is also available online at the www.lfcc.on.ca website.

In addition to published material, the Criminal Justice Branch in British Columbia redrafted relevant policies and practice directives so that Crown lawyers are guided to communicate to the children/adolescents what accommodations are available to them. This is done firstly by a letter that is sent out in advance in a case involving a child witness and subsequently when face-to-face meetings take place as part of court preparation. Crown lawyers are also encouraged to work with victim services programs throughout the provinces who play a key role in informing parents and children/adolescents of their right to these accommodations.

Support person: The concept of a support person is not new, and even before the legislative changes to the *Code* judges often did allow a support person to sit with the child. Section 486.1 clarifies that the support person is a person of the witness's choice who not only is present during the testimony but also sits close to the child. Even with this provision, some judges want the support person to sit out of view of the child for fear of influence and have been known to exclude a parent from court while the child testifies in the courtroom.

In choosing a support person, the parent and child may be assisted by these guidelines:

1. The support person:

   a. Should not be a witness named and not a potential witness in the trial (for example, the person who received the first complaint or was present in the same location at the time of the offences). The witness runs a risk that the defence may ask the support person be made available for questioning and even disqualified as a support person causing negativity at the last moment in the trial before the child starts testifying.

   b. Should be a mature person (that is, not another child) who is willing to sit with the witness without inappropriately interacting, providing them answers to questions or appearing to do so;

   c. May be the victim services worker. The advantages of having the worker in this role is the freeing up of family members to meet other commitments during the process and the familiarity the worker already has with the system. Occasionally there are events that occur in the separate CCTV room—such as a child needing a bathroom break, the child failing asleep, even a spider at the feet of the witness—and an experienced victim support worker will know how to deal with these contingencies without adding anxiety to an already stressful experience.

Testifying behind a screen or outside of the courtroom: The child witness has a choice of location, vis à vis the courtroom, when testifying. They may testify:

- in the courtroom without a screen or screening device (likely a partition and CCTV link);
- in the courtroom with a screen or screening device;

- outside the courtroom (which may be either in the court building or nearby).

This opportunity has existed since 1988, and even before then, as far back as the early 1900s, there is **case law** authority for the accused being asked to sit at the back of the courtroom to accommodate a child witness (*R. v. Smellie* (1919), 14 Cr. App. R. 128). Since the 1988 *Code* amendments (Bill C-15) further legislative changes in the *Code* have broadened the applicability to witnesses as well as victims and to cases where any offence is charged rather than restricting it to sexual crimes and crimes of violence upon application to the court and showing the need for same. In 2006 the Bill C-2 amendments eliminated the requirement to show need, and it is now presumed the appropriate procedure for children under 18 in cases of all offences.

Being outside the courtroom totally separates the witness from not only the accused person but also members of the public and around the courtroom. The experience is more relaxed, hence a need arises for an experienced support person who helps maintain the appropriate formality of the occasion.

At times, there are equipment challenges that flow from out-of-court testimony and delays occur. And, in some jurisdictions, the equipment challenges are so significant that the choice of this method of testimony is elusive. There are still locations in Canada where witnesses are not told of the options or the equipment is not available to make the choice a reality. In all cases, advance communication and preparation is key if out-of-court testimony is anticipated.

Some fairly young children express a desire to be in the courtroom to show others they are brave, because they like the accused and want to see him, are curious, or other. This may be without a mature understanding of the realities of the court scenario and a parent or the Crown may apply that a child testify outside the room in spite of the child's expressed wishes and the accommodation will still be allowed. An example is a young child who was in the house at the time of a domestic homicide and has not seen the alleged offending spouse who has been in jail since the date of the murder. In the case of older children and adolescents the procedure followed will be according to their request.

The constitutionality of these laws was challenged but subsequently upheld in 1993, by a unanimous Supreme Court of Canada decision. Madam Justice L'Heureux-Dubé wrote on behalf of the Court that one of the main goals of the court process is to seek the truth, and integral to that goal is the need that the evidence of all those involved, including children, be given in the way that is most favourable to eliciting the truth (*R. v. Levogiannis*, [1993] 4 S.C.R. 475, (1993), 85 C.C.C. (3d) 327). More recently, the amendments in 2005–2006 (Bill C-2) related to the absolution of the competence inquiry and the presumption in favour of the out-of-court testimony or screen were also constitutionally challenged unsuccessfully in the case of *R. v. S. (J.)* (2008), 252 C.C.C. (3d) 1 (S.C.C.).

Preventing cross-examination by the accused: The *Code* (s. 486.3) allows for the appointment of counsel to cross-examine the child/adolescent witness under 18 in a trial for any offence where the accused is not represented. The section is worded presumptively in favour of appointing counsel. The implementation of the section is complicated. The accused often does not inform the court of the absence of counsel until late in the process, is not named in the section as the party who applies for the lawyer (as it is perhaps assumed to be the accused's preference if he personally conducts the cross-examination of the child), and the Crown cannot play an active role in ensuring or determining who the new lawyer might be. If circumstances arise triggering a need for an s. 486.3 application, a delay of the trial proceedings for not only the appointment but

(continued)

also the preparation of the new lawyer appointed is highly likely. This may even occur on the day of trial where an accused has fired his lawyer and not informed the Crown.

Review Question

Many important and helpful aids have been conceived and implemented. However, what other challenges continue to confront children, and what strategies could be allowed to support them?

Source: Provided to Anastasia Bake by Wendy van Tongeren Harvey, Crown Counsel (British Columbia).

7.2 LAWS PROTECTING ADULTS FROM VIOLENCE AND HARM

The Canadian *Criminal Code* has no specific offence for the psychological or emotional abuse that takes place in the environment of a violent relationship. Yelling, insults, and put-downs are not crimes under the *Criminal Code*. Yet they cause harm and often are used to control and intimidate intimate partners. The legal provisions that most commonly apply to the acts of violence that have been described in this textbook include sexual assault, assault, murder, criminal harassment, sexual harassment, forcible confinement, and neglect. This section will begin with the *Criminal Code* offences that relate to sexual crimes.

Canadian Laws for the Sexually Victimized

The one thing that doesn't abide by majority rule is a person's conscience.

—**Atticus Finch in** *To Kill a Mockingbird,* **by Harper Lee**

In 1983, the *Criminal Code of Canada* underwent significant changes with the enactment of Bill C-127 (refer to Chapter 1). Three new "categories" of sexual assault offences were introduced, focusing on the violent rather than the sexual nature of the offence. The reforms also made it clear that the spouse of a victim could be charged with sexual assault. Additionally, one of the significant shortcomings of the earlier sexual assault legislation related to language. The specific description of rape was gender-biased. The new legislation clarified that males and/or females could be the victim of sexual assault. Yet despite the 1983 changes, challenges would continue within the Canadian justice system involving sexual assault cases.

Today, the Department of Justice Canada (2005) defines sexual assault as any form of sexual activity without a person's consent. This may include:

- any kissing, fondling, touching, oral/anal sex, or sexual intercourse without voluntary consent
- not stopping sexual contact when asked
- forcing someone to engage in sexual intercourse or any other sexual act

Further, in 1991 the Supreme Court of Canada ruled that the act of sexual assault does not depend solely on contact with any specific part of the human anatomy but rather on the act of a sexual nature that violates the sexual integrity of the victim (*R. v. Chase*, [1991] 2 S.C.R. 293). When investigating a sexual assault, there are certain relevant factors to consider:

a. the part of the body touched

b. the nature of the contact

c. the situation in which the contact occurred

d. the words and gestures accompanying the act

e. all other circumstances surrounding the act

f. any threats that may or may not be accompanied by force

But law is complex, and since Bill C-127 enactment numerous challenges have occurred to address the constitutionality of the law. What ultimately began to unfold after 1983 in courtrooms across Canada were legal challenges to clarify the issues of (1) access to complainants' (victims') **records**, and (2) the "meaning of consent" (or mistaken belief in consent). These important issues will now be discussed.

Access to Complainants' Records

Eight years had passed when, in 1991, Bill C-127 faced its first of many major tests; the Supreme Court of Canada in a 7–2 ruling struck down the so-called rape shield provision of the *Criminal Code* for sexual assault. The ruling was on two specific cases, *R. v. Seaboyer* and *R. v. Gayme*. The Court's decision vastly changed the face of Bill C-127, and set off a fireball of protests. What took place? The rape shield provision of the *Criminal Code* had specifically referred to two sections:

- section 276, which prevented evidence about the sexual history of the complainant with any person other than the accused.

- section 277, which declared admissible evidence of sexual reputation for the purpose of undermining the credibility of the complainant.

Attorneys in the Seaboyer and Gayme cases submitted to the Supreme Court of Canada the position that those subsections of the *Criminal Code* contravened their clients' *Charter* rights, which prevented them from mounting a full defence of the accusations against their client. The two areas of the *Charter* were sections 7 and 11(d). They read as follows:

- section 7: Everyone has the right to life, liberty and security of the person and the right not to be deprived thereof except in accordance with the principles of fundamental justice.

- section 11(d). Any person charged with an offence has the right to be presumed innocent until proven guilty according to law in a fair and public hearing by an independent and impartial tribunal

The attorneys argued that these two sections of the *Charter* prevented them from challenging the complainant's reputation and also prevented them from supporting a defence of "honest but mistaken belief in consent" (Tang, 1998).

The Supreme Court ultimately ruled that section 276 of the *Criminal Code,* which had allowed for a blanket exclusion of evidence, was flawed. The original purpose of this section was to abolish the "outmoded, sexist-based use of sexual conduct evidence," but the Supreme Court determined that Bill C-127 "overshoots the mark and renders inadmissible evidence which may be essential to the presentation of legitimate defences and hence to a fair trial" (*R. v. Seaboyer; R. v. Gayme* [1991] 2 S.C.R. 577 at 582).

In her judgment, Madam Justice Beverley McLachlin stated that the evidence of the complainant's sexual history with other men or with the accused may be necessary to support a defence of honest but mistaken belief in consent. This decision set the **precedent** for the inclusion of sexual history as admissible evidence (Schissel, 1996). McLachlin also justified striking down section 276 on the grounds that sexual stereotyping was a "universally discredited" practice in the present legal system (*R. v. Seaboyer; R. v. Gayme* [1991] 2 S.C.R. 577).

The 7–2 decision caused a sharp division of opinion within the Supreme Court. There were two dissenting positions in response to this case: Justice Claire L'Heureux-Dubé, and Justice Charles Gonthier. Justice L'Heureux-Dubé wrote the minority opinion and said that "Parliament enacted the 1983 law because it did not trust judges to make the correct decision about an issue still clouded by 'myths and stereotypes'" (*R. v. Seaboyer; R. v. Gayme* [1991] 2 S.C.R. 577).

Women's groups and activists shared Justice L'Heureux-Dubé's view. They too thought the Supreme Court decision could be potentially dangerous. Essentially, the decision to allow or exclude evidence regarding a victim's sexual history would no longer be

The Honourable Madam Justice Claire L'Heureux-Dubé. www.scc-csc.gc.ca/court-cour/ju/lheureux-dube/index-eng.asp

controlled by the *Criminal Code*. This decision would now be made on a case-by-case basis, leaving the decision to the discretion of individual trial judges.

Once again, vulnerability was created for those sexually victimized seeking justice. The possibility that a sexual assault complainant's personal records could be disclosed to the accused was again at hand (Gotell, 2002).

Introduction of Bill C-49 Following the Supreme Court decision, in 1992 Parliament went back to work to write a new bill that would govern sexual character evidence in sexual assault laws and create a new rape shield law with strict guidelines for when, and how, previous sexual conduct could be used by a defendant at trial. The outcome led to Bill C-49 (An Act to Amend the *Criminal Code* (prohibiting the admission of sexual history evidence), c.38, Ss.276, 276.1, 276.2).

Bill C-49 replaced the former *Criminal Code* section 276 with new procedures and criteria for determining the admissibility of evidence concerning a complainant's sexual conduct and use of a woman's past sexual history to discredit her. But before long, in 1995, the Supreme Court rendered another judgment in the case of British Columbia Bishop Hubert O'Connor *(R. v. O'Connor)* when it again struck down the rape shield law. This decision once again supported the rights of the accused; see "Canadian Headline News" Box 7.4.

7.4 Canadian Headline News: Bishop Hubert O'Connor

During Bishop Hubert Patrick O'Connor's Criminal trial the court heard vivid details about a predatory perpetrator who used his position to attain sex from Aboriginal girls. He maintained his innocence throughout the long court battle, arguing his accusers had consented to sex. Incidentally, he also admitted to fathering a child who was placed for adoption.

Following the court proceedings in 1996, he was convicted of committing rape and indecent assault on two young Aboriginal women during the 1960s when he was a priest. At the same time, a former secretary also testified that he had once presented her with a Christmas gift of a statue of the Virgin Mary before feeling her breasts and trying to kiss her. He would later be found guilty. He was sentenced to two and a half years in prison by Justice Oppal.

Following this decision, his defence attorney successfully argued that the existing law had prevented them from mounting a full defence of the accusations against their client (Hubert O'Conner), because the Crown failed to provide the records of the therapists and psychologists who treated the accuser's victims.

The Court stated that the medical and counseling records of a complainant in a sexual assault case that are held by a third party can be disclosed by order of the judge. In making this decision, the court struck down the rape shield law of 1983. This decision resulted in outcry, and the eventual enactment of Bill C-46 in 1997.

In life, one could say, timing is everything. Due to Hubert Patrick O'Connor's attorney's legal defence, combined with his crime and

(continued)

the timing of his victims' disclosure, O'Connor has now been firmly rooted in legal history, providing him "eternal" notoriety. Apart from being the successful defendant in a leading decision on disclosure of medical records by the Supreme Court of Canada, he will be remembered as a sexual predator who preyed upon powerless Aboriginal girls. The essence of his character will be read and re-read in the archives of the Supreme Court of Canada.

Reflection Question

This case may have challenged a particular section of the *Criminal Code*, but what other issues are raised that should concern Canadians?

Source: *R. v. O'Connor*, [1995] 4 S.C.R. 411.

Introduction of Bill C-46 In response to the *R. v. O'Connor* Supreme Court decision, then-Justice Minister Allan Rock and numerous women's groups went back to work. On May 12, 1997, Bill C-46, An Act to Amend the Criminal Code (production of records in sexual offence proceedings), became law.

This bill limited the production of a complainant's personal counselling records to the defence in sexual offence cases. Specific provisions regarding the **production** and **disclosure** of third-party records (therapists, counselling, medical) to the accused in sexual assault proceedings were addressed in Bill C-46 (s. 278.1). Moreover, Bill C-46 minimized the number of occasions in which a complainant's sexual character could be brought up in a sexual assault trial. For many feminists and politicians the enactment of Bill C-49 was viewed as a victory, providing the courts with a new rape shield law that would help victims.

Bill C-46 would be tested in *R. v. Mills*. This time, in 1999, the Supreme Court upheld the earlier conviction. Supreme Court decisions regarding access to complainants' records had been rendered. Bill C-46 would now hinder the routine legal invasions of complainants' private records.

Access to Records Challenged in the New Millennium In 2000, almost 10 years later, the Supreme Court was called upon to rule on the case involving Andrew Scott Darrach (*R. v. Darrach*, 2000 SCC 46, [2000] 2 S.C.R. 443). This trial became a pivotal Canadian case, which made its way to the Supreme Court of Canada. At the heart of his defence lawyer's argument was the concern that his client did not have full access to the complaints record, which prevented him from having a fair trial. During Darrach's trial his lawyer argued that the rape shield legislation violated his client's *Charter* rights. The trial judge refused, ruling that the accused failed to provide a connection between the complainant's sexual history (access to her records) and his defence of a mistaken belief of consent. Darrach was convicted and sentenced to nine months in prison.

Darrach's case was then appealed to the Ontario Court of Appeal, which upheld the trial judge's findings. It was then argued before the Supreme Court. The Supreme Court dismissed the appeal in a unanimous ruling. The Court found that all the rape shield provisions in the *Criminal Code* were constitutional. Nearly 10 years after the Seaboyer and Gayme cases, the Supreme Court of Canada had rendered its decision (*R. v. Darrach*, 2000 SCC 46, [2000] 2 S.C.R. 443).

Veritas, the statue of truth. One of two statues flanking the Supreme Court of Canada. Truth is vital! In 1993, Madam Justice L'Heureux-Dubé wrote on behalf of the Court that one of the main goals of the court process is to seek the truth, and integral to that goal is the need that the evidence of all those involved, including children, be given in the way that is most favourable to eliciting the truth (*R. v. Levogiannis,* [1993] 4 S.C.R. 475, (1993), 85 C.C.C. (3d) 327). www.scc-csc.gc.ca/details/art-stat-veritas2-eng.asp

Consent or Mistaken Belief in Consent

In Canada, no one has the legal right to touch another person sexually without their consent. This includes kissing, touching, sexual intercourse, anal intercourse, and oral sex. A sexual assault occurs when someone forces any form of sexual activity on another person without that person's consent. As straightforward as this definition might be, a central issue in cases of sexual assault is that of consent, and perhaps *truth*. The "honest belief" that the complainant (victim) in a sexual assault case consented would provide the evidence necessary for a successful defence, and therefore acquit the accused.

So what is consent and how does it occur in reality? In 1995, this particular issue was tested in the Supreme Court in *R. v. Park.* The Supreme Court ruled on the issue of a mistaken belief defence in this sexual assault trial. Daryl Park was first convicted in an Alberta court, but that conviction was later overturned in the Alberta Court of Appeal. The case was then sent to the Supreme Court of Canada, which ruled that the original conviction should be restored. "Canadian Headline News" Box 7.5 describes the details of the case.

7.5 Canadian Headline News: The Supreme Court Decision in *R. v. Park*

According to the Supreme Court, Park and the victim had discussed birth control during their first date, along with the fact that the complainant was a born-again Christian and did not believe in pre-marital sex. The night of the incident, the accused called the complainant to come over to her house and she greeted him at the door wearing only a bathrobe. According to the complainant's testimony she resisted actively, both verbally and physically, but he was stronger. She described the assault in detail.

Feeling his weight atop her, she had a flashback to a previous traumatic experience and went into "shock." The next thing she remembered was him pulling his penis out of her and ejaculating on her stomach. She fled to the bathroom and vomited. He dressed and kissed her goodbye on the cheek as he left.

The accused testified that the complainant was an active participant in the sexual activity and "when things began to get 'hot', he prematurely ejaculated on her stomach" (*R. v. Park* [1995] 2 S.C.R. 836 at 845). He testified that no intercourse took place, and at trial his defence was that "the complainant consented to the sexual activity or, in the alternative that he had an honest but mistaken belief that she was consenting" (*R. v. Park* [1995] 2 S.C.R. 836 at 837).

The Supreme Court ruled that the conviction should be restored. In this decision, the Court determined that there must be an "air of reality" to support a mistaken belief in consent. Writing for the majority, Madame Justice L'Heureux-Dubé outlined the cases in which mistaken belief in consent could be used in sexual assault cases. From a practical perspective, she wrote, there should be only two principal considerations in a discussion regarding mistaken consent. First, what the complainant communicated; and second, the evidence that explained how the accused understood that consent. This meant that the jury would act as objective observers and decide what reasonable grounds the accused had (i.e., subjectively) for his alleged honest belief.

Reflection Question

Reading a synopsis of a sexual assault can create feelings that range from *shocking* to very *upsetting, to rage. However*, what these cases teach us is the many ways in which sexual assaults actually take place. What is your reaction to these circumstances? How often do you think women (and men) are forced into sexual activity, regardless of whether they define it as assault?

Source: R. v. Park [1995] 2 S.C.R. 836 at 844 and 845.

A second case of Supreme Court significance was *R. v. Ewanchuk*. This case would ultimately clarify the issue of consent, which built upon the earlier assertions put forward by defence of mistaken belief discussed in *R. v. Park*. The unfolding process of this case was quite different from *R. v. Park*. An overview of the case details is provided in "Canadian Headline News" Box 7.6.

Ultimately, in February 1999 the Supreme Court affirmed that *no actually means no* in sexual assault cases. As *R. v. Ewanchuk* and *R. v. Park* illustrate, the complexities of the criminal prosecution of sexual crimes, and the concerns and fears for victims, are numerous. This issue continually confronts victims, defence lawyers, and Crown prosecutors, and has been persistently recorded and debated in the media.

7.6 Canadian Headline News: The Supreme Court Decision in *R. v. Ewanchuk*

In February 1999, the Supreme Court of Canada was once again called upon to define consent in sexual assault cases. In *R. v. Ewanchuk* the court was asked to rule on the concept of implied consent.

In June 1994, 44-year-old Steve Ewanchuk interviewed a 17-year-old woman for a sales clerk position. The interview took place in a trailer parked in a shopping mall parking lot in Edmonton. According to the Alberta Court of Appeal, during the two-and-a-half-hour interview, Ewanchuk made several sexual advances toward the woman. She said no to each of those advances and when she told the accused she wanted to leave, the interview was completed and the pair walked out of the trailer. The 17-year-old subsequently filed charges with police and Ewanchuk was acquitted of sexual assault in provincial court.

The Crown appealed to the Alberta Court of Appeal. Three justices were involved and all three justices of the Court of Appeal issued separate reasons. Judges John McClung and Robert Foisy dismissed the appeal, suggesting that "[c]onsent may be implied or expressed, and clearly this was a case of implied consent" (*R. v. Ewanchuk* (1998), 57 Alta.L.R. (3d) 236 (Alta. COA). Judge McClung wrote:

> Ewanchuk's advances to the complainant were far less criminal than hormonal. In a less litigious age going too far in the boyfriend's car was better dealt with on-site—a well-chosen expletive, a slap in the face, or, if necessary, a well-directed knee. What this accused tried to initiate hardly qualifies him for the lasting stigma of a conviction for sexual assault (*R. v. Ewanchuk* (1998), 57 Alta.L.R. (3d) 250 (Alta. COA).

At the same time, Chief Justice Catherine Fraser wrote her reason for her disagreement. She stated that Canada's sexual assault laws were supposed to, "protect women from the inappropriate use of stereotypical assumptions about women in cases of sexual assault" (*R. v. Ewanchuk* (1998), 57 Alta.L.R. (3d) 268 (Alta. COA)).

The Crown then appealed the case to the Supreme Court, and on February 25, 1999, the Supreme Court determined in unanimous decision that the trial judge in the Ewanchuk case made errors of law. At the centre of the case was the issue of implied consent. Justice Major wrote:

> . . . that the accused knew that the complainant was not consenting before each encounter. The trial judge ought to have considered whether anything occurred between the communication of non-consent and the subsequent sexual touching, which the accused could have honestly believed constituted consent. The trial record conclusively establishes that the accused's persistent and increasingly serious advances constituted a sexual assault for which he had no defence (*R. v. Ewanchuk* [1999], 1 S.C.R. 330 at 334).

By relying on the question of what constitutes consent and what does not, what the victim does not do may well be construed as consent. This was in essence how the defence built its case in Ewanchuk. The victim said no, but because she did not attempt to leave the trailer, she did not scream, and she did not appear scared, the defence put forth the argument that the accused believed she was consenting despite saying no.

Reflection Question

You just read the facts regarding one more sexual assault. To the reader, these are words on a page. How might the actual victim—or any victim—feel as they read how the details of a traumatic event can eventually be played out in the Canadian justice system, which inevitably includes the public domain? Is it therefore understandable why so few victims report their sexual assault?

Source: R. v. Ewanchuk [1999], 1 S.C.R. 330.

In May 2011, the question of consent would again appear before the Supreme Court, but this time the particulars of the case were quite different. The Supreme Court upheld a conviction of a man who had sodomized his longtime partner after she had agreed to let him choke her until she was unconscious. They had not agreed to intercourse when she was conscious, therefore consent had not been given. So what happened?

In a 6–3 decision, the Court ruled the man, known only as J.A., was guilty of sexual assault against the Ottawa woman, known as K.D. The majority concluded that the *Criminal Code* protects the right of an individual "to consent to particular acts and to revoke her consent at any time," and does not allow for an individual to provide consent to sexual activity if the individual is not conscious. Chief Justice Beverley McLachlin wrote in the ruling, "I conclude that the *Code* makes it clear that an individual *must be conscious throughout the sexual activity* in order to provide the requisite consent." She further wrote, "Parliament requires ongoing, conscious consent to ensure that women and men are not the victims of sexual exploitation, and to ensure that individuals engaging in sexual activity are capable of asking their partners to stop at any point" (*R. v. J.A.*, 2011 SCC 28).

Consent Today, no means no at any time *and* consent must be given. Sexual contact cannot take place or continue if an agreement has been denied. Additionally, no one else, such as a parent, spouse, or sponsor, can give consent on behalf of another person.

Further, simple silence or lack of resistance to sexual contact cannot be equated with consent. It recognizes that people cannot always speak up and say no. The Court will not accept a victim's silence or passivity as a form of consent; in other words, implied consent is not a defence of criminal sexual assault. It is now understood that a victim could be in some way disabled. Plus, it is impossible to predict how a victim (or any of us, for that matter) will respond during a moment of extreme fear. Numerous reactions are possible when facing a potentially life-threatening event. Victims freeze. What's more, fearing the possibility of death a victim might choose to not speak. Realistically, if a death threat is made, it is possible, after all, that at that point a violent assaulted is unfolding.

Over the years, sexual perpetrators have developed various methods of coercion to help force a sexual offence. Consent defined by section 273.1 of Canada's *Criminal Code* refers to the voluntary agreement of the complainant (victim) to engage in the sexual activity in question. Consent is NOT given if:

- it is given by someone else
- the person is unconscious, drunk, drugged, or sleeping
- it is an abuse of power, trust, or authority
- the person does not say yes, says no, or through words or behaviour implies no
- the person changes her/his mind

A Special Note Regarding Date Rape Legally speaking, the *Criminal Code* definition of sexual assault applies to cases that have been commonly termed date rape, or acquaintance rape. The coining of this term reflected the statistical reality—many

Table 7.3 Recap of Sexual Assault Cases: Legal Challenges and Resultant Decisions		
Criminal Code of Canada: rape becomes codified	**1892**	
The Canadian Charter of Rights and Freedoms	**1982**	
Bill C-127 enacted	**1983**	
	1991	SCC strikes down the rape shield law *R. v. Seaboyer & Gayme*
Bill C-49 enacted	**1992**	
	1995	SCC strikes down the rape shield law *R. v. O'Connor*
Bill C-46 enacted	**1997**	
	1999	SCC upholds Bill C-46 *R. v. Mills*
	1999	SCC upholds Bill C-46 *R. v. Ewanchuk* *defines consent
	2000	SCC upholds Bill C-46 *R. v. Darrach* Rape shield provisions are constitutional

women were being raped not by strangers lying in wait, but by their dates, or someone they knew. Yet the process is the same for any sexual victimization:

1. the manner in which a case might be investigated (if investigated)

2. the manner in which charges are laid

3. the manner in which the case is prosecuted (if prosecuted)

4. the manner in which the court proceedings occur

It is noteworthy that date rape rarely involves extreme force; rather, the male attempts to fulfill his sexual expectations while failing to recognize the resistance of his victim. This suggests that date rape has existed for years but has gone unreported. The fact that most sexual assaults are classified as a level one assault tells us that many of these forms of sexual assaults could not have been reported before the 1983 legislation (Rhynard & Krebs, 1999).

Stalking (Criminal Harassment)

In 1993, the offence of criminal harassment, also known as "stalking," was introduced in section 264(1) of the *Criminal Code*. Although criminal harassment is not gender-specific, the legislation was mainly introduced as a response to violence against women (Department of Justice Canada, 2004).

Criminal harassment is obsessive behaviour directed toward another person. Stalking can be broadly defined as willfully, maliciously, and repeatedly following or harassing another person. Being stalked can be a frightening—and, for some, a life-changing—experience. The behaviour can cause the victim to fear for their safety, or that of someone close to them. The law related to criminal harassment has undergone changes. Since its enactment in 1993 there have been additional amendments:

- in 1997: if a murder is committed in the course of stalking, whether it was planned or deliberate, a first-degree murder offence is applied.

- in 2002: the maximum penalty for criminal harassment was doubled to 10 years in prison.

- in 2006: the law was amended to limit the instances in which an accused can personally cross-examine a victim of criminal harassment, thus preventing any continuation of the harassment that might occur.

Sexual Harassment

Sexual harassment is against the law. Although the *Criminal Code* protects people from physical or sexual assault, it does not legally cover sexual harassment. The *Canadian Human Rights Act* (R.S., 1985, c. H-6) protects employees from harassment related to work. The *Canadian Human Rights Act* gives each of us an equal opportunity to work and live without being hindered by discriminatory practices. Sexual harassment turns the workplace into a hostile environment. The jurisdiction of the *Canadian Human Rights Act* covers *federal* government departments, agencies, and Crown corporations, as well as businesses and industries that fall under federal jurisdiction, such as banks, airlines, and railways. All other places of work and education are protected through provincial legislation. Therefore, all provinces/territories have some form of legislation which prohibits discrimination.

Since the *Canadian Human Rights Act* was first passed it has undergone many changes. One of the most important developments resulted from a Supreme Court decision in 1989. The Supreme Court recognized sexual harassment as a prohibited form of discrimination under human rights legislation. At the time the Court defined "sexual harassment" as "unwelcome conduct of a sexual nature that detrimentally affects the work environment or leads to adverse job-related consequences for the victims of harassment" (*Janzen v. Platy Enterprises Ltd.*). Ultimately, employers are responsible for work-related harassment. The Supreme Court stated the goal of the employer is to control the organization; they therefore are the only ones who can actually reverse the negative effects of harassment and ensure a healthy work or school environment. If harassment does occur, a school and/or workplace must show it did everything possible to prevent it or to alleviate its effects.

Spousal Violence

The legislation protecting women against violence has improved dramatically over the last century considering the husband once had the legal right to discipline his wife if she disobeyed him as long as the instrument was a "stick no bigger than his thumb." Even decades later, when laws existed to protect women, the response of police was uneven. It was not that long ago when police would not arrest an abusive husband unless the police officer had personally witnessed the violence; even then it was rare.

There were reasons to clarify the reluctance on the part of the police. Many stemmed from the very nature of domestic violence:

- many abused women would return to their abusive partners and police would become frustrated by these choices

- when a charge was laid, the abused spouse would not follow through with the charges

- police were aware of the lenience of court sentences, and the fact that many women return to the abuser

- concerns that an arrest would provoke more severe acts of violence

Change would occur. Since the 1980s, many police forces have adopted a mandatory arrest policy in domestic situations. Police officers do not have to see the violence occur; they only need to have *reasonable and probable grounds* to believe that it happened. Reasonable and probable grounds can be described as "to believe that (1) that a crime has been committed and (2) the defendant committed it" (Schmalleger, MacAlister, & McKenna, 2004, p. 16).

A mandatory arrest policy takes away the officer's discretion and forces the officer to make an arrest. However, there is still a minimal amount of judgment allowed for exceptional circumstances. Mandatory arrest policies have helped provide police with the tools to respond appropriately to spousal abuse. Yet the arrest is only an immediate solution to the violence. Crown Attorneys decide whether to prosecute or not. Prosecution is the next important step in ensuring the long-term safety of the victim.

Intimate Spousal (Domestic) Assault Cases

Although spousal abuse or domestic abuse is not classified differently in the *Criminal Code,* in many jurisdictions spousal assault cases are separately identified and prosecuted by specially appointed Crowns who almost exclusively deal with these types of acts of violence (allegations). When an assault takes place between two people who share a marital or common-law relationship, the case is labelled "domestic" and prosecuted by Crown Attorneys quite differently compared to other assault charges. The policy of the Crown Attorney in Ontario, for instance, as set out in the *Crown Policy Manual* is to prosecute these offences "with vigour." In doing so, Ontario as well as other provinces has adopted was has been referred to as a "no-drop policy."

No-Drop Policies No-drop policies began to be implemented in the 1980s, in response to what was perceived to be the criminal justice system's inadequate response to incidents of spousal violence. These policies were designed to counter the notion that spousal violence was a private affair, and to acknowledge that it was a serious social problem and a violation of the law.

In an effort to underscore the seriousness of this crime, and to strengthen support to abused women, investigating police officers and Crown prosecutors were seen as the critical ingredients needed to address this societal problem. Implementing the no-drop policy was an important step toward positive protective change.

What essentially changed was that the burden or responsibility of laying a charge was no longer placed upon the abused spouse; it was now the duty of the police. It had become clear that a victim had several reasons to deter her from laying a charge. The most obvious was fear of retaliation. By placing the onus on the police, and ultimately the Crown prosecutor who would prosecute the case, the victim could now indicate to her abusive spouse that the decision to lay a charge and proceed was not hers.

These policies, however, have placed Crown Attorneys in awkward positions when faced with an uncooperative victim. The victim's testimony is vital; without it the Crown may be forced to withdraw the charges or in some cases hold the victim in **contempt of court**. While Crowns want to carry on with charges, when a victim refuses to testify the case becomes seriously compromised. A victim who is unwilling or hesitant to testify can be arrested and brought to court pursuant to a material witness warrant. Placing an abused woman in jail is not an appropriate solution, yet neither is returning her to an abusive partner. Crowns face difficult decisions.

Most persons charged with domestic assault are held by police overnight for a bail hearing, which would take place the following day. The Crown might also seek to have the abusive spouse kept in custody until the charge is disposed of. This is often the desired action if the abuser has a criminal record for assault against the same victim, or if the present assault was vicious. If the court releases an individual who was charged with a domestic offence they are also likely to be put on strict bail conditions and most would restrict contact with the victim, even if the victim wanted contact. In virtually all cases, the court will order the released abuser to have no contact with the victim. The accused person will also likely be ordered to stay away from the victim's residence, regardless of legal ownership. If the victim continues to live there, the conditions will remain the same for as long as the criminal charge is before the court or otherwise modified by the judge.

The next section will address offences that would apply to a case of physical violence.

7.3 LAWS PROTECTING ALL CANADIANS FROM PHYSICAL VIOLENCE AND MALTREATMENT

In this section we will examine the legislation that addresses specific forms of physical violence that are considered a *Criminal Code* offence. The victim can be a female or male adult child or parent, heterosexual or GLBT citizen. The types of violent acts addressed are assault, manslaughter, second-degree murder, and murder. We will begin this module by examining the *Criminal Code* offences that would protect females and males. The sections that follow will address laws that specifically protect the elderly person from violence and maltreatment, and laws and rights specific to GLBT citizens.

Physical Violence

Throughout this text, various forms of physical violence have been highlighted, from slaps to stabbings to gunshots. Physical violence includes any intentional use of physical force that either injures or risks injuring someone. These crimes can be perpetrated against a date, a person with whom a person shares an intimate relationship, a spouse, or an elderly person.

In Canada, a number of crimes are listed in the *Criminal Code* that would cover the spectrum of physical violence. Specifically, there are three levels of physical assaults. Categories that are defined in the *Criminal Code* include common assault, assault with a weapon or causing bodily harm, and aggravated assault; these, along with sexual assault crimes, are outlined in Table 7.4.

Table 7.4 *Criminal Code* Categories of Assault		
Behaviour	**Crime**	*Criminal Code*
Accused touches victim accidentally	No Crime	
Accused touches a victim intentionally *Generally this "assault" is caused by the force from a person's extremities such as hands, elbow, legs or feet. A push or pinch in some cases may be sufficient to establish a criminal assault.*	Simple assault	s. 266
Accused touches a victim intentionally *Plus* bodily harm or with a weapon *The "weapon" could be an inanimate object such as a bat, a tool, knife, stick or a thrown object also be delivered by something other than an inanimate object, for instance if a dog was ordered to attack a person.*	Assault with a weapon or causing bodily harm	s. 267
Accused touches a victim intentionally *Plus* Wounding, maiming, disfiguring, or endangering life (with or without a weapon)	Aggravated assault	s. 268
Accused touches a victim intentionally *Plus* Sexual nature of assault	Level 1 Sexual assault	s. 271
Accused touches a victim intentionally *Plus* Sexual nature of assault and use of a weapon	Level 2 Sexual assault with a weapon	s. 272
Accused touches a victim intentionally *Plus* Sexual nature of assault and wounding, maiming, etc.	Level 3 Aggravated sexual assault	s. 273

Because these crimes build upon each other, the less serious version is included in the more serious one. For instance an accused could be charged with aggravated assault, but the judge or jury may find that the victim injuries do not meet the definition of wounding, maiming, disfiguring or endanger life. In this situation, the accused may be convicted of assault with a weapon or causing bodily harm.

Manslaughter, Second-Degree Murder, and Murder The last and most extreme example of physical violence includes the action of killing someone. The terms "murder" and "homicide" are often used interchangeably, but they are not one and the same. Homicide occurs when a person, directly or indirectly, by any means, causes the death of human being. Homicide, therefore, can be either culpable or non-culpable, or blameworthy or not blameworthy (Schmalleger & Volk, 2011).

- *Non-culpable homicide* consists of justifiable and/or excusable homicide. This might include a legally authorized act, such as a police officer killing someone in the line of duty. For instance, the officer shoots and kills a suspect when the suspect draws a weapon, or actually shoots at the officer. A further example of an excusable homicide includes acts of self-defence or the defence of others. "Canadian Headline News" Box 5.2 in Chapter 5 provided details of the Supreme Court's decision regarding the battered woman defence.

- *Culpable homicide* is a serious offence in Canada (called an **indictable offense**). Culpable homicide is considered an offence under the *Criminal Code* and includes murder, manslaughter, and infanticide. In Canada, murder is classified as either first-degree or second-degree murder.

Table 7.5 First-Degree Murder, Second-Degree Murder, Manslaughter, and Infanticide

Degree	Definition	
First-degree murder	Planned and deliberate	s. 229
	Contracted	
	While committing or attempting to commit sexual assault	
	While committing or attempting to commit sexual assault with a weapon	
	While committing or attempting to commit aggravated sexual assault	
	While committing or attempting to commit kidnapping and forcible confinement	
	While committing criminal harassment	
	While committing intimidation	
Second-degree murder	Which is not first degree murder	
	It could be "in the spur of the moment"	
Man-slaughter	Manslaughter is any culpable homicide which is *not* murder	
Infanticide	When a female considered disturbed from the effects of giving birth causes the death of her newborn child under the age of one.	

Sources: *Criminal Code of Canada*, R.S., 1985, c. C-46, s. 231; R.S., 1985, c. 27 (1st Supp.), ss. 7, 35, 40, 185(F), c. 1 (4th Supp.), s. 18(F); 1997, c. 16, s. 3, c. 23, s. 8; 2001, c. 32, s. 9, c. 41, s. 9.

- *Murder* (s. 229) occurs when one person intentionally causes the death of another or intends to cause bodily harm that consequently results in death. Murder is further classified into first-degree murder and second-degree murder (Schmalleger & Volk, 2011).

- *First-degree murder* is sometimes called "murder in the first degree" (s. 231, *Criminal Code*). It describes culpable homicide that is *planned* and deliberate. Crimes can also qualify for first-degree murder if, while committing another crime such as a sexual assault, someone is killed (see "Canadian Headline News" Box 7.7).

- *Second-degree murder* includes all murder that is not first-degree. In other words, it is intentional and unlawful *but not planned*.

- *Manslaughter* is considered to be a non-intentional homicide committed in response to a sudden provocation, as a result of impaired judgment due to alcohol or drug consumption, or as a result of recklessness or **carelessness**, without malice or deliberation.

For a summary of the various forms of homicide/murder, refer to Table 7.5.

7.4 LAWS THAT PROTECT ELDER CANADIANS

Elder persons, similar to young children, are often dependent upon others for their care. This could place them more at risk for harm. Omitting to provide needed medical care, pharmaceutical treatments, or adequate nutrition is part of neglect and could also lead to an injurious outcome.

Neglect of the Elderly Person

As mentioned earlier in this chapter, the "duty to provide necessaries of life to dependent persons" is a *Criminal Code* item (s. 215) that means there is a duty to provide necessaries for children under the age of 16, your spouse, and any invalids in your care. Notice that each spouse is legally obligated to provide the necessities of life to the other.

Duty to Provide Necessaries of Life The duty to provide necessaries of life is covered in section 215 of the *Criminal Code*. This section specifically speaks to those who are responsible for the welfare of others. Neglect, whether intentional or unintentional, is chronic, and usually involves repeated incidents that result in the failure to provide adequately for a dependent adult. Neglect may include failing to provide adequate nutrition, personal care, or a clean and safe living environment, or withholding or improperly providing medications, medical aids, assistive devices, or treatments. It may also include leaving an incapacitated older adult alone for too long or abandoning them. Some forms of neglect are crimes in Canada.

Failure to provide the necessities of life could lead to serious harm, or death. The *Criminal Code* provisions that could apply in these instances are criminal negligence causing bodily harm or death, ss. 219–221, and failure to provide the necessities of life, s. 2.15.

Criminal negligence is gross or extreme negligence, and proving it requires that specific behaviours demonstrate a noticeable departure from a normal standard of care, or conduct that shows a "wanton or reckless disregard for the lives or safety of other persons." Recklessness is usually described as a "malfeasance," which could be described as a hostile, aggressive action taken to injure. Recklessness, therefore, occurs when an individual knowingly exposes another person to the risk of injury (s. 219 *Criminal Code*).

Negligence shows the least level of culpability. From a legal perspective or in plain English, culpability describes the degree of one's blameworthiness in committing a crime. Negligence arises when a person has not actually foreseen the potentially adverse consequences to the planned actions and has gone ahead, subjecting a victim to the risk of suffering injury or loss.

Emotional or Psychological Abuse of the Elderly

Emotional or psychological abuse refers to insults, humiliation, putdowns, threats, and yelling. Although they are psychologically injurious and are often effectively used to control and intimidate a victim, they are not crimes under the *Criminal Code* (Department of Justice). However, depending on the manner in which the emotional abuse is being conducted, there are some *Criminal Code* provisions that may apply, which includes uttering threats and intimidation. Intimidation is defined in section 423(1) of the *Criminal Code.*

Threatening is a psychologically harmful action that would be addressed under the *Criminal Code.* It is considered an offence to knowingly utter or convey a threat to cause death or to cause bodily harm to someone. It is also an offence to threaten to burn, destory, or damage property, or to threaten to kill, poison, or injure an animal or bird that belongs to a person (s. 264.1).

What is critical for the prosecution when addressing this crime is to prove that the person uttering the threat was aware of the words used and the meaning they would convey. The Crown must also prove that the person making the threat intended the threat to be taken seriously. It must also be proven that there was the intention to intimidate or strike fear into the mind of the victim. In law it is *not necessary* that the person making the threat intended to carry it out, or be capable of doing so. Moreover, even if the abuser makes a threat that he/she could not carry out, they may still be found guilty of the offence. The central issue for the judge to determine is whether a threat occurred, and to decide whether the words were uttered (was it meant to be taken seriously so as to produce a reaction of alarm or fear in the mind of the recipient), *not* on the present ability to carry out the threat. The motive for making the threat is immaterial.

Counselling Suicide Although no Canadian should ever have to experience the fear of being pressured to end their life, this type of abuse does exist and would be more probable for the elderly. Pressuring or coercing the suicide of another person is a crime. In Canada, the increase in chronic conditions such as Alzheimer's disease and incurable diseases such as AIDS as well as some forms of cancer has meant an afflicted person could see their probable future before they become incapacitated (Tiedemann & Valiquet, 2008). In Canada, protection exists to prevent an individual from being pressured to make a decision to end one's life. This type of fear or threat is covered under s. 241 of the *Criminal Code* and is referred to as counselling suicide.

Physical Abuse of the Elderly

The elderly have additional risks to physical violence. Physical abuse specific to elder violence is the use of constraints or the action of organizing an elder person's environment in a manner that would confine. For instance, forcing them to remain in bed, or locking them up, or taking away medically needed equipment (e.g., a walker) that enables them to be mobile. Physical abuse against older adults may also include the unnecessary use or misuse of restraints (physical or pharmaceutical).

In Canada, it is a criminal offence to unjustly hold anyone against their will through the use of threats, duress, force, or the exhibition of force. This offence is called "forcible confinement" (s. 279), and is defined by the *Criminal Code* as depriving an individual of the liberty to move from one point to another by unlawfully confining, imprisoning, or forcibly seizing that person (Dauvergne, 2009). These types of harm do occur in Canadian society. A case in 2011 involved a 68-year-old woman suffering from dementia; for a description, see "Canadian Headline News" Box 7.7.

7.7 Canadian Headline News: 68-Year-Old Senior Found Freezing in Garage

A 68-year-old woman suffering from dementia was left alone in an uninsulated garage during the winter by her son and daughter-in-law. At the time she was discovered the woman was taken to hospital, where she suffered a stroke and was in serious condition. Medical staff told police she was unconscious and non-responsive. She was frostbitten, malnourished, and had likely been badly neglected for some time.

An investigation into what police allege is a serious case of elder abuse began after emergency services were called about an unconscious woman at the house in Scarborough, Ontario. After the woman was taken to hospital, police searched the garage. Inside they found a box of adult diapers, one piece of bread, and a mattress on top of a sheet of plywood. They further indicated that the woman was using a portable toilet and had only a bucket for washing. Police believe she had no access to the house. Police also told the CBC News that the garage had been converted into a makeshift bedroom and was unfit for human habitation. In February 2011, Kwong Yan, 43, and his wife Qi Tan, 28, were charged with failing to provide the necessities of life and with criminal negligence causing bodily harm. The woman was released from intensive care at the beginning of March 2011, and because she was no longer able to make her own personal care decisions due to dementia she moved to a nursing home in Scarborough.

(continued)

Later that year, in October, the Crown Attorney dropped the criminal negligence charge against Kwon Yan and he pleaded guilty to improperly caring for his 63-year-old mother. Consequently, he was sentenced in the Ontario Court of Justice to eight months in jail for one count of failing to provide the necessities of life.

Reflection Question

The demographics of Canada are changing. Do you think new laws should be enacted to address the unique vulnerabilities of seniors? If so, what changes or additional forms of protection would you suggest?

Sources: CBC News, 2011; O'Toole & Lodge, 2011.

Financial Abuse of Spouses and the Elderly

Economic or financial abuse includes acting without consent in a way that financially benefits one person at the cost of another. This is a type of violence that falls under the category of spousal violence and elder abuse. It may consist of stealing or using a spouse's or an older adult's money or property in a dishonest manner, or failing to use the person's assets for their welfare. Taking unjust advantage of them by forcing them to sign legal documents, pressuring them to provide financial support or care for others, or wrongfully using a power of attorney are also examples of financial abuse. Many acts of financial abuse are included in the *Criminal Code*; these include Theft s. 322, Theft by a Person Holding a Power of Attorney (s. 331), Fraud (s. 380), Extortion (s. 346), Stopping Mail with Intent (s. 345), and Forgery (s. 366).

Role of Provincial/Territorial Legislation: Other Protective Measures

Knowledge of the abuse of adults involves the duty to protect. The greatest percentage of legislative effort in Canada directed at protecting adults has focused on those individuals who are incompetent to make decisions regarding health care, or those who are vulnerable to financial abuse. Therefore, these laws protected an elderly person's interests in terms of physical or mental deterioration through guardianship, health law, substitute decision-making, and succession legislation. Some offences, such as abuse of power of attorney or contravention of the *Trustee Act*, are offences within provincial/territorial jurisdictions.

A different issue can and does arise in situations when an adult has been physically abused, neglected, or has experienced emotional cruelty by others, particularly by family members. Individuals who have knowledge of an abused adult could take action if they live in a province where protective legislation exists. It should be pointed out that only a few provinces in Canada have mandatory reporting laws. In Canada, the Atlantic Provinces have led the way in enacting adult protection legislation. Newfoundland was the first province to introduce adult protection legislation. The driving force of the time was the concern for the welfare of neglected rather than abused adults.

In some of these jurisdictions where adult protection and guardianship legislation are in place, statutory adult-protection service programs are offered in combination with legal, health, and social service interventions. These laws and policies were heavily influenced by the child welfare models. Some of these contain elements such as the legal power to investigate and mandatory reporting (2001). Since this time, various models of protection have been developing. Similar to child protection legislation, it is best to consult the legislation that exists within each province (Gordon, 2001).

Conclusion

Central to all laws and investigative procedures are the skills and sensitivity required to respectfully balance the protection of older adults with the need to value their independence. Many ongoing challenges will require further research in an effort to understand how the law will ensure that the rights of our elderly Canadians are met while respecting their needs in the justice system.

7.5 LAWS THAT PROTECT GLBT CITIZENS

Gay, lesbian, bisexual, and transgender persons are citizens who are entitled to the same legal protections that are extended to all members of Canadian society. However, for this population of Canadians additional sources of violence exist. When a group of people have been targeted as pathological, deviant, or criminal, and they have not had medical support and legal refuge from harm, their eventual protective needs are different. Equally concerning was their fight for the right to love and express commitment in an intimate or dating relationship or marriage; the right to marry has always been a heterosexual privilege. This section will discuss laws and rights that are specifically important for gay, lesbian, bisexual, and transgender Canadians, and how they have unfolded.

Sexual Orientation and Canadian Law

The fight for legal protection and equality for gays and lesbians did not appear or progress as quickly as it did for women and children; however, progress did occur. The first major breakthrough came when Pierre Trudeau (Justice Minister and Attorney General of Canada) introduced Bill C-150, which would ultimately decriminalize homosexuality in Canada. In 1969 Parliament passed an amendment to the *Criminal Code* that decriminalized same-sex behaviour between consenting adults.

At the time, Trudeau's advocacy was ignited by the very public debate involving Everett George Klippert, a mechanic from Pine Point in the Northwest Territories who had confessed to having consensual adult sex with another man. (Mr. Klippert's case was discussed in Chapter 1.) Klippert's case and the resultant *Criminal Code* changes, plus other major pieces of legislation, have benefited gay males and lesbians. Many of these important legal rights have been realized because of the enactment of the *Canadian Charter of Rights and Freedoms* in 1982. The *Charter* helped guide and build major structural changes that were necessary to help ensure Canada would become an advanced democratic society. Many challenges were directed at overtly oppressive laws that needed change. With the advent of the *Charter,* the role of the courts in Canada expanded greatly and provided new opportunity to use litigation to bring about much-needed legal and social change. Moreover, the *Charter* encouraged all social activists to seek constitutionally guaranteed rights as an end in themselves.

The Canadian Bill of Rights: The Movement Begins Prior to the *Charter of Rights and Freedoms*—in fact, almost 25 years earlier, in 1960—the *Canadian Bill of Rights* was enacted. It was introduced by Prime Minister John Diefenbaker's government, and was Canada's earliest expression of human rights law at the federal level. The *Bill of Rights* guaranteed the "right of the individual to equality before the law" and the protection of the law. Therefore, with this existing legislation, provinces and activists began to illuminate and address violations of gay and lesbian rights.

One of the first and most notable challenges and changes that unfolded was in 1975, when the Quebec National Assembly adopted the *Quebec Charter of Human Rights and Freedoms*. At that point there was no mention of sexual orientation as an illegal motive for discrimination. Later, in 1977, the Quebec National Assembly modified article 10 of the *Quebec Charter* to include sexual orientation as an illegal motive for discrimination. As such, Quebec has the notable distinction of becoming the first jurisdiction in North America and the second in the world (after Denmark), to prohibit discrimination based on sexual orientation (Hunt, 1999).

Timing was a significant obstacle for the momentum of the gay liberation groups. In the 1970s many gays were still in the closet. Therefore, the litigation and the movement that was essential to raise consciousness and create a political identity were challenged. But this would change with the inception and resultant advocacy of a national lobby group called Equality for Gays and Lesbians Everywhere. In 1986 it became a leader in lobbying for equality through the legal system (Hunt, 1999).

Lobbying efforts by gay liberation groups would take hold. The most imperative demand that ultimately took several years for all provinces to obtain was the necessary amendment to the *Charter of Rights and Freedoms*. The goal was to have "sexual orientation" read in as an area upon which an individual could not be discriminated against. The other demand was the right to legal marriage. We will begin with sexual orientation and human rights legislation, followed by the acquisition of the right to a same-sex legal marriage.

Sexual Orientation and Human Rights Legislation

Sexual orientation was slow to receive protection as a prohibited group of discrimination under Canadian law, and until recently only a few jurisdictions extended such protection. This would eventually become one of the principal demands made on behalf of the GLBT community. Following Quebec's earlier lead in 1977, the other provinces began to add prohibition of discrimination based on sexual orientation within their provincial *Human Rights Codes* (Hunt, 1999). By 2005, all the provinces except Alberta expressly prohibited discrimination on the basis of sexual orientation in their human rights statutes.

Federal amendments would follow in 1995, when by virtue of section 15 of the *Charter* the Supreme Court held that sexual orientation was among a group that was discriminated against under section 15 (*Egan v. Canada, 1995*). As such, in 1996 the Canadian House of Commons modified the *Charter* to include a prohibition of discrimination based on sexual orientation.

The last "right" or law to explore will end this chapter on a positive note. Although this law didn't affect the majority of Canadians, what it did do was provide *equality* to *all* Canadians. Protection from harm is not its goal, but this piece of legislation supports human dignity and entitlement—the right for gay and lesbian citizens to legally marry in Canada.

Marriage Laws

Marriage is found in all human societies. People in every known society sometimes—or nearly always—get married at least once. Statistics Canada (2006) estimates that three-quarters of Canadians who are in their thirties will marry at some point in their lives. But the right to enter into a legally binding marriage contract in Canada was not always extended to same-sex partners. Although it did not happen quickly, as with many momentous gains in our society, with our few "strong and free" who were willing to "step up" and "step out," incrementally significant gains and victories for same-sex couples have been achieved.

The first significant movement in the fight for same-sex marriage took place in 1999, when the Supreme Court of Canada ruled that the Province of Ontario's definition of spouse violated the *Charter of Rights and Freedoms* because it applied only to heterosexuals and not gay males and lesbians (*M. v. H.* [1999] 2 S.C.R. 3). Later, in 2002, the Ontario Supreme Court ruled that because the legal definition of marriage is discriminatory it should be changed to include same-sex couples. A year later, in 2003, gay and lesbian marriages were legalized in two Canadian provinces, Ontario and British Columbia. Following these decisions, the federal government announced on June 17, 2003 that it would *not* appeal the decisions of the courts of appeal in British Columbia and Ontario on the definition of marriage.

Although this signified a *fait accompli* for gay marriage in parts of Canada, popular opinion and research remained almost evenly divided, making it a difficult political issue for governments. Plus, many religious institutions were opposed to same-sex marriage. In fact, the Vatican launched a global campaign in a 12-page document approved by Pope John Paul II against gay marriages, warning Catholic politicians that support of same-sex unions is "gravely immoral." It further reiterated the Catholic position that marriage exists solely between a man and woman: "Marriage is holy, while homosexual acts go against the natural moral law" (CNN, 2003).

Although most Canadians accepted same-sex marriage, there was significant opposition from a determined minority. A 2003 national survey conducted by the Centre for

Research and Information on Canada found that 61 percent of Canadian adults approved of same-sex marriage (Hurst, 2003). In a separate national survey of Canadian young people, only a minority (23 percent) disapproved of same-sex marriage and even fewer (15 percent) said they would never vote for a gay or lesbian political candidate (Youthography Ping Survey, 2004). However, an opinion poll conducted in January 2004 found that 47 percent of the respondents agreed with the statement, "Prime Minister Martin should change Canada's marriage laws to include same-sex couples"; 48 percent disagreed, while 5 percent expressed no opinion (Lunman & Fagan, 2004).

Consequently, in 2003 the Canadian government asked the Supreme Court to rule on four questions:

1. Is the definition of marriage a federal government jurisdiction?

2. Does a law authorizing the marriage of same-sex couples conform to the *Charter of Rights*?

3. Does the *Charter of Rights* protect the right of religious institutions to refuse to celebrate marriages with which they do not agree?

4. Is the federal law that defines marriage as being between a man and a woman constitutional?

On December 9, 2004, the Supreme Court delivered a unanimous response to the questions and gave the go-ahead to the government to legalize same-sex marriages. The nine Supreme Court judges stated that, "Our constitution is a living tree which, given a progressive interpretation, adapts and responds to the realities of modern life. Interpreted in a liberal way, *the word marriage does not exclude marriage between people of the same sex.*" They further noted that:

- the federal government has the power to revise the traditional definition of marriage in order to allow spouses of the same sex to marry, *but*

- neither the federal nor provincial governments can force religious authorities to celebrate homosexual marriages against their will if this contravenes their beliefs or their traditions.

The Supreme Court refused to respond to the fourth question, which asked whether the traditional definition of marriage is constitutional (SCC 79, [2004] 3 S.C.R. 698).

Following the unanimous Supreme Court decision, in February 2005 then-Prime Minister Paul Martin presented a bill that would change the definition of marriage to the legitimate union of two people. The House of Commons adopted Bill C-38 on its third reading on June 28, 2005, by a majority vote (158 for, 133 against) recognizing civil marriage between people of the same sex. The *Civil Marriage Act* recognized same-sex marriage. The Senate would later adopt Bill C-38 in July 2005. These two subsequent votes made Canada the fourth country in the world to legalize same-sex marriage. Earlier in 2001, the Netherlands became the first; Belgium followed in 2003 and Spain in 2005 (Statutes of Canada S.C. 2005, c. 33).

CHAPTER CONCLUSION

A reoccurring pedagogical feature in this text is the Canadian Headline News Stories which highlighted cases. When authentic stories are available they provide priceless insight. Many cases exposed dark moments, but at the same time, they helped illuminate the potential strength and ethos of present day Canada. Opportunity exists to support courageous individuals who have the bravery to speak the truth and demand change. Sometimes this process brings about an acceptance of responsibility and an apology. Moreover, these publicly recorded victimizations have also demonstrated Canada's response to victims and their needs. And, as you will read they brought about the call for legislative changes, the enactment of new laws, essential services, and the realization that *all* Canadians can become advocates!

Multiple Choice Questions

1. In which of the following years was the United Nations *Convention on the Rights of the Child* declared?

   a. 1961   b. 1983
   c. 1991   d. 2004

2. All of the following statements are true regarding child abuse mandatory reporting EXCEPT which one?

   a. The legislation clearly states that it is not necessary for a person to be certain that a child is or may be in need of protection to make a report.
   b. If a report of suspected abuse is made a child protection investigation may or may not follow through.
   c. The legislation requires certain professionals to report cases of suspected child abuse or neglect to a designated authority for investigation.
   d. A professional or official who fails to report a suspicion that a child is or may be in need of protection could be fined.

3. Reasons were provide to explain why certain individuals who witness or suspect child abuse may NOT report. Which of the following was NOT identified?

   a. Want to avoid the demands of becoming "involved."
   b. They have a history of abusing their own child, and are worried about their own situation.
   c. Believe that reporting the abuse to the authorities is not in the child's best interest.
   d. Do not understand their responsibility to report abuse.

4. Which of the following best describes the *Criminal Code* offence of infanticide?

   a. occurs when a female, considered disturbed from the effects of giving birth, causes the death of her newborn child under the age of one
   b. occurs when a either a male or a female is considered disturbed from the effects of giving birth and causes the death of a newborn child under the age of one
   c. occurs when a child under the age of 5 kills a child under the age of one.
   d. occurs when any family member (through blood or marriage) kills a child under the age of one

5. In what year did Canada's age of sexual consent increase to 16?

    a. 1985   **b.** 2005
    c. 1995   **d.** 2008

6. Which of the following is NOT a true statement regarding the spanking law issue?

    a. Canada's Supreme Court upheld the spanking law in Canada.
    b. The issue at hand was section 43 of the *Criminal Code.* Advocates wanted this section of the *Code* repealed.
    c. Canada was censured by the United Nations for permitting spanking.
    d. The Supreme Court recognized that part of section 43 of the Criminal Code did violate a child's rights to security of the person and equality.

7. When police investigate a sexual assault, there are certain relevant factors to consider. Which of the following has NOT been identified?

    a. the part of the body touched
    b. the nature of the contact
    c. the victim's relationship to the accused
    d. the words and gestures accompanying the act

8. Access to a complainant's records in sexual assault cases dominated the criminal courts for almost 20 years. Which of the following Supreme Court decisions discussed in this chapter did NOT relate to a *complainant's records*?

    a. *R. v. Seaboyer*   **b.** *R. v. Gayme*
    c. *R. v. Ewanchuk*   **d.** *R. v. O'Connor*

9. Consent or mistaken belief of consent is a critical factor in sexual assault cases. What Supreme Court decisions related to the question of consent?

    a. *R. v. Park*   **b.** *R. v. Darrach*
    c. *R. v. Seaboyer*   **d.** *R. v. Mills*

10. If you lived in British Columbia and worked for Canada Post, and you believed you were the victim of sexual harassment, what piece of legislation would relate to this victimization?

    a. *Canadian Human Rights Act*
    b. *Criminal Code of Canada*
    c. *The British Columbia Human Rights Code*
    d. *Canadian Charter of Rights and Freedoms*

Discussion Questions

1. Identify and describe the Criminal Code legislation that specifically protects children from sexual harm in Canada?

2. Some elderly people live with caregivers who violently harm and maltreat them, yet they may refuse to ask the person to leave. Should a legislative body (for example, an adult protection worker) be allowed to compel this person to leave?

3. Briefly describe the legislative actions since 1983 that have been taken to protect sexual assault victims.

Key Terms

accused: a person against whom a criminal or quasi-criminal charge has been laid, but who has not yet been convicted.

acquittal: finding an accused not guilty of an offence.

adversarial system: the procedure used to determine truth in a criminal court system. According to this system, the burden is on the state to prove the charges against the accused beyond a reasonable doubt.

appeal: a review of a lower court decision or proceedings by a higher court.

carelessness: a level of intent (*mens rea*) where a person fails to appreciate a risk that a reasonable person would have foreseen.

case law: reported decision of judges from trial or appeals that are used to interpret the law.

contempt of court: includes but is not limited to the deliberate defiance or disobedience or any willful conduct that interferes with the proper administration of justice or to bring it into disrepute.

disclosure: the responsibility of the Crown to share information with the accused.

indictable offence: a serious crime that attracts more serious penalties and that is prosecuted using the more formal of two possible sets of criminal procedures.

infanticide: When a female considered disturbed from the effects of giving birth causes the death of her newborn child under the age of one.

mandated reporting: the requirement that suspected abuse be reported to the appropriate child protection agency.

negligence: the unintentional harm caused as a result of a breach of a legally recognized duty of care to individuals.

omission: a failure to do something that is required by statute or by common law.

precedent: a court decision that influences or binds future decision on the same issue or similar facts

production: any responsibility of a third party to fulfill the accused's right of full answer and defence.

records: in a sexual assault criminal court case, any form of record that contains personal information for which there is a reasonable expectation of privacy.

repealed: terminated the application of a statute or statuary.

Chapter 8
Services to Victims

In matters of truth and justice, there is no difference between large and small problems, for issues concerning the treatment of people are all the same.

Albert Einstein, German physicist (1879–1955)

Chapter Objectives

1 To present an overview of the criminal justice system and the professionals who work within it.

2 To present a description of various victim services.

3 To present a variety of initiatives that honour victims, raise awareness of violence in Canadian society, and work for positive change.

INTRODUCTION

As Canadian society slowly unearthed the sombre statistical prevalence of violence and the plight of its victims, public awareness and outrage grew. Many issues began to emerge, and two in particular were the need to address the rights of victims to participate in the criminal trial, and the responsibility to provide them some degree of support and protection.

Subsequently, the proponents of the victims' rights movement began to argue that integrating victims into the court system and guaranteeing their right to be involved would recognize their requests for status in a court proceeding (Hall, 1991). Promoting their role would also signify that a human life had suffered at the hands of a criminal. We would be deluding ourselves if we did not acknowledge that, at the end of the day, it is the victim and often their families who are left coping with the aftermath—*not* society. By providing victims the right to be heard in court, their dignity and worth would be acknowledged (Goff, 2008).

At the same time, opponents of the pro-victim reform movement argued that establishing victims' rights would challenge the very basis of the adversarial legal system—in particular, the idea that crime is a violation against the state rather than an individual. But as noted in previous chapters, laws addressing victim needs and rights did begin to materialize, and services slowly unfolded across Canada.

Over time, many victims' movements emerged, and one overall goal was to advocate for new laws or improved legislation. As such, the criminal justice system became viewed as a potential tool and place to assist a victim of violence. New legislation helped to treat personal violence (crime) seriously, to get funding for shelters, to make it possible to get restraining orders, and to sensitize judges and to mandate training in all these issues.

8.1 THE CANADIAN JUSTICE SYSTEM

To embark on our chapter on services to victims, for a number of reasons we will begin with an overview of Canada's justice system and how it is organized. Throughout this textbook many violent crimes have been discussed. In the process of describing these victimizations, various references were made regarding laws, legal terms, courts, and the key people involved in the administration of justice. To further enhance this chapter we will highlight cases discussed earlier to broaden our perspective and overall understanding.

The second benefit in understanding how the criminal justice system is organized enables us to determine when and at what stage specific victims' rights and services are provided. The objective of this section is to provide an overview of Canada's justice system, not a detailed description or an assessment of its efficiency. Further, if someone should find themselves in this system, it is advisable to seek out the advice and guidance of those qualified to work within this specialized and complex field. First, let's examine the principles of fundamental justice, and the individual rights guaranteed to all Canadians.

Principles of Fundamental Justice and Individual Rights

From the outset, it is important to underscore the fact that although acts of intimate personal violence are committed against individuals, in Canada when a crime is committed it is considered to be an offence against society as a whole. The Law Reform Commission of Canada (1988) states that a key function of Canada's criminal justice system is to bring those who commit crimes—the offenders—to justice. In doing so, Canada's legal system also ensures that a number of rights and protections exist for those accused of committing crimes in order to protect them from the enormous power of the state, and the potential of a wrongful conviction. These rights are entrenched in the values of the *Charter of Rights and Freedoms*. As such, when the police first learn that a crime has been committed, throughout the duration of the unfolding investigation explicit fundamental principles are guaranteed to all Canadian citizens.

These guarantees are noted in section 7 of the *Charter of Rights and Freedoms*, and these rights are referred to as principles of fundamental justice. The *Charter* specifically states, "Everyone has the right to life, liberty and security of the person and the right not to be deprived thereof except in accordance with the principles of fundamental justice." The *Charter* takes precedence over all other legislation because it is entrenched in Canada's Constitution: the supreme law. If you reflect back to earlier chapters, you will recall that Canadian history has unquestionably demonstrated the fact that equal rights, access to justice, and protection were not extended to all Canadians. Since its enactment the *Charter* has ensured the guaranteed rights of an accused person (Schmalleger, MacAlister, & McKenna, 2004).

When a victimization involves a **Criminal Code of Canada** offence, the crime may be either discovered by or reported to the police. In either situation an investigation would commence, and so too would an additional basic principle—the presumption of innocence. In other words, anyone in Canada accused of or charged with breaking the law is considered innocent until proven guilty in a court of law.

Additionally, every person who is accused of a *Criminal Code* offence has specific *Charter* rights: the right to consult a lawyer, and the right to remain silent, and even when they are questioned by the police. As Schmalleger and colleagues wrote, "Given the importance placed on recognizing this right by this Supreme Court of Canada, the right to silence also is typically stated in expressed terms by the police officer upon arresting a suspect" (2004, p. 14).

The second basic principle includes the process of impartiality and fairness. If and when a case makes its way to Canada's court system it is the responsibility of our courts to determine ultimately whether or not an accused has been proven guilty. Judges must make certain that throughout the investigation the state enforced the law in a way that did not go against the legal rights of a citizen. Goff (2008) has referred to these fundamental rights as guaranteed criminal procedures: "Criminal procedure is concerned with how criminal justice agencies operate during the interrogation of suspects, the gathering of evidence, and the process of the accused through the courts" (p. 13).

Our courts must also provide an autonomous and composed environment so that justice is applied consistently and fairly, and based on proven facts when determining whether the law has been broken, as well as determining the eventual consequence for those responsible (Schmalleger et al., 2004). So how is this achieved?

You might have noticed when the topic of justice is "visually" presented you often see a blindfolded women holding a set of scales in her hand. The entrance to the Supreme Court of Canada's building is flanked by two huge statues, *Justitia* (Justice) and *Veritas* (Truth). *Justitia* is portrayed as a woman holding a two-edged sword, but she does not wear the traditional blindfold (see Photo 8.1). Some have interpreted this to mean that the nine Supreme Court justices of Canada's highest court must without a doubt see the consequences of their decisions, and must communicate them to the Canadian public. Even in this text alone, a number of important Supreme Court decisions were discussed.

Justitia, therefore, serves as a reminder that justice is best achieved by weighing and assessing evidence without interference from outside influences. This is why an independent judiciary is a vital feature of Canada's justice system. This chapter will now address judicial independence and the system that helps to ensure it flourishes. And, as you have read throughout this textbook, many Supreme Court decisions have had an enormous impact on rights and various forms of protection.

Judicial Independence

Canada's Judges For most people, it is probably the judge who is the most closely associated with a criminal trial. In the courtroom the judge holds ultimate authority and the crucial duty of ensuring justice. Judges must ensure the rights of the accused are upheld (Goff, 2008). They also must rule on matters of law, weighing objections from

The statue *Justitia* (Justice), Supreme Court of Canada entrance.
www.scc-csc.gc.ca/details/art-stat-justitia2-eng.asp

either the Crown or defence attorney, or deciding on the admissibility of evidence. Additionally, it is the judge who disciplines anyone who challenges the order of the court (Schmalleger et al., 2004).

Judicial independence is the foundation of the Canadian judicial system. To support this process, three integral components exist: security of tenure, financial security, and administrative independence (Canadian Judicial Council, 2004). Further, each jurisdiction has a chief judge or chief justice. Besides serving on the bench as a trial judge, they must also administer the court system; for instance, assigning court cases to the various judges (Canadian Judicial Council, 2004; Schmalleger et al., 2004).

Judicial Ethics and Discipline Judges have the duty to uphold and defend judicial independence. It is not so much a privilege but a means to guarantee the constitutional rights of *every* Canadian (Canadian Judicial Council, 2004). As such, the Canadian Judicial Council (2004) states, "Judges should exhibit and promote high standards of judicial conduct so as to reinforce public confidence which is the cornerstone of judicial independence" (p. 13). The rule of law and the independence of the judiciary depend primarily upon public confidence, because, "lapses and questionable conduct by judges tend to erode that confidence" (p. 16).

Another factor that undermines public respect and confidence occurs if a judge's conduct in and out of court demonstrates a lack of integrity (Canadian Judicial Council, 2004). Judicial misconduct refers to "bad behaviour," but it is important to note that bad behaviour is not the same as a bad legal decision. When a defence or Crown attorney believes a judge has rendered a bad legal decision they can file an appeal (appeals will be discussed later in this chapter). When the concern is about judicial conduct, for instance when a judge behaves "badly," the decision as to whether a judge should continue in office can only be made through an inquiry. With respect to this action, Gall wrote, "it takes a very dramatic malfeasance before the removal provisions are brought into force" (1995, p. 300). This now begs the question, who judges the judge? The answer is the Canadian Judicial Council.

The Canadian Judicial Council The Canadian Judicial Council was created in 1971. It developed a set of ethical principles for judges, designed to assist judges in maintaining their independence, integrity, and impartiality. Each jurisdiction has a judicial council that has general responsibility for promoting professional standards and conduct (Schmalleger et al., 2004).

Managing complaints about judicial misconduct is also their responsibility (Schmalleger et al., 2004). From time to time a judge's questionable behaviour does become public. For instance, a situation arose in February 2011 during a sexual assault sentencing hearing. See "Canadian Headline News" Box 8.1 to read about how various news sources reported that Manitoba's Queen's Bench Justice Robert Dewar made what many believed to be a number of sexist and inappropriate remarks during a sexual assault sentencing hearing. A public outcry ensued, and so too did the process to speak to, report, and hold the judge accountable for his comments.

8.1 Canadian Headline News: Manitoba's Queen's Bench Justice Robert Dewar—"Sex Was in the Air"

Convicted rapist Kenneth Rhodes will not go to jail, because Manitoba judge Robert Dewar said the victim sent signals that "sex was in the air" through her suggestive attire and flirtatious conduct on the night of the attack.

During the sentencing, Justice Dewar specifically noted the women were wearing tube tops with no bra, high heels, and plenty of makeup. Dewar further stated, "They made their intentions publicly known that they wanted to party." He said the women spoke of going swimming in a nearby lake that night "notwithstanding the fact neither of them had a bathing suit."

However, the rape victim, advocating on her own behalf, slammed Justice Dewar's decision, which gave her attacker a lenient sentence on the basis she may have sent mixed signals about her sexual intentions. She specifically stated:

> "This is beyond sexist. I don't even know how to comment on it. No woman asks to be raped," the 26-year-old single mother told the *Winnipeg Free Press* in an exclusive telephone interview Thursday from her rural Manitoba home. "Nobody knows what it was like to be in this position. It's not something I'd ever want to go through again. No woman should have to."

Rhodes and a friend had met the woman (victim) and her girlfriend earlier that night outside a bar under what the judge called "inviting circumstances." The victim's comments to the judge's statement were, "I wasn't dressed like a skank. I was like 20 years old, wearing a tube top. It was summer," said the victim, who cannot be identified because she is the victim of a sexual assault.

The court was also told that the foursome left the parking lot in a vehicle and headed into the woods. Rhodes began making sexual advances toward the victim, who initially rejected him but later returned his kisses. Rhodes then forced himself upon the woman once they were alone.

Justice Robert Dewar further called Rhodes a "clumsy Don Juan" who may have misunderstood what the woman wanted when he forced intercourse along a darkened highway outside Thompson, Manitoba, in 2006. In response, the victim said,

> "That's bulls—. I did say no to him. I kept saying no. He knew that I didn't want (sex)."

The victim further stated, "It's impacted me in so many ways, . . . I'm a prisoner in my own home." She further noted she also bears a permanent reminder of what Rhodes did to her in the form of a scar on her knee, a sign of the violence the much larger man used to restrain her.

Rhodes pleaded not guilty at the trial on the basis he thought the woman had consented. Dewar rejected his defence—but said aspects of it could be considered in sentencing. But, Rhodes was found guilty and given a two-year conditional penalty, which allowed him to remain free in the community. He was placed under a 24-hour curfew for the first year of his conditional sentence, with exceptions to allow him to work and attend to medical appointments. His name was placed on the national sex offender registry. Rhodes was also ordered by the judge to write a letter of apology to his victim.

The Crown had requested at least three years behind bars, citing numerous case precedents including the Manitoba Court of Appeal, which suggested that the starting point for a major sexual assault involving intercourse is a penitentiary sentence—case law.

Dewar stated that the case was not "typical" of ones the courts often see and shouldn't be viewed as a precedent. "There is a different quality to this case than many sexual assaults," he said. "Not all guilty people are morally culpable to the same level. This difference is not to be reflected in conviction. It can be reflected in sentencing."

At the time of the sentencing, Karen Busby, a law professor at the University of Manitoba, suggested the comments blame the victim while partially exonerating her attacker. "I hope they appeal. I would like some justice . . . This sentencing will raise a number of issues relating to public confidence in the sentencing process," Crown Attorney Sheila Seesahai told court. She said the victim was at the mercy of her much larger attacker and his "repugnant and reprehensible" conduct. In a victim impact statement, the woman described her ongoing fear related to the attack.

As a reminder, 20 years earlier, in 1991, following a 7–2 decision, Supreme Court Justice Beverley McLachlin cited one of the reasons for "striking down" the so-called "rape shield law" was that sexual stereotyping was a "universally discredited" practice in the present legal system (see Chapter 7). "This is not real justice to me. It's a slap on the wrist," said the victim.

Reflection Question

What important points regarding victims are raised by this case?

Sources: McIntyre, 2011a, 2011b; *R. v. Kenneth Rhodes*, 2011; Reynolds, 2011.

The process to report concerns regarding judicial misconduct is outlined in the *Federal Judges Act,* section 63, which states: "the Council shall, at the request of the Minister or the attorney general of a province, commence an inquiry as to whether a judge of a Superior Court or of the Tax Court of Canada should be removed from office." This was in fact what unfolded after Justice Robert Dewar's comments were disclosed. Manitoba's attorney general filed a complaint.

The federal *Judges Act* (R.S.C., 1985, c. J-1) has also established the criteria under which the Canadian Judicial Council will recommend removal of a judge from office.

Judges and the Law Two pieces of federal legislation are essential to judges and their role: the *Judges Act* and the *Constitution Acts 1867 to 1982, Part VII, Canadian Legislation and Regulations.* The Constitution clearly indicates that the judiciary is separate from and independent of the other two branches of government, the executive and the legislative (Schmalleger et al., 2004).

An Alleged Crime Is Committed— The System Unfolds

A complaint is made and an investigation begins. The overarching question is then asked: Are there sufficient grounds (facts) to believe an offence has been committed? If the police believe there are not, then perhaps a warning is given by the police or no action is taken.

When the police believe a crime has been committed and an accused person is identified, the person accused might not be arrested. They may receive a **summons** after a charge has been laid before the court. A summons is an order to appear in court at a certain time to answer to the charge. If arrested, they are guaranteed the right to 1) consult a lawyer, 2) remain silent, 3) be informed promptly of the reasons for the arrest, to retain and instruct counsel without delay, and to be informed of that right, and 4) to have the validity of the detention determined by way of *habeas corpus* and to be released if the detention is not lawful. Additionally, as soon as possible after an arrest, or unless released more quickly by the police, an accused would appear before a justice of the peace or judge (Schmalleger et al., 2004).

At the bail hearing (sometimes referred to as a "show cause" hearing), the prosecutor (the State) must show and explain why the accused should remain in custody (Schmalleger et al., 2004). Bail is a vital part of the Canadian legal process; the *Charter* guarantees it. Section 11(e), specifically, states the right of the accused "not to be denied reasonable bail without just cause." At the same time, however, s. 457 of the *Criminal Code* states that bail may not be granted when it can be shown to be in the public interest or necessary for the protection or safety of the public, and/or when denial is necessary to ensure the appearance of the accuse on the designated date of the trial (Goff, 2008).

Consequently, in certain situations the accused must show why he/she should be released. If a judge decides to release the accused they could be released with or without conditions. In the case of a domestic assault, the Crown might also seek to have the abusive spouse kept in custody until the charge is disposed of. This is often the desired action if:

- the abuser has a criminal record for assault against the same victim
- the present assault was vicious

If the court releases an individual charged with a domestic offence, the person is likely to be put on strict bail conditions; most would also restrict contact with the victim, even if the victim wanted contact. If released on bail with conditions, and the conditions are breached, the individual would return to jail. Victims are entitled to copies of the bail order and information regarding the conditions of bail (Goff, 2008).

Plea Bargain

After a charge is laid, and throughout the judicial process, the Crown and defence may engage at any point in plea bargaining. Plea bargaining is not officially regulated, but it is sanctioned by the Supreme Court of Canada. In fact, Goff (2008) writes, "there is no formal definition of plea bargaining in the *Criminal Code*" (p. 233). Further, the Law Reform Commission states, "as a general definition, plea bargaining has been defined as any agreement by accused to plead guilty in return for the promise of some benefit" (1975, p. 45). As such, it is a process of negotiation that usually involves the defendant, prosecutor, and defence counsel. "This process may be viewed as being founded upon the mutual interest of all three parties involved" (Schmalleger et al., 2004, p. 235). Plea bargains are driven by the following:

1. Defence attorney and defendants will agree to a plea of guilt:
   a. When they are unsure of their ability to win an acquittal at trial
   b. Because of the possibility to reduce or combine charges
   c. For reduced legal fees
   d. For a lower sentence than might otherwise be anticipated
2. Prosecutors bargain when
   a. Their evidence is weaker than they would hope to have
   b. A quick conviction would result without the need to commit the time and resources necessary for trial

Plea bargaining is undoubtedly complex and unique to every alleged offender (Schmalleger et al., 2004). Judges are not involved in the plea bargaining process. Although common over the years, it is generally veiled in secrecy. Public opinion on plea bargaining is generally negative (Schmalleger et al., 2004). Schmalleger and colleagues wrote, in referring to research done by Doob's, that "the public might be more willing to accept the practice of plea bargaining if the process is more open and accountable" (Schmalleger et al., 2004, p. 236). This might, therefore, be a poignant place in this chapter to discuss the role of the Crown counsel.

Crown Counsel

Crown prosecutors are entrusted with the prosecution of all offences and appeals related to the *Criminal Code* of Canada. Crown prosecutors do not represent the government, the police, or the crime victim. And, as stated earlier, when a crime is committed against a victim it is considered a crime against our society as a whole. Therefore, prosecutors perform their function on behalf of the community (Daylen, Harvey, & O'Toole, 2006; Schmalleger et al., 2004).

Prosecutors occupy a unique position in the criminal justice system by virtue of the considerable prosecutorial discretion they yield. They have very broad powers that are not constrained by many controls (Schmalleger et al., 2004). Prosecutorial discretion includes the following:

1. authorizing or not authorizing a charge against a suspect

2. accepting bargained pleas

3. scheduling cases for trial

Depending on where you live in Canada, prosecuting lawyers have different names: Crown Attorney, Crown Counsel, Crown Prosecutor, or Public Prosecutor. Regardless of the label, all prosecutors are responsible for presenting the State's case against the accused person.

If and when there is a significant possibility of a perceived or real improper influence on the prosecution process, a special prosecutor is appointed to handle the case (Schmalleger et al., 2004). Whether it is a Crown Attorney or a special prosecutor who is assigned to a case, a prosecutor's foremost and ultimate responsibilities are to ensure:

- evidence is presented thoroughly and accurately
- the trial process is fair to all
- the independence and integrity of the justice process is maintained

The Crown's duty is not to obtain a conviction at any cost, but rather to make sure that justice is done in an efficient, impartial, fair, and respectful manner (Daylen et al., 2006; Schmalleger et al., 2004).

The Decision to Prosecute— The Trial Process Begins

A criminal charge and the possibility of a trial is a serious matter because a criminal conviction can ultimately result in loss of freedom, not to mention the consequential shame and stigma from a finding of guilt. A great deal is at stake for the accused person.

When someone is accused of a serious crime it is known as an **indictable offence**. For the most part, the types of *Criminal Code* offences discussed in this textbook would fall under this classification. When an indictable offence charge occurs the accused has the right to choose to be tried by a judge and jury, or by a judge alone in Superior Court. The right to choose to be tried by a jury has existed in Canada for almost 300 years (Goff, 2008). For any charge that could result in a prison term of five years or more, the right to be tried by one's peers is guaranteed in the *Charter* (Davison, 2005). When a person is charged with murder—considered to be the most serious of all crimes—he/she will automatically stand trial in Superior Court; however, they still may choose to be tried by a judge alone, and not a jury.

When a jury is chosen, its responsibly is to assess the facts of a case after a judge explains the law to them. The decision that follows is based on the jury's assessment. Sentencing is, however, the judge's responsibility.

The process begins with the option to have a preliminary inquiry, at which time the judge determines whether there is sufficient evidence for the case to proceed to trial.

The Preliminary Hearing

If the charge is an indictable offence, before a trial takes place in the higher court the accused person has the right to undergo a preliminary inquiry (also known as a preliminary hearing) at the provincial court level (see Figure 8.1). The purpose of this proceeding is to determine whether the Crown has enough evidence to justify sending the defendant to trial. Although a preliminary inquiry resembles a trial, the purpose is not to determine whether an accused person is guilty or innocent of the charge. During these hearings a judge examines the case to decide if there is enough evidence to proceed with the trial (Goff, 2008).

When preliminary inquiries take place, they are heard by a provincial court judge (see Figure 8.1). The preliminary inquiry unfolds much like a trial. The Crown presents witnesses, documents, and other evidence to support the allegations against the accused. The defence has an opportunity to review the evidence gathered by police and to question and challenge witnesses. Legal arguments over the admissibility of evidence will also be dealt with. Essentially, the preliminary inquiry functions like a filter. It exists to ensure that the Crown can convince the court that it has sufficient evidence to justify sending the case to a trial. It also allows courts to end prosecutions based on weak allegations, thus sparing citizens from an unnecessary trial. The Heikamp case discussed in "Canadian Headline News" Box 3.2 in Chapter 3 provides an example of a potential outcome of a preliminary hearing.

The Criminal Trial

During the criminal trial the Crown must present an adequate amount of evidence to demonstrate that the accused person is guilty of the charge **beyond a reasonable doubt**. Also, if any evidence was obtained in breach of the accused person's *Charter* rights, the judge may refuse to admit the evidence. An accused person does not have to prove they are innocent, nor are they legally required to testify or to present any other evidence (Schmalleger et al., 2004). These are also fundamental rights which are outlined in the *Charter of Rights and Freedoms.*

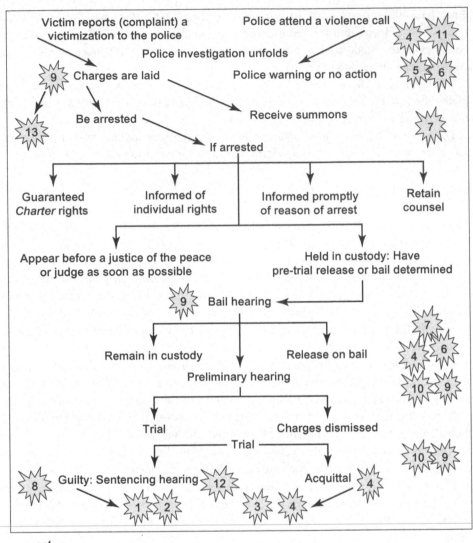

Victim reports (complaint) a victimization to the police

Police attend a violence call

4 11

Police investigation unfolds

9 Charges are laid

Police warning or no action

5 6

Be arrested

Receive summons

13

If arrested

7

Guaranteed *Charter* rights

Informed of individual rights

Informed promptly of reason of arrest

Retain counsel

Appear before a justice of the peace or judge as soon as possible

Held in custody: Have pre-trial release or bail determined

9 Bail hearing

7

Remain in custody

Release on bail

4 6

Preliminary hearing

10 9

Trial

Charges dismissed

Trial

10 9

8 Guilty: Sentencing hearing **12**

Acquittal **4**

1 2

3 4

Key: Services/Protection for Victims

1 Criminal Injuries Compensation
2 Civil Litigation
3 Coroner's Inquest
4 Child Protection Representation and Protection Order
5 Shelter
6 Peace Bond
7 Restraining Order

8 Victim Impact Statement
9 Victim Witness Assistant Services (Court-Based Service)
10 Crown-Based Service
11 Police-based victim services
12 The victim surcharge
13 Community-based services

Figure 8.1 Overview of the Unfolding Criminal Justice System and the Timing of Victim Services

The criminal trial ends with the announcement of a verdict: guilty or not guilty. If the accused is found not guilty, he or she will be **acquitted** and then is free to go. If a jury was involved, once its decision has been made the judge will thank and dismiss the jury members.

Sentencing

Following a verdict of guilt, the post-trial issues begin. One key issue involves sentencing. It is the judge who must decide the appropriate sentence. As Daylen and colleagues wrote, "Canadian law, and revenge is not the reason why judges impose sentences. The fundamental purpose of sentencing is specifically set out in the *Canadian Criminal Code*; it should contribute to respect for the law and maintenance of a just, peaceful and safe society" (2006, p. 336).

Sentencing is dealt with in great detail in s. 718 of the *Criminal Code*. When the judge passes a sentence that revokes an offender's freedom or imposes conditions, it is done with the following objectives in mind:

1. sending a message that the crime committed will not be tolerated

2. informing the offender and the public that the crime committed will have consequences

3. assisting the offender to rehabilitate to prevent further criminal acts

4. making reparation to the community and to the victim for the crime committed (Daylen et al., 2006).

"The court does not sentence those convicted of a criminal offence solely to satisfy the understandable, human emotional need to see offenders suffer in some way for their actions; sentencing is done with the greater good of society in mind" (Daylen et al., 2006, p. 336). Nor do judges reach their sentencing decision in an arbitrary way. Their opinions are restricted by law; this is referred to as the "structure of sentencing" (Goff, 2008). Previous cases are considered. Cases from the same province in which the crime was committed and Supreme Court decisions will be the most valuable case references; these are referred to as **precedent**. Precedent, however, is not the only variable a judge will consider.

Judges have certain parameters within which they can individualize sentences on the basis of the offender's characteristics (prior record) as well as **mitigating circumstances** and/or aggravating circumstances surrounding the crime itself (Goff, 2008). **Aggravating factors** are those circumstances that make the crime *more heinous* than it might otherwise be. Does the offender have a past criminal record for the same offence? If the answer is yes, then that variable is considered. Use of violence, use of a weapon, and injury to the victim are also examples of aggravating factors that may result in a harsher sentence (Daylen et al., 2006; Goff, 2008).

Mitigating factors are facts that can lead to a *less severe* sentence. Age of the offender, pleading guilty to a crime early on in the criminal process, and consenting to attend or already attending a rehabilitative program are also examples.

In all cases, the judge who sentences the offender is the same judge that presided in the trial. Once found guilty, if the sentence is for more than two years the offender will be sent to a federal penitentiary. If sentenced to two years or less they will go to a provincial prison. Judges have a number of dispositions available to them when punishing a convicted offender; the variables involved in sentencing are broad and complex.

Appeals

The verdict of the judge or jury in a criminal trial is not necessarily the final word. Judges make errors in a trial. The right to **appeal** a court's decision is therefore an important safeguard in the Canadian legal system. Appellate litigation (an appeal) is usually confined to questions of law. No new evidence is presented.

In most criminal cases, a decision made at one level of the court system can be appealed to a higher level. The decision of a provincial court judge in an indictable matter is appealed to the provincial and territorial Superior courts. The decisions of a Superior court judge or judge and jury must be appealed to the Provincial Court of Appeal.

In some cases the party who loses on appeal will bring a second appeal to the Supreme Court of Canada. This judgment is not subject to a further appeal. The higher court may deny the appeal, or affirm or reverse the original court decision. In some cases, the Supreme Court will order a new trial. Both sides in a criminal case, either the prosecution or defence, may appeal. A number of case examples have been presented in this text that describe court challenges, for instance the rape shield law in *R. v. Ewanchuk* (refer to Chapter 7). Although in this case the Supreme Court decision impacted the defendant and the victim, the outcome also significantly affected all Canadians, particularly those advocating for the protection of the sexually victimized in our society as the Supreme Court unanimously affirmed that *no actually means no* in sexual assault cases.

The next section will explain how the courts are organized in Canada.

Canada's Courts: How They Are Organized

As *R. v. Ewanchuk* illustrated, there are many layers of courts in Canada:

1. The provincial/territorial courts. They handle the greatest majority of cases that come into the system.
2. The provincial/territorial *superior* courts. These courts deal with more serious crimes and also take appeals from provincial/territorial court judgments. On the same level, but responsible for different issues, is the Federal Court.
3. The provincial/territorial *courts of appeal* and the Federal Court of Appeal.
4. The Supreme Court of Canada, the country's highest court.

For the most part, the *Criminal Code* cases discussed took place in the shaded section of the court system diagram shown in Figure 8.2.

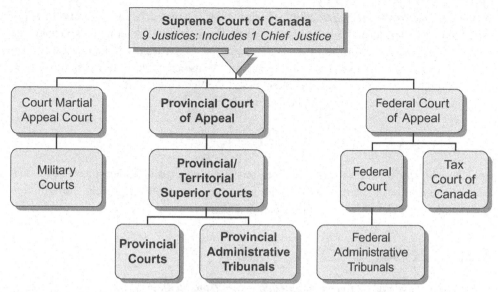

Figure 8.2 Outline of Canada's Court System

Source: Department of Justice Canada, 2005. Adapted with the permission of the Minister of Public Works and Government Services Canada, 2012. http://www.justice.gc.ca/eng/dept-min/pub/ccs-ajc/page3.html

The Supreme Court of Canada The Supreme Court of Canada has a dual role in Canadian society. First, it serves as the final court of appeal. Its nine judges represent the five major regions of the country; three of the justices must be from Quebec, in recognition of the civil law system. The Supreme Court of Canada wields immense power. It is the greatest authority with the capacity for judicial review of all lower court decisions (Schmalleger et al., 2004). As such, it hears appeals from decisions of the appeal courts in all the provinces/territories and from the Federal Court of Appeal.

In Canada each year there are several hundred requests for review, but only about 120 are actually heard (Schmalleger et al, 2004). The Court decides which are worthy of review, and generally it elects to review only cases that involve a substantial question of national importance.

Supreme Court judgments are final. Rarely are the decisions rendered unanimously (Schmalleger et al., 2004). The decision made by the majority of the court becomes the final judgment. Justices who do not agree with the majority decision write dissenting opinions. Those dissenting opinions offer new possibilities for successful appeals made at a later date (Schmalleger et al., 2004). In fact, one such view was described by Justice L'Heureux-Dubé when the rape shield law was struck down in 1992 (see Chapter 7).

The Supreme Court has a second vital function: it decides important questions, referred to as **Reference Questions**, concerning the Constitution and controversial or complicated areas of private and public law. A Reference Question is submitted by the federal or provincial governments asking for an advisory opinion on a major legal issue. Typically, the question concerns the constitutionality of legislation. Interested parties are able to apply for intervener status to make submissions during the hearing. The opinion given by the Supreme Court is in the form of a judicial decision but is not legally binding; however, to date, no government has ever ignored the opinion. A case example of this magnitude took place in 2003 when the federal government asked the Supreme Court to rule on four questions regarding same-sex marriage (see Chapter 7).

Conclusion

Canadian society provides the accused persons and convicted offenders many rights that are enshrined in our Canadian laws; we all need these protections. This chapter will now outline the rights and services that do exist for victims.

8.2: SERVICES TO VICTIMS

Great spirits have always found violent opposition from mediocrities.
The latter cannot understand it when a man does not thoughtlessly submit to hereditary prejudices, but honestly and courageously uses his intelligence and fulfills the duty to express the results of his thought in clear form.

—*Albert Einstein, physicist 1879—1955*

Albeit slowly, and not yet fully, the sun eventually shone a beam of light on the harm committed against victims and the potential breadth and scope of their trauma, loss, and needs. Minimally, the responsibility to offer support, compensation, acknowledgment, and services to the victimized person began. But other services that have emerged also provide a service of a different kind—awareness. Public knowledge, compassion, and advocacy can grow from awareness campaigns. In this module we will examine victim services.

To facilitate our understanding, Figure 8.1 indicates *when* services are available to victims and/or their families. For instance, *Star No. 1* refers to criminal injuries compensation.

The following services are included in this section, and are listed here with their "star number" from Figure 8.1: (1) criminal injuries compensation, (2) civil litigation, (3) coroner's inquest, (4) child protection representations and protection orders, (5) shelters, (6) peace bonds, (7) restraining orders, (8) victim impact statements, (9) Crown/court-based services, (10) court services for children, (11) police-based victim services, (12) the victim surcharge, and (13) community-based services.

Criminal Injuries Compensation: *Star No. 1*

Having just completed an overview of the criminal justice system, you now know that considerable emphasis is placed on ensuring that the civil liberties of the offender are respected and enforced. Legislation and services have also been established to provide assistance to victims. The first example or hint of redress for victims came about in 1969 when the province of Alberta developed legislation that would create a victim compensation program. In time many provincial governments followed Alberta's lead.

Victim compensation plans allow victims of violent crimes to recover some financial costs associated with the crimes that were perpetrated against them. Although a price cannot be put on the impact of victimization, there are often financial consequences for victims. Compensation may help with their loss of wages, medical bills, cost of therapy, and some compensation legislation awarded for pain and suffering. Despite its financial purpose, many victims do not view criminal injuries compensation as a form of economic assistance, but rather as a public acknowledgment that they were harmed.

An award for compensation is not dependent on a criminal conviction. Eligibility is determined by the criminal injuries boards that are established in each province.

Civil Litigation: *Star No. 2*

The next possible service to discuss is the non-criminal side of law: civil law. Enforcement of rights and obligations in civil law takes place in the context of litigations (lawsuits) in the civil courts, not in the context of the criminal justice system. Civil litigation provides a vital opportunity to hold those accountable for the injury they have caused others. It is not the intent of this chapter to discuss the complex components of civil law; however, a brief description will be presented.

The two legal disciplines from which civil law principles flow are contracts and torts. We will briefly explore tort law. **Tort** is a French word that means a "wrong." The law of torts deals with wrongs, or injuries (physical, sexual, economic), inflicted by one party on another, which takes place outside a contract.

The result of the inflicted "wrong" is that the injured party sues the wrongdoer, called a *tortfeasor,* for the injury suffered. In theory, most victims of criminal offences have the common-law right to sue the perpetrator of a *Criminal Code* offence in civil court under the law of tort, *regardless* of whether the offence was prosecuted in the criminal justice system (Daylen et al., 2006; Schmalleger et al., 2004).

The best course of action for those individuals who believe they have been harmed, or who have suffered a violation of their rights, is to consult a lawyer who specializes in tort law for advice regarding the risks and costs of a lawsuit. The financial cost for the victim who pursues civil litigation is therefore a consideration that will need to be addressed. This is quite different from the criminal justice system, because it poses no direct financial burden on the victim. In civil litigation it is ultimately the victim (generally referred to as a plaintiff) who decides to initiate a legal action (Schmalleger et al., 2004).

Generally speaking, there are main categories of harm that allow a victim of violence the right to sue: assault, battery, intentional infliction of mental suffering, and breach of fiduciary duty (Daylen et al., 2006; Klar, 2003; Schmalleger et al., 2004).

Claims can also be initiated against third parties based on negligence. Negligence refers to the unintentional harm caused as a result of a breach of a legally recognized duty of care to individuals. One issue that probably stands out for the reader is the number of victimizations committed by Catholic priests. Since the 1990s, civil litigation has increased as an avenue for victims of childhood sexual abuse and sexual assault to receive some form of justice and compensation. Positive outcomes are attainable. Justice and recognition of stolen human dignity can be achieved even decades later. Refer to Box 8.2 for the details of two cases where victims have won civil litigations against those who stole their childhood.

Civil suits do not seek punishment. If a civil case is found in favour of the complainant, damages for the person's injuries can be awarded. Damages are intended to be restitutionary in nature, designed to restore the victim to the position he or she would have been in if the wrongful act (tort) had not occurred. Awards can cover:

- pain and suffering
- loss of expectation of life
- all pretrial losses, such as loss of income, medical expenses
- future care cost
- loss of earning capacity

The means for calculating civil awards have been established in Supreme Court decisions.

8.2 Victims Win Civil Litigations Against Those Who Stole Their Childhood

Since 1974, when Rev. Barry Glendinning first pleaded guilty to six counts of gross indecency involving children, 22 additional priests from the London diocese (southwestern Ontario) have been convicted, charged, or sued for sexual abuse. Following Glendinning's criminal conviction, his victims sued and were eventually awarded a $1.4-million judgment against the London diocese.

In 2004, Superior Court Justice J. G. Kerr wrote, "It is undisputed that Glendinning was and is a pedophile, and was, at least between 1969 and 1974, a very promiscuous one." Further, during the civil trial a victim, referred to as T.L., said Glendinning abused him between 1967 and 1969. It was similar to what

was endured by the Swales brothers (other victims). The same victim, T.L., swore during the Swales civil trial that he was regularly seen by other residents at the seminary, and was asked by one of them to keep quiet.

Another victim also swore he was repeatedly brought to Glendinning's for overnight stays and sexually abused between 1969 and 1971. He said the priest never tried to conceal his presence, even though it was against the rules for children to stay at the seminary. Justice Kerr came to the "inescapable conclusion" that the diocese "encouraged secrecy, if not willful blindness on the part of its priests with respect to sexual deviance." Justice J. G. Kerr also stated, "It was an environment in which one heard no evil, saw no evil and spoke no evil. The diocese thus created and nurtured an environment in which Glendinning was free to carry on his sexual predation without fear of discovery."

Father Charles Sylvestre was another pedophile priest who preyed upon and sexually victimized numerous girl children for more than 40 years. Sylvestre confronted his multiple acts of violence (legally) on August 3, 2006, when at the age of 84 he pleaded guilty to 47 counts of indecent assault. On this day he was sentenced to three years in prison for sexually abusing young girls for almost four decades. The first report of his abuse was in 1954. London lawyer Rob Talach, with the firm Ledroit Beckett, launched the majority of those lawsuits. Talach noted that the number of

lawsuits specifically involving Sylvestre was pushing 100.

Review Questions

1. Glendinning and Sylvestre are two sexual offenders, but how many others do you think also knew about these victimizations and chose to do nothing and look the other way?

2. Do you think not helping a victim, omitting to report, or even blaming and shaming a victim is as serious (if not worse) as committing the actual crimes? What are your thoughts?

Sources: Wilhelm, 2006, 2011; *Windsor Star,* 2006; *K.M.M. v. The Roman Catholic Episcopal Corp.* 2011. ONSC 2143. Retrieved in June 2011 from www.ledroitbeckett.com/upload/files/reasons-for-judgment2011-04-21.pdf.

Coroner's Inquest: *Star No. 3*

A coroner's inquest can serve as another opportunity for victims to see justice and the truth revealed. An inquest serves an investigative function. For family members left behind, struggling to make sense of the death of a loved one, an inquest can help provide answers, and for some a pathway to closure. On another level, an inquest serves a social and preventative function. It involves a public examination of the conditions that may have caused or contributed to a death: It is a fact-finding process.

In Ontario, the motto for the Office of the Chief Coroner is "We Speak for the Dead to Protect the Living." The coroner is charged with the responsibility to review the circumstances around the death of a person in the hopes that a similar death can be prevented in the future. This is in fact the overarching responsibility of all coroners' offices in Canada.

A coroner's inquest is a public hearing held under the authority of the *Coroners Act.* During an inquest evidence is presented. The purpose of an inquest is not to place blame or make a finding of legal responsibility. If there are any criminal proceedings arising out of a death they must be resolved before an inquest can be held. Recall from Chapter 3 that this was precisely the process that unfolded after the death of 35-day-old Jordan Heikamp. First there was the criminal proceeding, which began and ended at the pre-trial stage; the case was dismissed due to insufficient evidence (see Box 3.2). Later, an inquest was conducted and the coroner declared that Jordan Hiekamp had died of starvation.

For the family of Lori Dupont, the inquest into their daughter's death provided the family some comfort in knowing meaningful positive change would come from their overwhelming loss and grief. Part one of the story was introduced in Chapter 4, Box 4.1. You will now read about part two of Lori's story, the coroner's inquest, in "From the Pen of . . ." Box 8.3.

8.3 From the Pen of Lawyer Greg Monforton: The Lori Dupont Story, Part 2

A coroner's inquest is not a trial. There is no accused. There is no finding of blame or fault. There are no fines imposed, compensation ordered, or punishment meted out. Rather, its purpose is to allow the coroner's jury to hear all of the evidence and make recommendations at the inquest's conclusion designed to prevent other deaths in similar circumstances.

Although a coroner's inquest is not a trial, its rules and overall method of proceeding are somewhat akin to a trial. It is presided over by a coroner. Representing the coroner's interests at the inquest is coroner's counsel. Coroner's counsel has the power to summons both people and records at the inquest. Standing is granted only to those individuals or entities directly involved in the death in question or who stand to suffer impugned integrity. Each party granted standing to participate is entitled to be represented by counsel.

All in all, the coroner's inquest into the deaths of Lori Dupont and Marc Daniel lasted well over nine weeks, beginning in September of 2007 and finishing in the early days of December. The coroner's brief of documentation consisted of over 8000 pages. Over 70 witnesses were called to give evidence.

Those granted standing by Coroner Dr. Andrew McCallum included the Dupont family (who I had the privilege to represent), the estate of Marc Daniel, Marc Daniel's treating psychiatrists Dr. Brian Burke and Dr. William Taylor, the Ontario Hospital Association, the Ontario Nurses Association, the Essex County Crown Attorney's Office, and the Ministry of Labour for the Province of Ontario.

Naturally, the Dupont family's motives in seeking the inquest were to find out precisely what took place in the months and weeks leading up to Lori's death, and to help achieve real, substantive, and pervasive change in workplace domestic violence. I, as their counsel, also had a number of specific questions that demanded answers:

1. Did the action or inaction of the hospital management hierarchy contribute to the circumstances leading up to Marc Daniel's murder of Lori?

2. Did the hospital fail to provide Lori with a safe place to work?

3. Did the hospital empower Daniel to do what he did?

4. In the months leading up to Lori's death, did the hospital take appropriate steps to confront Daniel?

5. Did the Physician's Health Program operated by the Ontario Medical Association properly monitor Daniel's actions, particularly upon his return to work in May of 2005?

6. Did the criminal justice system, once charges were laid by Lori against Daniel, proceed with sufficient dispatch and concern for Lori's safety?

7. Did the hospital's management structure provide sufficient accountability for those involved in Daniel's reintegration into the hospital workplace just a few months prior to Lori's murder?

The length constraints of this article do not provide sufficient space to detail all of what was learned during the many weeks of testimony from the dozens of witnesses and the hundreds of documents filed. Day after day, week after week, witness after witness told the same tragic story from slightly different perspectives.

Not a day passed during the inquest in which tears were not shed. More than once, I lay awake at night, haunted by my thoughts of what Lori's last and unspeakably horrible moments must have been like. And day after day, Lori's parents Barbara and John, and sister Christine, maintained their watch; listening to each day's proceedings with stoic dignity and simply unbelievable courage.

For the most part, the evidence of those testifying on behalf of the hospital's administrative and medical management teams focused on the unforeseeability of a tragedy fuelled only by the irrational and undetectable rage of Marc Daniel. Many on the hospital's management team tried to cast the tragedy not as a workplace tragedy but simply as a personal domestic relationship that simply happened to play out there. And they spoke of the adverse financial consequences which the hospital might have faced if it had wrongfully suspended Daniel's privileges prior to Lori's death.

On the other hand, the vast majority of Lori's nursing colleagues and friends told contrasting stories of steadily escalating harassment of Lori by Daniel, and a lack of sufficient and timely action on the part of both hospital management and the justice system to either confront Daniel or protect Lori.

One of the inquest's most compelling witnesses was Dr. Peter Jaffe. Dr. Jaffe is a professor in the Faculty of Education and Academic Director of the Centre for Research on Violence against Women and Children at the University of Western Ontario. Dr. Jaffe defined domestic violence and abuse as any form of psychological, physical, or sexual force, actual or threatened, in an intimate relationship. He noted that while both women and men can be victims of domestic violence, the overwhelming majority of this violence involves men abusing women. Dr. Jaffe characterized what took place in the months and weeks leading up to Lori's death as a pattern of assaultive and controlling behaviour on the part of Marc Daniel. He cited the fact that responsibility for safety is generally put on the victim and not on the perpetrator. He spoke of the importance of engaging with the abuser and holding him accountable rather than excusing his behaviour. He cited studies indicating that 70 percent of employed victims of domestic violence encounter harassment by their abusers at work.

Perhaps most strikingly, in reviewing Daniel's actions involving Lori and the hospital, Dr. Jaffe identified 16 risk factors in the Lori Dupont–Marc Daniel relationship. These included (but were not limited to) a history of violence and abusive behaviours, prior threats to kill Lori, Daniel's prior suicide attempt, his prior attempts to isolate Lori, his efforts to control her daily activities, and the escalation of violence.

Dr. Jaffe also spoke of critical events and opportunities. He defined "critical events" as warning signs and risk factors that, either by themselves or as part of a pattern of behaviour, should have raised the possibility of danger. Dr. Jaffe defined "opportunities" as chances to intervene and offer protection for the victim or accountability for the perpetrator.

All in all, Dr. Jaffe found 37 critical events and 84 missed opportunities occurring between October of 2003 and Lori's murder in November of 2005. Most importantly, Dr. Jaffe offered nine overarching recommendations designed to

(*continued*)

prevent the occurrence of a similar tragedy in the future; these recommendations focused on changes to workplace domestic violence and harassment policies, the government, the criminal justice system, and the education of health care providers.

At the conclusion of the inquest, the coroner's jury made a number of sweeping recommendations directed to, among others, the legislature of the Province of Ontario and the Ministry of Health and Long Term Care, the Ontario Hospital Association, Hotel-Dieu Grace Hospital and to all public hospitals in Ontario, to the Ontario Medical Association, the Director of the Physician Health Program, the College of Physicians and Surgeons of Ontario, the Ontario Hospital Association, and the Ontario Ministry of Labour.

All of the recommendations made by the coroner's jury were supported by the Dupont family; a fact that was stressed by me to the jury in the course of my closing remarks to them.

Before delving into the specific recommendations the Dupont family was urging the jury to make, I first spoke to the jury of the tremendous opportunity they had to make our province safer for the literally thousands of health care workers in our province and throughout our country who work tirelessly to cure our sick and ease their suffering. And in urging the jury to reject the anticipated requests by those speaking on behalf of some of the institutions granted standing at the inquest not to disturb the status quo too strongly. I spoke of the special kind of courage it takes to speak truth to those in power and to make genuine, lasting, and important change.

In the jury's preamble to its recommendations, they expressed their sincere condolences to the family of Lori Dupont and to the family of Marc Daniel. The jury told of their recognition of the profound effect that this tragedy had on Hotel-Dieu Hospital and the entire community.

In the simplest of terms, the jury's recommendations aimed to better protect those confronted with domestic violence in the workplace. The recommendations were made taking into account several of Lori's employer's failings, including recognition of the imbalance of power inherent in the relationship between a nurse and a doctor, and a review of the Public Hospitals Act. The Ontario Ministry of Labour was given a specific recommendation to review its Occupational Health and Safety Act and to "examine the feasibility of including domestic violence (from someone in the workplace), abuse and harassment as factors warranting investigation and appropriate action by the Ministry of Labour."

In the weeks and months that followed the inquest's conclusion, Lori's mother Barbara and others, including Michelle Schryer of the Chatham-Kent Sexual Assault Crisis Centre, worked tirelessly in urging the government of Ontario to make changes to the Occupational Health and Safety Act.

As a result of their efforts, legislation was passed by the government of Ontario in December of 2009. The new law in question, formally titled the Occupational Health and Safety Amendment Act, is the first legislation in Canada to recognize the dangers of domestic violence in the workplace.

Many advocates for the victims of workplace violence believe that this legislation falls somewhat short, failing to provide sufficient avenues for complaints in situations which do not include physical violence. But most agree that it is an important first step in making the workplace safer for those who find themselves victims of workplace violence.

It is every lawyer's dream to represent people they admire and whose cause they truly embrace. And it is every lawyer's goal to play a role in helping create actual changes in the law for the better. Although I never had the pleasure of meeting Lori Dupont, I do feel that in some small way I did come to know her during my representation of her family during the coroner's inquest.

I believe that Lori would have been extremely proud of her family. And I believe she would have been immensely grateful to them for all they have done to celebrate her life, protect and preserve her legacy, and give positive meaning to her tragic death.

Lori Dupont and her family will always have a very special place in my mind and heart. To represent them was a privilege I will always be grateful for and never forget.

Review Question

After reading about the inquest into the death of Lori Dupont, what levels of protective care can you see were ignored, not offered, or not available? Also reflect on Chapter 2: what forms of oppression (if any) might have been at play to have permitted this tragedy?

Source: Submitted to Anastasia Bake by Greg Monforton, www.gregmonforton.com.

Forms of Protection

Various services are provided that specifically focus on protection. The four services that will be discussed are child protection representations and protection orders, shelters, peace bonds, and restraining orders. An additional service that exists to protect the public from sexual predators, although quite different in appearance, is the National Sex Offender Registry.

Child Protection Representations and Protection Orders: *Star No. 4*

Children have the right to legal representations. In 1974, the Law Reform Commission of Canada recommended that children who are subject to family law proceedings be provided with independent legal counsel. Since 1991, this right became recognized when Canada ratified the United Nations *Convention on the Rights of the Child,* which gave children the right to representations views on legal matters that affect them either directly or through representations.

Apart from legal representation, child protection orders also provide protection for children from further or potential harm. Protection orders are civil court orders issued under provincial family violence (child welfare) legislation. If evidence is available, child protection orders will specifically address the existence of or the potential for harm. The legal "findings" of a child protection case will be stated, and a plan developed to address the concerns.

Shelters: *Star No. 5*
Battered women's shelters exist with the primary goal to provide immediate refuge for women seeking relief or escape from violence. All battered women's shelters have 24-hour hotlines, and generally accept women who are in imminent danger. Protection from harm is their purpose.

Information on shelters in Canada is collected through the Transition Home Survey (THS), a biennial census of all residential facilities for female victims of family violence (Sauvé & Burns, 2009). The THS was developed as part of the federal Family Violence Initiative, and provided an overview of shelters in Canada that offer residential services to abused women and their children. It also provided a profile of the people who used them. Since approximately 9 in 10 shelters prohibited the admission of men, information on men using these facilities is limited.

In the 2008 family violence survey, 569 facilities were included in the report. The delivery and mixture of types of sheltering facilities differs by province/territory. In 2008, about 70 percent of the shelters in Canada were located in three provinces: Ontario (28 percent), Quebec (22 percent), and British Columbia (19 percent). When one factors in population, however, Prince Edward Island had the greatest number of shelters per capita, (14 per 100 000 married, common-law, and separated women) (Sauvé & Burns, 2008). Nationally, there were approximately seven shelters for every 100 000 married, common-law, and separated women (Sauvé & Burns, 2008).

To put in perspective the need for shelters, on April 16, 2008 (this snapshot day) 4273 women were residing in shelters across Canada, and 3222 of them were attempting to escape an abusive situation. These women brought nearly 2900 children with them. The remaining women and children in shelters were seeking accommodation for reasons other than abuse. For instance, one of the reasons noted was the need for shelter (Sauvé & Burns, 2008).

An interesting note to make is that at the time of writing this textbook there was no standalone shelter for victims of same-sex domestic violence in Canada. However, a number of shelters have committed a specific number of beds to this population if and when a need is identified.

Peace Bonds: *Star No. 6* Not all victimized persons need to move to a place of safety when they have been harmed, yet there may be a real threat of danger to them and their children. Many want to remain in their own homes and carry out their lives and routines as normally as possible. Nonetheless, fear and threat exists. Two possible forms of protections exist to allow a person to obtain an added level of security: peace bonds and restraining orders.

The purpose of a peace bond is to prevent anticipated future harm by a feared individual. This can be initiated by a victim who fears they or their family might also be harmed by the offender. This action takes place through the Crown's office or the police. An abused woman, for instance, has the right to obtain a "peace bond" against her partner or husband in an attempt to prevent him from communicating with her or being around her.

To obtain a peace bond, a person must go to the local courthouse and see a justice of the peace and explain the circumstances. A lawyer is not needed. A peace bond may be issued under section 810 of the *Criminal Code* or under the court's common-law jurisdiction to bind a party over to keep the peace. If the person named agrees to the peace bond, it will be granted immediately by a judge. If the person named does not agree, a hearing will be ordered that must be attended by the victim.

A peace bond can be issued for a maximum of 12 months. If the complainant chooses to renew the bond a new hearing must be held. If the conditions of the peace bond are broken, the person named can be charged with a criminal offence.

Restraining Orders: *Star No. 7* A restraining order is an additional form of protection. Restraining orders are intended to protect victims who fear for their safety or the safety of someone known to them. For example, if there is a considerable risk of harassment following a spousal separation, a restraining order can be obtained by the estranged husband/wife, which may require the stalker/abuser to maintain a safe distance from the place of work or residence of the applicant and restrict any form of communication with him or her.

A restraining order is an order made under provincial civil law in family court. A lawyer is normally required to apply for a restraining order. Such an order is meant to keep the abuser from bothering the victim, which could include stalking. These orders are civil in nature, not criminal. Therefore, police helpfulness in enforcing them is often an issue.

The National Sex Offender Registry In 2004, the Government of Canada created a large database called the National Sex Offender Registry in order to provide the police with quick access to current critical information about convicted sex offenders. The database contains information about the offender's offences, aliases (if any), identifying marks (scars/tattoos), and current address and telephone numbers. It can be accessed only by police agencies. All person convicted of a sex offence are required to re-register annually with the police and/or every time they change their address or legal name (RCMP, 2008).

The Registry does not necessarily prevent a person from committing a sexual crime, but it does assist in the investigations of sexual crimes and identifying possible suspects known to reside near the place where an offence was committed. It is therefore possible that the registry acts as a **deterrent** to reoffended, because the offenders would know of its existence and as such would increase the odds they would be apprehended if they were to reoffend.

Victim Impact Statement: *Star No. 8*

Victims and victim advocates sought to have those who had been harmed recognized in the justice system. They wanted their voices heard and their experiences considered. A significant opportunity did materialize in 1988 when victim impact statements were legislated. Bill C-89, among other things amended the *Criminal Code* to provide victims the right to present victim impact statements. The **victim impact statement (VIS)** is a voluntary account that details the impact of a crime on a victim's physical, social, psychological, and financial functioning.

When this legislation was first passed, there was nothing that mandated a judge to consider the VIS. Amendments were subsequently made in 1996 when Bill C-41 was passed, which required judges to consider the statements. In 1999 (s. 745 *Criminal Code*) a further amendment occurred when the definition of "victim" was expanded to include relatives or a spouse (Department of Justice Canada, 2006; Littlefield, 2004).

Moreover, judges were now required by law to ask a Crown, before imposing a sentence, whether the victim had been informed of the opportunity to prepare a victim impact statement.

When a victim impact statement is filed, both the defence counsel and the sentencing judge receive copies. While it is mandatory for judges in criminal cases to make use of victim impact statements, they are not mandatory. Victims have an opportunity and a choice to make. For many victims, the simple act of telling the court how the crime impacted their life can be therapeutic and healing. As Daylen and colleagues point out, "At the time of sentencing, the accused is now the offender and neither the offender nor the defence can intimidate you as long as you follow the guidelines give to you by the Crown (2006, p. 364).

Given that a criminal justice process and the courtroom is not a therapeutic environment—and, potentially, a very stressful place, particularly for child and adult sexual assault victims (Herman, 2003)—the victim impact statement has been seen as an important opportunity to help many victims experience psychological catharsis (Erez, 1994). After participating many have felt validated—especially when comments from the victim impact statements are referred to by judges, because this communicates to victims that the community recognizes and validates the harm sustained (Erez & Rogers 1999; Meredith & Paquette, 2001).

Victim Impact Statements and Parole Hearings

Originally, victim impact statements were used only at sentencing hearings, but their use grew to include parole hearings, judicial reviews, and even bail hearings. In 1992, the *Corrections and Conditional Release Act* was adopted to include a clause to allow victims the right to present a VIS to the National Parole Board when it considers granting conditional release for an offender.

This marked the first time victims were formally recognized in federal legislation governing the correctional and conditional release system. At a parole hearing the victim impact statement can shine a light on the effects the crime had on the victim. The information can not only provide insight regarding the impact the crime had on the victim and the victim's family, but it also can provide the Board with insight and information not available elsewhere. As stated earlier, some offences are dealt with through a plea bargain; consequently, the impact the crime had on the victim or the victim's family may not have been heard in an *open* court process. Therefore, at a parole hearing the victim's impact is allowed.

Recall from "Canadian Headline News" Box 5.4 that Gavin Mandin was denied parole after admitting he felt justified for murdering his family ten years earlier. From a Canadian historical point, the legislative change had just occurred, allowing victims the right to present an *oral* impact statement at federal parole hearings, not simply in written form, which had previously existed. Consequently, in 2001 the first ever oral statement was given on behalf of the Mandin family by the aunt of Gavin Mandin and her father.

Many individuals affected by horrific crimes move forward and contribute to victim awareness. Following this family tragedy, Colette Mandin fought for victims' rights. In a demonstration of her commitment, Ms. Mandin generously provided her victim impact statement given in June 2001 at a parole hearing for Gavin Mandin. It appears in "From the Pen of . . ." Box 8.4.

8.4 From the Pen of Colette Mandin: Victim Impact Statement Given at Gavin Mandin Parole Hearing

**Victim Impact Statement: June 2001
Re: Gavin Joseph Mandin**

Intro: Although this is a very difficult thing to do, I have fought long and hard, at great personal cost, for victims to have a voice in the justice process. I am pleased that this has occurred on time for my family to benefit. I thank the National Parole Board for this opportunity.

When an impact statement is delivered after the crime, you have no idea what the impact is going to be two years from then, five years from then, ten years from then. You rarely know, at the time, the effect of trauma on individuals and the family on the long run.

Impact Statement

How can anyone truly describe the impact of this crime on me personally, on my immediate family, on our extended family and the surrounding community? Like any other trauma, it is almost impossible to measure, and difficult to voice.

Physical Impact: I will start with the physical impact because it is tangible and most people understand it.

The Mandin family lost five people in August 1991. Maurice, Susan, Islay and Janelle to murder and Gavin to crime and prison. I cannot describe the feeling that arises when there are family gatherings, forever changed, with five people missing. The loss is painful, intense, and difficult to describe. This loss has shifted the dynamics and the politics of the family and forever changed the relationships within it.

Can one measure the impact of such a crime on the physical and emotional health of the family? Over the last ten years, I have observed my parents age 25 years in 10. Myself and family members have struggled with anxiety, depression, fear, suicidal ideation, traumatic grief and symptoms of posttraumatic stress. Our individual health has been adversely affected just as anyone's who has suffered a trauma. The cost is not covered for us as it is for the offender. The financial burden has been enormous. We pay for our own security systems, our own counseling, our own medications, our own aftermath of this crime. The tens of thousands of dollars spent on the above as well as communications travel, lost work and divorce are gone. They could have better been invested in our futures.

Emotional Impact: Only those who understand the emotional impact of sudden loss and murder, or the impact of post traumatic stress and traumatic grief will truly know the emotional impact of this crime on me and my family. Although the symptoms and emotional triggers dull somewhat with time, they will remain with us till we die. They will likely be passed down

(continued)

as post-traumatic behaviour to the next generation as we struggle to deal with grief, shattered dreams, beliefs and relationships.

Spiritual Impact: Can anyone explain such a senseless act such as murdering four people, two who are children? This crime shattered my belief systems, my sense of trust and goodwill in humans, and my feeling of being secure in the world. What an assault to one's spirituality to have the sanctity of life of your loved ones so violated, so disrespected, so brutalized.

I had embraced, literally, Gavin as a family member when his mother married my brother. Gavin is of similar age as my sons. He became my nephew: someone to nurture to adulthood. How can I explain the feeling of betrayal of that trust in these murders? How can someone I had placed trust in murder his family, his sisters and desecrate the bodies of his parents? My feelings of repulsion of this act and betrayal of everyone in our family run deep and will likely never fade.

Safety: I do not believe members of my family and I will ever feel truly safe again. How could we? Gavin proved to us that we aren't.

Because of the way justice works, and the guilty plea to second degree murder, Gavin never had to own up for his actions to the public, nor to his family. We are unaware of his motivators and certainly not privy to any information about his rehabilitation.

We know how manipulative and sociopathic Gavin can be, we have been witness to it.

Gavin's maternal grandmother, years ago, described Gavin's childhood to me. Self-centered rages were not an unusual occurrence, certainly not the exception. That type of history and pattern of behavior is not likely to be well documented in this process. A person's formative years are age 0–12 and the person who would know his patterns of behaviour the best, his mother, is dead.

We can only make an informed guess, with limited information, as to whether Gavin poses a risk to our family and to society. Your information will involve the last ten years; ours will involve the 15 years before that. Our information has little opportunity to overlap with yours; victims are not interviewed for this purpose. Anything we say is not considered evidence and would be considered hearsay.

I do not believe, for a moment, that these murders were not premeditated, planned and executed. I do not trust that this would not happen again. I challenge anyone to convince me that there is no risk in releasing Gavin.

Review Question

In 2001, Colette Mandin read the first oral victim impact statement in a Canadian parole hearing. As this book goes to print, the Mandin family are continually notified and invited to attend each of Gavin Mandin's parole hearings. How do you think this continual process would or could affect victims?

Source: Submitted to Anastasia Bake by Colette Mandin.

Crown/Court-Based Services: *Star No. 9*

Most communities with courthouses have court-based services such as victim/witness assistance programs. Although today these programs exist and are designed to help victims and witnesses in the criminal justice system, the origin of their inception provides an example of how important initiatives begin. In "From the Pen of . . ." Box 8.5, Lynn Kainz provides a historical reflection up to and including a present-day account of a victim/witness program. Lynn Kainz had been an advocate for women and children for over 35 years when she would ultimately retire as the manager of the Ministry of the Attorney General's Victim/Witness Assistance Program in Windsor, Ontario, in July 2009.

Moreover, many provinces prepare and design materials that are written in language that is emotionally and cognitively appropriate for child victims. Some provinces also have websites designed to further teach and enhance a child's understanding. Given that these staffs are well trained and understand the impact and potential needs of victims, they also help by providing referrals to community agencies for counselling and other supportive services.

8.5 From the Pen of Lynn Kainz: Victim Witness Programs

When I first started working in the criminal justice system in the early 1980s there were very few services available to victims of crime. Those services were specific to particular groups of victims, for example the Sexual Assault Crisis Centre provided services to victims of sexual assault, and Hiatus House, a shelter for battered women, provided services to victims of domestic assault. Even then there were programs available for male batterers.

At that time there were no services available in Windsor to support victims and witnesses of crime through the criminal justice system. However, in the early 1980s the Salvation Army in London, Ontario was providing some services to victims and witnesses of crime. An information desk was set up at the courthouse to provide emotional support and information on the day of court. This information included:

1. Directions to determine where the appropriate courtrooms were located

2. How to determine who was the officer in charge of their particular court, in order to obtain their statement for review

3. Information; general facts about the layout of the courtroom and court process.

Victims and witnesses were also provided with practical assistance regarding where they could collect witness fees and the location of the washrooms.

While I was working as Corrections Coordinator at the Salvation Army in Windsor, Ontario in 1986 I learned of this service for victims and witnesses. Consequently, I approached the Windsor Courts about setting up an information desk at the Ontario Court of Justice. It was clear that this type of service had been extremely valuable to those attending court to testify in criminal matters. Soon we were provided with an information desk and a small waiting room away from the general public; victims could now wait in a safe and secure waiting area. At that time there were three separate court locations (buildings) in Windsor: the Ontario Court of Justice, Superior Court of Justice, and Family Court, which caused a fair bit of confusion.

Further issues became known as a result of our presence in the court buildings. For instance, on Mondays when jury selections were taking place, potential jurors would have to be redirected to the Superior Court of Justice. Many expressed their anxiety about having to serve as jurors, so it was not surprising to learn that those attending court

(continued)

because they had been subpoenaed to testify in criminal court matters were very worried and afraid.

Prior to the implementation of the Ministry of the Attorney General's Victim/Witness Assistance Program (VWAP) in 1987, victims and witnesses of crime would provide a statement to the police and would not hear BACK from anyone until months later when they were served with a subpoena to testify. Victims subpoenaed to court not only expressed fear for their safety, but fear of having to testify in an open court in front of the general public. Due to the lengthy passage of time they also expressed fear that they would not remember specific details about the case and would be subjected to a grueling cross-examination.

The Criminal Justice System is confusing and intimidating. Most people's knowledge of and information about the court system was minimal and they welcomed any information related to court.

Windsor would eventually become one of eight VWAP pilot projects in Ontario created by the Ministry of the Attorney General to deliver support to victims and witnesses of crime, and to help them receive the information and services they needed throughout the Criminal Justice system. I was hired as the Windsor Victim/Witness Coordinator in April 1987 and was responsible for implementing the program locally and setting up a volunteer program. Volunteers assisted at the information desk and provided court accompaniment to victims/witnesses on the day of trial.

Today, the VWAP's goals continue to be to enhance the victims'/witnesses' understanding of and participation in the criminal justice system, to ensure the coordination of services with community agencies that support victims and witnesses of crime, and to assist them in regaining a sense of well-being.

To accomplish these goals, VWAP staff provide crisis intervention, emotional support, case specific information such as court dates, bail [release] conditions, information about the court process and its protocol and decorum, court preparation and orientation, needs assessment, referrals to community agencies and assistance with victim impact statements. *Information is power.* Experience underscored that fact that once the victim or witness received information about the court process and their role as a witness within the criminal justice system, PLUS they had their fears and questions addressed by the Assistant Crown Attorney (VWAP staff do NOT discuss evidence), they became stronger witnesses.

As there is no fee for service, the majority of victims would avail themselves of the service. Services are offered shortly after charges are laid and continue until the matter is resolved. Services are available to women, men, and children. VWAP staff assess the needs of children and make recommendations to the Crown attorney with respect to testimonial aides to assist children to testify; for example, use of a screen, a support person, closed circuit TV, etc. *All* children are provided with courtroom orientation and preparation. The VWAP became a permanent program in 1989 and has expanded to 61 sites across the province.

One last reflection, if I may. Throughout the years I have witnessed many victims/witnesses who presented themselves at our office expressing their fear of testifying and their inability to cope with the demands of the criminal justice system. However, with information and with the assistance and support of the VWAP staff many realized the depth of their ability and would indeed successfully go forward and participate in the criminal court process!

Review Question

What services exist in your community to support victims and witnesses involved in the criminal justice system?

Source: Submitted to Anastasia Bake by Lynn Kainz.

Court Services for Children: *Star No. 10*

Prepare and prevent, don't repair and repent.

—Author Unknown

Numerous children are required to testify about their own victimization or about the violent acts they have witnessed in their lives. Testifying in an **adversarial system** is threatening and places a enormous emotional responsibility and burden on children. Over time, changes to legislation allowed for special courtroom procedures to help children. The provisions are sensitive to the needs of children in the court process and do not require special status in order to be implemented. These innovative legal reforms translated to concrete services for children. They include closed courtrooms, privacy protection, and videotaped statements. For a detailed explanation of how these services are introduced into the criminal court process, see "From the Pen of" Box 7.3 in Chapter 7.

Police-Based Victim Services: *Star No. 11*

Several communities have established police-based victim service units/programs where trained personnel work in affiliation with the local police department. These services are time limited, generally lasting only a couple weeks following the victimization. The overarching goal is to provide an instantaneous capable intervention during a crisis—emotional support is vital. Services vary from providing instant crisis intervention for victims and their families to following up for a specified period of time after the crime. During this time referrals are made to attend to the urgent and eventual needs of victims. Most of us do not plan to be victimized, so the immediacy of this help is vital and valued.

The Victim Surcharge: *Star No. 12*

The creation of the victim surcharge came into force in July 1989 and was designed to collect revenue for provincial victim assistance programs. The victim surcharge requires all those who are found guilty of an offence to pay something to support victim of crimes. Specifically, s. 737 of the *Criminal Code* dictates that the proceeds of this surcharge "shall be applied for the purposes of providing such assistance to victims of offences as the Lieutenant Governor in Council of the Province in which the surcharge is imposed may direct from time to time."

Community-Based Services: *Star No. 13*

Community-based services include sexual assault centres, distress centres, victim advocacy groups, and safe homes or shelters. These types of service will vary greatly due to the number of cities in Canada's provinces/territories.

Governmental Initiatives

Canada's federal and provincial/territorial governments over the years have provided numerous initiatives to address the needs of crime victims. They range from public education initiatives, to specialized agencies and ministries, to commitment of financial support, research, and publication. Declaring special dates in the calendar year or supporting initiatives that result from Canadian tragedies are a few examples. Although they are numerous in scope, the following examples will be highlighted: the Office of the Federal Ombudsman for Victims of Crime, the Family Violence Initiative (and the National Clearinghouse on Family Violence), the National Seniors Council on Elder Abuse, and victims' rights legislation.

The Office of the Federal Ombudsman for Victims of Crime Implemented in 2007, the Office of the Federal Ombudsman for Victims of Crime is an independent resource for victims in Canada created to ensure the federal government meets its responsibilities to victims of crime. The Ombudsman works to ensure that policy makers and other criminal justice personnel are aware of victims' needs and concerns and to identify important issues and trends that may negatively impact victims. The Office also provides information to victims regarding their rights under federal law, the services available to them, or to make a complaint about any federal agency or federal legislation dealing with victims of crime (Office of the Federal Ombudsman, website).

The Family Violence Initiative First announced in June 1988, the Family Violence Initiative (FVI) has represented a long-term commitment by the federal government; the FVI's mandate is to enhance awareness of family violence issues (Jamieson & Gomes, 2010).

One of the many services provided under the Family Violence Initiative umbrella is the management of the National Clearinghouse on Family Violence. It has become Canada's resource centre for information on violence within the family. Many new products, resources, research, and events are continually updated and are available to the Canadian public or any person interested in the issue of violence. Also available to those who are interested is a quarterly subscription to the *National Clearinghouse on Family Violence E-Bulletin* (Family Violence Initiative, website).

The National Seniors Council on Elder Abuse In an effort to learn about and continue to address the issues confronting the senior population in Canada, the National Seniors Council held five regional meetings to specifically address the topic of elder abuse. Fifty individuals, representing organizations serving seniors, law enforcement agencies, legal experts, service providers, and academics, participated in five meetings in various regions of Canada. The discussions were guided by the following objectives:

- enable the National Seniors Council to learn more about the issue of elder abuse

- share good practices for raising awareness, responding to and preventing elder abuse

- identify areas for possible federal government action (National Seniors Council, 2007).

Although each meeting was unique, six themes emerged that provided the content of their document, which has subsequently provided advice to the federal government. The National Seniors Council asked the federal government to consider the following summary and their action points, or goals. The six points that would guide the work of the National Seniors Council throughout the next few years were:

1. awareness
2. knowledge transfer and information sharing
3. education and training
4. research
5. resources for community responses to elder abuse
6. legal considerations

The National Seniors Council on Elder Abuse tabled these goals in its 2007 report. Continual progress will unfold. Research and statistics are key to better defining, confronting, and ameliorating elder abuse.

Similar to governmental services, other organizations exist that focus on education, awareness, and the distribution of knowledge that addresses critical questions in Canadian society. There are many such organizations in Canada; here, we will address the Canadian Association of Sexual Assault Centres and the Sisters in Spirit, a component of the Native Women's Association of Canada (NWAC).

Canadian Association of Sexual Assault Centres This is a pan-Canadian group of sexual assault centres that came together to implement the legal, social, and attitudinal changes necessary to prevent, and ultimately eradicate, rape and sexual assault. As feminist organizations they recognize that violence against women is one of the strongest indicators of prevailing societal attitudes toward women. The Canadian Association of Sexual Assault Centres (CASAC) aims to be a force for social change regarding violence against women at the individual, institutional, and political levels.

They provide the vehicle essential for communication and education to alleviate the political and geographical isolation of centres in Canada. They also support and encourage efforts to create a society in which all members have the rights of social, economic, and political equality.

CASAC has political alliances with other national groups whose work promotes women's equality and anti-violence. In addition to being CASAC members, many of the centres belong to the National Action Committee on the Status of Women (NAC), Canada's largest feminist coalition. For more information, visit http://casac.ca.

Sisters in Spirit: A Component of the Native Women's Association of Canada (NWAC) Sisters in Spirit is a research, education, and policy initiative driven and led by Aboriginal women. The primary goal was to conduct research and raise awareness of the staggeringly high rates of violence against Aboriginal women and girls in Canada.

The scope and breadth of this work has been published along with the stories of the women's lives in NWAC's "Voices of Our Sisters in Spirit: A Report to Families and Communities" (March 2009). SIS shares the Native Women's Association of Canada (NWAC) objective to educate and ensure effective access to justice for families of missing Aboriginal women through awareness of police training and resources to deal with reports of all missing Aboriginal women without discrimination. For more information on the NWAC's work and publications, see www.nwac.ca/programs/sisters-spirit.

Victims' Rights Legislation Canada's governments responded to the United Nations 1985 *Declaration of Basic Principles of Justice for Victims of Crime and Abuse of Power.* This Declaration provided a critical international document that acknowledged the need for governments of the world to take action. In recognition, various provincial governments agreed to uphold the basic principles of justice for victims of crime by enacting their own provincial legislation. Manitoba was the first province to lead, by enacting *Manitoba's Justice of Victims of Crime Act* (1986). British Columbia in 1996, and Ontario in 1995, would be the last provinces to enact legislation.

In 1988, all federal, provincial, and territorial ministers responsible for criminal justice endorsed the *Canadian Statement of Basic Principles of Justice for Victims of Crime* (1988). It was renewed again in 2003. The statement provides a comprehensive and valuable overview of how victims should be treated, particularly during the criminal justice process. However, because it is not law, it does not provide victims with additional rights beyond those outlined.

8.3 WORKING FOR POSITIVE CHANGE

All the evidence that we have indicates that it is reasonable to assume in practically every human being, and certainly in almost every newborn baby, that there is an active will toward health, an impulse towards growth, or towards the actualization.

—Abraham Maslow, psychologist (1908–1970)

Advocacy and a desire to help those who have been harmed are achieved in many ways. Some victim and victim advocates have fought to change laws, but other advocacy growth has also bloomed throughout Canada's history. For many victims and their families, destructive, unplanned, and unwanted life events have given rise to motivated, intelligent, and creative efforts to make communities more dignified and safe.

Some advocacy and social action efforts joined international campaigns (Take Back the Night), and others grew from Canadian tragedies (the Montreal Massacre). Some Canadian citizens were inspired to look back in time and speak for the voiceless victims (the British Home Children). This section, although not exhaustive, provides examples of the variety and manner in which Canadians have initiated creative ways to work for positive change. Relentless, courageous work takes place across Canada each day. The initiatives

Canada Post Commemorative Stamp: Year of the British Home Children

and accomplishments to be highlighted are the British Home Children, Take Back the Night, the White Ribbon Campaign, and the SlutWalk.

British Home Children

Canadians, through various means, have provided services to those who have been victimized. One example relates back in Canadian history to a time when child migration took place. In "From the Pen of . . ." Box 1.1 in Chapter 1, Marion Crawford provided an overview of an extraordinary effort to ensure the voiceless child victims from the past were acknowledged and honoured. Due to this hard work and advocacy, the Government of Canada designated 2010 as the Year of the British Home Child in Canada. It commemorates the Child Migration Scheme that brought 100 000 children from Britain to Canada from 1869 through to the late 1940s. Canada Post also honoured the Home Children with a commemorative stamp.

Take Back the Night

Over 35 years ago, women started to stand up and speak out against sexual violence under the banner of Take Back the Night. One of the first documented Take Back the Night events took place in 1976, at the International Tribunal on Crimes against Women in Brussels, Belgium, where 2000 women representing 40 countries gathered. The event rapidly took hold in cities across Europe and quickly crossed the ocean to North America. The universal impetus was to break and shatter the silence surrounding violence against women. Vancouver was the first Canadian city to organize a march, in 1978. Since 1981, the Canadian Association of Sexual Assault Centres has declared the third Friday in September as the date of the Take Back the Night march.

White Ribbon Campaign

The White Ribbon Campaign grew from the bold, brazen, and deadly act of violence directed at women known today as the Montreal massacre (see "Canadian Headline News" Box 4.3 in Chapter 4). This Canadian tragedy motivated a handful of men in 1991 to urge other men to speak out about violence against women. Soon, wearing a ribbon would symbolize a man's opposition to violence against women. With only six weeks of preparation, the original campaign was embraced by 100 000 men across Canada. They wore their white ribbons, which symbolized a personal pledge *to never commit, condone, or remain silent about violence against women and girls.*

Today, the White Ribbon Campaign (WRC) is the largest effort in the world of men working to end violence against women. Campaigns exist in more than 55 countries, and are led by both men and women; however, the focus is on educating men and boys. The campaign coincides with Canada's *National Day of Remembrance and Action on Violence Against Women,* which falls every year in December 6—the anniversary of the Montreal massacre.

The SlutWalk

In January 2011, a representative of the Toronto police force provided a shocking piece of advice to help women prevent being victims of sexual assault when he stated, "women should avoid dressing like sluts in order not to be victimized." This was not an off-the-cuff remark made by a police officer following a stressful shift. This officer was a representative of the Toronto police, the city's major protective service. This statement perpetuated the myth and stereotype of the "slut" and in doing so failed all women—particularly the sexually victimized.

As this textbook has revealed, sexual assault is the most profoundly underreported *crime* in Canada. As such, these blaming words were piercing. This viewpoint illuminated a serious, and erroneous, perception of thought, and gave rise to a grim reason to be even more cautious and calculating when considering reporting a sexual victimization to the police. These words also created a "call to action"—the SlutWalk. According to SlutWalk Toronto, the aim was to bring attention to the word "slut" by noting that it has historically carried with it a predominantly negative connotation (www.slutwalktoronto.com). The word "slut" was re-appropriated. As such, the overarching goals of the SlutWalk were to:

- call foul on the police force and demand change
- demand that Toronto Police Services take serious steps to regain the trust of women
- make a unified statement about sexual assault and victims' rights and to demand respect for all.

- ensure the message to the world is that for those who experience sexual assault it is not their fault—ever!

In achieving, if not surpassing, their goal, the SlutWalkers came together not only as women, but also as people from all gender expressions and orientations, all walks of life, levels of employment and education, all races, ages, abilities, and backgrounds, from all points of the city and elsewhere. The community united. In rapid speed, the SlutWalk has become a global movement. After an overwhelming affirming response, another Slut-Walk was set for the following year. Organizers are steadfast in their conviction to continue to raise awareness and fight for women's right to be safe and respected.

CHAPTER CONCLUSION

As far as service goes, it can take the form of a million things. To do service, you don't have to be a doctor working in the slums for free, or become a social worker. Your position in life and what you do doesn't matter as much as how you do what you do.

—*Elisabeth Kubler-Ross, psychologist (1926–2004)*

Social action and working for change can take many forms. It can be done through rowdy public demonstrations, from the abortion caravan of 1970 to the SlutWalk of 2011. It can also be realized through navigating the political system and involving various levels of governments. This was demonstrated as early as 1918 when Canadian women lobbied for the legal right to vote, and even more recently when 2010 was declared "The Year of the British Home Child." But it is even more profoundly witnessed when the advocacy comes from courageous victims who have chosen to speak out and tell their stories.

The goal of all these efforts is to raise awareness and to eradicate the stigma associated with intimate personal violence. This collective, continuous, and courageous work adds power and momentum that can force or inspire those in authority to be, or act, morally, ethically, and judiciously. Ultimately, the way in which we treat members of our society, particularly those who have been victimized, declares to each of us—and the rest of the world—how we define, respect, and honour human dignity. As American writer Walt Whitman once wrote: "*. . . and whoever walks a furlong without sympathy walks to his own funeral drest in his shroud.*" This is a thought worthy of reflection.

Multiple Choice Questions

1. Which of the following describes a sentence?
   a. decided by the judge based on precedent and relevant *Criminal Code* sections
   b. decided by the jury based on the relevant *Criminal Code* sections
   c. decide by the judge and the jury together based on precedent and relevant *Criminal Code* sections
   d. decided by the jury based on the relevant *Criminal Code* sections

2. Which of the following is NOT a rationale for punishment?

    a. deterrence
    b. rehabilitation
    c. revenge
    d. protection of society

3. Prosecutorial discretion includes all of the following EXCEPT one. Which one?

    a. to authorize or not authorize a charge against a suspect
    b. to determine the sentence
    c. to accept bargained pleas
    d. to schedule cases for trial

4. Which of the following victim advocacy initiatives did NOT originate in Canada?

    a. Year of the British Home Children
    b. Take Back the Night
    c. White Ribbon Campaign
    d. The SlutWalk

5. Which of the following best describes how the White Ribbon Campaign grew?

    a. the increased number of sexual assaults committed on college and university campuses.
    b. a high school initiative honouring the large number of children killed each year by a family member.
    c. a group of men responding to the Montreal massacre.
    d. the growing number of violent acts committed against Canada's senior population.

6. The Office of the Federal Ombudsman for Victims of Crime was implemented in which of the following years?

    a. 1987
    b. 1997
    c. 2007
    d. 2011

7. In which of the following years were victim impact statements first introduced in the criminal justice system?

    a. 1983
    b. 1988
    c. 1990
    d. 2001

8. Information on shelters in Canada is collected through which of the following surveys?

    a. The National Batterers Survey
    b. Transition Home Survey
    c. Official Guardian's Survey
    d. Federal Ombudsman Office Survey

9. In which of the following legal processes is the question of blame paramount?

    a. civil litigation
    b. coroner's inquest
    c. criminal preliminary hearing/trial
    d. criminal trial

10. Which of the following describes how the Canadian government honoured the British Home Children?

    a. It declared a week in their honour.
    b. It endorsed the creation of a commemorative coin.
    c. It endorsed Canada Post to create a commemorative stamp.
    d. Parliament supported the Prime Minister's public apology on behalf of Canada.

Discussion Questions

1. Briefly outline the key points in the criminal justice system when victims' services are introduced and briefly identify the service.

2. Of all the positive victim advocacy initiatives, which one do you most identify with and why?

Key Terms

acquitted: found not guilty of an offence.

adversarial system: the procedure used to determine truth in a criminal court system. According to this system, the burden is on the state to prove the charges against the accused beyond a reasonable doubt.

aggravating factors: in sentencing context, circumstances of the offence or the offender that supports a more serious punishment.

appeal: a review of a lower court decision or proceedings by a higher court.

Criminal Code of Canada: first enacted in 1892, the most important source of criminal law in Canada. It is divided into 28 parts and contains the full listing and explanation of criminal offences and procedure in Canada.

beyond a reasonable doubt: the standard used to determine the guilt or innocence of an accused.

deterrent: something that prevents a crime before it occurs by threatening an individual with criminal sanctions.

indictable offence: a serious crime that attracts more serious penalties and that is prosecuted using the more formal of two possible sets of criminal procedures.

mitigating circumstances: any circumstance accompanying the commission of a crime that may justify a lighter sentence.

precedent: a court decision that influences or binds future decision on the same issue or similar facts.

Reference Questions: Reference Questions are submitted to the Supreme Court of Canada by the federal or provincial government, which asks for an advisory opinion on a major legal issue.

summons: an order by the court requiring the appearance of the accused or a witness before it.

tort: a French word that means "a wrong."

victim impact statement (VIS): a written document that describes the losses, suffering, and trauma experienced by crime victims or by their survivors. Judges are expected to consider these effects in arriving at an appropriate sentence for the offender.

APPENDIX Answers to Multiple Choice Questions

Chapter 1

1. c
2. c
3. b
4. a
5. c
6. b
7. d
8. c
9. d
10. d

Chapter 2

1. c
2. a
3. a
4. d
5. a
6. a
7. d
8. c
9. a
10. b

Chapter 3

1. d
2. c
3. a
4. b
5. c
6. d
7. c
8. b
9. b
10. d

Chapter 4

1. c
2. a
3. b
4. c
5. a
6. c
7. a
8. d
9. c
10. a

Chapter 5

1. a
2. b
3. c
4. c
5. b
6. b
7. d
8. a
9. a
10. c

Chapter 6

1. b
2. c
3. c
4. c
5. a
6. a
7. a
8. a
9. b
10. c

Chapter 7

1. c
2. b
3. b
4. a
5. d
6. d
7. c
8. c
9. a
10. a

Chapter 8

1. a
2. c
3. b
4. b
5. c
6. c
7. b
8. b
9. d
10. c

Bibliography

Chapter 1

Aboriginal Healing Foundation. *Directory of Residential Schools in Canada.* To learn more about each residential school, go to http://www.afn.ca/residentialschools/history.html

Aboriginal Healing Foundation. *Map of Residential Schools in Canada.* Retrieved April 2011, from http://www.afn.ca/residentialschools/history.html

Aboriginal Justice Implementation Commission. (1999). The Justice System and Aboriginal People: Chapter 14: The "Sixties Scoop." Available online: http://www.ajic.mb.ca/volumel/chapter14.html#2

Absolon, K., Herbert, E., & MacDonald, K. (1996). *Aboriginal women and treaties project.* Victoria, B.C.: Ministry of Women's Equality.

Adam, B. D. (1987). *The rise of a gay and lesbian movement.* Boston: Twayne.

American Psychological Association. (1974). *Standards for educational and psychological tests.* Washington, DC: Author.

American Psychiatric Association. (1987). *Diagnostic and statistical manual of mental disorders* (3rd ed., revised). Washington, DC: Author.

American Psychiatric Association. (1994). *DSM-IV-TR sourcebook, Volume 1.* Washington, DC: Author.

American Psychological Association. (1975). Minutes of the Council of Representatives. *American Psychologist, 30,* 633.

American Psychological Association. (1987). *Policy statements on lesbian and gay issues.* Washington, DC: Author.

Assembly of First Nations. (1994). *Breaking the silence: An interpretive study of Residential School impact and healing as illustrated by the stories of First Nation individuals.* Ottawa: First Nations Health Secretariat.

Badgley, R. (1984). *Sexual offences against children: Report of the Committee on Sexual Offences against Children and Youths.* Volumes 1 and 2. Ottawa: Ministries of Justice, Attorney General, and Health and Welfare. Library of Parliament, Research Branch.

Barry, K. (1984). *Female sexual slavery.* New York: University Press.

Boswell, J. (1980). *Christianity, social tolerance, and homosexuality: Gay people in Western Europe from the beginning of the Christian era to the fourteenth century.* Chicago: University of Chicago Press.

Bourgeault, R. (1989). Race, class, and gender: Colonial domination of Indian women. In J. Forts et al. (Eds.), *Race, class and gender: Bonds and barriers* (2nd ed.). Toronto: Jargoned Press.

Brennan, S., & Taylor-Butts, A. (2008). Sexual assault in Canada, 2004 and 2007. *Canadian Centre for Justice Statistics Profile Series.* Statistics Canada. Catalogue no. 85F0033M-No. 19. Ottawa. Retrieved June 6, 2010, from http://www.statcan.gc.ca/pub/85f0033m/85f0033m2008019-eng.htm

British Home Children. http://www.britishhomechildren.org/

Bullough, V. L. (1979). *Homosexuality: A history.* New York: New American Library.

Cahill, B. L. (1992). *Butterbox babies: Baby sales, baby deaths—New revelations 15 years later.* Halifax: Fernwood Publishing.

Calixte, S., Johnson, J. L., & Motapanyane, J. M. (2010). Liberal, socialist, and radical feminism: An introduction to the three theories about women's oppression and social change. In N. Mandell (Ed.), *Feminist issues* (pp. 1–39). Toronto: Pearson Canada.

Carroll, J. L. (2010). *Sexuality now: Embracing diversity* (3rd ed.). Wadsworth Cengage Learning.

CBC. (2001). Bird Commission's 30th anniversary. Broadcast date March 8, 2001. Story number 9. Retrieved from http://archives.cbc.ca/politics/rights_freedoms/topics/86/

CBC. (2001). *Canada: A People's History—Women Get the Vote.* Retrieved from http://www.cbc.ca/history/EPISCONTENTSE1EP11CH4PA5LE.html

CBC. (1992). Broadcast date August 14, 1992. Story No. 1. Retrieved from http://archives.cbc.ca/society/youth/topics/1633/

CBC. (1992). *Reaction and response.* Broadcast date August 21, 1992. Story No. 2. Retrieved from http://archives.cbc.ca/society/youth/topics/1633/

CBC. (1993). Downie, P. *Man Alive. Life in an orphanage.* Broadcast date February 8, 1993. Story No. 3. Retrieved from http://archives.cbc.ca/society/youth/topics/1633/

CBC. (2004). *Medical experimentation.* Broadcast date June 18, 2004. Story No. 14. Retrieved from http://archives.cbc.ca/society/youth/topics/ 1633/

Committee on the Rights of the Child. (2003, October 27). Concluding observations of the Committee on the Rights of the Child: Canada. CRC/C15/Add.215.

Committee on the Rights of the Child. (2006). General comment No. 8: The right of the child to protection from corporal punishment and other cruel or degrading forms of punishment (articles 19, 28(2) and 37, inter alia). CRC/C/GC/8.

Convention on the Rights of the Child. (1989). UN Doc. A/RES/44/25(1989). Retrieved May 8, 2008, from http://www.unhchr.ch/html/menu3/b/k2crc.htm

Criminal Code of Canada R.S.C. 1985, c. C-46.

Danis, F. S. (2003, April 1). The criminalization of domestic violence: What social workers need to know. *Social Work.*

Davin Report. Nicholas Flood Davin, *Report on Industrial Schools for Indians and Half-Breeds* (March 14, 1879). Retrieved from http://www.canadiana.org/view/03651/0001

DeKeseredy, W., & Macleod, L. (1997). *Women abuse: A sociological story.* Toronto: Harcourt-Brace.

D'Emilio, J., & Freedman, E. B. (1988). *Intimate matters: A history of sexuality in America.* New York: Harper & Row.

Denham, D., & Gillespie, J. (1998). Setting the scene (section 1). In *Two steps forward . . . one step back: An overview of Canadian initiatives and resources to end woman abuse 1989–1997* (pp. 3–6). Ottawa: National Clearinghouse on Family Violence.

Department of Justice Canada. (n.p.) *Child abuse: A fact sheet.* Retrieved from www.justice.gc.ca

Dobash, R. E., & Dobash, R. (1979). Violence against wives: A case against the patriarchy. New York: Free Press. Cited in Danis, F. S. (2003, April 1). The criminalization of domestic violence: What social workers need to know. *Social Work.*

Dobash, R. E., & Dobash, R. (1992). *Women, violence and social change.* New York: Routledge.

Duberman, M. B., Vicinus, M., & Chauncey, G., Jr. (1989). *Hidden from history: Reclaiming the gay and lesbian past.* New York: New American Library.

Elkes, N. (2010). *Apology for the British Home Children Shipped to Canada.* West Midlands News. Retrieved from http://www.birminghampost.net/news/west-midlands-news/2010/02/18/apology-for-the-british-home-children-shipped-to-canada-65233-25864340/

Fontana, V. J. (1964). *The maltreated child: The maltreatment syndrome in children.* Springfield, Illinois: Charles C. Thomas.

Foucault, M. (1980). *The history of sexuality: Volume one—an introduction.* Trans. Robert Hurley. New York: Vintage Books.

Fournier, S., & Crey, E. (1997). *Stolen from our embrace: The abduction of First Nations children and the restoration of Aboriginal communities.* Vancouver: Douglas & McIntyre.

Gelles, R. (1980). Violence in the family: A review of research in the seventies. *Journal of Marriage and the Family, 42,* 873–885.

Giles, G. (2002). Why bother about homosexuals? Homophobia and sexual politics in Nazi Germany. Second printing. Assigned to the United States Holocaust Memorial Museum. Retrieved from **http://www.ushmm.org/research/center/publications/occasional/2002-04/paper.pdf**

Greenberg, D. F. (1988). *The construction of homosexuality.* Chicago: The University of Chicago Press.

Hartlen, R. (2001). *Butterbox survivors! Life after the ideal maternity home.* Halifax: Nimbus Books.

Hunt, R. J. (1999). *Historical dictionary of the gay liberation movement: Gay men and the quest for social justice.* Lanham, MD and London: Scarecrow Press.

Janovicek, N. (2007). *No place to go: Local histories of the battered women's shelter movement.* Vancouver: UBC Press.

Johnston, P. (1983). *Native children and the child welfare system.* Toronto: Canadian Council on Social Development in association with James Lorimer and Company.

Kempe, C. H., Silverman, F. N., Steel, B. F., Droegemueller, W., & Silver, H. K. (1962). The battered child syndrome. *Journal of the American Medical Association, 181,* 17–24.

Kohli, M. (2003). *The golden bridge: Young immigrants to Canada, 1833–1939.* Toronto: Natural Heritage Books.

Kuefler, M. (2006). *The Boswell thesis: Essays on Christianity, social tolerance, and homosexuality.* Chicago: University of Chicago.

Lemon, N. (1996). *Domestic violence law: A comprehensive overview of cases and sources.* San Francisco: Austin and Winfield.

Leslie, J. (1982). The Bagot Commission: Developing a corporate memory for the Indian Department. *Historical Papers—Canadian Historical Association.* Ottawa: Canadian Historical Association, pp. 31–52.

MacFarlane, B. A. (1992). Historical development of the offence of rape. In Wood and Peck, *100 Years of the Criminal Code in Canada: Essays Commemorating the Centenary of the Canadian Criminal Code.* Published by the Canadian Bar Association.

MacLeod, L. (1987). *Battered but not beaten: Preventing wife battering in Canada.* Ottawa: Canadian Advisory Council on the Status of Women.

MacLeod, L., & Cadieux, A. (1980). *Wife battering in Canada: The vicious circle.* Ottawa: Canadian Advisory Council on the Status of Women.

Mahony, M. R. (1994). Victimization or oppression? Women's lives, violence and agency. In M. A. Fineman & R. Mykitiuk (Eds.), *The public nature of private violence: The discovery of domestic abuse* (pp. 59–92). New York: Routledge.

Marcus, E. (1992). *Making history: The struggle for gay and lesbian equal rights, 1945–1990.* New York: HarperCollins.

Martin, D. (1976). *Battered wives.* New York: Pocket Books.

McHugh, P. R. (1999). How psychiatry lost its way. Commentary 108 (December 1999): 67–72. Retrieved April 10, 2011, from **http://www.scribd.com/doc/43529427/How-Psychiatry-Lost-Its-Way- McHugh-2011**

McKenna, T. (1970). CBC Digital Archives. The Toronto bathhouse raids. Retrieved from:**http://www.cbc.ca/archives/categories/politics/rights-freedoms/gay-and-lesbian-**

emergence-out-in-canada/the-toronto-bathhouse-raids.html

McNutty, F. (1980). *The burning bed.* New York: Houghton Mifflin Harcourt.

Milloy, J. (1999). *A national crime: The Canadian government and the Residential School system, 1879–1986.* Winnipeg: University of Manitoba Press.

National Archives of Canada. Record Group 10, vol. 6810, file 470-2-3, vol. 7, pp. 55 (L-3) and 63 (N-3). For a more accessible source, see John Leslie, *The historical development of the Indian Act* (2nd ed.). Ottawa: Department of Indian Affairs and Northern Development, Treaties and Historical Research Branch, 1978, p. 114.

Okun, L. (1986). *Woman abuse: Facts replacing myths.* New York: State University of New York.

Pizzey, E. (1974). *Scream quietly or the neighbours will hear.* Penguin: Harmondsworth.

Radbill, S. X. (1987). Children in a world of violence: A history of child abuse. In R. E. Helfer and R. S. Kempe (Eds.), *The battered child* (4th ed.) (pp. 3–22). Chicago: University of Chicago Press.

Regehr, C., & Glancy, G. (2010). *Mental health social work practice in Canada.* Oxford University Press.

Roberts, J. V., & Gebotys, R. (1992). Reforming rape laws: Effects of legislative change in Canada. *Law Human Behaviour, 16,* 555–573.

Roberts, J. &, Grossman, M. (1994). "Changing definitions of sexual assault: An analysis of police statistics." In J. Roberts and R. Mohr (eds.). *Confronting Sexual Assault: A Decade of Legal and Social Change* (pp. 57–83). Toronto: University of Toronto Press.

Roberts, J. V., Grossman, M. G., & Gebotys, R. J. (1996). Rape reform in Canada: Public knowledge and opinion. *Journal of Family Violence (11)*2, 133–148.

Royal Commission on the Status of Women. (1970). *Report of the Royal Commission on the Status of Women in Canada.* Ottawa: Information Canada.

Sanders, W. B. (1945). *Some early beginnings of the children's court movement in England.* New York: National Council on Crime and Delinquency.

Schechter, S. (1982). *Women and male violence.* Boston: South End Press.

Scott, D. C. National Archives of Canada, Record Group 10, Vol. 6810, file 470-2-3, vol. 7, pp. 55 (L-3) and 63 (N-3).

Siker, J. S. (1994). *Homosexuality in the Church: Both sides of the debate.* Louisville, KY: Westminster John Know Press.

Steakley, J. (1974, Jan./Feb.). The making of the image of the modern homosexual: Homosexuals and the Third Reich. *The Body Politic, 11.*

Stevenson, W. (1999). Colonialism and First Nations women in Canada. In E. Dua and A. Robertson (Eds.), *Scratching the surface: Canadian anti-racist feminist thought* (pp. 49–80). Toronto: Women's Press.

Tang, K. (1998). Rape law reform in Canada: The success and limits of legislation. *International Journal of Offender Therapy and Comparative Criminology, 42*(3), 258–270.

Thomson, A. (2008). *Winning choice on abortion: How British Columbia and Canadian Feminists Won the Battles of the 1970s and 1980s.* Trafford Publishing.

Turekheimer, D. (2004, June 22). Recognizing and remedying the harm of battering: A call to criminalize domestic violence. *Journal of Criminal Law and Criminology.*

Turner, J., & Turner, J. (2010). *Canadian social welfare.* (6th ed.). Toronto: Pearson Canada.

Tutty, L. (2006). *Effective practice in shelter women: Leaving violence in intimate relationships.* Phase II report prepared for the YMCA of Canada. Retrieved from http://ywcacanada.ca/data/publications/ 00000013.pdf

United Nations. (1948). *Universal Declaration of Human Rights*. Retrieved from **www.un.org/Overview/rights.html**

United Nations. (1989). *The United Nations Convention on the Rights of the Child.* Retrieved from **http://www2.ohchr.org/english/law/crc.htm**

Walker, G. (1990). *Family violence and the women's movement*: *The conceptual politics of struggle.* Toronto: University of Toronto Press.

Walker, L. (1979). *The battered woman.* New York: HarperCollins.

Walker, L. (1984). *The battered woman syndrome.* New York: Springer Publishing Company.

World Health Organization. (2010). *Gender and reproductive rights.* Retrieved July 5, 2010, from **http://who.int/reproductive-ealth/gender/index.html**

Chapter 2

Abel, G. G., Mittelman, M. S., & Becker, J. V. (1987). Sex offenders: Results of assessment and recommendations for treatment. In M. H Ben-Aron, S. J. Hucker, C. D. Webster (Eds.), *Clinical criminology: The assessment and treatment of criminal behavior* (pp. 207–220). Toronto: M&M Graphics.

Akers, R. L. (1973). *Deviant behavior: A social learning approach.* Belmont, CA: Wadsworth Publishing Company Inc.

Allen, L., & Santrock, J. (1993). *The contexts of behavior psychology.* Madison, WI: Brown & Benchmark Press.

American Psychiatric Association. (1994). *Diagnostic and statistical manual of mental disorders* (4th ed.). Washington, DC: Author.

American Psychiatric Association. (2000). *Diagnostic and statistical manual of mental disorders* (4th ed., revision). Washington, DC: Author.

American Psychological Association. (1953). *Ethical standards of psychologists.* Washington, DC: Author.

Babcock, J. C., Miller, S. A., & Siard, C. (2003). Toward a typology of abusive women: Differences between partner-only and generally violent women in the use of violence. *Psychology of Women Quarterly, 27,* 153–161.

Bandura, A. (1969). *Principles of behavior modification.* New York: Holt, Rinehart & Winston.

Bandura, A. (1973). *Aggression: A social learning analysis.* Englewood Cliffs, NJ: Prentice-Hall.

Bandura, A. (1975). *Social learning and personality development*: New Jersey: Holt, Rinehart & Winston.

Bandura, A. (1977). *Social learning theory.* New York: General Learning Press.

Bandura, A. (1997). *Self-efficacy: The exercise of control.* New York: W.H. Freeman.

Bandura, A., & Ribes-Inesta, E. (1976). *Analysis of delinquency and aggression.* New Jersey: Lawrence Erlbaum Associates.

Bandura, A., & Walters, R. H. (1959). *Adolescent aggression.* New York: Ronald Press.

Barlow, D. H., Durand, V. M., & Stewart, S. H. (2009). *Abnormal psychology: An integrative approach* (2nd Canadian ed.). Toronto: Nelson Education.

Beck, A. T., & Weishaar, M. (1995). Cognitive therapy. In R. J. Corsini & D. Wedding (Eds.), *Current psychotherapies*. Ithaca: F. E. Peacock Publishers.

Bishop, A. (2002). *Becoming an ally: Breaking the cycle of oppression* (2nd ed.). Crowns Nest, NSW, Australia: Allen and Unwin.

Boyd, D., Johnson, P., & Bee, H. (2009). *Lifespan development* (4th Canadian ed.). Toronto: Pearson Canada.

Broidy, L., Cauffman, E., Espelage, D. L., Mazerolle, P., & Piquero, A. (2003). Sex differences in empathy and its relation to juvenile offending. *Violence and Victims, 18,* 503–516.

Bronfenbrenner, U. (1979). Toward an experimental ecology of human development. *American Psychologist, 32,* 513–531.

Burke, R. H. (2005). *An introduction to criminological theory.* Portland, OR: Willan Publishing.

Butcher, J. M., Mineka, S., Hooley, J. H., Taylor, S., & Antony, M. M. (2009). *Abnormal psychology* (Canadian ed.). Toronto: Pearson Canada.

Chapple, C. L. (2003). Examining intergenerational violence: Violent role modeling or weak parental controls. *Violence and Victims, 18,* 143–162.

Choice, P., Dankoski, M. E., Keiley, M. K., Lloyd, S. A., Seery, B. L., & Thomas V. (2006). Affect regulation and the cycle of violence against women: New directions for understanding the process. *Journal of Family Violence, 21,* 327–339.

Ciccarelli, S., Harrigan, T., & Fritzley, H., V. (2009). *Psychology with MyPsychLab* (Canadian ed.). Toronto: Pearson Education Canada.

City News. (2007, December 14). Brother of slain murdered 16-year-old Aqsa Paraves freed on bail. Retrieved July 23, 2011, from **http://www.citytv.com/toronto/citynews/news/local/article/19064--brother-of-slain-16-year-old-aqsa-parvez-freed-on-bail**

City News. (2010, June 15). Father & brother of murdered teen Aqsa Paraves plead guilty. Retrieved July 23, 2011, from **http://www.citytv.com/toronto/citynews/news/local/article/79149--father-brother-of-murdered-teen-aqsa-parvez-plead-guilty**

Cohen, T. (2010). Honour killings on the rise in Canada: Expert. *Vancouver Sun.* Retrieved July 23, 2011, from **http://www.vancouversun.com/life/Honour+killings+rise+Canada+Expert/3165638/story.html**

Department of Justice. (2002, November). Review of the mental disorder provisions of the *Criminal Code.* Retrieved August 2, 2011, from **http://www.justice.gc.ca/eng/dept-min/pub/md-tm/defin. html**

Dutton, D. G. (1995). Male abusiveness in intimate relationships. *Clinical Psychology Review, 15,* 567–581.

Dutton, D. G. (1998). *The abusive personality: Violence and control in intimate relationships.* New York: Guilford Press.

Dutton, D. G. (2007). *The abusive personality: Violence and control in intimate relationship* (2nd ed.). New York: Guilford Press.

Dutton, D. G., & Starzomski, A. J. (1993). Borderline personality in perpetrators of psychological and physical abuse. *Violence & Victims, 8,* 327–337.

Eller, J. D. (2005). *Violence and culture: A cross-culture and interdisciplinary approach.* Australia: Thomson Wadsworth.

Elliott, D., Mihalic, S. W. (1997). A social learning theory model of marital violence. *Journal of Family Violence 12(1),* 21–47.

Emery, R., & Laumann-Billings, L. (1998). An overview of the nature, causes and consequences of abuse family relationships: Toward differentiating maltreatment and violence. *American Psychologist, 53,* 121–135.

Evans, R. I. (1989). *Albert Bandura: The man and his ideas—A dialogue.* New York: Praeger.

Fagan, A. A. (2005). The relationship between adolescent physical abuse and criminal offending: Support for an enduring and generalized cycle of violence. *Journal of Family Violence, 20(5),* 279–290.

Finkelhor, D. (1984). *Child sexual abuse: New theory and research.* New York: The Free Press.

Finkelhor, D. (1986). *A sourcebook on child sexual abuse.* Beverly Hills: Sage.

Finkelhor, D. (2008). *Childhood victimizations: Violence, crime and abuse in the lives of young people.* New York: Oxford Press.

Finney Hayward, R. (2000). *Breaking the earthenware jar: Lessons from South Asia to end violence against women and girls.* UNICEF. Regional Office for South Asia.

Frankl, V. (1963). *Man's search for meaning: An introduction to logotherapy.* Boston: Beacon Press.

Fry, M. (2001). Oppression. In P. S. Rothenberg (Ed.), *Race, class, and gender in the United States: An integrated study* (5th ed.) (pp. 239–243). New York: Worth Publishers.

Gill, A. (2006, January). Patriarchal violence in the name of "honour." *International Journal of Criminal Justice Sciences, 1*(1).

Groth, N. (1979). *Men who rape: The psychology of the offender.* New York: Plenum Press.

Groth, N. (1985). The incest offender. In S. Sgroi, *Handbook of clinical intervention in child sexual abuse.* Massachusetts: Lexington Books.

Groth, N. (1990). Rape: Myths and realities. In *Men Who Rape* (p. 5). New York: Plenum Press.

Hare, R. D. (1993). *Without conscience: The disturbing world of the psychopaths among us.* New York: Pocket Books.

Heise, L. L. (1998, June). Violence against women: An integrated, ecological framework. *Violence Against Women, 4*(3), 262–290.

Hofeller, K. (1982). *Social psychological and situational factors in wife abuse.* Palo Alto, CA: R&E Research Associates.

Hoffman, M. L. (1981). Is altruism part of human nature? *Journal of Personality and Social Psychology, 40,* 121–137.

Holtzworth-Munroe, A., & Stuart, G. L. (1994). Typologies of male batterers: Three subtypes and the differences among them. *Psychological Bulletin, 116,* 476–497.

Kempe, H., & Steele, B. F. (1962). The battered child syndrome. *Journal of the American Medical Association, 181,* 17–24.

Kindschi Gosselin, D. (2010). *Heavy hands: An introduction to the crimes of family violence* (4th ed.). New York: Prentice Hall.

Koestner, R., Franz, C., & Weinberger, J. (1990). The family origins of empathic concern: A 26-year longitudinal study. *Journal of Personality and Social psychology, 58,* 709–717.

Mahoney, J., & Nolen, S. (2011, June 22). Vicious attack in Bangladesh leaves UBC student blind; husband arrested. *Globe and Mail.* Retrieved July 7, 2011, from **http://www.theglobeandmail. com/news/national/british-columbia/ vicious-attack-in-bangladesh-leaves-ubc-student-blind-husband-arrested/article 2070667/**

MacLeod, L. (1989). *Battered but not beaten: Preventing wife battering in Canada.* Ottawa: Canadian Advisory Council on the Status of Women, 1987.

McMahon, M. (1999). Battered women and bad science: The limited validity and utility of battered woman syndrome. *Psychiatry, Psychology and Law, 6*(1), 23–49.

Mekerle, C., Wall, A. M., Leung, E., & Trocmé, N. (2007). Cumulative stress and substantiated maltreatment: The importance of caregiver vulnerability and adult partner violence. *Child Abuse and Neglect, 31,* 427–443.

Miller, P. A., & Eisenberg, N. (1988). The relation of empathy to aggressive and externalizing/antisocial behavior. *Psychological Bulletin, 103,* 324–344.

Milner, J. S., & Chilamkurti, C. (1991). Physical child abuse perpetrator characteristics. *Journal of Interpersonal Violence, 6* (3), 345–366.

Mullaly, B. (2007). *The new structural social work: Ideology, theory, practice* (3rd ed.). Oxford University Press.

Mullaly, B. (2010). *Challenging oppression and confronting privilege* (2nd ed.). Oxford University Press.

National Post. (2007, December 12). The double life of Aqsa Parvez. Retrieved July 23, 2011 from **http:// network.nationalpost.com/np/blogs/ toronto/archive/2007/12/12/the-double-life-of-aqsa-parvez.aspx**

Nicholas, K. B., & Rasmussen, E. H. (2006). Childhood abusive and supportive experiences, inter-parental violence, and parental alcohol use: Prediction of young adult depressive symptoms and aggression. *Journal of Family Violence, 21*(1), 43–61.

Parnell, T., &, Day, D. (1997). *Munchausen by proxy syndrome: Misunderstood child abuse.* Thousand Oaks, CA: Sage.

Pence, E., & Paymar, M. (1993). *Domestic violence information manual: The Duluth domestic abuse intervention project.* Springer Publishing Company, Inc.

Porter, S., Fairweather, D., Drugge, J., Herve, H., Birt, A., & Boer, D. P. (2000). Profiles of psychopath in incarcerated sexual offenders. *Criminal Justice & Behavior, 27,* 216–233.

Pizzey, E. (1977). *Scream quietly or the neighbors will hear.* Short Hills, NJ: R. Enslow Publishers.

Preston-Shoot, M. (1995). Assessing anti-oppressive practice. *Social Work Education, 14*(2), 11–29.

Roberts, J. &, Grossman, M. (1994). Changing definitions of sexual assault: An analysis of police statistics. In J. Roberts and R. Mohr (Eds.), *Confronting sexual assault: A decade of legal and social change* (pp. 57–83). Toronto: University of Toronto Press.

Roesler, A., & Witztum, E. (2000). Pharmacotherapy of paraphilias in the next millennium. *Behavior Science and the Law, 18*(1), 43–56.

Rosenberg, L., & Duffy, A. (2010). Violence against women. In N. Mandell (Ed.), *Feminist issues: Race, class and sexuality* (5th ed.). Toronto: Pearson Canada.

Rotter, J. (1990). Internal versus external control of reinforcement: A case history of a variable. *American Psychologist, 45*(4), 489–493.

Ruston, J. P., Fulker, D. W., Neale, M. C., Nias, D. K. B., & Eysenck, H. J. (1986). Altruism and aggression: The heritability of individual differences. *Journal of Personality and Social Psychology, 50,* 1192–1198.

Ryan, D. (2011). B.C. woman Rumana Monzur shocked at news of husband's death. *Vancouver Sun.* Retrieved December 28, 2011, from **http://www.vancouversun.com/woman+Rumana+Monzur+shocked+news+husband+death/5819297/story.html#ixzz1i2eFsdg4**

Schmalleger, F., & Volk, R. (2008). *Canadian criminology today: Theories and applications.* Toronto: Pearson Prentice Hall.

Schreier, H. A., & Libow, J. A. (1993). *Hurting for love: Munchausen by proxy syndrome.* New York: The Guilford Press.

Seigel, L. (1992). *Criminology.* West Publishing Company: St. Paul, Minnesota.

Sgroi, S. M. (1985). *Handbook of clinical intervention in child sexual abuse.* Massachusetts: Lexington Books.

Singh, G. (1996). Promoting anti-racist and black perspectives in social work education. *Social Work Education, 15*(2), 35–36.

Skinner, B. F. (1953). *Science and human behavior.* New York: Macmillan.

Skinner, B. F. (1957). *Verbal behavior.* New York: Prentice Hall.

Soler, H., Vinayak, P., & Quadagno, D. (2000). Biosocial aspects of domestic violence. *Psychoneuroendocrinolgy, 25,* 721–739.

Straus, M. (1993). Consequences of child abuse and neglect. Panel on research on child abuse and neglect, National Research Council. In *Understanding Child Abuse and Neglect.* The National Academies Press.

Switzer, J. (2011). Hypoglycemia defence gets officer who threatened to taser suspects probation. *National Post.* Retrieved August 2, 2011, from **http://www.financialpost.com/related/topics/Hypoglycemia+defence+gets+officer+threatened+Taser+suspects+probation/5014335/story.html**

Tammy, Z., Akay, G, Kilic, G., Peykerli, G., Devecioglu, E., Ones, U., &, Guler, N. (2007). Corrosive poisoning mimicking cicatricial pemphigoid: Munchausen by proxy. *Child: Care, Health and Development, 33,* 496–499.

The Daily Star. (2011, June 21). Rumana returns, sees nothing. Retrieved July 7, 2011 from http://www.thedailystar.net/newDesign/news-details.php?nid=190903

Todd, J., & Bohart, A. C. (1994). *Foundations of clinical and counseling psychology* (2nd ed.). New York: HarperCollins.

Tolman, R. M., & Bennett, L. W. (1990), A review of quantitative research on men who batter. *Journal of Interpersonal Violence, 5,* 87–118.

Toope, S. (2011a, June 15). Message to the community from the UBC president. Retrieved July 7, 2011, from http://president.ubc.ca/2011/06/15/message-to-the-community-from-the-ubc-president/

Toope, S. (2011b, June 21). Update: UBC responds to Rumana Monzur attack. Retrieved July 7, 2011, from http://president.ubc.ca/2011/06/21/update-ubc-responds-to-rumana-monzur-attack

Toronto Life. (2008). Girl interrupted. Retrieved July 23, 2011, from http://www.torontolife.com/features/girl-interrupted/

Van Dam, C. (2006). *The socially skilled child molester: Differentiating the guilty from the falsely accused.* New York: The Haworth Press.

Venneman, B., Bajanowski, Karger, B., Pfeiffer, H. Kohler, H., & Brinkmann, B. (2005). Suffocation and poisoning: The hard hitting side of Munchausen syndrome by proxy. *International Journal of Legal Medicine.*

Walker, L. E. (1977/78). Battered women and learned helplessness. *Victimology: An International Journal, 2*(3/4), 525–534.

Walker, L. E. (1984). *The battered woman syndrome.* New York: Springer Publishing Company.

Walker, L. E. (1991). Post traumatic stress disorder in women: Diagnosis and treatment of battered woman syndrome. *Psychotherapy, 28*(1), 21–29.

Walker, L. E. (1992). Battered women syndrome and self-defense: Symposium on women and the law. *Notre Dame Journal of Law, Ethics and Public Policy, 6*(2), 321–334.

Walker, L. E. (1995). Understanding battered woman syndrome. *Trial, 31*(2), 30–37.

Wekerle, C., & Wolfe, D. A. (1993). Prevention of child physical abuse and neglect: Promising new directions. *Clinical Psychology Review, 13,* 501–540.

Widiger, T. A. & Corbitt, E. M. (1995). Antisocial personality disorder. In W. J. Livesley (Ed.), *The DSM-IV personality disorders* (pp. 103–126). New York: Guilford.

Young, I. M. (1990). *Justice and the politics of difference.* Princeton, NJ: Princeton University Press.

Chapter 3

American Psychiatric Association. Retrieved June 9, 2011, from http://www.psych.org/MainMenu/Research/DSMIV.aspx

Berliner, L. (1991). The effects of sexual abuse on children. *Violence Update, 1*(10), 1, 8, 10–11.

Blanchard, C. (1999, March 2). *National Post.* Common ground between tragedies: The response of the Catholic CAS to two high-risk families. Retrieved from http://www.fact.on.ca/newpaper/np99030g.htm

Briere, J. (1992). *Child abuse trauma.* Newbury Park, CA: Sage Publications.

Briere, J., & Runtz, M. (1993). Childhood sexual abuse: Long-term sequelae and implications for psychological assessment. *Journal of Interpersonal Violence, 8* (3), 313–330.

CBC. (2006). The good father: Father Sylvestre, convicted pedophile. Retrieved from http://www.cbc.ca/fifth/goodfather/

CBC News. (2001a, March 15). Heikamp denies Jordan was skin and bones.

Retrieved from http://www.cbc.ca/news/story/2001/03/15/heikamp_testimony010315.html

CBC News. (2001b, March 21). Heikamp's case worker testifies at inquiry. Retrieved from http://www.cbc.ca/news/story/2001/03/21/heikamp_martin010321.html

CBC News. (2001c, April 11). Coroner's jury rules Heikamp's death a homicide. Retrieved from http://www.cbc.ca/news/story/2001/04/11/heikamp_homocide.html

Canadian Child Welfare Research Portal. http://www.cecw-cepb.ca/

Canadian Children's Rights Council. Child rights—virtual library, resource centre, archives and advocacy. http://www.canadiancrc.com/Age_of_consent_sex_in_Canada.aspx

Canadian Medical Association Journal. (2003, January 21). 168(2).

Centers for Disease Control and Prevention. (2006). *Adverse childhood experiences study.* Atlanta: National Centers for Injury Prevention and Control, Centers for Disease Control and Prevention. Retrieved from http://www.cdc.gov/NCCDPHP/ACE

Centres of Excellence for Children's Well-Being. Retrieved from http://www.cecw-cepb.ca/child-abuse-neglect

Child and Family Service Act of Ontario. R.S.O. (1990). Retrieved from http://www.e-laws.gov.on.ca/html/statutes/english/elaws_statutes_90c11_e.htm

Charter of Rights and Freedoms. (1982). Retrieved from http://laws.justice.gc.ca/eng/charter/

Conte, J. R. (1994). Child sexual abuse: Awareness and backlash. *The Future of Children, 4*(2), 224–232.

Convention on the Rights of the Child. (1989). UN Doc. A/RES/44/25 (1989). Retrieved May 8, 2008, from http://www.unhchr.ch/html/menu3/b/k2crc.htm

Criminal Code of Canada. R.S.C. 1985, c. C-46.

Cross, T., Finkelhor, D., & Ormrod, R. K. (2005). Police involvement in child protective services investigations. *Child Maltreatment, 10*(3), 224–244.

Dauvergne, M., & Johnson, H. (2001). Children witnessing family violence. *Juristat, 21*(6). Canadian Centre for Justice Statistics, Statistics Canada.

De Bellis, M., & Thomas, L. (2003). Biologic findings of post-traumatic stress disorder and child maltreatment. *Current Psychiatry Reports, 5,* 108–117.

Department of Justice Canada. *Sexual abuse and exploitation of children and youth: A fact sheet from the Department of Justice Canada.* Retrieved from http://www.justice.gc.ca/eng/pi/fv-vf/facts-info/sex_abu.html

Dubowitz, H. (1994). Neglecting the neglect of neglect. *Journal of Interpersonal Violence, 9*(40), 556–560.

Dubowitz, H., Papas, M. A., Black, M. M., & Starr, R. H., Jr. (2002). Child neglect: Outcomes in high-risk urban preschoolers. *Pediatrics, 109,* 1100–1107.

Durrant, J. (2006, Winter). Distinguishing physical punishment from physical abuse: Implications for professionals. *Developing Practice: The Child, Youth and Family Work Journal, 16,* 43–51.

Durrant, J., & Ensom, R. (2004). Joint statement on physical punishment of children and youth. Coalition on Physical Punishment of Children and Youth. Ottawa: The Canadian Child Welfare Research Portal. Retrieved from http://www.cecw-cepb.ca/publications/1008

Durrant, J. E., Trocmé, N., Fallon, B., Milne, C., & Black, T. (2009). Protection of children from physical maltreatment in Canada: An evaluation of the Supreme Court's definition of reasonable force. *Journal of Aggression, Maltreatment & Trauma, 18*(1), 64-87.

Egeland, B., Yates, T., Appleyard, K., & van Dulmen, M. (2002). The long-term consequences of maltreatment in the early years:

A developmental pathway model to anti-social behavior. *Children's Services, 5,* 249–260.

Erickson, M. F., Egeland, B., & Pianta, R. (1989). The effects of maltreatment on the development of young children. In D. Cicchetti & V. Carlson (Eds.), *Child maltreatment: Theory and research on the causes and consequences of child abuse and neglect* (pp. 647–684). New York: Cambridge University Press.

Eth, S., & Pynoos, R. S. (1994). Children who witness the homicide of a parent. *Psychiatry, 57*(4), 287–306.

Ethier, L. S., Couture, G., & Lacharite, C. (2004). Risk factors associated with the chronicity of high potential for child abuse and neglect. *Journal of Family Violence, 19,* 13–24.

Falconer, N. E., & Swift, K. (1983). *Preparing for practice: The fundamentals of child protection. Toronto:* Toronto Children's Aid Society.

Faller, K. (1981). *Social work with abused and neglected children*: A manual of interdisciplinary practice. New York: The Free Press.

Faller, K. (1988). *Child sexual abuse. An interdisciplinary manual for diagnoses, case management and treatment.* New York: Columbia University Press.

Fallon, B., Trocmé, N., MacLaurin, B., Knoke, D., Black, T., Daciuk, J., & Felstiner, C. (2005). *Ontario incidence study of reported child abuse and neglect, OIS-2003: Major FindingsReport.* Toronto: Centre of Excellence for Child Welfare.

Fantuzzo, J. W., & Lindquite, C. U. (1989). The effects of observing conjugal violence on children: A review and analysis of research methodology. *Journal of Family Violence, 4,* 77–90.

Felitti, V. J., Anda, R. F., Nordenberg, D., Williamson, D. F., Spitz, A. M., Edwards V., Koss M. P., & Marks, J. S. (1998). Relationship of childhood abuse and household dysfunction to many of the leading causes of death in adults: The adverse childhood experiences (ACE) study. *American Journal of Preventive Medicine, 14,* 245–258.

Finkelhor, D. (1979). Sexual victimization of children in a normal population. In D. Finkelhor, *Sexually victimized children.* New York: Free Press.

Finkelhor, D. (1986). *A sourcebook on child sexual abuse.* Newbury Park, CA: Sage Publication.

Finkelhor, D. (1994). Current information on the scope and nature of child sexual abuse. *The Future of Children, 4*(2), 31–53.

Finkelhor, D. (2008). *Child victimization: Violence, crime, and abuse in the lives of young people.* New York: Oxford University Press.

Finkelhor, D., & Brown, A. (1986). Initial and long-term effects: A review of the research. In D. Finkelhor et al. (Eds.), *A sourcebook on child sexual abuse.* Newbury Park, CA: Sage Publication.

Finkelhor, D., Ormrod, R. K., Turner, H. A., & Hamby, S. L. (2005). The victimization of children and youth: A comprehensive, national survey. *Child Maltreatment, 10*(1), 5–25.

Flaherty, E. G., et al. (2006). Effect of early childhood adversity on health. *Archives of Pediatrics and Adolescent Medicine, 160,* 1232–1238.

Fleury, T., & McLellan Day, K. (2009). *Playing with fire.* HarperCollins Canada.

Flynn, R., & Bouchard, D. (2005). Randomized and quasi-experimental evaluations of program impact in child welfare in Canada: A review. *Canadian Journal of Program Evaluation, 20*(3), 65–100.

Fontana, V. J. (1964). *The maltreated child: The maltreatment syndrome in children.* Soringfield, IL: Charles C. Thomas.

Fortin, A., &, Chamberland, C. (1995). Preventing the psychological maltreatment of children. *Journal of Interpersonal Violence, 10*(3), 275–295.

Frankl, V. (1963). *Man's search for meaning.* Washington Square Press.

Gannon, M. (2006). Family violence against older adults. In L. Ogrodnik (Ed.), *Family violence in Canada: A statistical profile, 2006.* Ottawa: Statistics Canada Catalogue no. 85-224-X.

Garrett, A., & Libbey, H. (1997). Common outcomes of abuse and neglect. *Theory and Research on the Outcomes and Consequences of Child Abuse and Neglect, 2.* Washington, DC: National Institute of Justice.

Groth, N., & Birnbaum, H. J. (1979). *Men who rape: The psychology of the offender.* New York: Plenum Press.

Harris, M. (1990). *Unholy orders: Tragedy at Mount Cashel.* Toronto: Penguin Books.

Hepworth, H. P. (1975). Services for abused and battered children. *Social Services in Canada, 3,* CCSD.

Indian and Northern Affairs Canada. Retrieved from **http://www.aadnc-aandc.gc.ca/eng/1100100010002**

Jaffe, P. G., Wolfe, D. A., & Crooks, C. V. (2003). Legal and policy responses to children exposed to domestic violence: The need to evaluate intended and unintended consequences. *Clinical Child and Family Psychology Review, 6*(3), 205–231.

Jaffe, P. G., Wolfe, D. A., & Wilson, S. K. (1990). *Children of battered women.* New York: Sage.

Johnson, R., Rew, L., & Sternglanz, R. W. (2006). The relationship between childhood sexual abuse and sexual health practices of homeless adolescents. *Adolescence, 41*(162), 221–234.

Kanani, K., Regehr, C., & Bernstein, M. (2002). Liability considerations in child welfare from Canada. *Child Abuse & Neglect, 26*(10), pp. 1029–1043.

Kaplan, S. J., Pelcovitz, D., & Labruna, V. (1999). Child and adolescent abuse and neglect research: A review of the past 10 years. Part 1: Physical and emotional abuse and neglect. *Journal of American Academy of Child and Adolescent Psychiatry, 38*(10), 1214–1221.

Kaufman, J., Kantor, G., & Little, L. (2003). Defining the boundaries of child neglect: When does domestic violence equate with parental failure to protect? *Journal of Interpersonal Violence, 18*(4), 338–355.

Kelley, B. T., Thornberry, T. P., & Smith, C. A. (1997). *In the wake of childhood maltreatment.* Washington, DC: National Institute of Justice. Retrieved April 27, 2006, from **www.ncjrs.gov/pdffiles1/165257.pdf**

Kelly, L. (1996). When woman protection is the best kind of child protection: Children, domestic violence and child abuse. *Administration, 44*(2), 118–135.

Kempe, C. H., Silverman, F. N., Steel, B. F., Droegemueller, W., & Silver, H. K. (1962). The battered child syndrome. *Journal of the American Medical Association, 181,* 17–24.

Kennedy, S. (2006). With James Grainger. *Why I didn't say anything.* Insomniac Press.

King, W. J., MacKay, M., Sirnick, A., & The Canadian Shaken Baby Study Group. (2003). Shaken baby syndrome in Canada: Clinical characteristics and outcomes of hospital cases. *Canadian Medical Association Journal, 168,* 155–159.

Knoke, D., & Trocmé, N. (2004). *Risk assessment in child welfare.* CECW Information Sheet #18E. Faculty of Social Work, University of Toronto.

Kolbo, J. R., Blakely, E. H., & Engelman, D. (1996). Children who witness domestic violence: A review of empirical literature. *Journal of Interpersonal violence, 11*(2), 281–293.

Krane, J., & Davies, L. (2000). Mothering and child protection practice: Rethinking risk assessment. *Child and Family Social Work, 5*(1), 35–45.

Krane, J., & Davies, L. (2007). Mothering under difficult circumstances: Challenges to working with battered women. *AFFILIA Journal of Women and Social Work, 22*(1), 23–38.

Kurtz, P. D., James M. Gaudin, J. M., Wodarski, J. S., & Howing, P. T. (1993, September-October). Maltreatment and the school-aged child: School performance consequences. *Child Abuse & Neglect, 17*(5), pp. 581–589.

LaPrairie, C. (1995). *Seen but not heard: Native people in the inner city.* Ottawa: Minister of Public Works and Government Services.

Monteleone, J. A., & Brodeur, A. F. (1994). Identifying, interpreting, and reporting injuries. In J. A. Monteleone & A. E. Brodeur (Eds.), *Clinical maltreatment: A clinical guide and reference.* St. Louis, MO: G. W. Medical Publishing.

Mount Cashel Orphanage. Retrieved from **http://archives.cbc.ca/on_this_day/11/27/**

Nemr, R. (2009). Fact sheet—Police-reported family violence against children and youth. Catalogue no. 85-224-X. Published by authority of the Minister responsible for Statistics Canada www.statcan.gc.ca

O'Brien, D. (1991). *Suffer little children: An autobiography of a foster child.* Breakwater Book, St. John's FD.

Paris, J. (1998). Does childhood trauma cause personality disorders in adults? *Canadian Journal of Psychiatry, 43*, 148–153.

Perreault, S., & Brennan, S. (2010). Criminal victimization in Canada, 2009. *Juristat, 30* (2). Ottawa: Statistics Canada Catalogue no. 85-002-X. **http://www.statcan.gc.ca/pub/85-002-x/2010002/article/11340-eng.pdf**

Portwood, S. G. (1999). Coming to terms with a consensual definition of child maltreatment. *Child Maltreatment, 4*(1), 56–68.

Russell, D. (1986). *The secret trauma.* New York: Basic Books Inc.

R. v. Heikamp and Martin, 1999.

Schleslinger, B. (1980). *Sexual abuse of children: An annotated bibliography 1937–1980.* Toronto: University of Toronto.

Schmalleger, F., MacAlister, D., & McKenna, P. (2004). *Canadian criminal justice today.* Toronto: Pearson Education Canada.

Sgroi, S. M. (1975, May-June). Sexual molestation of children: The last frontier in child abuse. *Children Today,* pp. 18–21.

Sgroi, S. M. (1982). *Handbook of clinical intervention in child sexual abuse.* Toronto: Lexington Books.

Silverman, A. B., Reinherz, H. Z., & Giaconia, R. M. (1996). The long-term sequelae of child and adolescent abuse: A longitudinal community study. *Child Abuse and Neglect, 20*(8), 709–723.

Springer, K. W., Sheridan, J., Kuo, D., & Carnes, M. (2007). Long-term physical and mental health consequences of childhood physical abuse: Results from a large population-based sample of men and women. *Child Abuse & Neglect, 31,* 517–530.

Statistics Canada. (2005). *General Social Survey on Victimization, Cycle 18: An Overview of Findings.* Statistics Canada. Ottawa.

Statistics Canada. (2007). Uniform Crime Reporting Survey (UCR). Retrieved from **http://www.statcan.gc.ca/cgibin/imdb/p2SV.pl?Function=getSurvey&SurvId=3302&SurvVer=0&InstaId=15093&InstaVer=9&SDDS=3302&lang=en&db=imdb&adm=8&dis=2**

Statistics Canada. (2010). Canadian Centre for Justice Statistics, Homicide Survey. Retrieved from **http://www.statcan.gc.ca/pub/85-002-x/2011001/article/11561-eng.htm**

Statistics Canada. (2011). Uniform Crime Reporting Survey (UCR). Retrieved from **http://www.statcan.gc.ca/cgibin/imdb/p2SV.pl?Function=getSurvey&SurvId=3302&SurvVer=0&InstaId=15093&InstaVer=12&SDDS=3302&lang=en&db=imdb&adm=8&dis=2**

Teicher, M. D. (2000). Wounds that time won't heal: The neurobiology of child abuse. *Cerebrum: The Dana Forum on Brain Science, 2*(4), 50–67.

Toronto Star. (2000). July 25, 2000, p. A17, **https://tspace.library.utoronto.ca/bitstream/ 1807/17383/1/sever.pdf**

Trocmé, N., & Wolfe, W. (2001). *Canadian incidence study of reported child abuse and neglect: Selected results, 2001.* Ottawa: Minister of Public Works and Government Services Canada. *Canadian Incidence Study of Reported Child Abuse and Neglect (1998) (CIS-1998): Final Report.*

Trocmé, N., Fallon, B., MacLaurin, B., Daciuk, J., Felstiner, C., & Black, T. (2005). *Canadian incidence study of reported child abuse and neglect, 2003: Major findings.* Ottawa: Minister of Public Works and Government Services Canada. Retrieved from **http://www.cecw-cepb.ca/sites/ default/files/publications/en/CIS2003_ MajorFindings_slides.pdf**

Trocmé, N., Fallon, B., MacLaurin, B., Sinha, V., Black, T., Fast, E., Felstiner, C., Hélie, S., Turcotte, D., Weightman, P., Douglas, J., Holroyd, J. (2010). *Canadian incidence study of reported child abuse and neglect, 2008: Major findings.* Ottawa: Minister of Public Works and Government Services Canada.

Trocmé, N., Lajoie, J., Fallon, B., & Felstiner, C. (2007). Injuries and deaths of children at the hands of their parents. *CECW Information Sheet #57E.* Toronto: University of Toronto Faculty of Social Work. Retrieved October 15, 2008, from **http://www.cecw-epb.ca/ publications/519**

Trocmé, N., MacLaurin, B., Fallon, B., Daciuk, J., Billingsley, D., Tourigny, M., Mayer, M., Wright, J., Barter, K., Burford, G., Hornick, J., Sullivan, R., & McKenzie, B. (2001). *Canadian incidence study of reported child abuse and neglect 1998: Final report.* Ottawa: Minister of Public Works and Government Services Canada.

Vandermeulen, G., Wekerle, C., & Ylagan, C. (2005). Introduction to the special issue on child welfare—Research collaborations: Teamwork, research excellence, and credible, relevant results for practice. *Ontario Association of Children's Aid Societies (OACAS) Journal, 49*(1), 2–3.

Chapter 4

AAUW (American Association of University Women). (1991). Shortchanging girls, shortchanging America. Retrieved from **http://www.aauw.org/learn/research/ upload/SGSA-2.pdf**

Aggarwal, A. P. (1987). *Sexual harassment in the workplace.* Toronto: Butterworths.

American Psychiatric Association. (1994). *DSM-IV-TR sourcebook, Volume 1.* Washington, DC: Author.

Amnesty International. (2004). *Stolen sisters: Discrimination and violence against Indigenous women in Canada.* Ottawa: Author.

Anderson, K. J., & Accomando, C. (1999). Madcap misogyny and romanticized victim-blaming: Discourses of stalking in "There's Something about Mary." *Women and Language, 22,* 24–28.

AuCoin, K. (Ed.). (2005). *Family violence in Canada: A statistical profile 2005.* Catalogue no. 85-224-XIE. Ottawa: Statistics Canada.

Bagley, C., Bolitho, F., & Bertrand, L. (1997). Sexual assault in school, mental health and suicidal behaviors in adolescent women in Canada. *Adolescence, 32,* 361–366.

Baker, R. L. (1995). *The social work dictionary* (3rd ed.). Washington, DC: National Association of Social Workers.

Beattie, S. (2003). Criminal harassment. In H. Johnson & K. AuCoin (Eds.), *Family violence in Canada: A statistical profile 2003.* Catalogue no. 85-224-XIE. Ottawa: Statistics Canada, Canadian Centre for Justice Statistics.

Becky, R. D., & Farren, P. M. (1997). Teaching students how to understand and avoid abusive relationships. *School Counselor, 44,* 303–308.

Brennan, S., & Taylor-Butts, A. (2008). Sexual assault in Canada, 2004 and 2007. *Canadian Centre for Justice Statistics Profile Series.* Catalogue no. 85F0033M–No. 19. Ottawa: Statistics Canada. Retrieved June 6, 2010, from **http://www.statcan.gc.ca/pub/ 85f0033m/85f0033m2008019-eng.htm**

Burgess, A., & Holmstrom, L. (1974). Rape trauma syndrome. *American Journal of Psychiatry, 131,* 981–986.

Burt, M. R., & Katz, B. L. (1987). Dimensions of recovery from rape. *Journal of Interpersonal Violence, 2,* 57–81.

Campbell, R. (2006). Rape survivors' experiences with the legal and medical systems: Do rape victim advocates make a difference? *Violence Against Women, 12*(1), 30–45.

Canadian Centre for Justice Statistics. (1999). *The Juristat Reader: A statistical overview of the Canadian justice system.* Toronto: Thompson Educational Publishing, Inc.

Canadian Human Rights Commission. (1983). *Unwanted sexual attention and sexual harassment: Results of a survey of Canadians.* Ottawa: Canadian Human Rights Commission.

Cass, A. (2007). Routine activities and sexual assault: An analysis of individual- and school-level factors. *Journal of Violence and Victims, 22*(3), 350–364.

CBC. (2010, September 17). CBC rave rape suspect arrested. Retrieved from **http:// www.cbc.ca/news/canada/british-columbia/story/2010/09/17/bc-gang-rape-high-school-police.html**

CBC. (2011, December 5). B.C. teen pleads guilty for alleged rape photos. Retrieved from **http://www.cbc.ca/news/canada/ british-columbia/story/2011/12/05/bc-gang-rape-facebook.html**

CBC News. (2009, December 6). Montreal massacre events mark 1989 shootings. Retrieved from **http://www.cbc.ca/ news/canada/montreal/story/2009/12/04/ montreal-massacre-victims.html**

CBC News (2010, July 30). Robert Pickton won't get new trial: Top court. Retrieved from **http://www.cbc.ca/canada/story/ 2010/07/30/pickton-supreme030.html**

Charney, D., & Russell, R. (1994). An overview of sexual harassment. *American Journal of Psychiatry, 151,* 10–17.

Criminal Code, 1892, S.C. 1892, c. 29.

Crocker, D., & Kalemba, V. (1999, November). The incidence and impact of women's experiences of sexual harassment in Canadian workplaces. *Canadian Review of Sociology and Anthropology.*

Dansky, B., & Kilpatrick, D. (1997). Effects of sexual harassment. In W. O'Donahue (Ed.), *Sexual harassment: Theory, research, and treatment* (pp. 152–174). Boston: Allyn & Bacon.

Dauvergne, M., & Turner, J. (2009). Police-reported crime statistics in Canada, 2009. *Juristat* Article Component of Statistics Canada Catalogue no. 85-002-X. *Juristat.* Retrieved from **http://www.statcan.gc.ca/pub/85-002-x/ 2010002/article/11292-eng.pdf**

David-Herndon, C., & Hertz, C. (2007, December). Electronic media, violence, and adolescents: An emerging public health problem. *Journal of Adolescent Health.*

David-Herndon C., & Hertz, M. F. (2009). Electronic media and youth violence: A CDC issue brief for researchers. Atlanta: Centers for Disease Control.

DeKeseredy, W., & Kelly, K. (1993). The incidence and prevalence of woman abuse in Canadian university and college dating relationships: Results from a national survey. Ottawa: Health Canada.

Department of Justice Canada. (2005). *Dating violence: A fact sheet from the Department of Justice Canada.* Ottawa: Author.

Dickinson, L. M., DeGruy, F. U. III, Dickinson, W. P., & Candib, L. M. (1999). Health related quality of life and symptom profiles of female survivors of sexual abuse. *Archives of Female Medicine, 8*(1), 35–43.

Farley, M., Lynne, J., & Cotton, A. J. (2005). Prostitution in Vancouver: Violence and the colonization of First Nations women. *Transcultural Psychiatry, 42,* 24.

Frazier, P. A. (2000). The role of attributions and perceived control in recovery from rape. *Journal of Personal and Interpersonal Loss, 5*(2/3), 203–225.

Frazier, P. A. (2003). Perceived control and distress following sexual assault: A longitudinal test of a new model. *Journal of Personality and Social Psychology, 84,* 1257–1269.

Gannon, M., & Mihorean, K. (2005). Criminal victimization in Canada, 2004. *Juristat, 25*(7). Catalogue no. 85-002-XPE. Ottawa: Statistics Canada.

Gross, L. (1995). *To have or to harm: True stories of stalkers and their victims.* New York: Warner Books.

Gutek, B. A., & Koss, M. P. (1993). Changed women and changed organizations: Consequences of and coping with sexual harassment. *Journal of Vocational Behavior, 42*(1), 28–48.

Hackett, K. (2000). Criminal harassment. *Juristat, 20*(11). Catalogue no. 85-002-XIE. Ottawa: Statistics Canada.

Hampton, H. L. (1995). Care of the women who have been raped. *New England Journal of Medicine, 332*(4), 234–237.

Hotton Mahony, T. (2010). Police-reported dating violence in Canada, 2008. *Juristat* article. Component of Statistics Canada Catalogue no. 85-002-X *Juristat*. Retrieved from **http://www.statcan.gc.ca/pub/85-002-x/2010002/article/11242-eng.pdf**

Indian and Northern Affairs Canada. (1996, Summer). *Aboriginal women: A demographic, social and economic profile.* Ottawa: Author.

Johnson, H. (2006). *Measuring violence against women: Statistical trends 2006.* Ottawa; Canadian Centre for Justice Statistics, Ministry of Industry.

Kong, R. (1996). Criminal harassment. *Juristat, 16*(12). Catalogue no. 85-002-XPE. Ottawa: Statistics Canada.

Kong, R., Johnson, H., Beattie, S., & Cardillo, A. (2003). Sexual offences in Canada. *Juristat, 23*(6). Catalogue no. 85-002-XIE. Ottawa: Statistics Canada.

Koss, M. P. (1988). Hidden rape: Sexual aggression and victimization in the national sample of students in higher education. In M. A. Pirog-Good & J. E. Stets (Eds.), *Violence in dating relationships: Emerging social issues* (pp. 145–168). New York: Praeger.

Koss, M. P., & Dinero, T. E. (1988). A discriminant analysis of risk factors among a national sample of college women. *Journal of Consulting and Clinical Psychology, 57,* 133–147.

Koss, M. P., Figueredo, A. J., & Prince, R. J. (2002). Cognitive mediation of rape's mental, physical, and social health impact: Test of four models in cross-sectional data. *Journal of Consulting & Clinical Psychology, 55,* 162–170.

Koss, M. P., & Harvey, M. R. (1991). *The rape victim: Clinical and community intervention.* Newbury Park, CA: Sage.

Larkin J. (1994). Walking through walls: The sexual harassment of high school girls. *Gender Education, 6,* 263–280.

LePard, D. (2010). *Missing women investigation review.* Vancouver: Vancouver Police Department. Retrieved from **http://vancouver.ca/police/media/2010/mw-summary-report.pdf**

Levan, M. B. (2003). *Creating a framework for the wisdom of the community: Victim services in Nunavut: Needs and recommendations.* Ottawa: Department of Justice Canada.

Levinthal, C. (2010). *Drugs, behavior and modern society* (6th ed.). Boston: Allyn & Bacon.

Loy, P. H., & Stewart, L. P. (1984). The extent and effects of the sexual harassment of working women. *Sociological Focus, 17*(1), 31–43.

Macy, R. J., Nurius, P. S., & Norris, J. (2006). Responding in the best interests: Contextualizing women's coping with acquaintance sexual aggression. *Violence Against Women, 12*(5), 478–500.

Makepeace, J. M. (1997). Courtship violence as process: A development theory. In A. P. Cardarelli, *Violence between intimate partners: Patterns, causes and effects* (pp. 29–47). Boston: Allyn and Bacon.

Malik S., Sorenson, S. B., & Aneshensel C. S. (1997). Community and dating violence among adolescents: Perpetration and victimization. *Journal of Adolescent Health, 21,* 291–302.

Mazar, D. B., & Percival, E. F. (1989). Students' experiences of sexual harassment at a small university. *Sex Roles, 20,* 1–22.

McFarlane, A. C., & DeGirolamo, G. (1996). The nature of traumatic stressors and the epidemiology of posttraumatic reactions. In B.A. van der Kolk, A.C. McFarlane, & L. Weisaeth (Eds.), *Traumatic stress: The effects of overwhelming experience on mind, body, and society* (pp. 129–154). New York: Guilford.

McFarlane, J. J., Campbell, J. C., & Watson, K. (2002). Intimate partner stalking and femicide: Urgent implications for women's safety. *Behavioral Sciences and the Law, 20,* 51–68.

McGregor, M. J., Ericksen, J., Ronald, L. A. Janseen, P. A. Van Vliet, A., & Schulzer, M. (2004). Rising incidence of hospital-reported drug-facilitated sexual assault in a large urban community in Canada. *Canadian Journal of Public Health, 95*(6), 441–445.

McMaster, L. E., Connolly, J., Pepler, D., & Craig, W. M. (2002). Peer to peer sexual harassment in early adolescence: A developmental perspective. *Development and Psychopathology, 14,* 91–105.

Melton, H. C. (2007). Predicting the occurrences of stalking in relationships characterized by domestic violence. *Journal of Interpersonal Violence, 22*(1), 3–25.

Mercer, S., (1987). *Not a pretty picture: An exploratory study of violence against women in dating relationships.* Toronto: Education Wife Assault.

Milligan, S. (2009). Criminal harassment in Canada, 2009. *Juristat Bulletin* article. Component of Statistics Canada Catalogue no. 85-005-X. Retrieved from http://www.statcan.gc.ca/pub/85-005-x/2011001/article/11407-eng.pdf

Ministry of the Solicitor General. (1982). *Canadian urban victimization survey.* Ottawa: Ministry of Supply and Services.

Missing Women Commission of Inquiry Website. Retrieved from http://www.missingwomeninquiry.ca/

Mohandie, K., Hatcher, C., & Raymond, D. (1998). False victimization syndromes in stalking. In R. Meloy (Ed.), *The psychology of stalking: Clinical and forensic perspectives* (pp. 225–256). New York: Academic Press.

Mohandie, K. C., Meloy, J. R., McGowan, M. G., & Williams, J. (2006). The RECON typology of stalking: Reliability and validly based upon a large sample of North American stalkers. *Journal of Forensic Science, 51*(1), 147–155.

Mullen, P., Pathe, M., Purcell, R., & Stuart, G. W. (1999). Study of stalkers. *American Journal of Psychiatry, 156,* 1244–1249.

Native Women's Association of Canada Website: http://www.nwac.ca/

Ontario Human Rights Commission. (1993). *Policy statement on sexual harassment and inappropriate gender-related comment and conduct.* Toronto: Ontario Human Rights Commission Policy and Research Unit.

Orenstein, P. (1997). *School girls: Young women, self-esteem and the confidence gap.* New York: Doubleday.

Oxman-Martinez, J., Lacroix, M., & Hanley, J. (2005). *Victims of trafficking in persons: Perspectives from the Canadian community sector.* Ottawa: Department of Justice Canada.

Pacific Association of First Nations Women. (2005). BC Women's Hospital & Health Centre and BC Association of Specialized Victim Assistance and Counselling Programs. *Researched to death: B.C. Aboriginal women and violence.* Eva BC Publishing. **http://www.endingviolence.org/node/305**

Palarea, R., Zona, M., Lane, J., & Langhinrichsen-Rohling, J. (1999). The dangerous nature of intimate relationship stalking: Threats, violence, and associated risk factors. *Behavioral Sciences and the Law, 17,* 269–283.

Perreault, S. (2004). *Visible minorities and victimization.* Canadian Centre for Justice Statistics Profile Series No. 015. Catalogue no. 85F0033MIE. Ottawa: Statistics Canada. Retrieved from **http://www.statcan.gc.ca/pub/85f0033m/85f0033m2008015-eng.pdf**

Perreault, S., & Brennan, S. (2010). Criminal victimization in Canada, 2009. *Juristat, 30*(2). Catalogue no. 85-002-X. Ottawa: Statistics Canada. Retrieved from **http://www.statcan.gc.ca/pub/85-002-x/85-002-x2010002-eng.htm**

Perreault, S., Sauvé, J., & Burns, M. (2004). *Multiple victimization in Canada.* Catalogue no. 85F0033M No. 22. Ottawa: Canadian Centre for Justice Statistics. Retrieved from **http://www.statcan.gc.ca/pub/85f0033m/85f0033m2010022-eng.pdf**

Pipher M. (1994). *Reviving Ophelia: Saving the selves of adolescent girls.* New York: Ballantine Books.

Polusny, M. A., & Arbisi, P. A. (2006). Assessment of psychological distress and the disability after sexual assault in adults. In G. Young, et al. (Eds.), *Psychological knowledge in court: PTSD, Pain and TBI* (pp. 97–125). Berlin, Germany: Springer Science + Business Media.

Pottie Bunge, V. (2002). National trends in intimate partner homicides, 1974–2000. *Juristat, 22*(5). Catalogue no. 85-002-XIE. Ottawa: Statistics Canada.

Reimer, M. S. (1999). Gender, risk, and resilience in the middle school context. *Children and Schools, 24*(1), 35–47. A journal of the National Association of Social Workers.

Roberts, J. V., & Gebotys, R. (1992). Reforming rape laws: Effects of legislative change in Canada. *Law Human Behaviour, 16,* 555–573.

Resnick, H., Acierno, R., Kilpatrick, D., & Jager, N. (1999). Prevention of post-rape psychopathology: Preliminary findings of a controlled acute rape treatment study. *Journal of Anxiety Disorders, 13,* 359–370.

Royal Canadian Mounted Police. (2006). *Control or regulation of prostitution in Canada: Implications for police.* Ottawa: Research and Evaluation—Community, Contract and Aboriginal Policing Services Directorate.

R. v. Chase, [1987] 2 S.C.R. 293

R. v. Darrach, 000 SCC 46, 2000] 2 S.C.R. 443.

R. v. Ewanchuk [1999], 1 S.C.R. 330 at 334.

R. v. O'Connor, [1995] 4 S.C.R. 411

R. v. Park [1995] 2 S.C.R. 836 at 837.

R. v. Seaboyer; R. v. Gayme. [1991] 2 S.C.R. 577 at 582.

Sable, M. R., Danis, F., Mauzy, D. L., & Gallagher, S. K. (2006). Barriers to reporting sexual assault for women and men: Perspectives of college students. *Journal of American College Health, 55*(3), 157–161.

Schmalleger, F., & Volk, R. (2004). *Canadian criminology today: Theories and applications* (3rd ed.). Toronto: Pearson Canada.

Schmalleger, F., & Volk, R. (2011). *Canadian criminology today: Theories and applications*. Toronto: Pearson Canada.

Schneider, K. T., Swan, S., & Fitzgerald, L. F. (1997). Job related and psychological effects of sexual harassment in the workplace: Empirical evidence from two organizations. *Journal of Applied Psychology, 82*(3), 401–15.

Smith, D. (1995). Sexual harassment in the workplace: The silent oppression. *Social Worker, 63*(2), 85–88.

Statistics Canada. (2005). General Social Survey on Victimization (GSS). Cycle 18. Retrieved from **http://prod.library. utoronto.ca/datalib/codebooks/cstdli/gss/ gss18/gssc18gid-version2.pdf**

Statistics Canada. (2007). Uniform Crime Reporting Survey (UCR). Retrieved from **http://www.statcan.gc.ca/cgibin/ imdb/p2SV.pl?Function=getSurvey& SurvId=3302&SurvVer=0&InstaId= 15093&InstaVer=9&SDDS=3302&lang= en&db=imdb&adm=8&dis=2**

Statistics Canada. (2010). Canadian Centre for Justice Statistics, Homicide Survey. Retrieved from **http://www.statcan.gc.ca/ pub/85-002-x/2011001/article/11561-eng. htm**

Statistics Canada. (2011). Uniform Crime Reporting Survey (UCR). Retrieved from **http://www.statcan.gc.ca/cgibin/ imdb/p2SV.pl?Function=getSurvey& SurvId=3302&SurvVer=0&InstaId= 15093&InstaVer=12&SDDS=3302&lang= en&db=imdb&adm=8&dis=2**

Tjaden, P., & Thoennes, N. (1998). Stalking in America: Findings from the National Violence Against Women Survey. Research in Brief. NCJ 169592. Washington: National Institute of Justice.

Wakelin, A. (2003). Effects of victim gender and sexuality on attributions of blame to rape victims. *Sex Roles, 49*(9/10), 477–487.

Wekerle, C., & Wolfe, D. A. (1999). Dating violence in mid-adolescents: Theory, significance and emerging prevention issues. *Clinical Psychology Review, 19*, 435–456.

Chapter 5

Aboriginal Healing Foundation. (1999). *Aboriginal Healing Foundation program handbook* (2nd ed.). Ottawa: Aboriginal Healing Foundation.

Airdrie, K. (2008). *Angelina Napolitano, domestic violence victim: First battered wife syndrome defence in Canada*. Retrieved from **http://kathleen-airdrie.suite101.com/ immigrant-angelina-napolitano-a81771**

American Psychological Association. (2001). *Publication manual of the American Psychological Association* (5th ed.). Washington DC: Author.

Amnesty International. 2004. *Stolen sisters: Discrimination and violence against indigenous women in Canada*.

Archer, J. (2000). Sex differences in aggression between heterosexual partners: A meta-analytic review. *Psychological Bulletin, 126*, 651–680.

Baker, A. A. (1975). Granny battering. *Modern Geriatrics, 5*, 20–4.

Basile, K. C. (2008). Histories of violent victimizations among women who reported unwanted sex in marriages and intimate relationships. *Violence Against Women, 14*, 29–52.

Besserer, S., Brzozowski, J., Hendrick, D., Ogg, S., & Trainor, C. (2001*). A Profile of Criminal Victimization: Results of the 1999 General Social Survey*. Statistic Canada. Catalogue no. 85-553-XIE. Ottawa.

Blatchford, C. (2011a, October 20). *National Post*. "I would do it again." Retrieved from **http://fullcomment.nationalpost.com/ 2011/10/20/christie-blatchford-%E2% 80%98i-would-do-it-again%E2%80%99- court-hears-horror-of-an-alleged-honour- killing/**

Blatchford, C. (2011b, December 5). *National Post*. "Honour is men's need to control women's sexuality," expert tells Shafia murder trial. Retrieved from http://fullcomment.nationalpost.com/2011/12/05/christie-blatchford-in-some-honour-killings-fathers-see-the-attack-as-part-of-the-continuum-of-love-shafia-trial-hears/

Bobyk-Krumins, J. F. L., & Holosko, M. J. (2004). Abuse and neglect of the elderly person. In M. Holosko & M. Feit (Eds.), *Social work practice with the elderly* (3rd ed.). Toronto: The Canadian Scholar's Press Inc.

Brennan, S. (2011). Self-reported spousal violence, 2009. In *Family violence in Canada: A statistical profile*. Catalogue no. 85-224-X. Ottawa: Statistics Canada Canadian Centre for Justice Statistics. Retrieved November 2011 from http://www.statcan.gc.ca/pub/85-224-x/85-224-x2010000-eng.pdf

Browne, A. (1987). *When battered women kill*. New York: Macmillan/Free Press.

Browne, A. (1993). Violence against women by male partners: Prevalence, outcomes and policy implications. *American Psychologist, 48*, 1077–1087.

Brown, J. B., Lent, B., Brett, P. J., & Pederson, L. L. (1996). Development of the woman abuse screening tool for use in family practice. *Family Medicine, 28*(6), 422–8.

Brzozowski, J. (2004). Family violence against children and youth. In J. Brzozowski (Ed.), *Family violence in Canada: A statistical profile*.

Brzozowski, J., Taylor-Butts, A., & Johnson, S. (2006). Victimization and offending among the Aboriginal population in Canada. *Juristat, 26*(3). Catalogue no. 85-002-XIE. Ottawa: Statistics Canada.

Burston, G. R. (1975). *Granny-battering*. British Medical Journal, 3(5983), 592.

Byers, B., & Hendricks, J. (Eds.). (1993). *Adult protective services: Research and practice*. Springfield, IL: Charles C. Thomas.

Campbell, J., Poland, M., Walder, J., & Ager, J. (1992). Correlates of battering during pregnancy. *Research in Nursing and Health, 15*(3), 219–226.

Campbell, J. C., Oliver C., & Bullock, L. (1993). Why battering during pregnancy? *AWHONNS Clinical Issues in Perinatal and Women's Health Nursing, 4*(3), 343–9.

Carden, A. (1994). Wife abuse and wife abuser: Review and recommendations. *The Counseling Psychologist, 22*(4), 539–582.

Chartrand, L., & McKay, C. (2006). *First Nations, Metis and Inuit people*. Policy Centre for Victim Issues, Research and Statistics Division, Department of Justice. Retrieved from http://www.justice.gc.ca/eng/pi/rs/rep-rap/2006/rr06_vic1/rr06_vic1.pdf

Daly, M., Singh, L., & Wilson, M. (1993). Children fathered by previous partners: A risk factor for violence against women. *Canadian Journal of Public Health, 84*, 209–210.

De Léséleuc, S., & Brzozowski, J. (2004). *Victimization and offending in Canada's territories*. Canadian Centre for Justice Statistics Profile Series. Catalogue no. 85F0033MIE. Ottawa: Statistics Canada. Retrieved from http://www.statcan.gc.ca/pub/85f0033m/85f0033m2006011-eng.pdf

Department of Justice. (2007). *Family violence: Department of Justice Canada overview paper*. Retrieved from http://www.justice.gc.ca/eng/pi/fv-vf/facts-info/fv-vf/index.html

Department of Justice Canada Website: http://canada.justice.gc.ca/eng/pi/fv-vf/facts-info/fv-vf/fv1-vf1.html

Dictionary of Canadian Biography. (n.d.). Angelina Napolitano. Retrieved from http://www.biographi.ca/009004-119.01-e.php?&id_nbr=7952

Dobash, R. E., & Dobash, R. B. (1979). Violence against wives. New York: Free Press.

Dasgupta D. S. (1998). Defining violence against women by immigration, race and class. In R.K. Bergen (Ed.), *Issues *in intimate violence* (pp. 208–219). Thousand Oaks, CA: Sage.

Edleson, J. L., & Tolman, R. M. (1992). Intervention for men who batter: An ecological approach. Newbury Park, CA: Sage Publication.

Edwards, P., & Mawani, A. (2006, September). *Healthy aging in Canada: A new vision, a vital investment: From evidence to action.* Retrieved from http://www.phac-aspc.gc.ca/seniors-aines/publications/pro/healthy-sante/haging_newvision/vison-rpt/index-eng.php

Fiebert, M. S., & Gonzalez, D. M. (1997). College women who initiate assaults on their male partners and the reasons offered of such behaviour. *Psychological Reports, 80,* 583–590.

Frieze, I. H. (1983). Investigating the causes and consequence of marital rape. *Signs, 8,* 532–553.

Frieze, I. H., & Browne, A. (1989). Violence in marriage. In L. Ohlin & M. Tonry (Eds.), *Family violence* (pp. 163–218). Chicago: University of Chicago Press.

Frieze, I. H., Hymer, S., & Greenberg, M. S. (1987). Describing the crime victim: Psychological reactions to victimizations. *Professional Psychology Research and Practice, 18,* 299–315.

Frieze, I. H., & McHugh, M. C. (1992). Power and influence strategies in violent and non-violent marriages. *Psychology of Women Quarterly, 16,* 449–466.

Gannon, M., & Mihorean, K. (2005). Criminal victimization in Canada, 2004. *Juristat, 25*(7). Catalogue no. 85-002-XIE. Ottawa: Statistics Canada.

Gelles, R. J. (1972). Abused wives: Why do they stay? *Journal of Marriage and the Family, 38*(4), 659–666.

Gelles, R. J., & Cornell, C. P. (1985). *Intimate violence in families.* Beverly Hills, CA: Sage.

Hamby, S. L., & Gray-Little, B. (2003). Labeling partner violence: When do victims differentiate among acts? *Violence and Victims, 15,* 173–186.

Health Canada. (2002). *Canada's aging population.* Minister of Public Works and Government Services Canada 2002. Cat. no. H39-608/2002E. Retrieved from http://publications.gc.ca/collections/Collection/H39-608-2002E.pdf

Helton, A., McFarlane, J., & Anderson, E. (1987). Battered and pregnant: A prevalence study. *American Journal of Public Health, 77,* 1337–1339.

Herman, J. (1997). *Trauma and recovery: The aftermath of violence, from domestic abuse to political terror.* New York: Basic Books.

Holtzworth-Monroe, A., & Stuart, G. L. (1994). Typologies of male batterers: Three subtypes and the differences among them. *Psychological Bulletin, 116*(3), 476–497.

Hotton, T. (2001). Spousal violence after marital separation. *Juristat, 21*(7). Cat. No. 85-002-XPE. Ottawa: Canadian Centre for Justice Statistics, Statistics Canada.

Huth-Bocks, A. C., Levendosky, A. A., & Semel, M. A. (2001). The direct and indirect effects of domestic violence on young children's intellectual functioning. *Journal of Family Violence, 16*(3), 269–290.

Huth-Bocks, A. C., Levendosky, A. A., & Bogat, G. A. (2002). The effects of domestic violence during pregnancy on maternal and infant health. *Violence and Victims, 17,* 169–185.

Johnson, H. (1996a). Violent crime in Canada. *Juristat, 16*(6). Ottawa: Canadian Centre for Justice Statistics, Statistics Canada.

Johnson, H. (1996b). *Dangerous domains: Violence against women in Canada.* Scarborough: Nelson Canada.

Johnson, H. (2000). Trends in victim-reported wife assault. In V. Pottie Bunge and D. Locke (Eds.), *Family violence in Canada: A statistical profile, 2000.*

Catalogue no. 85-224-XIE. Ottawa: Statistics Canada.

Johnson, H., & Hotton. T. (2001). Spousal violence. In C. Trainor and K. Mihorean (Eds.), *Family violence in Canada: A statistical profile, 2001*. Catalogue no. 85-224-XPE. Ottawa: Statistics Canada.

Johnson, H., & Hotton, T. (2003). Losing control: Homicide risk in estranged and intact intimate relationships. *Homicide Studies, 7*(1), 58–84.

Johnson, H., & Hotton, T. (2003). Losing control: Homicide risk in estranged and intact intimate relationships. *Homicide Studies, 7*(1), 58–84.

Johnson, M. P. (1995). Patriarchal terrorism and common couple violence: Two forms of violence against women. *Journal of Marriage and the Family, 75*, 283–294.

Johnson, M. P., & Ferraro, K. J. (2000). Research on domestic violence in the 1990s: Making distinctions. *Journal of Marriage and the Family, 62*, 948–963.

Klymchuk, K. L, Cooper, M., & Pacey, K. (2002). *Children exposed to partner violence: An overview of key issues*. Vancouver: BC Institute Against Family Violence.

Krane, J., & Davies, L. (2007). Mothering under difficult circumstances: Challenges to working with battered women. *AFFILIA Journal of Women and Social Work, 22*(1), 23–38.

LaPrairie, C. (1995). *Seen but not heard: Native people in the inner city*. Ottawa: Minister of Public Works and Government Services.

Lehmann, P. (1997). The development of posttraumatic stress disorder (PTSD) in a sample of child witnesses to mother assault. *Journal of Family Violence, 12*(3), 241–257.

Levendosky, A. A., & Graham-Bermann, S. A. (2001). Parenting in battered women: The effects of domestic violence on women and their children. *Journal of Family Violence, 16*(2), 171–192.

Looking for Angelina (movie) . (2004).

MacLeod, L. (1980). *Wife battering is every woman's issue: A summary report of the CACSW consultation on wife battering*. Ottawa: Canadian Advisory Council on the Status of Women.

MacLeod, L., Cadieux, A.. (1980). *Wife battering in Canada: The vicious circle*. Ottawa: Canadian Advisory Council on the Status of Women.

Marra, O., Al, J.C. (Chair). (2002). *Domestic violence death review committee: Annual report to the Chief Coroner: Ottawa*.

Marra, O., Al, J.C. (Chair). (2004). *Domestic violence death review committee: Annual report to the chief coroner: Ottawa*.

Marra, O., Al, J.C. (Chair). (2005). *Domestic violence death review committee: Annual report to the chief coroner: Ottawa*.

McDonald, L., & Collins, A. (2000). *Abuse and neglect of older adults: A discussion paper for the Family Violence Prevention Unit, Health Canada*. Retrieved from **http://publications.gc.ca/collections/Collection/H88-3-30-2001/pdfs/violence/abuse_e.pdf**

McFarlane, J. (1992). Battering in pregnancy. In C.M. Sampselle (Ed.), *Violence against women: Nursing research, education and practice issues* (pp. 205–225). New York: Hemisphere Publications.

McFarlane, J. (1993). Abuse during pregnancy: The horror and the hope. *AWHONNS Clinical Issues in Perinatal and Women's Health Nursing, 4*(3), 350–62.

McFarlane J., Parker B., Soeken K., & Bullock L. (1992). Assessing for abuse during pregnancy: Severity and frequency of injuries and associated entry into prenatal care. *Journal of the American Medical Association, 267*, 3176–8.

McLachlin, B. (2008). *The law's response to an aging population: Remarks of the Right Honourable Beverley McLachlin, P.C.*

Chief Justice of Canada, World Elder Abuse Awareness Day 2008. Retrieved from **http://www.cnpea.ca/Ottawa% 20Presentations%202008_files/Cheif%20 Justice's%20speech%20final.pdf**

Mihorean, K. (2005). Trends in self-reported spousal violence. In K. AuCoin (Ed.), *Family violence in Canada: A statistical profile, 2005.* Catalogue no. 85-224-XIE. Ottawa: Statistics Canada.

Muhajarine, N., & D'Arcy, C. (1999). Physical abuse during pregnancy: Prevalence and risk factors. *Canadian Medical Association Journal, 160*(7), 1007–11.

National Seniors Council. (2007). *Report of the National Seniors Council on elder abuse.* Seniors Council, Government of Canada. Retrieved from **http:// www.seniorscouncil.gc.ca/eng/research_ publications/elder_abuse/2007/hs4_38/ page06.shtml**

OAITH. (1996). *Locked in, left out: Impacts of the Progressive Conservative budget cuts and policy initiatives on abused women and their children in Ontario.* Toronto: Ontario Association of Interval and Transition Houses.

OAITH. (1998). *Falling through the gender gap: How Ontario government policy continues to fail abused women and their children.* Toronto: Ontario Association of Interval and Transition Houses.

Ogrodnik, L. (2007). Seniors as victims of crime, 2004 and 2005. *Canadian Centre for Justice Statistics Profile Series.* Catalogue no. 85F0033M. No. 14. Ottawa: Statistics Canada.

Ogrodnik, L. (2009). Fact sheet: Family homicides. In *Family violence in Canada: A statistical profile.* Catalogue no. 85-224-X. Ottawa: Canadian Centre for Justice Statistics, Statistics Canada. Retrieved from **http://www.statcan.gc. ca/pub/85-224-x/85-224-x2010000-eng. pdf**

Ogrodnik, L. (Ed.). (2008). *Family violence in Canada: A statistical profile, 2008.*

Catalogue no. 85-224-X. Ottawa: Statistics Canada.

Pagelow, M. D. (1981). *Women-battering: Victims and their experiences.* Beverly Hills, CA: Sage.

Pagelow, M. D. (1984). *Family violence.* New York: Praeger.

Parker B., McFarlane J., & Soeken, K. (1994). Abuse during pregnancy: Effects on maternal complications and birth weight in adults and teenage women. *Obstetrics & Gynecology, 84*, 323–8.

Pence, E., & Paymar, M. (1993). *Education groups for men who batter.* New York: Springer Publishing Company.

Perreault, S., & Brennan, S. (2009). Criminal victimization in Canada, 2009. *Juristat, 30*(2). Catalogue no. 85-002-X. Ottawa: Statistics Canada. Retrieved from **http:// www.statcan.gc.ca/pub/85-002-x/85-002- x2010002-eng.htm**

Pillemer, K., & Finkelhor, D. (1988). The prevalence of elder abuse: A random sample survey. *Gerontologist, 28*(1), 51–57.

Podnieks, E., Pillemer, K., Nicholson, P., Shillington, T., & Frizzell, A. (1990). *National survey on abuse of the elderly in Canada.* Toronto: Ryerson Polytechnical Institute.

Podnieks, E., & Wilson, S. (2003). *Elder abuse awareness in faith communities: Findings from a Canadian pilot study.* The Haworth Press.

Pottie Bunge, V., & Locke, L. (Eds.). (2000). *Family violence in Canada: A statistical profile, 2000.* Catalogue no. 85-224-XIE. Ottawa: Canadian Centre for Justice Statistics, Statistics Canada.

Proulx, J., & Perrault, S. (2000). *No place for violence: Canadian Aboriginal alternatives.* Halifax: Fernwood Publishing Company.

Public Health Agency of Canada. (2009). *What mothers say: The Canadian maternity experiences survey.* Ottawa: Author.

Purwar, M. B., Jeyaseelan, L., Varhadpande, U., Motghare, V., Pimplakute, S. (1999). Survey of physical abuse during pregnancy GMCH, Nagpur, India. *Journal of Obstetrics and Gynaecology Research., 25*(3), 165–71.

Quinn, M. J., & Tomita, K. S. (1997). *Elder abuse and neglect: Causes, diagnosis, and intervention strategies* (2nd ed.). New York: Springer.

Russell, D. E. H. (1982). *Rape in marriage.* New York: Macmillan.

R. v. Lavallee, [1990] 1 S.C.R. 852. http://scc.lexum.umontreal.ca/en/1990/1990scr1-852/1990scr1-852.html

R. v. Whynot, [1983] N.S.J. No. 544, 9 C.C.C. (3d) 449 (N.S.C.A.).

Schecter, S., & Ganley, A. (1995). Understanding domestic violence. In *Domestic violence: A national curriculum for family preservation practitioners.* San Francisco: Family Violence Prevention Fund.

Seniors Resource Centre Association of Newfoundland and Labrador. (2005). *Strategic plan to address elder abuse in Newfoundland and Labrador: A five-year plan for 2005 to 2010.* Retrieved from http://www.seniorsresource.ca/docs/StrategicPlan.pdf

Shields, N., & Hanneke, C. R. (1983). Battered wives' reactions to marital rape. In D. Finkelhor, R. J. Gelles, G. T. Hotaling, & M. A. Straus (Eds.), *The dark side of families* (pp. 131–148). Beverly Hills, CA: Sage.

Sinha, M. (2009). Police-reported family violence against seniors, 2009. In *Family violence in Canada: A statistical profile.* Catalogue no. 85-224-X. Ottawa: Canadian Centre for Justice Statistics, Statistics Canada. Retrieved November 2011 from: http://www.statcan.gc.ca/pub/85-224-x/85-224-x2010000-eng.pdf

Statistics Canada. (2000, July 25). Family violence. *The Daily.* Ottawa: Statistics Canada. Retrieved from http://www.statcan.gc.ca/daily-quotidien/000725/dq000725b-eng.htm

Statistics Canada. (2007, July 17). 2006 census: Age and sex. *The Daily.* Ottawa: Statistics Canada. Retrieved from http://www.statcan.gc.ca/daily-quotidien/070717/dq070717-eng.pdf

Statistics Canada. (2011). *Family violence in Canada: A statistical profile.* Catalogue no. 85-224-X. Ottawa: Canadian Centre for Justice Statistics, Statistics Canada. Retrieved from http://www.statcan.gc.ca/pub/85-224-x/85-224-x2010000-eng.pdf.

Statistics Canada/VAWS. (1993). *Violence against women survey.* Retrieved from http://www.unece.org/fileadmin/DAM/stats/gender/vaw/surveys/Canada/1993_VAW_instrument.pdf

Stewart, D. E. (1994). Incidence of postpartum abuse in women with a history of abuse during pregnancy. *Canadian Medical Association Journal, 151*(11), 1601–04.

Stewart, D. E., & Cecutti, A. (1993). Physical abuse in pregnancy. *Canadian Medical Association Journal, 149*(9), 1257–63.

Straus, M. A. (1979). Measuring intrafamily conflict: The Conflict Tactics (CT) scales. *Journal of Marriage and the Family, 41,* 75–88.

Straus, M. A. (1993a). Identifying offenders in criminal justice research on domestic assaults. *American Behavioral Scientist, 36*(5), 587–599.

Straus, M. A. (1993b). Physical assaults by wives: A major social problem. In R. Gelles & D. Loseky (Eds.), *Current controversies on family violence* (pp. 67–87). Newbury Park, CA: Sage.

Straus, M. A. (2004). Prevalence of violence against dating partners by male and female university students worldwide. *Violence Against Women, 10*(7), 790–811.

Straus, M. A., & Gelles, R. (1986). Societal change and change in family violence from 1975 to 1985 as revealed by two national surveys. *Journal of Marriage and Family, 48,* 465–79.

Tatara, T. (1996). *Elder abuse: Questions and answers—An information guide for professionals and concerned citizens.* Washington, DC: National Centre on Elder Abuse.

Taylor-Butts, A. (2007). Canada's shelters for abused women, 2005/2006. *Juristat: Canadian Centre for Justice Studies.* Retrieved from www.statcan.ca/bsolc/english/bsolc?catno=85-002-X&CHROPG

Taylor-Butts, A. (2010). *Family violence in Canada: A statistical profile.* Catalogue no. 85-224-X. Ottawa: Canadian Centre for Justice Statistics, Statistics Canada. Retrieved from http://www.statcan.gc.ca/pub/85-224-x/85-224-x2010000-eng.pdf

Taylor-Butts, A., & Porter, L. (2011). Family-related homicides, 2000 to 2009. In *Family violence in Canada: A statistical profile.* Catalogue no. 85-224-X. Ottawa: Canadian Centre for Justice Statistics, Statistics Canada. Retrieved November 2011 from http://www.statcan.gc.ca/pub/85-224-x/85-224-x2010000-eng.pdf

Toews, M. L., McKenry, P. C., & Catlett, B. S. (2003). Male-initiated partner abuse during marital separation prior to divorce. *Violence and Victims, 18,* 387–402.

Toronto Star. (2000, July 25). p. A17.

Torres, S., Campbell, J., Campbell, D. W., Ryan, J., King, C., Price, P., Stalling, R. Y., Fuchs, S. C., & Laude, M. (2000). Abuse during and before pregnancy: Prevalence and cultural correlates. *Violence and Victims, 15,* 303–321.

Vaillancourt, R. (2009). Fact sheet: Police-reported family violence against older adults. In *Family violence in Canada: A statistical profile.* Catalogue no. 85-224-X. Ottawa: Canadian Centre for Justice Statistics, Statistics Canada. Retrieved from http://www.statcan.gc.ca/pub/85-224-x/85-224-x2010000-eng.pdf

Violence Prevention Initiative. (2005). Government of Newfoundland and Labrador. http://www.Gov.nf.ca/vpi/facts/elders.html

Walker, L. (1979). *The battered woman.* New York: Harper Perennial.

Walker, L. (1984). *The battered woman syndrome.* New York: Springer Publishing Company.

Wilson, M., & Daly, M. (1994). Spousal homicide. *Juristat, 14*(8). Ottawa: Canadian Centre for Justice Statistics, Statistics Canada.

Wilson M. I., & Daly, M. (1993). Spousal homicide risk and estrangement. *Violence and Victims, 8,* 3–16.

Wesley-Esquimaux, C. C., & Smolewski, M. (1999). *Historic trauma and Aboriginal healing.* Aboriginal Healing Foundation. Retrieved from http://www.ahf.ca/downloads/historic-trauma.pdf

World Health Organization. (2002). *The Toronto declaration on the global prevention of elder abuse.* Retrieved from http://www.who.int/ageing/projects/elder_abuse/alc_toronto_declaration_en.pdf

Wolf, R. (1992). Victimization of the elderly: Elder abuse and neglect. *Reviews in Clinical Gerontology, 2*(3), 269–76.

Wolf, R. S. (1988). Elder abuse: Ten years later. *Journal of the American Geriatrics Society, 36*(8), 758–62.

Wolf, R. S., & Pillemer, K. (1989). *Helping elderly victims: The reality of elder abuse.* New York: Columbia University Press.

Chapter 6

Allen, C., & Leventhal, B. (1999). History, culture, and identity. In B. Leventhal & S. E. Lundy (Eds.), *Same sex domestic violence: Strategies for change* (pp. 73–81). Thousand Oaks, CA: Sage Publications.

American Psychiatric Association Website: http://www.psych.org/MainMenu/Research/DSMIV.aspx

American Psychological Association. (1975). Minutes of the Council of Representatives. *American Psychologist, 30,* 633.

American Psychological Association. (1987). *Policy statements on lesbian and gay issues.* Washington, DC: Author.

Archer, J. (2000). Sex differences in physical aggression to partners A reply to Frieze (2000), O'Leary (2000), and White, Smith, Koss and Figueredo (2000). *Psychological Bulletin, 126,* 696–702.

Bayer, R. (1987). *Homosexuality and American psychiatry: The politics of diagnosis* (2nd ed.). Princeton, NJ: Princeton University Press.

Beauchamp, D. L. (2004). *Sexual orientation and victimization.* Catalogue no. 85F0033M, No. 016. Ottawa: Canadian Centre for Justice Statistics. Retrieved from **http://www.albertahatecrimes.ca/ 09/images/file/Documents/Resources/ Sexual%20Orientation%20and%20 Victimization%20(STATS%20Canada% 202004).pdf**

Berkeman, C. S., & Zinberg, G. (1997). Homophobia and heterosexism in social workers. *Social Work, 42,* 319–332.

Bernstein, M., & Kostelac, C. (2002). Lavender and blue: Attitudes about homosexual and behavior toward lesbians and gay men among police officers. *Journal of Contemporary Criminal Justice, 18*(3), 302–328.

Bill C-38: The Civil Marriage Act. Retrieved June 7, 2011, from **http://www.parl.gc.ca/ About/Parliament/LegislativeSummaries/ bills_ls.asp?ls=c38&Parl=38&Ses=1**

Bornstein, D. R., Fawcett, J., Sullivan, M., Senturia, K. D., & Shiu-Thornton, S. (2006). Understanding the experiences of lesbian, bisexual and trans survivors of domestic violence: A qualitative study. Co-published simultaneously in *Journal of Homosexuality, 51*(I), 159–181 and *Current Issues in Lesbian, Gay, Bisexual and Transgender Health* (Ed. J. Harcourt), Harrington Park Press, an imprint of The Haworth Press.

Brand, P. A., & Kidd, A. H. (1986). Frequency of physical aggression in heterosexual and female homosexual dyads. *Psychological Reports, 59,* 1307–1313.

Carroll, J. L. (2010). *Sexuality now: Embracing diversity* (3rd ed.). Wadsworth Cengage Learning.

CBC News. (2002. April 9). *Catholic school board rules against gay prom date.* Retrieved from **http://www.cbc.ca/news/ canada/story/2002/04/09/hall_prom020409. html**

CBC News. (2012, April 16). Gay activists demand Wildrose remove candidate. Retrieved from **http://www.cbc.ca/ news/canada/calgary/story/2012/04/16/ albertavotes2012-wildrose-hunsperger-gay. html**

Carlson, B. E. (1992). Questioning the party line on family violence. *AFFILIA Journal of Women and Social Work, 7*(2), 94–110.

Dobash, R. E., & Dobash, R. (1992). *Women, violence and social change.* New York: Routledge.

Dutton, D. (1995). *The batterer: A psychological profile.* New York: Basic Books.

Elliot, P. (1996). Shattering illusions: Same-gender domestic violence. *Journal of Gay & Lesbian Social Services, 4*(1), 1–8.

Ellis, D., & DeKeseredy, W. (1997). Rethinking estrangement, interventions, and intimate femicide. *Violence Against Women, 34,* 590–609.

Farley, N. (1996). A survey of factors contributing to gay and lesbian domestic violence. *Journal of Gay & Lesbian Social Services, 4*(1), 35–42.

Freedner, N. L., Freed, H., Yang, Y. W., & Austin. S. B. (2002). Dating violence among gay, lesbian, and bisexual adolescents: Results for a community survey. *Journal of Adolescent Health, 31*(6), 469–474.

Girshick, L. (2001). Sexual violence within lesbian battering. *Off Our Backs, 31*(9), 31–42.

Hall vs. Hall (Litigation guardian of) v. Powers between George Smitherman in his capacity as litigation guardian of Marc Hall, plaintiff, and Michael Powers and the Durham Catholic District School Board, defendant. Retrieved July 11, 2011, from http://www.samesexmarriage.ca/docs/MacKinnon_Hall.pdf

Harris, R. J., & Cook, C. A. (1994). Attributions about spouse abuse: It matters who the batterers and victims are. *Sex Roles, 30*, 553–565.

Hart, B. J. (1986). Lesbian battering: An examination. In K. Lobel (Ed.), *Naming the violence* (pp. 173–189). Seattle: Seal Press.

Henderson, L. (2003). *Prevalence of domestic violence among lesbians and gay men.* London: Sigma Research, 2003.

Herek, G. (2004). Beyond homophobia: Thinking about sexual prejudice and stigma in the twenty-first century. *Sexuality Research and Social Policy, 1*(2), 6–24.

Herek, G. M., Gillis, J. R., & Cogan, J. C. (2009). Internalized stigma among sexual minority adults: Insights from a social psychological perspective. *Journal of Counseling Psychology, 56,* 32–43.

Hester, M., & Donovan, C. (2009). Researching domestic violence in same-sex relationships: A feminist epistemological approach to survey development. *Journal of Lesbian Studies, 13,* 161–173.

Hester, M., Pearson, C., Harwin, N., & Abrahams, H. (2007). *Making an impact: Children and domestic violence—A reader* (2nd ed.). London: Jessica Kingsley.

Hotton Mahony, T. (2010). Police-reported dating violence in Canada, 2008. *Juristat* article. Component of Statistics Canada Catalogue no. 85-002-X *Juristat.*

Island, D., & Letellier, P. (1991). *Men who beat the men who love them: Battered gay men and domestic violence.* New York: Haworth Press.

Istar, A. (1996). Couple assessment: Identifying and intervening in domestic violence in lesbian relationships. *Journal of Gay & Lesbian Social Services, 4*(1), 93–106.

Johnson, M. P., & Ferraro, K. J. (2000). Research on domestic violence in the 1990s: Making distinctions. *Journal of Marriage and the Family, 62*(4), 948–963.

Kite, M. (2002). When perceptions meet reality: Individual differences in reactions to lesbians and gay men. In A. Coyle & C. Kitzinger (Eds.), *Lesbian and gay psychology: New perspectives* (pp. 25–53). Malden: Blackwell.

Klinger, R. L. (1995). Gay violence. *Journal of Gay & Lesbian Psychotherapy, 2*(3), 119–134.

Kulkin, H. S., Williams, J., Borne, H. F., de la Bretonne, D., & Laurendine, J. (2007). A review of research on violence in same-gender couples: A resource for clinicians. *Journal of Homosexuality, 53*(4), 77–87.

Kurz, D. (1989). Social science perspectives on wife abuse: Current debates and future directions. *Gender and Society, 3,* 489–505.

Landolt, M. A., & Dutton, D. G. (1997). Power and personality: An analysis of gay male intimate abuse. *Sex Roles, 37,* 335–359.

Lie, G. Y., & Gentlewarrier, S. (1991). Intimate violence in lesbian relationships: Discussion of survey findings and practice implications. *Journal of Social Service Research, 15,* 41–59.

Lie, G., Schilit, R., Bush, J., Montagne, M., & Reyes, L. (1991). Lesbians in currently aggressive relationships: How frequently do they report aggressive past relationships? *Violence and Victims, 6,* 121–135.

Lobel, K. (Ed.). (1986). *Naming the violence: Speaking out about lesbian battering.* Seattle: Seal Press.

Lockhart, L. L., White, B. W., Causby, V., & Isaac, A. (1994). Letting out the secret: Violence in lesbian relationships. *Journal of Interpersonal Violence, 9,* 469–492.

Loulan, J. (1987). *Lesbian passion: Loving ourselves and each other.* San Francisco: Spinsters/Aunt Lute.

M. v. H. (1999). 2 S.C.R. 3.

Margolies, L., & Leeder, E. (1995). Violence at the door: Treatment of lesbian batterers. *Violence Against Women, 1*(2), 139–157.

McClennen, J. R. (2005). Domestic violence between same-gendered partners: Recent findings and further research. *Journal of Interpersonal Violence, 20,* 149–154.

Merrill, G. S., & Wolfe, V. A. (2000). Battered gay men: An exploration of abuse, help seeking, and why they stay. *Journal of Homosexuality, 39*(2), 1–30.

Mullaly, B. (2007). *The new structural social work: Ideology, theory, practice* (3rd ed.). Oxford University Press.

Mullaly, B. (2010). *Challenging oppression and confronting privilege* (2nd ed.). Oxford University Press.

Osier, M. (2001). Lesbian battering dynamics: A new approach. *Off our backs, 36-39.* October

Patterson, J. P. (2000). Family relationships of lesbians and gay men. *Journal of Marriage and the Family, 62*(4), 1052–1069.

Pence, E., & Paymar, M. (1993). *Power and control: Tactics of men who batter.* Duluth: Minnesota Program Development, Inc.

Pharr, S. (1986). Two workshops on homophobia. In K. Lobel (Ed.), *Naming the violence: Speaking out about lesbian battering* (pp. 202–222). Seattle, WA: Seal Press.

Puzone, C. A., Saltzman, L. E., Kresnow, M. J., & Mercy, J. (2000). National trends in intimate partner homicide. *Violence Against Women, 6*(4), 409–426.

Renzetti, C. M. (1988). Violence in lesbian relationships: A preliminary analysis of causal factors. *Journal of Interpersonal Violence, 3*(4), 381–399.

Renzetti, C. M. (1992). *Violent betrayal: Partner abuse in lesbian relationships.* Thousand Oaks, CA: Sage.

Renzetti, C. M., & Miley, C. H. (1996). *Violence in gay and lesbian domestic partnerships.* Binghamton, NY: Harrington Park Press.

Scherzer, T. (1998). Domestic violence in lesbian relationships: Findings of the lesbian relationships research project. *Journal of Lesbian Studies, 2*(1), 29–7.

Schilit, R., Lie, G. Y, Bush, J., Montagne, M., & Reyes, L. (1991). Intergenerational transmission of violence in lesbian relationships. *AFFILIA Journal of Women and Social Work, 6*(1), 72–78.

Sue, D. W., & Sue, D. (2008). *Counseling the culturally diverse: Theory and practice* (5th ed.). Hoboken, NJ: John Wiley & Sons Inc.

Szymanski, D. (2004). Relations among dimensions of feminism and internalized heterosexism in lesbians and bisexual women. *Sexual Roles, 51*(3/4), 145–159.

Tjaden, P., & Thoennes, N. (2000). *Full report of the prevalence, incidence and consequences of violence against women: Findings from the National Violence Against Women Survey.* Washington, DC: U.S. Department of Justice.

Tjaden, P., Thoennes, N., & Allison, C. J. (1999). Comparing violence over the life span in samples of same-gender and opposite-gender cohabitants. *Violence and Victims, 14*(4), 413–425.

Tomsen, S., & Markwell, K. (2009). Violence, cultural display and the suspension of sexual prejudice. *Sexuality & Culture, 13,* 201–217.

Tully, C. (2000). *Lesbians, gays, and the empowerment perspective.* New York: Columbia University Press.

Turrell, S. C. (2000). A descriptive analysis of same-gender relationship violence for a diverse sample. *Journal of Family Violence, 15*(3), 281–293.

Waldner-Haugrud, L. K., Gratch, L. V., & Magruder, B. (1997). Victimization and perpetration rates of violence in gay and lesbian relationships: Gender issues explored. *Violence and Victims, 12*(2), 173–184.

Wise, A. J., & Bowman, S. L. (1997). Comparison of beginning counselors' responses to lesbian vs. heterosexual partner abuse. *Violence and Victims, 12*(2), 127–135.

World Health Organization (WHO). (1992). The ICD-10 classification of mental and behavioural disorders. Geneva: World Health Organization.

Zinn, R. W., & Brethour, P. P. (2004). *The law of human rights in Canada.* Aurora, ON: Canada Law Book.

Chapter 7

Ainsworth, F. (2002). Mandatory reporting of child abuse and neglect: Does it really make a difference? *Child and Family Social Work, 7,* 57–63.

Bala, N. (1990). "Double Victims: Child Sexual Abuse and the Criminal Justice System" , *Queen's Law Journal* 1990 (15 (1)), 3–32

Bala, N. (2004). *The* Charter of Rights *and child welfare law. For Law Society of Upper Canada program on Conduct of a Child Protection File.* http://www.canadacourtwatch.com/legal_documents/charter&childwelfare2004.pdf

Bill C-22. (2010, May 6). An Act respecting the mandatory reporting of Internet child pornography by persons who provide an Internet service. Retrieved from http://www2.parl.gc.ca/Sites/LOP/Legislative Summaries/Bills_ls.asp?lang=E&ls=c22&source=library_prb&Parl=40&Ses=3

Bill C-46. (1997). An Act to amend the *Criminal Code* (production of records in sexual offence proceedings), 2d Sess., 35th Parl. 1997 (assented to 25 April 1997), S.C. 1997, c.30.

Bill C-49. (1992). An Act to amend the *Criminal Code* (prohibiting the admission of sexual history evidence), c.38, Ss.276, 276.1, 276.2.

Bill C-127 (1983).

Bill C-150 (1969). *The Criminal Law Amendment Act,* 1968–69.

Canada Evidence Act (R.S.C., 1985, c. C-5).

Canada. Library of Parliament. Canada's legal age of consent to sexual activity. Ottawa: Revised April 12, 2001. No: PRB99-3E. Retrieved from http://www2.parl.gc.ca/Content/LOP/ResearchPublications/prb993-e.htm

Canada. Library of Parliament. Legislative summary of Bill C-22: An Act respecting the mandatory reporting of Internet child pornography by persons who provide an Internet service. No. 40-3-C22E http://www2.parl.gc.ca/Sites/LOP/Legislative Summaries/Bills_ls.asp?lang=E&ls=c22&source=library_prb&Parl=40&Ses=3

Canada. Library of Parliament. Legislative summary of Bill S-2: Protecting Victims from Sex Offenders Act. Prepared by Dupuis, Tanya. Legal and Legislative affairs division Parliamentary information and research service library of Parliament, March 19, 2010. http://www2.parl.gc.ca/Sites/LOP/LegislativeSummaries/Bills_ls.asp?lang=E&ls=s2&source=library_ prb&Parl=40&Ses=3

Canada. Department of Justice. Safeguarding the future and healing the past: The Government of Canada's response to the Law Commission's Report: Restoring dignity: Responding to child abuse in Canadian institutions, 2003.

Canada. Department of Justice. (1985). *The Experience of the rape victim with the criminal justice system prior to Bill C-127,* by Marilyn G. Stanley.

Canada. Library of Parliament. The "spanking" law: Section 43 of the *Criminal Code.* No. PRB 05-10E. http://www2.parl.gc.ca/Content/LOP/ResearchPublications/prb 0510-e.htm

Canada. Library of Parliament. Bill C-15A: An Act to amend the *Criminal Code* and to amend other acts: Legislative history of Bill C-15A. Legislative summary LS-410E. Ottawa: Revised September 30, 2002. Available from **http://www.parl.gc.ca/About/Parliament/LegislativeSummaries/bills_ls.asp?ls=C15A&Parl=37&Ses=1**

Canada. Library of Parliament, Bill C-2: An Act to amend the *Criminal Code* (protection of children and other vulnerable persons) and the Canada Evidence Act, Legislative summary LS-480E. Ottawa: Revised February 18, 2005. Available from **http://www.parl.gc.ca/common/Bills_ls.asp?Parl=38&Ses=1&ls=C2.**

Canada. Library of Parliament. Canada's legal age of consent to sexual activity. Ottawa: Revised April 12, 2001. No. PRB99-3E. **http://www2.parl.gc.ca/Content/LOP/ResearchPublications/prb993-e.htm**

Canada. Library of Parliament. Legislative summary of Bill C-22: An Act respecting the mandatory reporting of Internet child pornography by persons who provide an Internet service. No. 40-3-C22E. **http://www2.parl.gc.ca/Sites/LOP/Legislative Summaries/Bills_ls.asp?lang=E&ls=c22&source=library_prb&Parl=40&Ses=3**

Canada. Library of Parliament. The "spanking" law: Section 43 of the *Criminal Code*. No. PRB 05-10E. **http://www2.parl.gc.ca/Content/LOP/Research Publications/prb0510-e.htm**

Canadian Centre for Justice Statistics. (2005). *Family violence in Canada: A statistical profile 2005*. Cat. No. 85-224-XIE, 2005. Ottawa: Statistics Canada.

Canadian Charter of Rights and Freedoms. (1982). Retrieved from **http://laws.justice.gc.ca/eng/charter/**

Canadian Child Welfare Research Portal, **http://www.cecw-cepb.ca/**

Canadian Children's Rights Council Child Rights, Virtual Library, Resource Centre, Archives and Advocacy, **http://www.canadiancrc.com/Age_of_consent_sex_in_Canada.aspx**

CBC News. (2011, February 28). Senior found freezing in couple's garage: Son, daughter-in-law charged with failing to provide necessities of life. Retrieved from **http://www.cbc.ca/news/canada/toronto/story/2011/02/28/toronto-senior-garage-police485.html**

CBC News. (2011, October 12). Son pleads guilty in case of freezing senior. Retrieved from **http://www.cbc.ca/news/canada/toronto/story/2011/10/12/guilty-plea-senior-toronto458.html**

Child and Family Services Act. (1990). R.S.O. 1990. (CFSA). Retrieved from **http://www.e-laws.gov.on.ca/html/statutes/english/elaws_statutes_90c11_e.htm**

Child Witness Project. Retrieved from http://www.lfcc.on.ca/cwp.htm.

Civil Marriage Act, SC (2005), c 33 Statutes of Canada S.C. 2005, c. 33. Retrieved from **http://www.canlii.org/en/ca/laws/stat/sc-2005-c-33/latest/sc-2005-c-33.html**

CNN News. (2003). Vatican fights gay marriages. Retrieved from **http://articles.cnn.com/2003-07-31/world/vatican.gay.marriages_1_gay-marriages-civil-unions-gay-couples?_s=PM:WORLD**

Cohen, E., & Walthall, B. (2003). *Silent realities: Supporting young children and their families who experienced violence*. Washington, DC: The National Child Welfare Resource Centre for Family-Centered Practice.

Committee on the Rights of the Child. (2003, 27 October). Concluding observations of the Committee on the Rights of the Child: CANADA, CRC/C15/Add.215.

Committee on the Rights of the Child. (2006). General Comment No. 8. The right of the child to protection from corporal punishment and other cruel or degrading forms of punishment (articles 19, 28(2) and 37, inter alia), CRC/C/GC/8.

Convention on the Rights of the Child. (1989). UN Doc. A/RES/44/25 (1989). Retrieved May 8, 2008, from **http://www.unhchr.ch/html/menu3/b/k2crc.htm**

Criminal Code of Canada R.S.C. 1985, c. C-46.

Dauvergne, M. (2009). Forcible confinement in Canada, 2007. Component of *Juristat, 29*(1). Catalogue no. 85-002-X. Ottawa: Statistics Canada.

Dauvergne, M., & Brennan, S. (2011). Police-reported hate crime in Canada 2009. Component of *Juristat.* Catalogue no. 85-002-X. Ottawa: Statistics Canada.

Durrant, J. E., Trocmé, N., Fallon, B., Milne, C., & Black, T. (2009). Protection of children from physical maltreatment in Canada: An evaluation of the Supreme Court's definition of reasonable force. *Journal of Aggression, Maltreatment & Trauma, 18*(1), 64–87.

Egan v. Canada, [1995] 2 S.C.R. 513. Retrieved from **http://www.canlii.org/ en/ca/scc/doc/1995/1995canlii98/1995 canlii98.pdf**

Goff, C. (2008). *Criminal justice in Canada* (4th ed.). Toronto: Nelson Education.

Gordon, R. M. (2001). Adult protection legislation in Canada: Models, issues, and problems. *International Journal of Law and Psychiatry, 24,* 117–134.

Gotell, L. (2002, Summer). Confidential records and sexual assault complainants post-Mills: Still vulnerable? *Jurisfemme Publications, 21*(2).

Hunt, R. J. (1999). *Historical dictionary of the gay liberation movement: Gay men and the quest for social justice.* Lanham, MD, & London: The Scarecrow Press, Inc.

Hurst, L. (2003). A long trip to the altar. *Toronto Star.*

Janzen v. Platy Enterprises Ltd., [1989] 1 S.C.R. 1252.

Jaffe, P., Wolfe, D., Wilson, S., & Zak, L. (1986). Similarities in behavioral and social maladjustment among child victims and witnesses to family violence. American Journal of Orthopsychiatry, 56, 142-146.

Lunman, K., & Fagan, D. (2004, September 17). Marriage divides the House. *The Globe and Mail,* A1.

M. v. H. [1999] 2 S.C.R. 3.

Mathews, B., & Kenny, M. (2007). Mandatory reporting legislation in the USA, Canada and Australia: A cross-jurisdictional review of key features, differences and issues. *Child Maltreatment,* in press.

Mathews, B. P., & Bross, D. C. (2008). Mandated reporting is still a policy with reason: Empirical evidence and philosophical grounds. *Child Abuse and Neglect, 32*(5), 511–516.

Melton, G. (1992). The law is a good thing (psychology is, too): Human rights in psychological jurisprudence. *Law and Human Behavior, 16*(4), 381–398.

Melton, G. (2005). Mandated reporting: A policy without reason. *Child Abuse & Neglect, 29*(1), 9–18.

Ogg-Moss v. The Queen, [1984] 2 S.C.R. 173, Dickson J. at p. 193.

O'Toole, M., & Lodge, E. (2011, February 28). Couple charged after mother found in freezing garage. *National Post.* Retrieved from **http://news.nationalpost. com/2011/02/28/couple-charged-for-keeping-mother-in-uninsulated-garage-since-november/**

Pilon, M. (1999, January 25). Canada's legal age of consent to sexual activity. Law and Government Division. Revised April 12, 2001.

R. v. Chase, [1991] 2 S.C.R. 293).

R. v. Darrach, 2000 SCC 46, [2000] 2 S.C. R. 443.

R. v. Ewanchuk (1998), 57 Alta. L.R. (3d) 236 (Alta. COA).

R. v. Gayme, [1991] 2 S.C.R. 577

R. v. J.A., 2011 SCC 28

R. v. Lavallee, [1990] 1 S.C.R. 852 (1990)

*R. v. Levogiannis, [*1993*]* 4 S.C.R. 475, (1993), 85 C.C.C. (3d) 327).

R. v. O'Connor, [1995] 4 S.C.R. 411

*R. v. Park [*1995*]* 2 S.C.R. 836 at 844 and 845.).

R. v. Seaboyer; R. v. Gayme, [1991] 2 S.C.R. 577 (1991)

Repeal Committee. Retrieved at http://www.repeal43.org/

Rhynard, J., & Krebs, M. (1999). Sexual assault in dating relationships. *Journal of School Health, 67*(3). (From EBSCO Publishing.) Retrieved September 29, 1999 from http://www.epnet.com/ehost/login.html

Roberts, J. V., Grossman, M. J., & Gebotys, R. J. (1996). Rape reform in Canada: Public knowledge and opinion. *Journal of Family Violence, 11*(2), 133–148.

Schissel, B. (1996). Law reform and social change: A time-series analysis of sexual assault in Canada. *Journal of Criminal Justice, 24*(2), 123–138.

Schmalleger, F., MacAlister, D., & McKenna, P. (2004). *Canadian criminal justice today.* Toronto: Pearson Education Canada.

Schmalleger, F., & Volk, R. (2011). *Canadian criminology today: Theories and applications.* Toronto: Pearson Canada.

Statistics Canada. (2006). Census: Family portrait—Continuity and change in Canadian families and households in 2006. National portrait—Individuals. Retrieved from http://www12.statcan.ca/census-recensement/2006/as-sa/97-553/p4-eng.cfm

Tang, K. (1998). Rape law reform in Canada: The success and limits of legislation. *International Journal of Offender Therapy and Comparative Criminology, 42*(3), 258–270.

Tiedemann, M., & Valiquet, D. (2008). *Euthanasia and assisted suicide in Canada.* Parliamentary Information and Research Centre. Retrieved from http://www.parl.gc.ca/Content/LOP/researchpublications/919-e.htm

Trocmé, N., Fallon, B., MacLaurin, B., Daciuk, J., Felstiner, C., & Black, T. (2005). *Canadian incidence study of reported child abuse and neglect, 2003: Major findings.* Ottawa: Minister of Public Works and Government Services Canada. Retrieved from http://www.cecw-cepb.ca/sites/default/files/publications/en/CIS2003_MajorFindings_slides.pdf

United Nations *Convention on the Rights of the Child.* (1989). Retrieved from http://www2.ohchr.org/english/law/crc.htm

Youthography Ping Survey. (2004, February). Canadian youth (13–29).

Zabjek, A. (2011). Killing newborn earns suspended sentence. *Edmonton Journal.* Retrieved from http://www2.canada.com/edmontonjournal/news/story.html?id=cb85f50a-650f-4797-83a0-96d0bba2e116

Chapter 8

Canadian Judicial Council. (2004). *The conduct of judges, and the role of the Canadian Judicial Council.* Catalogue No. JU11-4/2004E-PDF. Retrieved April 10, 2011, from http://www.cjc-ccm.gc.ca/cmslib/general/news_pub_judicialconduct_CJCRole_2004_en.pdf

Canadian Legislation and Regulations. Justice Laws Website. Retrieved June 2011, from http://laws.justice.gc.ca/eng/

Canadian Statement of Basic Principles of Justice for Victims of Crime. (1988). Retrieved April 17, 2011, from http://www.justice.gc.ca/eng/pi/pcvi-cpcv/pub/03/princ.html

CBC. (2011, February 24). Judge's sex assault comments wrong: professor. No jail for "clumsy Don Juan." Retrieved July 25, 2011, from http://www.cbc.ca/news/canada/manitoba/story/2011/02/24/mb-professor-concerns-sex-assault-sentence-manitoba.html

Colin, M., & Paquette., C. (2001). *Summary report on victim impact statement focus groups.* Ottawa: Policy Centre for Victims Issues, Research and Statistics Division, Department of Justice Canada.

Constitution Acts, 1867 to 1982. Retrieved January 2011, from http://laws.justice.gc.ca/eng/Const/Const_index.html

Coroners Act of Ontario. R.S.O. 1990, Chapter C.37. Retrieved July 2011, from http://www.e-laws.gov.on.ca/html/statutes/english/elaws_statutes_90c37_e.htm

Criminal Code of Canada. http://www.canlii.org/en/ca/laws/stat/rsc-1985-c-c-46/latest/rsc-1985-c-c-46.html

Davison, D. B. (2005). The value of a jury trial. *Law Now, 30,* 37–38.

Daylen, J., van Tongeren Harvey, W., & O'Toole, D. (2006). *Trauma, trials, and transformation: Guiding sexual assault victims through the legal system and beyond.* Toronto: Irwin Law.

Department of Justice Canada. (2006, December 12). *Victim impact statement fact sheet.* Retrieved January 31, 2007, from http://justice.gc.ca/en/news/nr/1999/doc_24286.html

Erez, E. (1994). Victim participation in sentencing: And the debate goes on. *International Review of Victimology, 3,* 17–32.

Erez, E., & Rogers. L. (1999). Victim impact statements and sentencing outcomes and processes: The perspectives of legal professionals. *British Journal of Criminology, 39*(2): 216–239.

Gall, G. L. (1995). *The Canadian legal system* (4th ed.). Carswell Legal Publishing.

Goff, C. (2008). *Criminal justice in Canada* (4th ed.). Nelson Education.

Hall, D. J. (1991). Victims' voices in criminal court: The need for restraint. *American Criminal Law Review, 28,* 233–266.

Herman, J. L. (2003). The mental health of crime victims: Impact of legal intervention. *Journal of Traumatic Stress, 16*(2), 159–166.

Jamieson, W., & Gomes, L. (2010). Family violence initiative performance report for April 2004 to March 2008. Her Majesty the Queen in Right of Canada. Catalogue No. HP-2/2008 ISBN: 978-1-100-50728-6

Judges Act, R.S.C. 1985, c.J-1, s.55.

Justice Canada. How the courts are organized. Retrieved April 2010, from http://www.justice.gc.ca/eng/dept-min/pub/ccs-ajc/page3.html

Klar, L. N. (2003). *Tort law* (3rd ed.). Toronto: Thompson.

K.M.M. v. The Roman Catholic Episcopal Corp. (2011). ONSC 2143. Retrieved June 2011 from http://www.ledroitbeckett.com/upload/files/reasons-for-judgment2011-04-21.pdf

Law Reform Commission of Canada. (1975). *Criminal procedure: Control of the process.* Ottawa: Minister of Supply and Services Canada.

Law Reform Commission of Canada. (1988). *Compelling appearance, interim release, and the pre-trial detention.* Ottawa: Law Reform Commission of Canada.

Littlefield, D. (2004). *Legislative history for victim impact statements.* Department of Justice, Ontario Regional Office, Federal Prosecution Service. Retrieved from http://www.bankofcanada.ca/wp-content/uploads/2010/09/history_statement.pdf

McIntyre, M. (2011a, February 25). No woman asks to be raped. *Winnipeg Free Press.* Retrieved July 25, 2011, from http://news.nationalpost.com/2011/02/25/no-woman-asks-to-be-raped-victim-slams-judges-decision/

McIntyre, M. (2011b, February 24). Rape victim "inviting," so no jail: Judge rules woman's clothes, conduct ease blame on attacker. *Winnipeg Free Press.* Retrieved from http://www.winnipegfreepress.com/breakingnews/rape-victim-inviting-so-no-jail--rape-victim-inviting-so-no-jail-116801578.html

Meredith, C., & Paquette, C. (2001). *Summary report on victim impact statement focus groups.* Ottawa: Policy Centre for Victims' Issues, Research and Statistics Division, Department of Justice Canada.

R. v. Budreo. (2000). Retrieved February 2011 from http://vancouver.ca/police/justice/documents/NJCManual/RvBudreo.pdf

R. v. Ewanchuk, [1999] 1 S.C.R. 330. Retrieved April 2010 from http://scc.lexum.org/en/1999/1999scr1-330/1999scr1-330.html

R. v. Kenneth Rhodes. (2011, February 11). Transcript of Justice Dewar's decision. Retrieved from http://www.scribd.com/fullscreen/50396234

Reynolds, L. (2011, February 25). Outdated thinking horribly pervasive: Old views should die—because they're stupid. *Winnipeg Free Press.* Retrieved from http://www.winnipegfreepress.com/local/outdated- thinking-horribly-pervasive-116903908.html

Roach, K. (1999). Four models of the criminal process. *Journal of Criminal Law and Criminology, 89,* 671–716.

Roberts, J., & Allen, E. (2003). Victim impact statements at sentencing: Perceptions of the judiciary in Canada. *International Journal of Victimology 1*(4), 1–11.

RCMP (2008). National Sex Offender Registry. Retrieved June 2011 from http://www.rcmp-grc.gc.ca/tops-opst/bs-sc/nsor-rnds/prog-eng.htm

Sauvé, J., & Burns, M. (2009). Residents of Canada's shelters for abused women, 2008. Retrieved January 2011 from http://www.phac-aspc.gc.ca/ncfv-cnivf/pdfs/fem-residents-eng.pdf

Schmalleger, F., MacAlister, D., & McKenna, P. F. (2004). *Canadian criminal justice today.* Toronto: Pearson.

SlutWalk Toronto. Retrieved April 2011 from Http://www.slutwalktoronto.com/

Supreme Court of Canada Website. Retrieved January 11, 2012, from http://www.scc-csc.gc.ca/home-accueil/index-eng.asp

The National Sex Offender Registry. Retrieved May 2011, from http://www.rcmp-grc.gc.ca/tops-opst/bs-sc/nsor-rnds/prog-eng.htm

Wilhelm, T. (2006). Priest won girls' trust. *Windsor Star.* Retrieved August 3, 2011, from http://www.canada.com/windsorstar/news/story.html?id=e46aab3b-862e-422a-8adb-f58898cc3f80&k=79060

Wilhelm, T. (2011, July 22). 22 priests, hundreds of victims: Sexual abuse cases haunt Church's London Diocese. *Windsor Star.* Retrieved August 3, 2011, from http://www.windsorstar.com/news/priests+hundreds+victims/5139863/story.html

Wilhelm, T. (2011, April). Judge blasts diocese for Sylvestre abuse 'coverup.' *Windsor Star.* Retrieved August 3, 2011, from http://www.abolishsexabuse.org/index.php?option=com_content&view=article&id=986:judge-blasts-diocese-for-sylvestre-abuse-coverup&catid=71:world-news&Itemid=181

Transition Home Survey (THS). Retrieved March 2011, from http://www.statcan.gc.ca/cgi-bin/imdb/p2SV.pl?Function=getSurvey&SDDS=3328&lang=en&db=imdb&adm=8&dis=2

Photo Credits

Chapter 1 p. 11: LAC, PA-123681; p. 22: Hudson's Bay Company HBCA 1982/17/1; p. 28: LAC, PA-135131

Chapter 5 p. 173: The Canadian Press

Chapter 7 p. 254: Tom Hanson/The Canadian Press; p. 257: Supreme Court of Canada, Photgrapher: Philippe Landreville

Chapter 8 p. 281: Supreme Court of Canada, Photgrapher: Philippe Landreville; p. 311: © Canada Post Corporation 2010. Reproduced with Permission. LAC, 11047381

Index